Functional Programming with Scala, Second Edition

Praise for the First Edition

The definitive guide to functional programming for Scala and Java 8 developers!
—William E. Wheeler, TekSystems

Shows you the approach and mindset to raise your Scala way beyond 'a better Java.'
—Fernando Dobladez, Code54

The coding challenges are challenging, fun, and informative for real-world use.
—Chris Nauroth, Hortonworks

Learn by doing—rather than just reading.
—Douglas Alan, Eli and Edythe L. Broad Institute of Harvard and MIT

Functional Programming
with Scala

SECOND EDITION

MICHAEL PILQUIST
RÚNAR BJARNASON
PAUL CHIUSANO

FOREWORDS BY MARTIN ODERSKY AND DANIEL SPIEWAK

MANNING
SHELTER ISLAND

For online information and ordering of this and other Manning books, please visit
www.manning.com. The publisher offers discounts on this book when ordered in quantity.
For more information, please contact

    Special Sales Department
    Manning Publications Co.
    20 Baldwin Road
    PO Box 761
    Shelter Island, NY 11964
    Email: orders@manning.com

Manning Publications Co.   Development editor: Dustin Archibald
20 Baldwin Road   Technical development editor: Jerry Kuch
PO Box 761   Review editor: Aleksandar Dragosavljević
Shelter Island, NY 11964   Production editor: Deirdre Hiam
     Copy editor: Christian Berk
     Proofreader: Melody Dolab
     Technical proofreader: Jerry Kuch
     Typesetter: Gordan Salinovic
     Cover designer: Irene Scala

ISBN 9781617299582
Printed and bound by CPI Group (UK) Ltd, Croydon, CR0 4YY

brief contents

contents

foreword to the first edition

Functional Programming in Scala is an intriguing title. After all, Scala is generally called a functional programming language, and there are dozens of books about Scala on the market. Are all these other books missing the functional aspects of the language? To answer the question, it's instructive to dig a bit deeper. What is *functional programming*? For me, it's simply an alias for *programming with functions*—that is, a programming style that puts the focus on the functions in a program. What are *functions*? Here we find a larger spectrum of definitions. While one definition often admits functions that may have side effects in addition to returning a result, pure functional programming restricts functions to be as they are in mathematics: binary relations that map arguments to results.

Scala is an impure functional programming language in that it admits impure as well as pure functions and in that it does not try to distinguish between these categories by using different syntax or giving them different types. It shares this property with most other functional languages. It would be nice if we could distinguish between pure and impure functions in Scala, but I believe we have not yet found a way to do so that is lightweight and flexible enough to be added to Scala without hesitation.

To be sure, Scala programmers are generally encouraged to use pure functions. Side effects such as mutation, I/O, or using exceptions are not ruled out, and they can indeed come in quite handy sometimes, be it for reasons of interoperability, efficiency, or convenience. But overusing side effects is generally not considered good style by experts. Nevertheless, since impure programs are possible—and even convenient to write—in Scala, there is a temptation for programmers coming from a more imperative background to keep their style and not make the necessary effort to adapt to the functional mindset. In fact, it's quite possible to write Scala as if it were Java without the semicolons.

So to properly learn functional programming in Scala, should one make a detour via a pure functional language, such as Haskell? Any argument in favor of this approach has been severely weakened by the appearance of *Functional Programming in Scala*.

What Paul and Rúnar do, put simply, is treat Scala as a pure functional programming language. Mutable variables, exceptions, classical input/output, and all other traces of impurity are eliminated. If you wonder how one can write useful programs without any of these conveniences, you need to read the book. Building up from first principles and extending all the way to incremental input and output, they demonstrate that, indeed, one can express every concept using only pure functions. And they show that it is not only possible but that it also leads to beautiful code and deep insights into the nature of computation.

The book is challenging, both because it demands attention to detail and because it might challenge the way you think about programming. By reading the book and completing the recommended exercises, you will develop a better appreciation of what pure functional programming is, what it can express, and what its benefits are.

What I particularly liked about the book is that it is self-contained. It starts with the simplest possible expressions, and every abstraction is explained in detail before further abstractions are built on them in turn. In a sense, the book develops an alternative Scala universe, where mutable state does not exist and all functions are pure. Commonly used Scala libraries tend to deviate a bit from this ideal; often they are based on a partly imperative implementation with a (mostly) functional interface. That Scala allows the encapsulation of mutable state in a functional interface is, in my opinion, one of its strengths. But it is a capability that is also often misused. If you find yourself using it too often, *Functional Programming in Scala* is a powerful antidote.

—MARTIN ODERSKY, CREATOR OF SCALA

foreword to the second edition

The eight years since Paul and Rúnar created the first edition of *Functional Programming in Scala* have seen a remarkable transition, both in the Scala ecosystem and the industry at large. In some senses, the way we look at *Functional Programming in Scala*, or *the red book*, as it is often denoted, has mirrored this evolution.

Eight years ago, functional programming, and particularly *pure* functional programming, with all its attendant terminology, abstractions, and baggage, was considered a niche discipline at best. Frameworks such as Scalaz were arcana, and their practitioners were wizards advancing a strange religion. Meanwhile, the vast majority of the Scala ecosystem settled into an equilibrium best typified by frameworks like Akka and Spark—weakly higher-order APIs encouraging immutability and careful thought about side effects but with limited abstraction ultimately built on ad hoc (rather than compositional) foundations.

Since then, a quiet revolution has taken hold as more and more of these ideas have moved closer to the Scala mainstream. Highly compositional frameworks, like Cats and Fs2, are no longer unwelcome interlopers—their secrets known only to a rare few. Today Scala applications written on top of Http4s are just as common as those written on top of Play. The average Scala application developer may be expected to encounter `Monad` and `Functor` about as often as they encounter `ActorSystem`, and *the red book* is no longer a kitsch tome describing an obscure dialect of a major programming language but *the* standard guide to *advanced Scala*.

Functional programming in Scala, both the technique and the book, have entrenched themselves firmly within the landscape of the language and ecosystem.

With that have come new pressures and challenges but also new opportunities and discoveries. New ideas and requirements are attendant to large-scale adoption; the continued evolution of the broader industry; and even more specific inflections, such as the release of Scala 3. Just as the past eight years have brought about a sea change in the nature of the Scala ecosystem and the context in which we evaluate and employ functional techniques, so too will the coming eight years bring about evolution and innovation. Perhaps when it comes time to update this volume once again, names such as Cats Effect will seem as dated and ancestral as Scalaz seems to us today.

The second edition of *Functional Programming in Scala* is as much a thorough rewrite as it is a refresh. Mike's detailed firsthand knowledge of today's state of the art is matched only by his directional insight and ideas on how to shape the future. All of this is distilled into the pages herein, and the result is not only a worthy successor to the seminal original work but an effective companion for the community inventing tomorrow.

—DANIEL SPIEWAK, CREATOR OF CATS EFFECT

preface to the second edition

When I was asked to write the second edition of *Functional Programming in Scala*, I was both excited and apprehensive. I was excited because the first edition had a profound impact on my journey as a functional programmer. It taught me a new way to think about programming, more so than any other programming book I had ever encountered. And I was apprehensive for the same reason—would I be able to do justice to the first edition?

The first edition was published in 2014 and quickly became regarded as a classic text in functional programming. It's been used by university courses and study groups, hobbyists, and the world's largest companies, and it's been translated into multiple languages. The first edition also had a reputation for being very challenging, with many readers getting stuck on some of the exercises.

A lot has changed in Scala since 2014. At the time of publication, Scala 2.10 had been recently released and the Scala FP ecosystem was in its infancy. Major open source projects like doobie (http://github.com/tpolecat/doobie) and http4s (http://http4s.org) were just getting started; the Cats (http://typelevel.org/cats/) library didn't yet exist; and FS2 (https://github.com/typelevel/fs2), which grew out of the code presented in chapter 15, had just been published. Interoperability between libraries was cumbersome, and the Scala language had some key limitations that made FP less accessible than it could have been.

The second edition of *Functional Programming in Scala* does not stray far from the first. I cover the same main topics and in the same style, avoiding teaching any specific library and instead focusing on teaching the underlying concepts powering libraries like Cats, doobie, http4s, and FS2. The text has been updated for Scala 3 and other changes to the standard library since the original publication. Some new concepts are included throughout, particularly coverage of typeclasses and context parameters, as well as some other advanced features that show up in part 4.

Perhaps controversially, I've decided to include annotated answers to the exercises. I hope that by doing so, readers who were discouraged after getting stuck will instead find the inline answers illuminating and continue with the text. I encourage all readers to try the exercises before reading the answers, as practice with FP concepts is essential to understanding. The exercises and answers, updated for Scala 3, are also available on the book's Github repository: http://github.com/fpinscala/fpinscala.

I hope you enjoy the second edition of *Functional Programming in Scala* and that it lives up to the reputation of the first edition.

—MICHAEL PILQUIST

acknowledgments

I'd like to give special thanks to the Manning team: development editor Dustin Archibald, reviewing editor Aleksandar Dragosavljević, technical development editor and proofer Jerry Kutch, production editor Deirdre Hiam, copyeditor Christian Berk, and page proofreader Melody Dolab.

Also, to all the reviewers: Alain Couniot, Alessandro Campeis, Anastasios Makris, Andres Sacco, Anton Trunov, Atul Shriniwas Khot, Bob Resendes, Dan Sheikh, Daniela Zapata, Domenico Vistocco, Ernesto Bossi Carranza, Fernando Bernardino, Filip Krikava, Gary Kirrene, Gilberto Taccari, Giri S. Swaminathan, Igor Karp, Jacek Sokulski, Jedidiah Clemons-Johnson, Jeremy Townson, Joao Azevedo, João David Costa, Kristof Semjen, Mark Elston, Nathan B. Crocker, Özay Duman, Peter Pfister, Prabhuti Prakash, Raushan Jha, Richard Tobias, Sébastien Nichele, Vincent Theron, and William E. Wheeler, your suggestions helped make this a better book.

Thank you to Miles Sabin for always encouraging and believing in me. Thank you to the various members of the open source Scala community who have accompanied me on this FP journey, of which there are too many to name, but in particular, Rob Norris, Ross Baker, Daniel Spiewak, Fabio Labella, Christopher Davenport, Erik Osheim, Lars Hupel, Arman Bilge, Stew O'Connor, Cody Allen, Oscar Boykin, Raúl Raja, Luka Jacobowitz, Diego E. Alonso Blas, Alexandru Nedelcu, Pavel Chlupacek, Adam Rosien, Gabriel Volpe, Seth Tisue, Vasil Vasilev, Josh Suereth, Adriaan Moors, Martin Snyder, Brian Clapper, Jamie Allen, Matt Hughes, Steve Buzzard, Michael Smith, Dave Cleaver, Guillaume Martres, Darja Jovanovic, and Anton Sviridov. Thank you to my current and former colleagues at Comcast, particularly Tim Walsh, Stephen Abert, and Gary Henson, for helping me build a world-class Scala organization.

To Paul and Rúnar, thank you for entrusting me with the second edition of this book, and thank you for all of the support and mentoring over the last decade. It has truly been an honor, and I consider myself fortunate for having the opportunity to work with each of you.

Lastly, thank you to my wife Allison, who has suffered through my enthusiastic ramblings about applicative functors with patience and grace and who has supported me throughout both the writing of this book and my participation in the functional programming community.

about this book

This is not a book about Scala—this book is an introduction to *functional programming*, a radical, principled approach to writing software. We use Scala as the vehicle to get there, but you can apply the lessons herein to programming in any language. As you work through this book, our goal is for you to gain a firm grasp of functional programming concepts, become comfortable writing purely functional programs, and be able to absorb new material on the subject, beyond what we cover here.

How this book is structured

Functional Programming in Scala, Second Edition is organized into four parts. In part 1, we discuss exactly what functional programming is and introduce some core concepts. The chapters in this first part provide an overview of fundamental techniques, including how to organize small functional programs, define purely functional data structures, handle errors, and deal with state.

Building on this foundation, part 2 contains a series of tutorials on *functional design*. We work through some examples of practical functional libraries, laying bare the thought process that goes into designing them.

While working through the libraries in part 2, it will become clear that these libraries follow certain patterns and contain some duplication. This will highlight the need for new and higher abstractions for writing more generalized libraries, which we introduce in part 3. These are very powerful tools for reasoning about your code; once you master them, you will have the tools to be an extraordinarily productive programmer.

Part 4 then provides the final tools you'll need for writing real-world applications that perform I/O (e.g., working with databases, files, or video displays) and making use of mutable state, all in a purely functional way. Throughout the book, we rely heavily on programming exercises, carefully sequenced to help you internalize the material. It's not enough to learn abstract theory when trying to understand functional programming—you have to fire up your text editor and write some code. It's crucial that you take the theory that you have learned and put it into practice in your work.

We've also provided online notes for every chapter. Each chapter has a section with discussion related to that chapter, along with links to further material. These chapter notes are meant to be expanded upon by the community of readers and are available as an editable wiki at https://github.com/fpinscala/fpinscala/wiki.

Audience

This book is intended for readers with at least some programming experience. While writing the book, we had a particular kind of reader in mind: an intermediate-level Java or C programmer who is curious about functional programming. However, we believe this book is well suited for programmers coming from any language, at any level of experience.

Prior expertise is not as important as motivation and curiosity. Functional programming is a lot of fun, but it's a challenging topic. It may be especially challenging for very experienced programmers because it requires such a different way of thinking than they might be used to. No matter how long you have been programming, you must come prepared to be a beginner once again.

This book does not require any prior experience with Scala, but we won't spend a lot of time and space discussing Scala's syntax and language features. Instead, we will introduce them as we go, with minimal ceremony, mostly as a consequence of covering other material. These introductions to Scala should be enough to get you started with the exercises. If you have further questions about the Scala language, you should supplement your reading with another book on Scala (see https://docs.scala-lang.org/books.html) or look up specific questions in the Scala language documentation (http://scala-lang.org/documentation/).

How to read this book

Although the book can be read sequentially, the sequencing of the four parts is designed such that you can comfortably break between them, apply what you have learned to your own work, and then come back later for the next part. For example, the material in part 4 will make the most sense after you have a strong familiarity with the functional style of programming developed in parts 1, 2, and 3. After part 3, it may be a good idea to take a break and try getting more practice writing functional programs beyond the exercises we work on in the chapters. Of course, this is ultimately up to you.

Most chapters in this book have a similar structure. We introduce some new idea or technique, explain it with an example, and then work through a number of exercises. We strongly suggest you download the exercise source code and do the exercises as you go through each chapter. Exercises, hints, and answers are all available at https://github.com/fpinscala/fpinscala. We also encourage you to use the Discussions feature of GitHub for questions and discussion and join the #fpis-red-book channel on the Typelevel Discord server (https://discord.gg/vRP4FUpxWT).

Exercises are marked for both their difficulty and importance. We mark exercises we consider hard or optional, but these designations are only meant to give you some idea of what to expect—you may find some unmarked questions difficult and some questions marked *hard* quite easy. The *optional* designation is for exercises that are informative but can be skipped without impeding your ability to follow further material.

The exercises have the following icons in front of them to denote whether they are optional:

■ — EXERCISE 15.1 ——————————————————————————

A filled-in square next to an exercise means the exercise is critical.

——

□ — EXERCISE 15.2 ——————————————————————————

An open square means the exercise is optional.

——

Examples are presented throughout the book, and they are meant to be *tried* rather than just read. Before you begin, you should have the Scala interpreter running and ready. We encourage you to experiment on your own with variations of what you see in the examples; a good way to understand something is to change it slightly and see how the change affects the outcome.

Sometimes we will show a Scala interpreter session to demonstrate the result of running or evaluating some code. This will be marked by lines beginning with the scala> prompt of the interpreter. Code that follows this prompt is to be typed or pasted into the interpreter, and the line just below it shows the interpreter's response—like this:

```
scala> println("Hello, World!")
Hello, World!
```

Code conventions and downloads

This book contains many examples of source code both in numbered listings and in line with normal text. In both cases, source code is formatted in a fixed-width font like this to separate it from ordinary text. Sometimes code is also **in bold** to high-light code that has changed from previous steps in the chapter, such as when a new feature adds to an existing line of code.

In many cases, the original source code has been reformatted; we've added line breaks and reworked indentation to accommodate the available page space in the book. In rare cases, even this was not enough, and listings include line continuation markers (➥). Additionally, comments in the source code have often been removed from the listings when the code is described in the text. Code annotations accompany many of the listings, highlighting important concepts. You can get executable snippets of code from the liveBook (online) version of this book at https://livebook.manning.com/book/functional-programming-in-scala-second-edition/welcome. The complete code for the examples in the book is available for download from the Manning website at https://www.manning.com/books/functional-programming-in-scala-second-edition, and from GitHub at https://github.com/fpinscala/fpinscala.

Setting expectations

Although FP has a profound impact on the way we write software at every level, it takes time to build up to that—it's an incremental process. Don't expect to be blown away by how amazing functional programming is in the first chapter. The principles laid out in the beginning are quite subtle and may even seem like they're just common sense. If you think to yourself, *That's something I can already do without knowing FP*, then that's great! That's exactly the point. Most programmers are already doing FP to some extent without even knowing it. Many things most people consider to be best practices (e.g., making a function have only a single responsibility or data immutable) are implied by accepting the premise of FP. We are simply taking the principles underlying those best practices and carrying them all the way to their logical conclusion.

It's highly likely that in reading this book, you will simultaneously learn both Scala syntax and FP. As a result, at first it may seem to you that the code is very alien, the techniques are unnatural, and the exercises are brain bending. That is perfectly normal—do not be deterred. If you get stuck, look at the hints and answers (https://github.com/fpinscala/fpinscala), or take your questions to GitHub Discussions or the Discord channel (#fpis-red-book on Typelevel Discord).

Above all, we hope this book will be a fun and rewarding experience for you and FP makes your work easier and more enjoyable, as it has done for us. This book's purpose, when all is said and done, is to help you be more productive in your work. It should make you feel less like the software you are writing is a collection of dirty hacks and more like you are creating a thing of beauty and utility.

liveBook discussion forum

Purchase of *Functional Programming in Scala, Second Edition* includes free access to liveBook, Manning's online reading platform. Using liveBook's exclusive discussion features, you can attach comments to the book globally or to specific sections or paragraphs. It's a snap to make notes for yourself, ask and answer technical questions, and receive help from the author and other users. To access the forum, go to https://livebook.manning.com/book/functional-programming-in-scala-second-edition/discussion. You can also learn more about Manning's forums and the rules of conduct at https://livebook.manning.com/discussion.

Manning's commitment to our readers is to provide a venue where a meaningful dialogue between individual readers and between readers and the author can take place. It is not a commitment to any specific amount of participation on the part of the author, whose contribution to the forum remains voluntary (and unpaid). We suggest you try asking the author some challenging questions lest their interest stray! The forum and the archives of previous discussions will be accessible from the publisher's website for as long as the book is in print.

about the authors

MICHAEL PILQUIST started programming on an IBM AT using the BASICA programming language. In college, he was introduced to Standard ML but entered industry and focused on C++, Java, and C#. It would be nearly a decade before he returned to functional programming.

Michael is an Engineering Fellow at Comcast, where he is responsible for the end-to-end architecture of video distribution systems. Michael introduced Scala at Comcast, gradually transitioning organizations from enterprise Java with Spring to functional programming flavored Scala. The adoption of functional programming in these organizations directly led to more resilient systems that were easier to evolve to the changing needs of the business.

Michael is the author of many functional open source libraries including FS2, Scodec, and Simulacrum, and he's a co-maintainer of many other libraries including Cats, Cats Effect, and Skunk.

RÚNAR BJARNASON is a renowned software developer and functional programming expert with a passion for the Scala programming language. Alongside Paul Chiusano, Rúnar co-authored the influential book *Functional Programming in Scala*, which is widely considered a seminal text for learning functional programming concepts in Scala. In addition to his work in Scala, Rúnar has contributed to the development of the Unison programming language, a modern, statically-typed purely functional language designed to simplify building and maintaining large distributed systems.

PAUL CHIUSANO is a longtime Scala and Haskell developer and one of the creators of the Unison programming language. He lives in New Orleans with his family.

Part 1

Introduction to
functional programming

We begin this book with a radical and restrictive premise: we will be constructing programs using only pure functions with no side effects, such as reading from files or mutating memory. This idea, of FP, leads to a very different way of writing programs than you may be used to. We therefore start from the very beginning, relearning how to write the simplest of programs in a functional way.

In the first chapter, we'll explain exactly what FP means and give you some idea of its benefits. The rest of the chapters in part 1 introduce the basic techniques for functional programming in Scala. Chapter 2 introduces the Scala language and covers fundamentals, including writing loops functionally and manipulating them as ordinary values. Chapter 3 deals with in-memory data structures that may change over time, and chapter 4 talks about handling errors in pure functions. Chapter 5 then introduces the notion of non-strictness, which can be used to improve the efficiency and modularity of functional code. Finally, chapter 6 introduces modeling stateful programs using pure functions. The intent of this first part of the book is to get you thinking about programs purely in terms of functions from inputs to outputs and teach you the techniques you'll need in part 2 when we start writing some practical code.

What is functional programming?

Functional programming (FP) is based on a simple premise with far-reaching implications: we construct our programs using only *pure functions*—in other words, functions that have no *side effects*. But what are side effects? A function has a side effect if it does something other than simply return a result. This includes, for example, the following cases:

- Modifying a variable
- Modifying a data structure in place
- Setting a field on an object
- Throwing an exception or halting with an error

3

- Printing to the console or reading user input
- Reading from or writing to a file
- Drawing on the screen

We'll provide a more precise definition of side effects later in this chapter, but consider what programming would be like without the ability to do these things or with significant restrictions on when and how these actions could occur. It may be difficult to imagine. How would it be possible to write useful programs at all? If we can't reassign variables, how would we write simple programs like loops? What about working with data that changes or handling errors without throwing exceptions? How could we write programs that must perform input/output (I/O), like drawing to the screen or reading from a file?

The answer is that functional programming is a restriction on *how* we write programs but not on *what* programs we can express. Over the course of this book, we'll learn how to express all of our programs without side effects, including programs that perform I/O, handle errors, and modify data. We'll learn how following the discipline of FP is tremendously beneficial because of the increase in modularity we gain from programming with pure functions. Because of their modularity and lack of side effects, pure functions are easier to test, reuse, parallelize, generalize, and reason about. Furthermore, pure functions are much less prone to bugs.

In this chapter, we'll look at a simple program with side effects and demonstrate some of the benefits of FP by removing these side effects. We'll also discuss the benefits of FP more generally and define two important concepts: *referential transparency* and the *substitution model.*

1.1 *Understanding the benefits of functional programming*

Let's look at an example that demonstrates some of the benefits of programming with pure functions. The point here is just to illustrate some basic ideas that we'll return to throughout this book. This will also be your first exposure to Scala's syntax. We'll talk through Scala's syntax in much greater depth in the next chapter, so don't worry too much about following every detail. The goal of this chapter is simply to gain a basic idea of what the code is doing.

1.1.1 *A program with side effects*

Suppose we're implementing a program to handle purchases at a coffee shop. We'll begin with a Scala 3[1] program that uses side effects in its implementation (also called an *impure* program). Don't worry too much about Scala syntax at this point; we'll take a closer look at that in the next chapter.

---

[1] Throughout this book, we use Scala 3, which is significantly different from Scala 2 in some cases. The concepts explored throughout the book are relevant to both Scala 3 and Scala 2, but porting code snippets to Scala 2 requires some syntactic transformations.

Listing 1.1 A Scala program with side effects

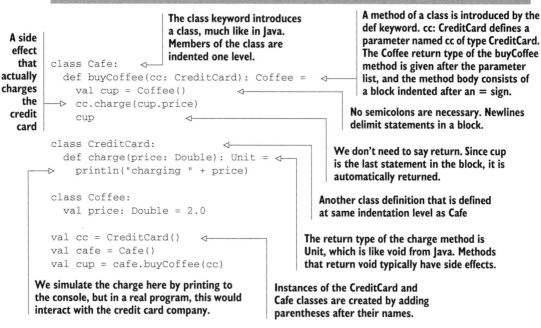

A side effect that actually charges the credit card

The class keyword introduces a class, much like in Java. Members of the class are indented one level.

A method of a class is introduced by the def keyword. cc: CreditCard defines a parameter named cc of type CreditCard. The Coffee return type of the buyCoffee method is given after the parameter list, and the method body consists of a block indented after an = sign.

No semicolons are necessary. Newlines delimit statements in a block.

We don't need to say return. Since cup is the last statement in the block, it is automatically returned.

Another class definition that is defined at same indentation level as Cafe

The return type of the charge method is Unit, which is like void from Java. Methods that return void typically have side effects.

We simulate the charge here by printing to the console, but in a real program, this would interact with the credit card company.

Instances of the CreditCard and Cafe classes are created by adding parentheses after their names.

The line `cc.charge(cup.price)` is an example of a side effect. Charging a credit card involves some interaction with the outside world; suppose it requires contacting the credit card company via some web service, authorizing the transaction, charging the card, and (if successful) persisting some record of the transaction for later reference. But our function merely returns a Coffee, and these other actions are happening *on the side* (hence the term *side effect*). Again, we'll define side effects more formally later in this chapter.

As a result of this side effect, the code is difficult to test. We don't want our tests to actually contact the credit card company and charge the card! This lack of testability suggests a design change; arguably, CreditCard shouldn't have any knowledge about how to contact the credit card company to execute a charge baked into it, nor should it have knowledge of how to persist a record of this charge in our internal systems. We can make the code more modular and testable by letting CreditCard be ignorant of these concerns and passing a Payments object into buyCoffee.

Listing 1.2 Adding a `Payments` object

```
class Cafe:
  def buyCoffee(cc: CreditCard, p: Payments): Coffee =
    val cup = Coffee()
    p.charge(cc, cup.price)
    cup

class CreditCard
```

The CreditCard class no longer has any methods, so we don't need the colon after the class name.

```
trait Payments:                              ◀─────────────
    def charge(cc: CreditCard, price: Double): Unit ◀──────┐

class SimulatedPayments extends Payments:
    def charge(cc: CreditCard, price: Double): Unit =
        println("charging " + price + " to " + cc)

class Coffee:
    val price: Double = 2.0

val cc = CreditCard()
val p = Payments()
val cafe = Cafe()
val cup = cafe.buyCoffee(cc, p)
```

The trait keyword introduces a new interface. Traits are more powerful than interfaces from other languages, but we'll get into those details later in the book.

We define the signature of the charge method on the Payments trait. Implementations of Payments must then provide the behavior of charge.

The SimulatedPayments class implements the Payments trait using the extends keyword.

We've extracted the charging logic into the Payments interface—in essence employing *dependency injection.* Though side effects still occur when we call p.charge(cc, cup.price), we have at least regained some testability. We can write a stub implementation of the Payments interface that is suitable for testing, but that isn't ideal either. We're forced to make Payments an interface when a concrete class may have been fine otherwise, and any stub implementation would be awkward to use. For example, it might contain some internal state tracking the charges that have been made. We'll have to inspect that state after the call to buyCoffee, and our test will have to make sure this state has been appropriately modified (*mutated*) by the call to charge. We can use a *mock framework* or similar to handle this detail for us, but this all feels like overkill if we just want to test that buyCoffee creates a charge equal to the price of a cup of coffee.[2]

Aside from the concern of testing, there's another problem: it's difficult to reuse buyCoffee. Suppose a customer, Alice, would like to order 12 cups of coffee. Ideally, we could just reuse buyCoffee for this, perhaps calling it 12 times in a loop. But as it is currently implemented, that will involve contacting the payment system 12 times, authorizing 12 separate charges to Alice's credit card! That adds more processing fees and isn't good for Alice or the coffee shop.

What can we do about this? We could write an entire new function, buyCoffees, with special logic for batching up the charges.[3] Here, that might not be such a big deal, since the logic of buyCoffee is so simple, but in other cases, the logic we need to duplicate may be nontrivial, and we should mourn the loss of code reuse and composition!

---

[2] Some mocking frameworks even support mocking concrete classes, which allow us to avoid creating the Payments interface entirely, instead intercepting calls to charge on the CreditCard class. There are various trade-offs to this technique, which we don't explore here.

[3] We could also write a specialized BatchingPayments implementation of the Payments interface that somehow attempts to batch successive charges to the same credit card. This gets complicated, though. How many charges should it try to batch up? And how long should it wait? Do we force buyCoffee to indicate that the batch is finished, perhaps by calling closeBatch? And how would it know when it's appropriate to do that, anyway?

1.1.2 A functional solution: Removing the side effects

The functional solution is to eliminate side effects and have `buyCoffee` return the charge as a value in addition to returning the `Coffee`. The concerns of processing the charge by sending it off to the credit card company, persisting a record of it, and so on will be handled elsewhere. A functional solution might look like the following:

buyCoffee now returns a pair of a Coffee and Charge, indicated with the type (Coffee, Charge). The system that processes payments is not involved at all here.

To create a pair, we put the cup and Charge in parentheses, separated by a comma.

```
class Cafe:
  def buyCoffee(cc: CreditCard): (Coffee, Charge) =
    val cup = Coffee()
    (cup, Charge(cc, cup.price))
```

Here we've separated the concern of *creating* a charge from the *processing* or *interpretation* of that charge. The buyCoffee function now returns a Charge as a value along with the Coffee. We'll see shortly how this lets us reuse it more easily to purchase multiple coffees with a single transaction. But what is Charge? It's a data type we just invented containing a CreditCard and an amount equipped with a handy function, combine, for combining charges with the same CreditCard:

A case class has one primary constructor whose argument list comes after the class name (Charge, in this case). The parameters in this list become public, unmodifiable (immutable) fields of the class and can be accessed using the usual object-oriented dot notation, as in other.cc.

An if expression has a similar syntax as in Java, but it also returns a value equal to the result of whichever branch is taken. If cc == other.cc, then combine will return Charge(..); otherwise, the exception in the else branch will be thrown.

```
case class Charge(cc: CreditCard, amount: Double):
  def combine(other: Charge): Charge =
    if cc == other.cc then
      Charge(cc, amount + other.amount)
    else
      throw Exception("Can't combine charges with different cards")
```

A case class can be created without the keyword new. We just use the class name followed by the list of arguments for its primary constructor.

The syntax for throwing exceptions is the same as in Java and many other languages. We'll discuss more functional ways of handling error conditions in a later chapter.

Now let's look at buyCoffees (figure 1.1) to implement the purchase of n cups of coffee. Unlike previously, this can now be implemented in terms of buyCoffee, as we had hoped. Note there's a lot of new syntax and methods in this implementation, which we'll gradually become familiar with over the next few chapters.

> **Listing 1.3 Buying multiple cups with `buyCoffees`**

```
class Cafe:

  def buyCoffee(cc: CreditCard): (Coffee, Charge) = ...

  def buyCoffees(
    cc: CreditCard, n: Int
  ): (List[Coffee], Charge) =
```

List[Coffee] is an immutable, singly linked list of Coffee values. We'll discuss this data type more in chapter 3.

```
val purchases: List[(Coffee, Charge)] =
    List.fill(n)(buyCoffee(cc))
val (coffees, charges) = purchases.unzip
val reduced =
    charges.reduce((c1, c2) => c1.combine(c2))
(coffees, reduced)
```

List.fill(n)(x) creates a List with n copies of x. More precisely, fill(n)(x) really returns a List with n successive evaluations of x. We'll talk about evaluation strategies more in chapter 5.

We simulate the charge here by printing to the console, but in a real program, this would interact with the credit card company.

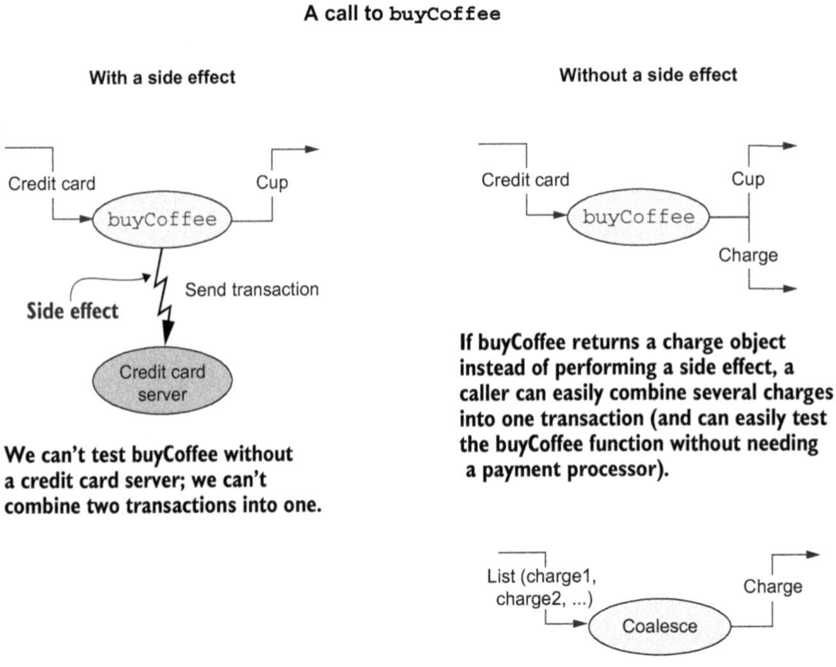

unzip splits a list of pairs into a pair of lists. Here we're destructuring this pair to declare two values (coffees and charges) on one line.

A call to buyCoffee

With a side effect

Without a side effect

We can't test buyCoffee without a credit card server; we can't combine two transactions into one.

If buyCoffee returns a charge object instead of performing a side effect, a caller can easily combine several charges into one transaction (and can easily test the buyCoffee function without needing a payment processor).

Figure 1.1 A call to buy coffee

Overall, this solution is a marked improvement; we're now able to reuse buyCoffee directly to define the buyCoffees function, and both functions are trivially testable without having to define complicated stub implementations of some Payments interface. In fact, the Cafe is now completely ignorant of how the Charge values will be processed. We can still have a Payments class for actually processing charges, of course, but Cafe doesn't need to know about it.

Making Charge into a first-class value has other benefits we might not have anticipated, since we can more easily assemble business logic for working with these charges. For instance, Alice may bring her laptop to the coffee shop and work there for a few hours, making occasional purchases. It might be nice if the coffee shop could combine these purchases Alice makes into a single charge, again saving on credit card processing fees. Since `Charge` is first-class, we can write the following function to coalesce any same-card charges in a `List[Charge]`:

```
def coalesce(charges: List[Charge]): List[Charge] =
  charges.groupBy(_.cc).values.map(_.reduce(_.combine(_))).toList
```

We're passing functions as values to the `groupBy`, `map`, and `reduce` methods. You'll learn to read and write one-liners like this over the course of the next several chapters. The `_.cc` and `_.combine(_)` are syntax for *anonymous functions*, which we'll introduce in the next chapter. As a preview, `_.cc` is equivalent to `c => c.cc`, and `_.combine(_)` is equivalent to `(c1, c2) => c1.combine(c2)`.

   You may find this kind of code difficult to read because the notation is very compact. But as you work through this book, reading and writing Scala code like this will become second nature very quickly. This function takes a list of charges, groups them by the credit card used, and then combines them into a single charge per card. It's perfectly reusable and testable without any additional mock objects or interfaces. Imagine trying to implement the same logic with our first implementation of `buyCoffee`!

   This is just a taste of the benefits of functional programming, and this example is intentionally simple. If the series of refactorings used here seems natural, obvious, unremarkable, or standard practice, that's good. FP is a discipline that merely takes what many consider a good idea to its logical endpoint, applying the discipline even in situations where its applicability is less obvious. As you'll learn over the course of this book, the consequences of consistently following the discipline of FP are profound, and the benefits are enormous. FP is a truly radical shift in how programs are organized at every level—from the simplest of loops to high-level program architecture. The style that emerges is quite different, but it's a beautiful and cohesive approach to programming that we hope you come to appreciate.

What about the real world?

We saw in the case of `buyCoffee` how we could separate the creation of the `Charge` from the interpretation or processing of that `Charge`. In general, we'll learn how this sort of transformation can be applied to any function with side effects to push these effects to the outer layers of the program. Functional programmers often refer to this as implementing programs with a pure core and a thin layer on the outside that handles effects.

But even so, surely at some point we must actually have an effect on the world and submit the `Charge` for processing by some external system. And aren't there other useful programs that necessitate side effects or mutation? How do we write such programs? As we work through this book, we'll discover how many programs that seem to necessitate side effects have some functional analogue. In other cases, we'll find ways to structure code so that effects occur but aren't observable. (For example, we can mutate data that's declared locally in the body of some function if we ensure it can't be referenced outside that function, or we can write to a file as long as no enclosing function can observe this occurring.)

1.2   *Exactly what is a (pure) function?*

We discussed earlier that FP refers to programming with pure functions, and a pure function is one that lacks side effects. In our discussion of the coffee shop example, we worked off an informal notion of side effects and purity. Here we'll formalize this notion to pinpoint more precisely what it means to program functionally. This will also give us additional insight into one of the benefits of functional programming: pure functions are easier to reason about.

A function f with input type A and output type B (written in Scala as a single type, A => B, which is pronounced *A to B*) is a computation that relates every value a of type A to exactly one value b of type B such that b is determined solely by the value of a. Any changing state of an internal or external process is irrelevant to computing the result f(a). For example, a function intToString having type Int => String will take every integer to a corresponding string. Furthermore, if it really is a *function*, it will do nothing else.

In other words, a function has no observable effect on the execution of the program aside from computing a result given its inputs; we say that it has no side effects. We sometimes qualify such functions as *pure* functions to make this more explicit, but this is somewhat redundant. Unless we state otherwise, we'll often use *function* to imply there are no side effects.[4]

You should be familiar with many pure functions already. Consider the addition (+) function on integers. It takes two integer values and returns an integer value. For any two given integer values, it will always return the same integer value. Another example is the length function of a String in Java, Scala, and many other languages in which strings can't be modified (are immutable). For any given string, the same length is always returned, and nothing else occurs.

We can formalize this idea of pure functions using the concept of *referential transparency* (RT). This is a property of *expressions* in general–not just functions. For the purposes of our discussion, consider an expression to be any part of a program that can be evaluated to a result—anything you could type into the Scala interpreter and get an answer. For example, 2 + 3 is an expression that applies the pure function + to the values 2 and 3 (which are also expressions). This has no side effect. The evaluation of this expression results in the same value, 5, every time. In fact, if we saw 2 + 3 in a program, we could simply replace it with the value 5, and it wouldn't change a thing about the meaning of our program.

This is all it means for an expression to be referentially transparent—in any program, the expression can be replaced by its result without changing the meaning of the program. And we say that a function is *pure* if calling it with RT arguments is also RT. We'll look at some examples next.

---

[4] *Procedure* is often used to refer to some parameterized chunk of code that may have side effects.

> ### Referential transparency and purity
> An expression e is *referentially transparent* if for all programs p, all occurrences of e in p can be replaced by the result of evaluating e without affecting the meaning of p. A function f is *pure* if the expression f(x) is referentially transparent for all referentially transparent x.[5]

1.3 *Referential transparency, purity, and the substitution model*

Let's see how the definition of RT applies to our original buyCoffee example:

```
def buyCoffee(cc: CreditCard): Coffee =
  val cup = Coffee()
  cc.charge(cup.price)
  cup
```

Whatever the return type of cc.charge(cup.price) (perhaps it's Unit, Scala's equivalent of void in other languages), it's discarded by buyCoffee. Thus, the result of evaluating buyCoffee(aliceCreditCard) will be merely cup, which is equivalent to a new Coffee(). For buyCoffee to be pure, by our definition of RT, it must be the case that p(buyCoffee(aliceCreditCard)) behaves the same as p(Coffee()) for any program p. This clearly doesn't hold; the program Coffee() doesn't do anything, whereas buyCoffee(aliceCreditCard) will contact the credit card company and authorize a charge. We already have an observable difference between the two programs.

Referential transparency forces the invariant that everything a function does is represented by the value that it returns according to the result type of the function. This constraint enables a simple and natural mode of reasoning about program evaluation called the *substitution model*. When expressions are referentially transparent, we can imagine that computation proceeds much like the way we'd solve an algebraic equation. We fully expand every part of an expression, replacing all variables with their referents, and then we reduce it to its simplest form. At each step, we replace a term with an equivalent one; computation proceeds by substituting *equals* for *equals*. In other words, RT enables *equational reasoning* about programs.

Let's look at two more examples—one in which all expressions are RT and can be reasoned about using the substitution model and one in which some expressions violate RT. There's nothing complicated here; we're just illustrating something you likely already understand.

Let's try the following in the Scala interpreter (also known as the read-eval-print loop (REPL), pronounced like *ripple* but with an *e* instead of an *i*). The interpreter is an interactive prompt that lets us enter a program. The interpreter then evaluates that program, prints the result, and prompts us for another program. When the interpreter is ready for a program to be entered, it prompts with scala>. When printing the result of

---

[5] There are some subtleties to this definition, and we'll refine it later in this book. See the chapter notes at our GitHub site (https://github.com/fpinscala/fpinscala/wiki) for more discussion.

a program, the interpreter displays a name for the result, the type of the result, and the value of the program.

Note that in Java and Scala, strings are immutable. A *modified* string is really a new string, and the old string remains intact:

```
scala> val x = "Hello, World"
x: java.lang.String = Hello, World

scala> val r1 = x.reverse
r1: String = dlroW ,olleH

scala> val r2 = x.reverse        ◁——— r1 and r2 are the same.
r2: String = dlroW ,olleH
```

Suppose we replace all occurrences of the term x with the expression referenced by x (its *definition*) as follows:

```
scala> val r1 = "Hello, World".reverse
r1: String = dlroW ,olleH

scala> val r2 = "Hello, World".reverse   ◁——— r1 and r2 are still the same.
r2: String = dlroW ,olleH
```

This transformation doesn't affect the outcome. The values of r1 and r2 are the same as before, so x was referentially transparent. What's more, r1 and r2 are referentially transparent as well, so if they appeared in some other part of a larger program, they could, in turn, be replaced with their values throughout, and it would have no effect on the program.

Now let's look at a function that is not referentially transparent. Consider the append function on the java.lang.StringBuilder class. This function operates on the StringBuilder in place. The previous state of the StringBuilder is destroyed after a call to append. Let's try this out:

```
scala> val x = new StringBuilder("Hello")
x: java.lang.StringBuilder = Hello

scala> val y = x.append(", World")
y: java.lang.StringBuilder = Hello, World

scala> val r1 = y.toString
r1: java.lang.String = Hello, World

scala> val r2 = y.toString
r2: java.lang.String = Hello, World        ◁——— r1 and r2 are the same.
```

So far, so good. Now let's see how this side effect breaks RT. Suppose we substitute the call to append like we did earlier, replacing all occurrences of y with the expression referenced by y:

```
scala> val x = new StringBuilder("Hello")
x: java.lang.StringBuilder = Hello

scala> val r1 = x.append(", World").toString
r1: java.lang.String = Hello, World

scala> val r2 = x.append(", World").toString
r2: java.lang.String = Hello, World, World  ◁——— rl and r2 are no longer the same.
```

This transformation of the program results in a different outcome. We therefore conclude that `StringBuilder.append` is not a pure function. What's going on here is that although r1 and r2 look like they're the same expression, they are in fact referencing two different values of the same `StringBuilder`. By the time r2 calls x.append, r1 will have already mutated the object referenced by x. If this seems difficult to think about, that's because it is. Side effects make reasoning about program behavior more difficult.

Conversely, the substitution model is simple to reason about, since effects of evaluation are purely local (they affect only the expression being evaluated), and we need not mentally simulate sequences of state updates to understand a block of code. Understanding requires only local reasoning. We need not mentally track all the state changes that may occur before or after our function's execution to understand what our function will do; we simply look at the function's definition and substitute the arguments into its body. Even if you haven't used the name *substitution model*, you have certainly used this mode of reasoning when thinking about your code. [6]

Formalizing the notion of purity this way gives insight into why functional programs are often more *modular*. Modular programs consist of components that can be understood and reused independently of the whole such that the meaning of the whole depends only on the meaning of the components and the rules governing their composition; that is, they are *composable*. A pure function is modular and composable because it separates the logic of the computation itself from what to do with the result and how to obtain the input; it's a black box. The input is obtained in exactly one way: via the argument(s) to the function. And the output is simply computed and returned. By keeping each of these concerns separate, the logic of the computation is more reusable; we may reuse the logic wherever we want without worrying about whether the side effect being performed with the result or the side effect requesting the input are appropriate in all contexts. We saw this in the `buyCoffee` example: by eliminating the side effect of payment processing being done with the output, we were more easily able to reuse the logic of the function, both for purposes of testing and further composition (like when we wrote `buyCoffees` and `coalesce`).

1.4   Conclusion

In this chapter, we introduced functional programming and explained exactly what FP is and why you might use it. Though the full benefits of the functional style will

---

[6] In practice, programmers don't spend time mechanically applying substitution to determine if code is pure—it will usually be obvious.

become clearer over the course of this book, we illustrated some of the benefits of FP using a simple example. We also discussed referential transparency and the substitution model and talked about how FP enables simpler reasoning about programs and greater modularity.

In this book, you'll learn the concepts and principles of FP as they apply to every level of programming, starting from the simplest of tasks and building on that foundation. In subsequent chapters, we'll cover some of the fundamentals: How do we write loops in FP? How do we implement data structures? How do we deal with errors and exceptions? We need to learn how to do these things and get comfortable with the low-level idioms of FP. We'll build on this understanding when we explore functional design techniques in parts 2, 3, and 4.

Summary

- Functional programming is the construction of programs using only pure functions—functions that do not have side effects.
- A side effect is something a function does aside from simply returning a result.
- Examples of side effects include modifying a field on an object, throwing an exception, and accessing the network or file system.
- Functional programming constrains the way we write programs but does not limit our expressive power.
- Side effects limit our ability to understand, compose, test, and refactor parts of our programs.
- Moving side effects to the outer edges of our program results in a pure core and thin outer layer, which handles effects and results in better testability.
- Referential transparency defines whether an expression is pure or contains side effects.
- The substitution model provides a way to test whether an expression is referentially transparent.
- Functional programming enables local reasoning and allows the embedding of smaller programs within larger programs.

Getting started with functional programming in Scala

2

This chapter covers

- Introducing the Scala language
- Explaining objects and namespaces
- Working with higher-order functions (passing functions to functions)
- Working with polymorphic functions (abstracting over types)
- Following types to implementations

Now that we have committed to using only pure functions, a question naturally emerges: How do we write even the simplest of programs? Most of us are used to thinking of programs as sequences of instructions that are executed in order, where each instruction has some kind of effect. In this chapter, we'll begin learning how to write programs in the Scala language by just combining pure functions.

15

This chapter is mainly intended for those readers who are new to Scala, functional programming, or both. Immersion is an effective method for learning a foreign language, so we'll just dive in. The only way Scala code will look familiar rather than foreign is by looking at a lot of Scala code. We've already seen some in the first chapter, and in this chapter, we'll start by looking at a small but complete program. We'll then break it down piece by piece to examine what it does in some detail to better understand the basics of the Scala language and its syntax. Our goal in this book is to teach functional programming, but we'll use Scala as our vehicle, and need to know enough of the Scala language and its syntax to get going.

Once we've covered some of the basic elements of the Scala language, we'll introduce some of the basic techniques of writing functional programs. We'll discuss how to write loops using *tail-recursive functions*, and we'll introduce *higher-order functions*. Higher-order functions are functions that take other functions as arguments and may themselves return functions as their output. We'll also look at some examples of *polymorphic* higher-order functions where we use types to guide us toward an implementation.

There's a lot of new material in this chapter. Some of the material related to higher-order functions may be brain bending if you have a lot of experience programming in a language without the ability to pass functions around like that. Remember, it's not crucial to internalize every single concept in this chapter or solve every exercise. We'll come back to these concepts again from different angles throughout the book, and our goal here is just to give you some initial exposure.

2.1 Introducing Scala the language

The following is a complete program listing in Scala, which we'll talk through. We aren't introducing any new concepts of functional programming here. Our goal is just to introduce the Scala language and its syntax.

Listing 2.1 A simple Scala program

```scala
// A comment!
/* Another comment */
/** A documentation comment */
object MyProgram:
  def abs(n: Int): Int =
    if n < 0 then -n
    else n

  private def formatAbs(x: Int) =
    val msg = "The absolute value of %d is %d"
    msg.format(x, abs(x))


@main def printAbs: Unit =
  println(formatAbs(-42))
```

Declares a singleton object, which simultaneously declares a class and its only instance

abs takes an integer and returns an integer.

Returns the negation of n if it's less than zero

A private method can only be called by other members of MyProgram. Specifying the return type is optional, and when omitted, like here, the return type is inferred from the last expression in the block.

A string with two placeholders for numbers marked as %d

Replaces the two %d placeholders in the string with x and abs(x), respectively

Unit serves the same purpose as void in languages like Java or C.

We declare an object named `MyProgram`. This is simply to give our code a place to live and a name so we can refer to it later. We put our code inside the object by indenting each member.[1] We'll discuss objects and classes in greater detail shortly. For now, we'll just look at this particular object.

The object keyword

The `object` keyword creates a new *singleton type*, which is like a `class` that only has a single named instance. If you're familiar with Java, declaring an `object` in Scala is a lot like creating a new instance of an anonymous class. Scala has no equivalent to Java's `static` keyword, and an object is often used in Scala where you might use a class with static members in Java.

The `MyProgram` object has three *methods*, introduced with the `def` keyword: abs, formatAbs, and printAbs. We'll use the term *method* to refer to some function defined within an object or class using the `def` keyword. Let's now go through the methods of `MyProgram` one by one.

The abs method is a pure function that takes an integer and returns its absolute value:

```
def abs(n: Int): Int =
  if n < 0 then -n
  else n
```

The def keyword is followed by the name of the method, which is followed by the parameter list in parentheses. In this case, abs takes only one argument: n of type Int. Following the closing parenthesis of the argument list, an optional type annotation (the : Int) indicates that the type of the result is Int (the colon may be pronounced *has type*).

The body of the method itself comes after a single equals sign (=). We'll sometimes refer to the part of a declaration that goes before the equals sign as the *left-hand side* or *signature* and the code that comes after the equals sign as the *right-hand* side or *definition*. Note the absence of an explicit `return` keyword. The value returned from a method is simply whatever value results from evaluating the right-hand side. All expressions, including `if` expressions, produce a result. Here the right-hand side is a single expression whose value is either -n or n, depending on whether n < 0.

The formatAbs method is another pure function:

```
private def formatAbs(x: Int) =
  val msg = "The absolute value of %d is %d."      format is a standard library
  msg.format(x, abs(x))                            method defined on string.
```

Here we're calling the `format` method on the `msg` object, passing in the value of x along with the value of abs applied to x. This results in a new string with the occurrences of %d in msg replaced with the evaluated results of x and abs(x), respectively.

---

[1] The `MyProgram` object is optional in this case because Scala supports top-level definitions. We could remove the `MyProgram` object entirely, but here we use the object to group the various related members together.

This method is declared `private`, which means it can't be called from any code outside of the `MyProgram` object. This function takes an `Int` and returns a `String`, but note that the return type is not declared. Scala is usually able to infer the return types of methods, so they can be omitted, but it's generally considered good style to explicitly declare the return types of methods you expect others to use. This method is private to our object, so we omit the type annotation.

The body of the method contains two statements, each indented the same number of spaces. A series of statements indented to the same level is called a *block*. Statements are separated by newline characters or semicolons. In this case, we're using a newline to separate our statements, so a semicolon isn't necessary. Scala supports surrounding blocks with curly braces, like in Java or C, but these can often be omitted. In this book, we omit curly braces when possible.

The first statement in the block declares a `String` named `msg` using the `val` keyword. It's simply there to give a name to the string value, so we can refer to it again. A `val` is an immutable variable, so inside the body of the `formatAbs` method, the name `msg` will always refer to the same `String` value. The Scala compiler will complain if you try to reassign `msg` to a different value in the same block. Scala supports declaring *mutable* variables with the `var` keyword, though `val` is used more frequently.

Remember, a method simply returns the value of its right-hand side, so we don't need a `return` keyword. In this case, the right-hand side is a block. In Scala, the value of a multistatement block is the same as the value returned by the last expression in the block. Therefore, the result of the `formatAbs` method is just the value returned by the call to `msg.format(x, abs(x))`.

Finally, our `printAbs` method is an outer shell that calls into our purely functional core and prints the answer to the console. We'll sometimes call such methods *procedures* (or *impure functions*), rather than functions, to emphasize the fact that they have side effects:

```
@main def printAbs(): Unit =
  println(formatAbs(-42))
```

We chose to define `printAbs` with an empty parameter list. Instead, we could have left the parentheses out entirely:

```
@main def printAbs: Unit =
  println(formatAbs(-42))
```

By convention,[2] parentheses are included on procedures (that is, impure functions) that take no parameters. If a method's parameter list is defined with empty parentheses, then the method must be called with an empty parameter list.

---

[2] The general idea is to signal the presence of side effects via parentheses. This indication of pure versus impure only applies to parameterless methods, though. For methods that take parameters, the parentheses are always required, and not all libraries follow this convention. As a result, some Scala programmers find the convention confusing. We'll look at other ways to differentiate pure functions from impure functions later in this book.

The printAbs method is annotated with @main, signaling to Scala that this method is the entry point of a program. It takes no arguments, and its return type is Unit. Scala supports parsing program arguments, but we're not doing that here.

Unit serves a similar purpose to void in programming languages like C and Java. In Scala, every method has to return some value as long as it doesn't crash or hang. But printAbs doesn't return anything meaningful, so there's a special type, Unit, that is the return type of such methods. There's only one value of this type, and the literal syntax for it is (), a pair of empty parentheses (pronounced *unit*, just like the type). Usually, a return type of Unit is a hint that the method has a side effect.

The body of our printAbs method prints the String returned by the call to formatAbs to the console. Note that the return type of println is Unit, which happens to be what we need to return from printAbs.

2.1.1   *Running our program*

This section discusses the simplest possible way of running your Scala programs, suitable for short examples. More typically, you'll build and run your Scala code using either scala-cli, a command-line tool for interacting with Scala, or sbt, a popular build tool for Scala. Alternatively, you might use an IDE like IntelliJ or Visual Studio Code. There are also various web-based options, like Scastie (http://scastie.scala-lang.org). See the book's source code repo on GitHub (https://github.com/fpinscala/fpinscala) for more information on getting set up with scala-cli and sbt.

The simplest way we can run this Scala program is from the command line by invoking the Scala compiler directly ourselves. First download the Scala 3 compiler from the official Scala website at https://docs.scala-lang.org/getting-started. Once Scala is installed, we start by putting the code in a file called MyProgram.scala or something similar. We can then compile it to Java bytecode using the scalac compiler:

```
> scalac MyProgram.scala
```

This will generate some files ending with the .class suffix and others ending with the .tasty suffix.[3] These files contain compiled code that can be run with the Java Virtual Machine (JVM). The code can be executed using the scala command-line tool, specifying the name of the @main method to run:

```
> scala printAbs
The absolute value of -42 is 42.
```

Actually, it's not strictly necessary to compile the code first with scalac. A simple program like the one we've written here can be run using just the Scala interpreter by passing it to the scala command-line tool directly:

```
> scala MyProgram.scala
The absolute value of -42 is 42.
```

---

[3] See https://mng.bz/vXX1 for more information on .tasty files.

This can be handy when using Scala for scripting. The interpreter will look for any object within the MyProgram.scala file that has an @main method with the appropriate signature, and then it will call it.

An alternative approach is using the Scala interpreter's interactive mode, the REPL, which can be started by running scala with no arguments. It's a great idea to have a REPL window open so you can try things out while you're programming in Scala. We can load our source file into the REPL and try things out (your actual console output may differ slightly):

```
> scala
Welcome to Scala.
Type in expressions for evaluation. Or try :help.

scala> :load MyProgram.scala                ◄─────
// defined object MyProgram

scala> MyProgram.abs(-42)        ◄────
val res0: Int = 42   ◄────
```

:load is a command to the REPL to interpret a Scala source file. (Note that, unfortunately, this won't work for Scala files with package declarations.)

We can type Scala expressions at the prompt.

The REPL evaluates our Scala expression and prints the answer. It also gives the answer a name, res0, that we can refer to later and shows its type, which in this case is Int.

It's also possible to copy and paste lines of code into the REPL. It's a good idea to get familiar with the REPL and its features because it's a tool you'll use a lot as a Scala programmer. To exit the REPL type :quit or press Ctrl-D or Ctrl-C.

2.2 *Objects and namespaces*

In this section, we'll discuss some additional aspects of Scala's syntax related to objects and namespaces. In the preceding REPL session, to refer to our abs method, we had to say MyProgram.abs because abs was defined in the MyProgram object. We say that MyProgram is its *namespace*. Aside from some technicalities, every value in Scala is what's called an *object*,[4] and each object may have zero or more *members*. A member can be a method declared with the def keyword, or it can be another object declared with val or object. Objects can also have other kinds of members, which we'll ignore for now.

We access the members of objects with the typical object-oriented dot notation, which is a namespace (the name that refers to the object) followed by a dot (the period character), and then followed by the name of the member, as in MyProgram .abs(-42). To use the toString member on the object 42, we use 42.toString. The implementations of members within an object can refer to each other unqualified (without prefixing the object name), but if needed, they have access to their enclosing object using a special name: this.[5]

---

[4] Unlike in Java, values of primitive types like Int are also considered objects for the purposes of this discussion.

[5] Note that in this book, we'll use the term *function* to refer more generally to either so-called standalone functions like sqrt or abs or members of some class, including methods. When it's clear from the context, we'll also use the terms *method* and *function* interchangeably, since what matters is not the syntax of invocation (i.e., obj.method(12) vs. method(obj, 12) but the fact that we're talking about some parameterized block of code.

Note that even an expression like 2 + 1 is just calling a member of an object. In that case, what we're calling is the + member of the object 2. It's really syntactic sugar for the expression 2.+(1), which passes 1 as an argument to the method + on the object 2. Any single argument method that has a symbolic name can be used infix like that (omitting the dot and parentheses). In a future version of Scala, methods with alphanumeric names will only be allowed to be called infix if they are defined as an infix def or are surrounded with backticks. For example, instead of MyProgram.abs(42), we can write MyProgram `abs` 42 and get the same result. This infix enforcement can be enabled now by adding -source:future and -deprecation compiler flags (these flags are enabled in the build contained in this book's GitHub repository).

We can bring an object's member into scope by *importing* it, which allows us to call it unqualified from then on:

```scala
scala> import MyProgram.abs
import MyProgram.abs

scala> abs(-42)
val res0: 42
```

We can bring all of an object's (nonprivate) members into scope by using the asterisk syntax:

```scala
import MyProgram.*
```

2.3   Higher-order functions: Passing functions to functions

Now that we've covered the basics of Scala's syntax, we'll move on to covering some of the basics of writing functional programs. The first new idea is this: functions are values. And just like values of other types—such as integers, strings, and lists—functions can be assigned to variables, stored in data structures, and passed as arguments to functions.

When writing purely functional programs, we'll often find it useful to write a function that accepts other functions as arguments, or higher-order functions—we'll look next at some simple examples of higher-order functions to illustrate. In later chapters, we'll see how useful this capability really is and how it permeates the functional programming style. But to start, suppose we wanted to adapt our program to print out both the absolute value of a number and the factorial of another number. Here's a sample run of such a program:

```
The absolute value of -42 is 42
The factorial of 7 is 5040
```

2.3.1   A short detour: Writing loops functionally

First let's write factorial:

```scala
def factorial(n: Int): Int =
  def go(n: Int, acc: Int): Int =
    if n <= 0 then acc
    else go(n - 1, n * acc)

  go(n, 1)
```

> This is an inner function or a local definition. It's common in Scala to write functions that are local to the body of another function. In functional programming, we shouldn't consider this more important than local integers or strings.

We write loops functionally, without mutating a loop variable, by using a recursive function. Here we're defining a recursive helper function inside the body of the factorial function. Such a helper function is often called go or loop by convention. In Scala, we can define functions inside any block, including within another function definition. Since it's local, the go function can only be referred to from within the body of the factorial function, just like a local variable would. The definition of factorial, finally, just consists of a call to go with the initial conditions for the loop.

The arguments to go are the state for the loop. In this case, they're the remaining value n and the current accumulated factorial acc. To advance to the next iteration, we call go recursively with the new loop state (here, go(n - 1, n * acc)), and to exit from the loop, we return a value without a recursive call (here, we return acc in the case that n <= 0). Scala detects this sort of *self-recursion* and compiles it to the same sort of bytecode as would be emitted for a while loop,[6] so long as the recursive call is in *tail position*. See the sidebar for the technical details on this, but the basic idea is that this optimization[7] (called *tail call elimination*) is applied when there's no additional work left to do after the recursive call returns.

We can manually trace the execution of a recursive function to get a better understanding how evaluation proceeds. An execution trace of factorial(5) might look like the following:

```
factorial(5)
  go(5, 1)
    go(4, 5)
      go(3, 20)
        go(2, 60)
          go(1, 120)
            go(0, 120)
              120
```

In this trace, each recursive call increases the indent level of the trace. We may choose to render tail recursive calls without increasing the indent level. Since the recursive call in go is in tail position, we could write the trace as

```
factorial(5)
  go(5, 1)
  go(4, 5)
  go(3, 20)
  go(2, 60)
  go(1, 120)
  go(0, 120)
  120
```

---

[6] We can write while loops by hand in Scala, but it's rarely necessary and considered bad form, since it hinders good compositional style.

[7] The term *optimization* is not really appropriate here. An optimization usually connotes some nonessential performance improvement, but when we use tail calls to write loops, we generally rely on them being compiled as iterative loops that don't consume a call stack frame for each iteration (which would result in a StackOverflowError for large inputs).

Manually writing out such traces is often very helpful for understanding recursive functions.

Tail calls in Scala

A call is said to be in *tail position* if the caller does nothing other than return the value of the recursive call. For example, the recursive call to go(n - 1, n * acc) that we discussed earlier is in tail position since the method returns the value of this recursive call directly and does nothing else with it. On the other hand, if we said 1 + go(n - 1, n * acc), go would no longer be in tail position since the method would still have work to do when go returned its result (namely, adding 1 to it).

If all recursive calls made by a function are in tail position, Scala automatically compiles the recursion to iterative loops that don't consume call stack frames for each iteration. By default, Scala doesn't tell us if tail call elimination was successful, but if we're expecting this to occur for a recursive function we write, we can tell the Scala compiler about this assumption using the tailrec annotation (https://mng.bz/499D) so it can give us a compile error if it's unable to eliminate the tail calls of the function. Here's the syntax for this:

```
def factorial(n: Int): Int =
  @annotation.tailrec
  def go(n: Int, acc: Int): Int =
    if n <= 0 then acc
    else go(n - 1, n * acc)

  go(n, 1)
```

We won't talk much more about annotations in this book (you can find more information at https://mng.bz/nYvV), but we'll use @annotation.tailrec extensively.

NOTE   See the preface for information on the exercises.

EXERCISE 2.1

Write a recursive function to get the nth Fibonacci number (http://mng.bz/C29s). The first two Fibonacci numbers are 0 and 1. The nth number is always the sum of the previous two—the sequence begins 0, 1, 1, 2, 3, 5. Your definition should use a local, tail-recursive function:

```
def fib(n: Int): Int
```

2.3.2 *Writing our first higher-order function*

Now that we have `factorial`, let's edit our previous program to include it.

Listing 2.2   A simple program including the factorial function

```
object MyProgram:                        │ Definitions of abs and
  ...                          ←─────────┤ factorial go here.
  private def formatAbs(x: Int) =
    val msg = "The absolute value of %d is %d."
    msg.format(x, abs(x))

  private def formatFactorial(n: Int) =
    val msg = "The factorial of %d is %d."
    msg.format(n, factorial(n))

  @main def printAbsAndFactorial: Unit =
    println(formatAbs(-42))
    println(formatFactorial(7))
```

The two functions, `formatAbs` and `formatFactorial`, are almost identical. If we like, we can generalize these to a single function, `formatResult`, which accepts the function as an argument to apply to its argument:

```
                                                    │ f is required to be a
def formatResult(name: String, n: Int, f: Int => Int) =  ←─┤ function from Int to Int.
  val msg = "The %s of %d is %d."
  msg.format(name, n, f(n))
```

Our `formatResult` function is a higher-order function that takes another function, called `f` (see the variable-naming conventions sidebar). We give a type to `f`, as we would for any other parameter. Its type is `Int => Int` (pronounced *int to int* or *a function from int to int*), which indicates that `f` expects an integer argument and will also return an integer.

Our previous abs function matches that type: it accepts an `Int` and returns an `Int`. Likewise, `factorial` accepts an `Int` and returns an `Int`, which also matches the `Int => Int` type. We can therefore pass abs or `factorial` as the `f` argument to `formatResult`:

```
scala> formatResult("absolute value", -42, abs)
val res0: String = "The absolute value of -42 is 42."

scala> formatResult("factorial", 7, factorial)
val res1: String = "The factorial of 7 is 5040."
```

Variable-naming conventions

It's a common convention to use names like `f`, `g`, and `h` for parameters to a higher-order function. In functional programming, we tend to use very short variable names—even one-letter names.

This is usually because higher-order functions are so general that they have no opinion on what the argument should actually do. All they know about the argument is its type. Many functional programmers feel that short names make code easier to read since they make the structure of the code easier to see at a glance.

2.4 *Polymorphic functions: Abstracting over types*

So far we've defined only *monomorphic* functions, or functions that operate on only one type of data. For example, abs and factorial are specific to arguments of type Int, and the higher-order function formatResult is also fixed to operate on functions that take arguments of type Int. Often, and especially when writing higher-order functions, we want to write code that works for any type it's given. These are called *polymorphic functions*,[8] and in the chapters ahead, you'll get plenty of experience writing such functions. Here we'll just introduce the idea.

2.4.1 *An example of a polymorphic function*

We can often discover polymorphic functions by observing that several monomorphic functions all share a similar structure. For example, the following monomorphic function, findFirst, returns the first index in an array where the key occurs, or -1 if it's not found. It's specialized for searching for a String in an Array of String values.

Listing 2.3 Monomorphic function to find a String in an array

```
def findFirst(ss: Array[String], key: String): Int =
  @annotation.tailrec
  def loop(n: Int): Int =
    if n >= ss.length then -1       If n is past the end of the array, return -1
    else if ss(n) == key then n     indicating the key doesn't exist in the array.
    else loop(n + 1)                Otherwise, increment n, and keep looking.

  loop(0)                           Start the loop at the first element of the array.
```

ss(n) extracts the nth element of the array ss. If the element at n is equal to the key, return n, indicating the element appears in the array at that index.

The details of the code aren't too important here. What's important is that the code for findFirst will look almost identical if we're searching for a String in an Array[String], an Int in an Array[Int], or an A in an Array[A] for any given type A. We can write findFirst more generally for any type A by accepting a function to use for testing a particular A value. Note that this last generalization isn't strictly necessary—we could instead just take the target key, of type A, to search for. But doing so assumes the type has a useful equals method, which may not be true.

---

[8] We're using the term *polymorphism* in a slightly different way than you might be used to if you're familiar with object-oriented programming, where that term usually connotes some form of subtyping or inheritance relationship. There are no interfaces or subtyping in this example. The kind of polymorphism we're using here is sometimes called *parametric polymorphism*.

Listing 2.4   Polymorphic function to find an element in an array

```
def findFirst[A](as: Array[A], p: A => Boolean): Int =
  @annotation.tailrec
  def loop(n: Int): Int =
    if n >= as.length then -1
    else if p(as(n)) then n
    else loop(n + 1)

  loop(0)
```

← Instead of hardcoding String, take a type A as a parameter. And instead of hardcoding an equality check for a given key, take a function with which to test each element of the array.

← If the function p matches the current element, we've found a match, and we return its index in the array.

This is an example of a polymorphic function, sometimes called a *generic* function. We're abstracting over the type of the array and the function used for searching it. To write a polymorphic function as a method, we introduce a comma-separated list of *type parameters*, surrounded by square brackets (here just a single [A]), following the name of the function (in this case findFirst). We can call the type parameters anything we want—[Foo, Bar, Baz] and [TheParameter, another_good_one] are valid type parameter declarations—though by convention, we typically use short, one-letter, uppercase type parameter names, like [A, B, C].

The type parameter list introduces *type variables* that can be referenced in the rest of the type signature (exactly analogous to how variables introduced in the parameter list to a function can be referenced in the body of the function). In findFirst, the type variable A is referenced in two places: the elements of the array are required to have the type A (since it's an Array[A]), and the p function must accept a value of type A (since it's a function of type A => Boolean). The fact that the same type variable is referenced in both places in the type signature implies that the type must be the same for both arguments, and the compiler will enforce this fact anywhere we try to call findFirst. If we try to search for a String in an Array[Int], for instance, we'll get a type mismatch error.

2.4.2   *Calling higher-order functions with anonymous functions*

When using higher-order functions, it's often convenient to be able to call these functions with *anonymous functions* or *function literals*, rather than having to supply some existing named function. For instance, we can test the findFirst function in the REPL as follows:

```
scala> findFirst(Array(7, 9, 13), (x: Int) => x == 9)
val res2: Int = 1
```

There is some new syntax here. The expression Array(7, 9, 13) is an *array literal*. It constructs a new array with three integers in it. Note the lack of a keyword like new to construct the array.

The syntax (x: Int) => x == 9 is a *function literal*, or *anonymous function*. Instead of defining this function as a method with a name, we can define it inline using this convenient syntax. This particular function takes one argument called x of type Int, and it returns a Boolean, indicating whether x is equal to 9.

In general, the arguments to the function are declared to the left of the => arrow, and we can then use them in the body of the function to the right of the arrow. For example, if we want to write an equality function that takes two integers and checks if they're equal to each other, we could write that like this:

```
scala> (x: Int, y: Int) => x == y
val res0: (Int, Int) => Boolean = Lambda$1240/0x00000008006dc840@121cf6f4
```

The (Int, Int) => Boolean notation given by the REPL indicates that the value of res0 is a function that takes two integer arguments and returns a Boolean. The Lambda$1240/0x00000008006dc840@121cf6f4 is a string representation of the function instance obtained by calling toString. The string value is not very useful, and we generally ignore it. When the type of the function's inputs can be inferred by Scala from the context, the type annotations on the function's arguments may be elided—for example, (x,y) => x < y. We'll see an example of this in the next section and lots more examples throughout the book.

EXERCISE 2.2

Implement isSorted, which checks whether an Array[A] is sorted according to a given comparison function, gt, which returns true if the first parameter is greater than the second parameter:

```
def isSorted[A](as: Array[A], gt: (A, A) => Boolean): Boolean
```

Your implementation of isSorted should return the following results:

```
scala> isSorted(Array(1, 2, 3), _ > _)
val res0: Boolean = true

scala> isSorted(Array(1, 2, 1), _ > _)
val res1: Boolean = false

scala> isSorted(Array(3, 2, 1), _ < _)
val res2: Boolean = true

scala> isSorted(Array(1, 2, 3), _ < _)
val res3: Boolean = false
```

2.5   *Following types to implementations*

As you might have seen when writing isSorted, the universe of possible implementations is significantly reduced when implementing a polymorphic function. If a function is polymorphic in some type A, the only operations that can be performed on that A are those passed into the function as arguments (or that can be defined in terms of these given operations).[9] In some cases, you'll find that the universe of possibilities for a given polymorphic type is constrained such that only one implementation is possible!

Let's look at an example of a function signature that can only be implemented in one way. It's a higher-order function for performing what's called *partial application*. This function, partial1, takes a value and a function of two arguments and returns a function of one argument as its result. The name comes from the fact that the function is being applied to some but not all of the arguments it requires:

```
def partial1[A, B, C](a: A, f: (A, B) => C): B => C
```

The partial1 function has three type parameters: A, B, and C. It then takes two arguments. The argument f is itself a function that takes two arguments of types A and B, respectively, and returns a value of type C. The value returned by partial1 will also be a function of type B => C.

How would we go about implementing this higher-order function? It turns out there's only one implementation that compiles, and it follows logically from the type signature. It's like a fun little logic puzzle. And even though it's a fun puzzle, this isn't a purely academic exercise. Functional programming in practice involves a lot of fitting building blocks together in the only way that makes sense. The purpose of this exercise is to get practice using higher-order functions and using Scala's type system to guide your programming.

Let's start by looking at the type of thing we have to return. The return type of partial1 is B => C, so we know we have to return a function of that type. We can begin by writing a function literal that takes an argument of type B:

```
def partial1[A, B, C](a: A, f: (A, B) => C): B => C =
  (b: B) => ???
```

This may feel strange at first if you're not used to writing anonymous functions. Where did that B come from? Well, we've just written, "Return a function that takes a value b of type B." On the right-hand side of the => arrow (where the question marks are now) comes the body of that anonymous function. We're free to refer to the value b in there for the same reason that we're allowed to refer to the value a in the body of partial1.[10]

In the body of the anonymous function ??? is the name of a built-in Scala function that simply throws a NotImplementedError. It's very common to use ??? to incrementally build up functionality. The full definition of ??? is

```
def ??? = throw NotImplementedError
```

---

[9] Technically, all values in Scala can be compared for equality (using ==) and turned into strings with toString and integers with hashCode. But this is something of a wart inherited from Java.

[10] Within the body of this inner function, the outer a is still in scope. We sometimes say that the inner function *closes over* its environment, which includes a.

Let's keep going. Now that we've asked for a value of type B, what do we want to return from our anonymous function? The type signature says it has to be a value of type C, and there's only one way to get such a value. According to the signature, C is the return type of the function f. So the only way to get that C is by passing an A and a B to f. That's easy:

```
def partial1[A, B, C](a: A, f: (A, B) => C): B => C =
  (b: B) => f(a, b)
```

And we're done! The result is a higher-order function that takes a function of two arguments and partially applies it. That is, if we have an A and a function that needs both A and B to produce C, we can get a function that just needs B to produce C (since we already have the A). It's like saying, "If I can give you a carrot for an apple and a banana, and you already gave me an apple, you just have to give me a banana, and I'll give you a carrot."

Note that the type annotation on b isn't needed here. Since we told Scala the return type would be B => C, Scala knows the type of b from the context, and we could just write b => f(a,b) as the implementation. Generally speaking, we'll omit the type annotation on a function literal if it can be inferred by Scala.

EXERCISE 2.3

Let's look at another example, currying,[11] which converts a function f of two arguments into a function of one argument that partially applies f. Here again there's only one implementation that compiles. Write this implementation:

```
def curry[A, B, C](f: (A, B) => C): A => (B => C)
```

Note the type A => (B => C) can be read as a function that takes an A and returns a new function from B to C.

EXERCISE 2.4

Implement uncurry, which reverses the transformation of curry. Note that since => associates to the right, A => (B => C) can be written as A => B => C:

```
def uncurry[A, B, C](f: A => B => C): (A, B) => C
```

---

[11]This is named after the mathematician Haskell Curry, who discovered the principle. It was independently discovered earlier by Moses *Schoenfinkel*, but Schoenfinkelization didn't catch on.

Let's look at a final example, *function composition*, which feeds the output of one function to the input of another function. Again, the implementation of this function is fully determined by its type signature.

■ **EXERCISE 2.5** ──

Implement the higher-order function that composes two functions:

```
def compose[A, B, C](f: B => C, g: A => B): A => C
```

──

This is such a common process that Scala's standard library provides `compose` as a method on `Function1` (the interface for functions that take one argument). To compose two functions, f and g, we say f compose g.[12] It also provides an `andThen` method. `f andThen g` is the same as `g compose f`:

```
scala> val f = (x: Double) => math.Pi / 2 - x
val f: Double => Double = <function1>

scala> val cos = f andThen math.sin
val cos: Double => Double = <function1>
```

It's all well and good to puzzle together little one-liners like this, but what about programming with a large, real-world code base? In functional programming, it turns out to be exactly the same. Higher-order functions like `compose` don't care whether they're operating on huge functions backed by millions of lines of code or functions that are simple one-liners. Polymorphic, higher-order functions often end up being extremely widely applicable, precisely because they say nothing about any particular domain and are simply abstracting over a common pattern that occurs in many contexts. For this reason, programming in the large has much the same flavor as programming in the small. We'll write several widely applicable functions over the course of this book, and the exercises in this chapter are a taste of the style of reasoning you'll employ when writing such functions.

2.6   *Conclusion*

In this chapter, we learned enough of the Scala language to get started, as well as some preliminary functional programming concepts. We learned how to define simple functions and programs, including how we can express loops using recursion; then we introduced the idea of higher-order functions, and we got some practice writing polymorphic functions in Scala. We saw how the implementations of polymorphic functions are often significantly constrained such that we can often simply follow the types to the correct implementation. This is something we'll see a lot of in the chapters ahead.

──

[12]Solving the `compose` exercise by using this library function is considered cheating.

Although we haven't yet written any large or complex programs, the principles we've discussed here are scalable and apply equally well to programming in the large and programming in the small. Next we'll look at using pure functions to manipulate data.

Summary

- Scala is a mixed paradigm language, blending concepts from both objected-oriented programming and functional programming.
- The `object` keyword creates a new singleton type. Objects contain members such as method definitions, values, and additional objects.
- Scala supports top-level definitions, but objects provide a convenient way to group related definitions.
- Methods are defined with the `def` keyword.
- The definition of a method can be a single expression or a block with multiple statements.
- Method definitions can contain local definitions, such as nested methods.
- The result of a method is the value of its right-hand side. There's no need for an explicit `return` statement.
- The `@main` annotation defines an entry point of a program.
- The `Unit` type serves a similar purpose to `void` in C and Java. There's one value of the `Unit` type, which is written as `()`.
- The `import` keyword allows us to reference the members of a namespace (that is, an object or package) without writing out their fully qualified names.
- Recursive functions allow the expression of looping without mutation. All loops can be rewritten as recursive functions and vice versa.
- Tail-recursive functions are recursive functions that limit recursive calls to the tail position—that is, the result of the recursive call is returned directly, with no further manipulation.
- Tail recursion ensures the stack does not grow with each recursive call.
- Higher-order functions are functions that take one or more functions as parameters.
- Polymorphic functions, also known as generic functions, are functions that use one or more type parameters in their signature, allowing them to operate on many types.
- A function with no type parameters is monomorphic.
- Polymorphic functions allow us to remove extraneous detail, resulting in definitions that are easier to read and write and are reusable.
- Polymorphic functions constrain the possible implementations of a function signature. Sometimes there is only a single possible implementation.
- Determining the implementation of a polymorphic function from its signature is known as following types to implementations or type-driven development.

Exercise answers

ANSWER 2.1

```scala
def fib(n: Int): Int =
  @annotation.tailrec
  def go(n: Int, current: Int, next: Int): Int =
    if n <= 0 then current
    else go(n - 1, next, current + next)

  go(n, 0, 1)
```

Like `factorial`, we define a local tail recursive function called go, which recurses on n, decrementing by 1 on each recursive call. Besides n, the go function takes parameters specifying the current (nth) and next (nth + 1) Fibonacci numbers. When n reaches 0, we've computed the nth value and simply return the current Fibonacci number. Otherwise, we recurse, shifting the next Fibonacci number into the current position and computing the new next as the sum of the Fibonacci numbers passed to this iteration.

ANSWER 2.2

```scala
def isSorted[A](as: Array[A], gt: (A,A) => Boolean): Boolean =
  @annotation.tailrec
  def loop(n: Int): Boolean =
    if n + 1 >= as.length then true
    else if gt(as(n), as(n + 1)) then false
    else loop(n + 1)

  loop(0)
```

This implementation is very similar to the definition of `findFirst`, using a local tail recursive function to iterate through the elements of an array. We call the gt function with the nth and nth + 1 elements of the array, returning `false` if the nth element is greater than the nth + 1 element. Otherwise, we recurse, terminating recursion when we've reached the end of the array.

■ **ANSWER 2.3**

```
def curry[A, B, C](f: (A, B) => C): A => (B => C) =
  a => b => f(a, b)
```

The solution uses the trick we used in the definition of partial1, but this time, we use it twice—once to get a value of type A and again to get a value of type B. We then apply the two received parameters to the function.

■ **ANSWER 2.4**

```
def uncurry[A, B, C](f: A => B => C): (A, B) => C =
  (a, b) => f(a)(b)
```

We again use the trick used in partial1 and curry, but this time, we return a function that accepts two parameters: a value of type A and another of type B. In the definition of that function, we apply a to the original function f, resulting in a new function from B => C. We then apply b to that function to get the final value of type C.

■ **ANSWER 2.5**

```
def compose[A, B, C](f: B => C, g: A => B): A => C =
  a => f(g(a))
```

We return an anonymous function from A to C. In the definition of that anonymous function, we have the parameter a and the outer values f: B => C and g: A => B. The only way we can make some progress is by applying a to the function g, resulting in a value of type B. The only thing we can do with that B is apply it to f, which gives us the exact type we need to return.

Functional
data structures

We said in the introduction that functional programs don't update variables or modify mutable data structures. This raises pressing questions: What sort of data structures can we use in functional programming? How do we define them in Scala? And how do we operate on them? In this chapter, we'll learn the concept of *functional data structures* and how to work with them. We'll use this as an opportunity to introduce how data types are defined in functional programming, learn about the related technique of *pattern matching*, and get practice writing and generalizing pure functions.

This chapter has many exercises, particularly dealing with writing and generalizing pure functions. Some of these exercises may be challenging; the answers are provided, but try to work through each exercise before looking at the answer, as these techniques require practice to fully grasp. You can also consult our GitHub site (https://github.com/fpinscala/fpinscala), which provides a build environment for the exercises and answers.

3.1 Defining functional data structures

A functional data structure is (not surprisingly) operated on using only pure functions. Remember, a pure function must not change data in place or perform other side effects. Therefore, functional data structures are, by definition, immutable. For example, the empty list (written `List()` or `Nil` in Scala) is as eternal and immutable as the integer values 3 or 4. And just as evaluating 3 + 4 results in a new number, 7, without modifying either 3 or 4, concatenating two lists together (the syntax for this is a ++ b for two lists a and b) yields a new list and leaves the two inputs unmodified.

Doesn't this mean we end up doing a lot of extra copying of the data? Perhaps surprisingly, the answer is no, and we'll talk about exactly why that is. But first, let's examine what is likely the most ubiquitous functional data structure: the singly linked list. The definition here is identical in spirit to (though simpler than) the `List` data type defined in Scala's standard library. Throughout this chapter, we'll develop and use our own `List` data type, though subsequent chapters will use the built-in `List`. The following listing introduces a lot of new syntax and concepts, which we'll talk through in detail.

Listing 3.1 Singly linked lists

```
package fpinscala.datastructures
```
A List data constructor representing the empty list

```
enum List[+A]:
  case Nil
  case Cons(head: A, tail: List[A])
```
Another data constructor representing nonempty lists. Note that tail is another List[A], which may be Nil or another Cons.

```
object List:
  def apply[A](as: A*): List[A] =
    if as.isEmpty then Nil
    else Cons(as.head, apply(as.tail*))
```
This is the List companion object. It contains functions for creating and working with lists.

List the data type parameterized on a type: A.

This is variadic function syntax, which lets us construct a List[Int] with syntax like List(l, 2, 3).

Let's look first at the definition of the data type, which begins with the keyword `enum`. An enum is a data type that consists of a series of *data constructors*, each defined by the case keyword. Scala enumerations are similar to enumerations from Java or C, but instead of being limited to a set of values (e.g., Red, Green, Blue), Scala enumerations can have data constructors that take arbitrary arguments.[1]

---

[1] Enumerations were introduced in Scala 3. In Scala 2, we used a `sealed trait` and a series of `case class` and `case object` instead, where each case was a subtype of the trait. See the enums versus sealed traits section at the end of this chapter for more information.

The `List` enumeration has two such data constructors, which represent the two possible forms a `List` can take. As figure 3.1 shows, a `List` can be empty, denoted by the data constructor `Nil`, or it can be nonempty, denoted by the data constructor `Cons` (traditionally, short for *construct*). A nonempty list consists of an initial element, head, followed by a `List` (possibly empty) of remaining elements (the `tail`):

```
case Nil
case Cons(head: A, tail: List[A])
```

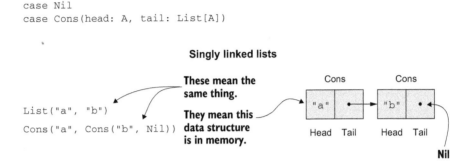

Figure 3.1   Constructing singly linked lists

Just as functions can be polymorphic, data types can be as well, and by adding the type parameter `[+A]` after enum List, we declare the `List` data type to be polymorphic in the type of elements it contains, which means we can use this same definition for a list of `Int` elements (denoted `List[Int]`), `Double` elements (denoted `List[Double]`), `String` elements (`List[String]`), and so on. (The + indicates that the type parameter A is *covariant*; see the "More about variance" sidebar for more information.)

A data constructor declaration gives us a function to construct that form of the data type. Here are a few examples:

```
val ex1: List[Double] = List.Nil
val ex2: List[Int] = List.Cons(1, List.Nil)
val ex3: List[String] = List.Cons("a", List.Cons("b", List.Nil))
```

The case `Nil` lets us write `List.Nil` to construct an empty `List`, and the case `Cons` lets us write `List.Cons(1, List.Nil)`, `List.Cons("a", List.Cons("b", List.Nil))`, and so on to build singly linked lists of arbitrary lengths.[2] Note that because `List` is parameterized on a type, A, these are polymorphic functions that can be instantiated with different types for A. Here ex2 instantiates the A type parameter to `Int`, while ex3 instantiates it to `String`. The ex1 example is interesting: `Nil` is being instantiated with

---

[2] Scala generates a default `def toString: String` method for enumerations, which can be convenient for debugging. You can see the output of this default `toString` implementation if you experiment with `List` values in the REPL, which uses `toString` to render the result of each expression. `List.Cons(1, List.Nil)` will be printed as the string `"Cons(1, Nil)"`, for instance. But note that the generated `toString` will be naively recursive and will cause stack overflow when printing long lists, so you may wish to provide a different implementation.

type `List[Double]`, which is allowed because the empty list contains no elements and can be considered a list of whatever type we want!

Each data constructor also introduces a *pattern* that can be used for *pattern matching*, as in the functions `sum` and `product`. We'll examine pattern matching in more detail next.

More about variance

In the declaration `enum List[+A]`, the + in front of the type parameter A is a *variance annotation* that signals that A is a *covariant* parameter of `List`. This means that, for instance, `List[Dog]` is considered a subtype of `List[Animal]`, assuming `Dog` is a subtype of `Animal`. (More generally, for all types X and Y, if X is a subtype of Y, then `List[X]` is a subtype of `List[Y]`). We could leave out the + in front of the A, which would make `List` *invariant* (or *nonvariant*) in that type parameter.

Note that `Nil` extends `List[Nothing]`; we could have explicitly stated this (via `case Nil extends List[Nothing]`), but since we didn't, Scala inferred that relationship. `Nothing` is a subtype of all types, which means in conjunction with the *variance annotation*, `Nil` can be considered a `List[Int]`, a `List[Double]`, and so on, exactly as we want.

These concerns about variance aren't very important for the present discussion and are more of an artifact of how Scala encodes data constructors via subtyping, so don't worry if this is not completely clear right now. It's certainly possible to write code without using variance annotations at all, and function signatures sometimes end up simpler (whereas type inference often gets worse). We'll use variance annotations throughout this book where it's convenient to do so, but you should feel free to experiment with both approaches (see https://mng.bz/QnnR for more details).

Variadic functions in Scala

The function `apply` in the `object List` is a *variadic function*, meaning it accepts zero or more arguments of type A:

```scala
def apply[A](as: A*): List[A] =
  if as.isEmpty then Nil
  else Cons(as.head, apply(as.tail*))
```

For data types, it's a common idiom to have a variadic `apply` method in the companion object to conveniently construct instances of the data type. By calling this function `apply` and placing it in the companion object, we can invoke it with syntax like `List(1, 2, 3, 4)` or `List("hi", "bye")`, with as many values as we want separated by commas (we sometimes call this the *list literal* or simply *literal* syntax).

Variadic functions just provide a little syntactic sugar for creating and passing a `Seq` of elements explicitly. `Seq` is the interface in Scala's collections library implemented by sequence-like data structures, such as lists, queues, and vectors.

(continued)

Inside `apply`, the argument as will be bound to a `Seq[A]` (see the documentation at http://mng.bz/f4k9), which has the functions `head` (which returns the first element) and `tail` (which returns all elements but the first). The special `*` annotation allows us to pass a `Seq` to a variadic method.

3.2   *Pattern matching*

Let's look in detail at the functions `sum` and `product`, which we place in the object `List`, sometimes called the *companion object* to `List` (see companion objects in Scala sidebar). Both these definitions make use of pattern matching:

```
object List:

  def sum(ints: List[Int]): Int = ints match
    case Nil => 0
    case Cons(x, xs) => x + sum(xs)

  def product(doubles: List[Double]): Double = doubles match
    case Nil => 1.0
    case Cons(0.0, _) => 0.0
    case Cons(x, xs) => x * product(xs)
```

As you might expect, the `sum` function states that the sum of an empty list is 0, and the sum of a nonempty list is the first element, x, plus the sum of the remaining elements, xs.[3] Likewise, the `product` definition states that the product of an empty list is 1.0, the product of any list starting with 0.0 is 0.0, and the product of any other nonempty list is the first element multiplied by the product of the remaining elements. Note that these are recursive definitions, which are common when writing functions that operate over recursive data types like `List` (which refers to itself recursively in its `Cons` data constructor).

Pattern matching works a bit like a fancy `switch` statement that may descend into the structure of the expression it examines and extract subexpressions of that structure. It's introduced with an expression (the *target* or *scrutinee*) like `ds` followed by the keyword `match` and a sequence of cases. Each case in the match consists of a pattern (like `Cons(x, xs)`) to the left of the `=>` and a result (like `x * product(xs)`) to the right of the `=>`. If the target *matches* the pattern in a case (discussed next), the result of that case becomes the result of the entire match expression. If multiple patterns match the target, Scala chooses the first matching case.

---

[3] We could call x and xs anything there, but it's a common convention to use xs, ys, as, or bs as variable names for a sequence of some sort and x, y, a, or b as the name for a single element of a sequence. Another common naming convention is h or hd for the first element of a list (the *head* of the list), t or tl for the remaining elements (the *tail*), and l for an entire list.

> ### Companion objects in Scala
>
> We'll often declare a *companion object* in addition to our data type and its data constructors. This is just an `object` with the same name as the data type (in this case, `List`) where we put various convenience functions for creating or working with values of the data type.
>
> If, for instance, we wanted a function, `def fill[A](n: Int, a: A): List[A]`, that created a `List` with n copies of the element a, the `List` companion object would be a good place for it. Companion objects have access to private and protected members of the type with the same name but are otherwise like any other object. We could have called this object `Foo` or `ListFunctions` if we wanted, but calling it `List` makes it clear that the object contains functions relevant to working with lists.

Let's look at a few more examples of pattern matching:

- `List(1,2,3) match { case _ => 42 }` results in 42. Here we're using a variable pattern, _, which matches any expression. We could say x or foo instead of _, but we usually use _ to indicate a variable whose value we ignore in the result of the case.[4]
- `List(1,2,3) match { case Cons(h, _) => h }` results in 1. Here we're using a data constructor pattern in conjunction with variables to *capture* or *bind* a subexpression of the target. This pattern match is depicted in figure 3.2.
- `List(1,2,3) match { case Cons(_, t) => t }` results in `List(2, 3)`.
- `List(1,2,3) match { case Nil => 42 }` throws a `MatchError` at runtime. A `MatchError` indicates that none of the cases in a match expression matched the target.[5]

In many of these examples, Scala warns us that our pattern match may not be exhaustive—and hence risks throwing a `MatchError` at runtime.

Matching a list

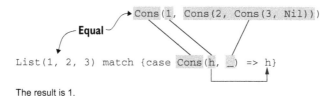

The result is 1.

Figure 3.2 Pattern matching on a list

---

[4] The _ variable pattern is treated somewhat specially in that it may be mentioned multiple times in the pattern to ignore multiple parts of the target.

[5] Scala is often able to determine at compile time if a match expression does not cover all cases. In such cases, the compiler reports a warning.

What determines if a pattern matches an expression? A pattern may contain *literals*, like 3 or "hi"; *variables*, like x and xs, which match anything, indicated by an identifier starting with a lowercase letter or underscore; and data constructors, like Cons(x, xs) and Nil, which match only values of the corresponding form. (Nil as a pattern matches only the value Nil, and Cons(h, t) or Cons(x, xs) as a pattern only matches Cons values.) These components of a pattern may be nested arbitrarily; Cons(x1, Cons(x2, Nil)) and Cons(y1, Cons(y2, Cons(y3, _))) are valid patterns. A pattern matches the target if there exists an assignment of variables in the pattern to subexpressions of the target that make it *structurally equivalent* to the target. The resulting expression for a matching case will then have access to these variable assignments in its local scope.

■ **EXERCISE 3.1** ──

What will be the result of the following match expression?

```
import List.*                        ◁──────────┐  This allows us to write Cons and Nil
                                                 │  instead of List.Cons and List.Nil.
val result = List(1,2,3,4,5) match
  case Cons(x, Cons(2, Cons(4, _))) => x
  case Nil => 42
  case Cons(x, Cons(y, Cons(3, Cons(4, _)))) => x + y
  case Cons(h, t) => h + sum(t)
  case _ => 101
```

You're strongly encouraged to try experimenting with pattern matching in the REPL to get a sense of how it behaves. When working in the REPL, it is convenient to import all the members of the List companion object via import List.* to enable writing Cons(1, Nil) instead of List.Cons(1, List.Nil).

When working in the REPL, take care to import the List type defined in this chapter instead of the built-in List type. If using the code in the companion GitHub project, it looks like this:

Imports the List type defined in the fpinscala.exercises
.datastructures package, shadowing the built-in Scala List

Imports Cons and Nil (and some other members) from the List companion object, shadowing the built-in Scala Nil

```
scala> import fpinscala.exercises.datastructures.List     ◁──┘

scala> import List.*                                       ◁──────────────────┘

scala> val x: List[Int] = Cons(1, Nil)                     ◁────────────┐
val x: fpinscala.exercises.datastructures.List[Int] = Cons(1,Nil)       │
```

Constructs a value of fpinscala.exercises.datastructures
.List[Int], not a value of the built-in Scala List[Int]

3.3   *Data sharing in functional data structures*

When data is immutable, how do we write functions that, for example, add or remove elements from a list? The answer is simple. When we add an element 1 to the front of an existing list, say xs, we return a new list—in this case, Cons(1, xs). Since lists are immutable, we don't need to actually copy xs; we can just reuse it. This is called *data sharing*. Sharing of immutable data often lets us implement functions more efficiently; we can always return immutable data structures without having to worry about subsequent code modifying our data. There's no need to pessimistically make copies to avoid modification or corruption.[6]

In the same way, to remove an element from the front of a list val mylist = Cons(x, xs), we simply return its tail, xs. There's no real removing going on. The original list, mylist, is still available, unharmed. We say that functional data structures are *persistent*, meaning existing references are never changed by operations on the data structure. Data sharing is depicted in figure 3.3.

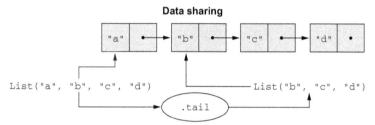

Data sharing

Both lists share the same data in memory. `.tail` does not modify the original list; it simply references the tail of the original list. Defensive copying is not needed because the list is immutable.

Figure 3.3   Data sharing of lists

Let's try implementing a few different functions for modifying lists in different ways. You can place this, and other functions we write, inside the List companion object.

■ EXERCISE 3.2

Implement the function tail for removing the first element of a List (note that the function takes constant time). You can use sys.error("message") to throw an exception if the List is Nil. In the next chapter, we'll look at different ways of handling errors. Be careful to use the List enum and the Nil case defined here and not the built-in Scala List and Nil types.

---

[6] Pessimistic copying can become a problem in large programs. When mutable data is passed through a chain of loosely coupled components, each component has to make its own copy of the data because other components might modify it. Immutable data is always safe to share, so we never have to make copies. We find that, in the large, FP can often achieve greater efficiency than approaches that rely on side effects due to much greater sharing of data and computation.

EXERCISE 3.3

Using the same idea, implement the function `setHead` for replacing the first element of a `List` with a different value.

3.3.1 *The efficiency of data sharing*

Data sharing often lets us implement operations more efficiently. Let's look at a few examples.

EXERCISE 3.4

Implement the function `drop`, which removes the first n elements from a list. Dropping n elements from an empty list should return the empty list. Note that this function takes time proportional only to the number of elements being dropped—we don't need to make a copy of the entire `List`:

```
def drop[A](as: List[A], n: Int): List[A]
```

EXERCISE 3.5

Implement `dropWhile`, which removes elements from the `List` prefix as long as they match a predicate:

```
def dropWhile[A](as: List[A], f: A => Boolean): List[A]
```

A more surprising example of data sharing is the following function, which adds all the elements of one list to the end of another:

```
def append[A](a1: List[A], a2: List[A]): List[A] =
  a1 match
    case Nil => a2
    case Cons(h, t) => Cons(h, append(t, a2))
```

Note that this definition only copies values until the first list is exhausted, so its runtime and memory usage are determined only by the length of a1. The remaining list then just points to a2. If we were to implement this same function for two arrays, we'd be forced to copy all the elements in both arrays into the result. In this case, the immutable linked list is much more efficient than an array!

Not everything works out so nicely. Implement a function, init, that returns a List consisting of all but the last element of a List, so given List(1,2,3,4), init will return List(1,2,3). Why can't this function be implemented in constant time (that is, runtime that's proportional to the size of the list) like tail?

```
def init[A](as: List[A]): List[A]
```

Because of the structure of a singly linked list, any time we want to replace the tail of a Cons, even if it's the last Cons in the list, we must copy all the previous Cons objects. Writing purely functional data structures that support different operations efficiently is all about finding clever ways to exploit data sharing. We're not going to cover these data structures here; for now, we're content to use the functional data structures others have written. As an example of what's possible, in the Scala standard library, there's a purely functional sequence implementation, Vector (see the documentation at http://mng.bz/aZqm), with constant-time random access, updates, head, tail, init, and effectively constant-time additions to either the front or rear of the sequence.

3.3.2 *Recursion over lists and generalizing to higher-order functions*

Let's look again at the implementations of sum and product. We've simplified the product implementation slightly so as not to include the *short-circuiting* logic of checking for 0.0:

```
def sum(ints: List[Int]): Int = ints match
  case Nil => 0
  case Cons(x, xs) => x + sum(xs)

def product(ds: List[Double]): Double = ds match
  case Nil => 1.0
  case Cons(x, xs) => x * product(xs)
```

Note how similar these two definitions are. They're operating on different types (List[Int] versus List[Double]), but aside from this, the only differences are the value to return in the case that the list is empty (0 in the case of sum and 1.0 in the case of product) and the operation to combine results (+ in the case of sum and * in the case of product). Whenever you encounter duplication like this, you can generalize it away by pulling subexpressions out into function arguments. If a subexpression refers to any local variables (the + operation refers to the local variables x and xs introduced by the pattern and similarly for product), turn the subexpression into a function that accepts these variables as arguments. Let's do that now. Our function

44 CHAPTER 3 *Functional data structures*

will take as arguments the value to return in the case of the empty list and the function
to add an element to the result in the case of a nonempty list.[7]

Listing 3.2 Right folds and simple uses

```
def foldRight[A, B](as: List[A], acc: B, f: (A, B) => B): B =
  as match
    case Nil => acc
    case Cons(x, xs) => f(x, foldRight(xs, acc, f))

def sumViaFoldRight(ns: List[Int]) =
  foldRight(ns, 0, (x,y) => x + y)

def productViaFoldRight(ns: List[Double]) =
  foldRight(ns, 1.0, _ * _)
```

_ * _ **is more concise
notation for (x,y) => x * y.**

foldRight is not specific to any one type of element, and we discover while generalizing that the value that's returned doesn't have to be of the same type as the elements
of the list! One way of describing what foldRight does is that it replaces the constructors of the list, Nil and Cons, with acc and f, as illustrated here:

```
Cons(1, Cons(2, Nil))
f   (1, f   (2, acc))
```

Let's look at a complete example. We'll trace the evaluation of foldRight(Cons(1,
Cons(2, Cons(3, Nil))), 0)((x,y) => x + y) by repeatedly substituting the definition
of foldRight for its usages. We'll use program traces like this throughout the book:

```
foldRight(Cons(1, Cons(2, Cons(3, Nil))), 0, (x,y) => x + y)
1 + foldRight(Cons(2, Cons(3, Nil)), 0, (x,y) => x + y)
1 + (2 + foldRight(Cons(3, Nil), 0, (x,y) => x + y))
1 + (2 + (3 + (foldRight(Nil, 0, (x,y) => x + y))))
1 + (2 + (3 + (0)))
6
```

**Replace foldRight
with its definition.**

Note that foldRight must traverse all the way to the end of the list (pushing frames
onto the call stack as it goes) before it can begin collapsing it. In fact, the name fold-
Right is a reference to the way collapsing each element begins at the rightmost end of
the list and works its way back toward the start.

---

[7] In the Scala standard library, foldRight is a method on List, and its arguments are curried, resulting in
usage like as.foldRight(acc)(f). Type inference in Scala 2 worked on each parameter list to a function in
succession—meaning the type of acc would be inferred and then constrain the type of f. In Scala 3, type
inference is not limited in this manner, and hence, there's less motivation for defining multiple parameter
lists. However, there's still a syntax advantage to defining higher-order functions to take their final function
argument as a distinct parameter list. Doing so allows syntax like as.foldRight(acc): a => … or
as.foldRight(acc) { a => … }.

Underscore notation for anonymous functions

The anonymous function $(x,y) => x + y$ can be written as $\_ + \_$ in situations where the types of x and y could be inferred by Scala. This is a useful shorthand in cases where the function parameters are mentioned just once in the body of the function. Each underscore in an anonymous function expression like $\_ + \_$ introduces a new (unnamed) function parameter and references it. Arguments are introduced in left-to-right order. Here are a few more examples:

_ + _   ⟵——— **(x, y) => x + y**

_ * 2   ⟵——— **x => x * 2**

_.head   ⟵——— **xs => xs.head**

_ drop _   ⟵——— **(xs, n) => xs.drop(n)**

Use this syntax judiciously. Its meaning in expressions like `foo(_, g(List(_ + 1), _))` can be unclear. There are precise rules about the scoping of these underscore-based anonymous functions in the Scala language specification, but if you have to think about it we recommend just using ordinarily named function parameters.

EXERCISE 3.7

Can `product`, implemented using `foldRight`, immediately halt the recursion and return `0.0` if it encounters a `0.0`? Why or why not? Consider how any short circuiting might work if you call `foldRight` with a large list. This is a deeper question, which we'll return to in chapter 5.

EXERCISE 3.8

See what happens when you pass `Nil` and `Cons` themselves to `foldRight`, like this: `foldRight(List(1, 2, 3), Nil: List[Int], Cons(_, _))`.[8] What do you think this says about the relationship between `foldRight` and the data constructors of `List`?

---

[8] The type annotation `Nil: List[Int]` is needed here because otherwise Scala infers the `B` type parameter in `foldRight` as `List[Nothing]`.

■ **EXERCISE 3.9**

Compute the length of a list using `foldRight`:

```
def length[A](as: List[A]): Int
```

■ **EXERCISE 3.10**

Our implementation of `foldRight` is not tail recursive and will result in a `StackOver-flowError` for large lists (we say it's not *stack safe*). Convince yourself that this is the case, and then write another general list-recursion function, `foldLeft`, that is tail recursive, using the techniques we discussed in the previous chapter. Start collapsing from the leftmost start of the list. Here is its signature:

```
def foldLeft[A, B](as: List[A], acc: B, f: (B, A) => B): B
```

■ **EXERCISE 3.11**

Write `sum`, `product`, and a function to compute the length of a list using `foldLeft`.

■ **EXERCISE 3.12**

Write a function that returns the reverse of a list (i.e., given `List(1,2,3)`, it returns `List(3,2,1)`). See if you can write it using a fold.

□ **EXERCISE 3.13**

Hard: Can you write `foldRight` in terms of `foldLeft`? How about the other way around? Implementing `foldRight` via `foldLeft` is useful because it lets us implement `foldRight` tail recursively, which means it works even for large lists without overflowing the stack.

---

[9] Again, `foldLeft` is defined as a method of `List` in the Scala standard library, and it is curried similarly for better type inference, so you can write `mylist.foldLeft(0.0)(_ + _)`.

■ **EXERCISE 3.14**

Recall the signature of append:

```
def append[A](a1: List[A], a2: List[A]): List[A]
```

Implement append in terms of either foldLeft or foldRight instead of structural recursion.

■ **EXERCISE 3.15**

Hard: Write a function that concatenates a list of lists into a single list. Its runtime should be linear in the total length of all lists. Try to use functions we have already defined.

3.3.3 *More functions for working with lists*

There are many more useful functions for working with lists. We'll cover a few more here to get additional practice with generalizing functions and some basic familiarity with common patterns when processing lists. After finishing this section, you're not going to emerge with an automatic sense of when to use each of these functions; just get in the habit of looking for possible ways to generalize any explicit recursive functions you write to process lists. If you do this, you'll (re)discover these functions for yourself and develop an instinct for when to use each one.

■ **EXERCISE 3.16**

Write a function that transforms a list of integers by adding 1 to each element (that is, given a list of integers, it returns a new list of integers where each value is one more than the corresponding value in the original list).

■ **EXERCISE 3.17**

Write a function that turns each value in a List[Double] into a String. You can use the expression d.toString to convert some d: Double to a String.

■ **EXERCISE 3.18**

Write a function, map, that generalizes modifying each element in a list while maintaining the structure of the list. Here is its signature:[10]

```
def map[A, B](as: List[A], f: A => B): List[B]
```

■ **EXERCISE 3.19**

Write a function, filter, that removes elements from a list unless they satisfy a given predicate. Use it to remove all odd numbers from a List[Int]:

```
def filter[A](as: List[A], f: A => Boolean): List[A]
```

■ **EXERCISE 3.20**

Write a function, flatMap, that works like map except that the function given will return a list instead of a single result, ensuring that the list is inserted into the final resulting list. Here is its signature:[11]

```
def flatMap[A, B](as: List[A], f: A => List[B]): List[B]
```

For instance, flatMap(List(1, 2, 3), i => List(i,i)) should result in List(1, 1, 2, 2, 3, 3).

■ **EXERCISE 3.21**

Use flatMap to implement filter.

■ **EXERCISE 3.22**

Write a function that accepts two lists and constructs a new list by adding corresponding elements. For example, List(1,2,3) and List(4,5,6) become List(5,7,9).

_____

[10]In the standard library, map is a method on List.
[11]In the standard library, flatMap is a method on List.

■ **EXERCISE 3.23**

Generalize the function you just wrote so it's not specific to integers or addition.

LISTS IN THE STANDARD LIBRARY

List exists in the Scala standard library (API documentation at http://mng.bz/y9qE), and we'll use the standard library version in subsequent chapters. The main difference between the List developed here and the standard library version is that Cons is called ::, which associates to the right,[12] so 1 :: 2 :: Nil is equal to 1 :: (2 :: Nil), which is equal to List(1,2). When pattern matching, case Cons(h,t) becomes case h :: t, which avoids having to nest parentheses if writing a pattern like case h :: h2 :: t to extract more than just the first element of the List.

There are a number of other useful methods on the standard library lists. You may want to try experimenting with these and other methods in the REPL after reading the API documentation. These are defined as methods on List[A] rather than as standalone functions, as we've done in this chapter:

- def take(n: Int): List[A]—It returns a list consisting of the first n elements of this.
- def takeWhile(f: A => Boolean): List[A]—It returns a list consisting of the longest valid prefix of this whose elements all pass the predicate f.
- def forall(f: A => Boolean): Boolean—It returns true if and only if all elements of this pass the predicate f.
- def exists(f: A => Boolean): Boolean—It returns true if any element of this passes the predicate f.
- scanLeft and scanRight—These are similar to foldLeft and foldRight, but they return the List of partial results rather than just the final accumulated value.

We recommend you look through the Scala API documentation after finishing this chapter to see what other functions there are. If you find yourself writing an explicit recursive function for doing some sort of list manipulation, check the List API to see if something like the function you need already exists.

3.3.4 *Loss of efficiency when assembling list functions from simpler components*

One of the problems with List is that although we often express operations and algorithms in terms of general-purpose functions, the resulting implementation isn't always efficient—we may end up making multiple passes over the same input or else have to write explicit recursive loops to allow early termination.

---

[12]In Scala, all methods whose names end in : are right associative. That is, the expression x :: xs is actually the method call xs.::(x), which in turn calls the data constructor ::(x,xs). See the Scala language specification for more information.

■ **EXERCISE 3.24**

Hard: Implement hasSubsequence to check whether a List contains another List as a subsequence. For instance, List(1,2,3,4) would have List(1,2), List(2,3), and List(4) as subsequences, among others. You may have some difficulty finding a concise and purely functional implementation that is also efficient—that's OK.

Implement the function in whatever manner comes most naturally. We'll return to this implementation in chapter 5 and hopefully improve upon it. Note that any two values x and y can be compared for equality in Scala using the expression x == y.

```
def hasSubsequence[A](sup: List[A], sub: List[A]): Boolean
```

3.4   *Trees*

List is just one example of what's called an *algebraic data type* (ADT). (Somewhat confusingly, ADT is sometimes used elsewhere to stand for *abstract data type*.) An ADT is just a data type defined by one or more data constructors, each of which may contain zero or more arguments. We say that the data type is the *sum* or *union* of its data constructors, and each data constructor is the *product* of its arguments—hence the name *algebraic* data type.[13]

Tuple types in Scala

Pairs and tuples of higher arities (e.g., triples) are also algebraic data types. They work just like the ADTs we've been writing here but have special syntax:

```
scala> val p = ("Bob", 42)
val p: (String, Int) = (Bob,42)
scala> p(0)
val res0: String = Bob
scala> p(1)
val res1: Int = 42
scala> p match { case (a, b) => b }
val res2: Int = 42
```

In this example, ("Bob", 42) is a pair whose type is (String, Int), which is syntactic sugar for Tuple2[String, Int] (see the API: http://mng.bz/1F2N). We can extract the first or second element of this pair by index, and we can pattern match on this pair much like any other case class. If we try passing an invalid index—e.g., 3 or -1—we get a *compilation* error, not a runtime error. Higher arity tuples work similarly; try experimenting with them in the REPL if you're interested.

---

[13]The naming is not coincidental. There's a deep connection, beyond the scope of this book, between the "addition" and "multiplication" of types to form an ADT and the addition and multiplication of numbers.

Algebraic data types can be used to define other data structures. Let's define a simple binary tree data structure:

```
enum Tree[+A]:
  case Leaf(value: A)
  case Branch(left: Tree[A], right: Tree[A])
```

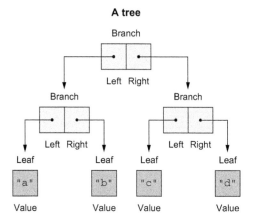

A tree

```
Branch(Branch(Leaf("a"), Leaf("b")),
       Branch(Leaf("c"), Leaf("d")))
```

Figure 3.4   Example tree structure

Pattern matching again provides a convenient way of operating over elements of our ADT. Let's write a function, size, that counts the number of nodes (leaves and branches) in a tree:

```
enum Tree[+A]:
  case Leaf(value: A)
  case Branch(left: Tree[A], right: Tree[A])

  def size: Int = this match
    case Leaf(_) => 1
    case Branch(l, r) => 1 + l.size + r.size
```

Pattern match on this to determine whether size is getting called on a Leaf or a Branch.

Invokes the size method on each branch

The size operation is defined as a method on Tree, allowing the method to be called in an object-oriented style. This simplifies both the definition of the size function as well as its usage. Consider the definition of size as a standalone function:

```
object Tree:
  def size[A](t: Tree[A]): Int = t match
    case Leaf(_) => 1
    case Branch(l, r) => 1 + size(l) + size(r)
```

Theses two definitions are very similar! The method syntax allows simpler call sites (t.size instead of size(t)) and simpler method signatures. When writing data structures we have the choice of using methods or functions—experiment with both.

Extension methods

The `size` method is defined for every tree, regardless of the type the tree is instantiated with; it works on `Tree[Int]`, `Tree[Double]`, and so on. Can we use method syntax to define methods for a more specific type?

Consider a function defined for `Tree[Int]` that returns the first positive integer in the tree (or, if none exists, returns the last visited value):

```
def firstPositive(t: Tree[Int]): Int = t match
  case Leaf(i) => i
  case Branch(l, r) =>
    val lpos = firstPositive(l)
    if lpos > 0 then lpos else firstPositive(r)
```

If we try to define this function as a method on `Tree`, we'll run into a problem because this is a `Tree[A]`, not a `Tree[Int]`. Instead, we can define `firstPositive` as an *extension method* on any `Tree[Int]`:

```
extension (t: Tree[Int]) def firstPositive: Int = t match
  case Leaf(i) => i
  case Branch(l, r) =>
    val lpos = l.firstPositive
    if lpos > 0 then lpos else r.firstPositive
```

This says that for any `Tree[Int]`, there exists a method named `firstPositive`, which takes no arguments and returns an `Int`. The definition of `firstPositive` can reference the tree on which it was called as the value `t` due to the `(t: Tree[Int])` clause after the extension keyword—just like a regular method can reference `this`.

When the compiler sees an expression like `myTree.firstPositive`, it will notice that there is no regular method named `firstPositive` and search for an extension method with that name. The search is limited to specific locations, so we need to define our extension method in one of those locations. In this case, we'll put the `firstPositive` extension method into the companion object for `Tree`. Extension methods defined in the companion are always available to callers. For more details on extension method syntax and where they can be placed, see the documentation (http://mng.bz/MgYm).

The choice between extension methods and standalone functions (usually defined in companion objects) is purely aesthetic. We use both forms throughout this book.[14]

---

[14]In general, we'll use this object-oriented style of syntax where possible for functions that have a single, primary operand (like `firstPositive`, which operates on a target `Tree[Int]`, or `map`, which operates on a target `Tree[A]`), and the standalone function style otherwise.

■ **EXERCISE 3.25** ──────────────────────────────

Write a function, `maximum`, that returns the maximum element in a `Tree[Int]`. (Note that in Scala you can use `x.max(y)` to compute the maximum of two integers x and y.) Let's try writing a few more functions.

■ **EXERCISE 3.26** ──────────────────────────────

Write a function, `depth`, that returns the maximum path length from the root of a tree to any leaf.

■ **EXERCISE 3.27** ──────────────────────────────

Write a function, `map`, analogous to the method of the same name on `List` that modifies each element in a tree with a given function.

ADTs and encapsulation

One might object that algebraic data types violate encapsulation by making public the internal representation of a type. In FP, we approach concerns about encapsulation differently—we don't typically have delicate mutable state that could lead to bugs or violation of invariants if exposed publicly. Exposing the data constructors of a type is often fine, and the decision to do so is approached much like any other decision about what the public API of a data type should be.[15]

We typically use ADTs for situations in which the set of cases is *closed* (i.e., known to be fixed). For `List` and `Tree`, changing the set of data constructors would significantly change what these data types are. `List` is a singly linked list—that is its nature—and the two cases `Nil` and `Cons` form part of its useful public API. We can certainly write code that deals with a more abstract API than `List` (we'll see examples of this later in the book), but this sort of information hiding can be handled as a separate layer rather than being baked into `List` directly.

---

[15]It's also possible in Scala to expose patterns like `Nil` and `Cons` independent of the actual data constructors of the type.

■ EXERCISE 3.28

Generalize `size`, `maximum`, `depth`, and `map`, writing a new function, `fold`, that abstracts over their similarities. Reimplement them in terms of this more general function. Can you draw an analogy between this `fold` function and the left and right folds for `List`?

Enums versus sealed traits

We've defined the `List` and `Tree` algebraic data types with the enum feature of Scala. Alternatively, we could define them with sealed traits (this is how algebraic data types were defined in Scala 2, which didn't support enumerations).

A `trait` defines an abstract interface of common methods (or values or other member types). Traits are abstract in the sense that they cannot be instantiated as values—rather, values are introduced via subtypes.

A class (or object) extends a trait, and each instantiated value of that class is an instance of the trait. Traits may define both abstract and concrete methods, and as of Scala 3, they may define parameters (http://mng.bz/XrYa), making them very similar to abstract classes. A class or object can extend multiple traits but only a single abstract class. There are some other small differences that are not significant for the purposes of this book (see https://mng.bz/Xaa1 for more details).

Defining an ADT with a sealed trait involves enumerating the data constructors as subtypes of the trait, normally as case classes and case objects defined in the companion object of the trait. The `sealed` modifier requires all subtypes to be defined in the same source file as the defining type. This is particularly important when defining ADTs, as we don't want folks to be able to define new data constructors; otherwise, all our pattern matches would fail. The compiler can even check whether all data constructors are handled when pattern matching on a sealed trait, giving a warning if any cases are missing. The following is what the sealed trait encoding of `List` looks like:

```
sealed trait List[+A]:
  import List.{Cons, Nil}

  def size: Int = this match
    case Cons(_, tl) => 1 + tl.size
    case Nil => 0

object List:
  case class Cons[+A](head: A, tail: List[A]) extends List[A]
  case object Nil extends List[Nothing]
```

We could even define `size` as an abstract method and provide implementations on each subtype:

```
sealed trait List[+A]:
  def size: Int

object List:
  case class Cons[+A](head: A, tail: List[A]) extends List[A]:
    def size: Int = 1 + tail.size
  case object Nil extends List[Nothing]:
    def size: Int = 0
```

The choice is largely driven by aethestic preferences, though the abstract method encoding tends to shift the focus to operations and away from thinking about the data. We'll use the `enum` encoding throughout this book, since it avoids a lot of boilerplate, but note that the `trait` encoding allows for more customization.

3.5 Conclusion

In this chapter, we covered a number of important concepts. We introduced algebraic data types and pattern matching and showed how to implement purely functional data structures, including the singly linked list. We hope that, after completing the exercises in this chapter, you are more comfortable writing pure functions and generalizing them. We'll continue to develop these skills in the chapters ahead.

Summary

- Functional data structures are immutable and are operated on using only pure functions.
- Algebraic data types (ADTs) are defined via a set of data constructors.
- ADTs are expressed in Scala with enumerations or sealed trait hierarchies.
- Enumerations may take type parameters, and each data constructor may take zero or more arguments.
- Singly linked lists are modeled as an ADT with two data constructors: `Cons(head: A, tail: List[A])` and `Nil`.
- Companion objects are objects with the same name as a data type. Companion objects have access to the private and protected members of the companion type.
- Pattern matching lets us destructure an algebraic data type, allowing us to inspect the values used to construct the algebraic data type.
- Pattern matches can be defined to be exhaustive, meaning one of the cases is always matched. A non-exhaustive pattern match may throw a `MatchError`. The compiler often warns when defining a non-exhaustive pattern match.
- Purely functional data structures use persistence, also known as structural sharing, to avoid unnecessary copying.

- With singly linked lists, some operations can be implemented with no copying, like prepending an element to the front of a list. Other operations require copying the entire structure, like appending an element to the end of a list.
- Many algorithms can be implemented with recursion on the structure of an algebraic data type, with a base case associated with one data constructor and recursive cases associated with other data constructors.
- foldRight and foldLeft allow us to compute a single result by visiting all the values of a list.
- map, filter, and flatMap are higher-order functions that compute a new list from an input list.
- Extension methods allow object-oriented style methods to be defined for a type in an ad hoc fashion separate from the definition of the type.

3.6   *Exercise answers*

 ANSWER 3.1 ──────────────────────────────────────

3

The cases are checked in order of appearance:

- The first case fails to match because the innermost Cons in the pattern requires a 4, but the value being matched contains a 3 in that position.
- The second case fails to match because our list of five elements starts with a Cons value, not a Nil.
- The third case binds 1 to x and 2 to y, matches 3 and 4, and then discards the final Cons(5, Nil) using the wildcard pattern. Since the third case matches, the right-hand side of the case (after the =>) is evaluated with the x = 1 and y = 2 bindings, resulting in the value 3.
- The final two cases are not consulted at all, since the third case matched, but both of them would have matched as well! Experiment with commenting out the various cases.

──────────────────────────────────────

ANSWER 3.2 ──────────────────────────────────────

```
def tail[A](as: List[A]): List[A] = as match
  case Cons(_, tl) => tl
  case Nil => sys.error("tail of empty list")
```

This definition starts by pattern matching on the supplied list. Our list can be either a Cons constructor or a Nil constructor. In the case of the Cons constructor, we use the _ pattern binding to ignore the head, and we bind the name tl to the tail, which allows us to return `tl` as the result of the function. If instead our list is a `Nil`, we raise an error. Alternatively, we could have chosen the tail of an empty list to be an empty list—that is, `case Nil => Nil`. Doing so is reasonable but risks masking mistakes; calling `tail` on an empty list is often a bug, and hence it's better to fail immediately, keeping the error close to the place where the nonempty assumption was wrong.

■ **ANSWER 3.3**

```
def setHead[A](as: List[A], hd: A): List[A] = as match
  case Cons(_, tl) => Cons(hd, tl)
  case Nil => sys.error("setHead of empty list")
```

We use the same technique as in the definition of `tail`, pattern matching on the input list and handling each data constructor. Like in `tail`, if we encounter a `Cons` constructor, we ignore its head and bind its tail to the name `tl`. We then return a new `Cons` value, passing our new head `hd` and the bound `tl`. If we encounter the `Nil` constructor, we error. Instead, we could choose to return an empty list in this case.

■ **ANSWER 3.4**

```
def drop[A](as: List[A], n: Int): List[A] =
  if n <= 0 then as
  else as match
    case Cons(_, tl) => drop(tl, n - 1)
    case Nil => Nil
```

We first check if the requested number of elements to drop is 0 or below, and if so, return the input list (`as`) without modification; otherwise, we pattern match on the list. If we encounter a `Cons` constructor we discard the head value and recursively call `drop` on the tail, decrementing the number of elements to drop by 1 to account for the discarded head. If instead we encounter a `Nil` value, we just return `Nil`.

Like the implementations of `tail` and `setHead`, we could have chosen to raise an error if we've been asked to drop more elements than there are in the list. We chose differently in this implementation since `drop` is often used in cases where the number of elements is computed. Had we decided to raise an error, callers would have had to check the size of the list before calling drop (e.g., `drop(as, n min size(as))`). Both design choices are valid. As you practice writing functional libraries, you'll develop an instinct for such decisions.

```
def dropWhile[A](as: List[A], f: A => Boolean): List[A] =
  as match
    case Cons(hd, tl) if f(hd) => dropWhile(tl, f)
    case _ => as
```

We pattern match on the list, but our cases are a little different this time. Our first case matches a Cons constructor, which has a head that passes the supplied predicate. We implement this using a *pattern guard*—a conditional on the pattern expressed using if <condition>. In this case, we bind hd and tl to the head and tail of the Cons constructor and use the guard if f(hd). This case only matches when f(hd) evaluates to true, in which case we call dropWhile recursively on tl. The remaining cases—a Cons constructor for which f(hd) evaluates to false and the Nil constructor—match the wildcard case and result in returning the input list.

Note that we didn't need to use pattern guards here. Instead, we could have matched solely on the structure of the input list:

```
def dropWhile[A](as: List[A], f: A => Boolean): List[A] =
  as match
    case Cons(hd, tl) =>
      if f(hd) then dropWhile(tl, f)
      else as
    case Nil => as
```

Either approach is fine in such a small example. It's good to be familiar with both approaches and choose the one that's easier to read on a case-by-case basis.

```
def init[A](as: List[A]): List[A] = as match
  case Nil => sys.error("init of empty list")
  case Cons(_, Nil) => Nil
  case Cons(hd, tl) => Cons(hd, init(tl))
```

We pattern match on the input list. If we encounter a Nil, we immediately error (like we did in tail). If instead we encounter a Cons(_, Nil), we know we have a list of one element, which we discard and return Nil. Otherwise, we must have a Cons(hd, tl) where tl is nonempty (that is, it's not equal to Nil, or we would have matched it already). Hence, we compute the init of the tail and then cons our hd on to the result.

The runtime of init is proportional to the length of the list as a result of traversing each Cons value. Furthermore, we have to build up a copy of the entire list, as there's no structural sharing between the initial list and the result of init. Finally, this implementation uses a stack frame for each element of the list, resulting in the potential for stack overflow errors for large lists. We'll see how to write recursive functions without accumulating stack frames in a bit.

■ **ANSWER 3.7**

No, this is not possible. `foldRight` recurses all the way to the end of the list before invoking the function. A full traversal has occurred before the supplied function is ever invoked. We'll cover early termination in chapter 5.

■ **ANSWER 3.8**

`foldRight(List(1, 2, 3), Nil: List[Int], Cons(_, _))` evaluates to `Cons(1, Cons(2, Cons(3, Nil)))`. Recall that `foldRight(as, acc, f)` replaces `Nil` with `acc` and `Cons` with `f`. When we set `acc` to `Nil` and `f` to `Cons`, our replacements are all identities.

■ **ANSWER 3.9**

```
def length[A](as: List[A]): Int =
  foldRight(as, 0, (_, acc) => acc + 1)
```

We call `foldRight` with an initial accumulator of 0 and a function that adds 1 to the accumulator for each element it encounters.

■ **ANSWER 3.10**

```
@annotation.tailrec
def foldLeft[A, B](as: List[A], acc: B, f: (B, A) => B): B =
  as match
    case Nil => acc
    case Cons(hd, tl) => foldLeft(tl, f(acc, hd), f)
```

We pattern match on the supplied list: if it's `Nil`, we return the accumulated result, and if it's a `Cons`, we compute a new accumulator by calling `f` with the current accumulator and the head of the `Cons` cell. We then recursively call `foldLeft`, passing the tail and the new accumulator. This implementation is tail recursive because there is no additional work to do after the recursive call completes. We have the Scala compiler ensure it is tail recursive by adding the `@annotation.tailrec` annotation.

■ ANSWER 3.11

```
def sum(ints: List[Int]): Int =
  foldLeft(ints, 0, _ + _)

def product(ds: List[Double]): Double =
  foldLeft(ds, 1.0, _ * _)

def length[A](as: List[A]): Int =
  foldLeft(as, 0, (acc, _) => acc + 1)
```

■ EXERCISE 3.12

```
def reverse[A](as: List[A]): List[A] =
  foldLeft(as, Nil: List[A], (acc, a) => Cons(a, acc))
```

We use `foldLeft` with an initial accumulator of an empty list and Cons(a, acc) as the combining function. As a result of `foldLeft` walking through the elements left to right, the resulting list is built right to left, yielding a list in the reverse order.

■ ANSWER 3.13

A simple and stack-safe implementation of `foldRight` makes two passes through the List:

```
def foldRightViaFoldLeft[A, B](as: List[A], acc: B, f: (A, B) => B): B =
  foldLeft(reverse(as), acc, (b, a) => f(a, b))
```

We first reverse the input list and then `foldLeft` with the result, flipping the order of the parameters passed to the combining function.

A different technique is interesting for theoretical reasons and works equally well for `foldRight` in terms of `foldLeft` as well as `foldLeft` in terms of `foldRight`. The trick is to accumulate a function B => B instead of accumulating a single value of type B. In both cases, we start with the identity function on type B as the initial accumulator: (b: B) => b. When implementing `foldRight` via `foldLeft` and using an accumulator of type B => B, the combining function passed to `foldLeft` ends up with the type (B => B, A) => (B => B). This is a function of two arguments; the first argument is a function from B to B, and the second argument is an A. The function returns a new function from B to B.

That's a bit hard to follow, so let's write out some types. Our combining function will take the following shape: (g: B => B, a: A) => ???: (B => B). Since we need to return a function from B to B, we can return an anonymous function. Expanding that, we get (g: B => B, a: A) => (b: B) => ???: B. We can follow the types from here; we have an a: A, a b: B, a function g: B => B, and a function f: (A, B) => B. We can apply a and b to f and apply the result to g. Putting all of that together gives us our implementation:

```
def foldRightViaFoldLeft[A, B](as: List[A], acc: B, f: (A, B) => B): B =
  foldLeft(as, (b: B) => b, (g, a) => b => g(f(a, b)))(acc)
```

Note that the result of foldLeft(as, (b: B) => b, (g, a) => b => g(f(a, b))) gives us a final function of B => B. We apply the initial acc to that function to get our result B.

We can use the same trick to implement foldLeft in terms of foldRight:

```
def foldLeftViaFoldRight[A, B](as: List[A], acc: B, f: (B, A) => B): B =
  foldRight(as, (b: B) => b, (a, g) => b => g(f(b, a)))(acc)
```

Note that neither of these tricky implementations are stack safe as a result of function composition not being stack safe. Each iteration through the combining function grows our accumulator by an additional anonymous function. Nonetheless, these implementations are hinting at something deeper, which we'll revisit in chapter 10.

ANSWER 3.14

```
def append[A](xs: List[A], ys: List[A]): List[A] =
  foldRight(xs, ys, Cons(_, _))
```

Recall that foldRight replaces Nil with the initial accumulator. Hence, we replace Nil in the first list with the entire second list.

ANSWER 3.15

```
def concat[A](l: List[List[A]]): List[A] =
  foldRight(l, Nil: List[A], append)
```

We combine each inner list with the accumulated List[A] using our append function from exercise 3.14.

ANSWER 3.16

```
def incrementEach(l: List[Int]): List[Int] =
  foldRight(l, Nil: List[Int], (i, acc) => Cons(i + 1, acc))
```

We use `foldRight`, so we can build the result list in the correct order while using `Cons` as our combining function. Before we create a `Cons` value, we increment the integer passed to the combining function.

◼ **ANSWER 3.17**

```
def doubleToString(l: List[Double]): List[String] =
  foldRight(l, Nil: List[String], (d, acc) => Cons(d.toString, acc))
```

We use the same strategy here as we did in `incrementEach`: a `foldRight` that uses `Cons` in the combining function. The only difference is calling `d.toString` instead of `i + 1`.

◼ **ANSWER 3.18**

```
def map[A, B](as: List[A], f: A => B): List[B] =
  foldRight(as, Nil: List[B], (a, acc) => Cons(f(a), acc))
```

We again use the same strategy of a `foldRight`, with `Cons` as the combining function. We've simply factored out the common structure between `incrementEach` and `doubleToString`. Note that our implementation is only stack safe if `foldRight` is stack safe. Our initial implementation of `foldRight` wasn't stack safe, but we showed one way it could be made stack safe by using `reverse` and `foldLeft` internally.

◼ **ANSWER 3.19**

```
def filter[A](as: List[A], f: A => Boolean): List[A] =
  foldRight(as, Nil: List[A], (a, acc) => if f(a) then Cons(a, acc) else acc)
```

This implementation is similar to `map`, except we only create a new `Cons` cell when the predicate passes.

◼ **ANSWER 3.20**

```
def flatMap[A, B](as: List[A], f: A => List[B]): List[B] =
  foldRight(as, Nil: List[B], (a, acc) => append(f(a), acc))
```

Here we `foldRight` again, first converting an A to a `List[B]` and then combining that with our accumulated `List[B]`. Alternatively, we could use `map` and `concat`:

```
def flatMap[A, B](as: List[A], f: A => List[B]): List[B] =
  concat(map(as, f))
```

ANSWER 3.21

```
def filter[A](as: List[A], f: A => Boolean): List[A] =
  flatMap(as, a => if f(a) then List(a) else Nil)
```

ANSWER 3.22

```
def addPairwise(a: List[Int], b: List[Int]): List[Int] = (a, b) match
  case (Nil, _) => Nil
  case (_, Nil) => Nil
  case (Cons(h1, t1), Cons(h2, t2)) => Cons(h1 + h2, addPairwise(t1, t2))
```

We construct a pair from our input lists and pattern match on the result. If either input list is empty, we return an empty list. Otherwise, both are Cons cells, so we bind names to their heads (h1 and h2) and tails (t1 and t2) and then construct a new Cons cell whose head is h1 + h2 and whose tail is the result of calling addPairwise on the tails. This implementation is not tail recursive because the result of the recursive call is used to subsequently create a Cons cell.

ANSWER 3.23

```
def zipWith[A, B, C](a: List[A], b: List[B], f: (A, B) => C): List[C] =
  (a, b) match
    case (Nil, _) => Nil
    case (_, Nil) => Nil
    case (Cons(h1, t1), Cons(h2, t2)) => Cons(f(h1, h2), zipWith(t1, t2, f))
```

We've made two generalizations here; first, we factored out the + operation into a function that's passed to zipWith as a parameter, and second, we allowed the types of each list to be different. Hence, we need three type parameters—two for the input lists and one for the result list. To make this stack safe, we can pass the accumulated value into our recursive call instead of first recursing and then using the result in subsequent computation:

```
def zipWith[A, B, C](a: List[A], b: List[B], f: (A, B) => C): List[C] =
  @annotation.tailrec
  def loop(a: List[A], b: List[B], acc: List[C]): List[C] =
    (a, b) match
      case (Nil, _) => acc
      case (_, Nil) => acc
      case (Cons(h1, t1), Cons(h2, t2)) => loop(t1, t2, Cons(f(h1, h2), acc))
  reverse(loop(a, b, Nil))
```

Here we've introduced a local function loop, which takes an additional acc argument of type List[C]. When we recurse, we pass Cons(f(h1, h2), acc) as the new accumulator. By doing so, our accumulator ends up in reverse order, so we reverse the answer before returning from zipWith.

ANSWER 3.24

We first create a helper function that checks whether a list 1 starts with another list prefix:

```
@annotation.tailrec
def startsWith[A](l: List[A], prefix: List[A]): Boolean = (l, prefix) match
  case (_, Nil) => true
  case (Cons(h, t), Cons(h2, t2)) if h == h2 => startsWith(t, t2)
  case _ => false
```

We recurse on the structure of both lists. If the prefix is Nil, then 1 trivially starts with prefix. Otherwise, we check if the head of 1 is equal to the head of prefix and, if so, recurse on the tails. Using this helper function, we can implement hasSubsequence:

```
@annotation.tailrec
def hasSubsequence[A](sup: List[A], sub: List[A]): Boolean = sup match
  case Nil => sub == Nil
  case _ if startsWith(sup, sub) => true
  case Cons(h,t) => hasSubsequence(t, sub)
```

We pattern match on the structure of sup. If sup is empty, then we return true if sub is also empty and false otherwise. If sup is nonempty, then we first check if sup starts with sub. If so, we're done, and we return true; if not, we recurse on our tail, checking if the tail has sub as a subsequence.

ANSWER 3.25

```
object Tree:
  extension (t: Tree[Int]) def maximum: Int = t match
    case Leaf(n) => n
    case Branch(l, r) => l.maximum.max(r.maximum)
```

We define an extension method on Tree[Int] in the companion object for Tree, and we pattern match on the data constructors of t. If we are at a leaf, then the maximum is trivially the value of that leaf. If we're at a branch, we compute the maximum of both the left and right branches and return whichever is larger. Note this implementation is not tail recursive.

■ **ANSWER 3.26**

```
enum Tree[+A]:
  def depth: Int = this match
    case Leaf(_) => 0
    case Branch(l, r) => 1 + (l.depth.max(r.depth))
```

This function works on any tree, so we define it as a method on the Tree type. We use the same structural recursion approach as used in maximum. The only differences are in the values used on the right-hand side of => in each case.

■ **ANSWER 3.27**

```
enum Tree[+A]:
  def map[B](f: A => B): Tree[B] = this match
    case Leaf(a) => Leaf(f(a))
    case Branch(l, r) => Branch(l.map(f), r.map(f))
```

This implementation is very similar to the initial implementation of map on List, where we use structural recursion, and on each match, we construct a new value of the same corresponding data constructor. With List we converted Nil to Nil and Cons to Cons. With Tree we've converted each Leaf to Leaf and each Branch to Branch, applying map recursively on the branches.

■ **ANSWER 3.28**

First let's define fold:

```
enum Tree[+A]:
  def fold[B](f: A => B, g: (B,B) => B): B = this match
    case Leaf(a) => f(a)
    case Branch(l, r) => g(l.fold(f, g), r.fold(f, g))
```

We pattern match on the structure of the tree. If we encounter a leaf, we transform its value using the supplied f: A => B. If we encounter a branch, we fold each of its subtrees and then combine the results using a g: (B, B) => B. We can then use this to implement each of the functions we implemented previously:

```
enum Tree[+A]:
  def size: Int =
    fold(a => 1, 1 + _ + _)
```

```
def depth: Int =
  fold(a => 0, (d1,d2) => 1 + (d1 max d2))

def map[B](f: A => B): Tree[B] =
  fold(a => Leaf(f(a)), Branch(_,_))

object Tree:
  extension (t: Tree[Int]) def maximum: Int =
    t.fold(a => a, _ max _)
```

Handling errors
without exceptions

This chapter covers
- Discussing the disadvantages of exceptions
- Introducing the `Option` data type
- Introducing the `Either` data type
- Introducing the `Try` data type

We noted briefly in chapter 1 that throwing exceptions is a side effect. If exceptions aren't used in functional code, what is used instead? In this chapter, we'll learn the basic principles for raising and handling errors functionally. The big idea is that we can represent failures and exceptions with ordinary values, and we can write higher-order functions that abstract out common patterns of error handling and recovery. The functional solution of returning errors as values is safer and retains referential transparency, and through the use of higher-order functions, we can preserve the primary benefit of exceptions: *consolidation of error-handling logic.* We'll see how this works over the course of this chapter after we take a closer look at exceptions and discuss some of their problems.

For the same reason that we created our own `List` data type in the previous chapter, we'll recreate two Scala standard library types in this chapter: `Option` and `Either`. Our aim here is to enhance your understanding of how these types can be used for handling errors. After completing this chapter, you should feel free to use the Scala standard library version of `Option` and `Either` (though you'll notice that the standard library versions of both types are missing some of the useful functions we define in this chapter).

4.1   *The good and bad aspects of exceptions*

Why do exceptions break referential transparency, and why is that a problem? Let's look at a simple example; we'll define a function that throws an exception and call it.

Listing 4.1   Throwing and catching an exception

```
def failingFn(i: Int): Int =
  val y: Int = throw Exception("fail!")    ◁─┐
  try
    val x = 42 + 5
    x + y
  catch
    case e: Exception => 43    ◁─┐
```

val y: Int = ... declares y as having the type Int and sets it equal to the right-hand side of =.

A catch block is just a pattern-matching block like the ones we've seen. case e: Exception is a pattern that matches any Exception, and it binds this value to the identifier e. The match returns the value 43.

Calling `failingFn` from the REPL results in an exception being thrown:

```
scala> failingFn(12)
java.lang.Exception: fail!
  at failingFn(<console>:8)
  ...
```

We can prove y is not referentially transparent. Recall that any RT expression may be substituted with the value it refers to, and this substitution should preserve program meaning. If we substitute `throw Exception("fail!")` for y in x + y, it produces a different result because the exception will now be raised inside a `try` block that will catch the exception and return 43:

```
def failingFn2(i: Int): Int =
  try
    val x = 42 + 5
    x + ((throw Exception("fail!")): Int)    ◁─┐
  catch
    case e: Exception => 43
```

A thrown Exception can be given any type; here we're annotating it with the type Int.

We can demonstrate this in the REPL:

```
scala> failingFn2(12)
res1: Int = 43
```

Another way of understanding RT is knowing that the meaning of RT expressions does not depend on context and may be reasoned about locally, whereas the meaning of non-RT expressions is context-dependent and requires more global reasoning. For instance, the meaning of the RT expression 42 + 5 doesn't depend on the larger expression it's embedded in—it's always and forever equal to 47. But the meaning of the expression throw Exception("fail") is very context dependent; as we just demonstrated, it takes on different meanings depending on which try block (if any) it's nested within.

There are two main problems with exceptions:

- *Exceptions break RT and introduce context dependence.* This moves us away from the simple reasoning of the substitution model, making it possible to write confusing, exception-based code. This is the source of the folkloric advice that exceptions should be used only for error handling, not for control flow.
- *Exceptions are not type safe.* The type of failingFn, Int => Int tells us nothing about the fact that exceptions may occur, and the compiler will certainly not force callers of failingFn to make a decision about how to handle those exceptions. If we forget to check for an exception in failingFn, this won't be detected until runtime.

Checked exceptions

While Java's checked exceptions force a decision about whether to handle or reraise an error, they result in significant boilerplate for callers. More importantly, they don't work for higher-order functions,[1] which can't possibly be aware of the specific exceptions that could be raised by their arguments. For example, consider the map function we defined for List:

```
def map[A, B](l: List[A], f: A => B): List[B]
```

This function is clearly useful, highly generic, and at odds with the use of checked exceptions; we can't have a version of map for every single checked exception that could possibly be thrown by f. Even if we wanted to do this, how would map know what exceptions were possible? This is why generic code, even in Java, so often resorts to using RuntimeException or some common checked Exception type.

We'd like an alternative to exceptions without these drawbacks, but we don't want to lose out on the primary benefit of exceptions: they allow us to consolidate and centralize error-handling logic, rather than be forced to distribute this logic throughout our codebase. The technique we use is based on an old idea: instead of throwing an exception, we return a value indicating that an exceptional condition has occurred. This idea might be familiar to anyone who has used return codes in C to handle exceptions, but instead of using error codes, we introduce a new generic type for these *possibly defined*

---

[1] This is an active area of research, and Scala 3 has some experimental features that attempt to address this. See https://mng.bz/yaao for details.

values and use higher-order functions to encapsulate common patterns of handling and propagating errors. Unlike C-style error codes, the error-handling strategy we use is completely type safe, and we get full assistance from the type checker in forcing us to deal with errors, with a minimum of syntactic noise. We'll see how all of this works shortly.

4.2 Possible alternatives to exceptions

Let's now consider a realistic situation in which we might use an exception and look at different approaches we could use instead. Here's an implementation of a function that computes the mean of a list, which is undefined if the list is empty:

```
def mean(xs: Seq[Double]): Double =     ◁─┤  Seq is the common interface of various linear
  if xs.isEmpty then                          sequence-like collections. Check the API docs
    throw new ArithmeticException("mean of empty list!")   (http://mng.bz/f4k9) for more information.
  else xs.sum / xs.length   ◁──┐
                                │  sum is defined as a method on Seq only if the elements of the
                                │  sequence are numeric. The standard library accomplishes
                                │  this trick with implicits, which we won't go into here.
```

The mean function is an example of what's called a *partial function*, meaning it's not defined for some inputs. A function is typically partial because it makes some assumptions about its inputs that aren't implied by the input types.[2] You may be used to throwing exceptions in this case, but we have a few other options. Let's look at these for our mean example.

The first possibility is to return some sort of bogus value of type Double. We could simply return xs.sum / xs.length in all cases, resulting in 0.0/0.0 when the input is empty, which is Double.NaN;, or we could return some other sentinel value. In other situations, we might return null instead of a value of the needed type. This general class of approaches is how error handling is often done in languages without exceptions, and we reject this solution for a few reasons:

- *It allows errors to silently propagate.* The caller can forget to check this condition and won't be alerted by the compiler, which might result in subsequent code not working properly. Often the error won't be detected until much later in the code.
- *It results in a fair amount of boilerplate code at call sites, with explicit* if *statements to check whether the caller has received a real result.* This boilerplate is magnified if you happen to be calling several functions, each of which uses error codes that must be checked and aggregated in some way.

---

[2] A function may also be partial if it doesn't terminate for some inputs. We won't discuss this form of partiality here, since it's not a recoverable error, so there's no question of how best to handle it. See the chapter notes (https://github.com/fpinscala/fpinscala/wiki) for more about partiality.

- *It's not applicable to polymorphic code.* For some output types, we might not even have a sentinel value of that type even if we wanted to! Consider a function like `max`, which finds the maximum value in a sequence according to a custom comparison function: `def max[A](xs: Seq[A])(greater: (A,A) => Boolean): A`. If the input is empty, we can't invent a value of type `A`, nor can `null` be used here, since `null` is only valid for nonprimitive types, and `A` may in fact be a primitive like `Double` or `Int`.

- *It demands a special policy or calling convention of callers.* Proper use of the `mean` function would require callers to do something other than call `mean` and make use of the result. Giving functions special policies like this makes it difficult to pass them to higher-order functions, which must treat all arguments uniformly.

The second possibility is forcing the caller to supply an argument that tells us what to do in case we don't know how to handle the input:

```
def mean(xs: Seq[Double], onEmpty: Double): Double =
  if xs.isEmpty then onEmpty
  else xs.sum / xs.length
```

This makes `mean` into a total function, but it has drawbacks; it requires immediate callers to have direct knowledge of how to handle the undefined case and limits them to returning a `Double`. What if `mean` is called as part of a larger computation and we'd like to abort that computation if `mean` is undefined? Or perhaps we'd like to take some completely different branch in the larger computation in this case. Simply passing an `onEmpty` parameter doesn't give us this freedom. We need a way to defer the decision of how to handle undefined cases so they can be dealt with at the most appropriate level.

4.3   *The Option data type*

The solution is explicitly representing that a function may not always have an answer in the return type. We can think of this as deferring to the caller for the error-handling strategy. We introduce a new type: `Option`. As mentioned earlier, this type also exists in the Scala standard library, but we're recreating it here for pedagogical purposes:

```
enum Option[+A]:
  case Some(get: A)
  case None
```

`Option` has two cases: it can be defined, in which case it will be a `Some`, or it can be undefined, in which case it will be `None`. We can use `Option` for our definition of `mean` like so:

```
import Option.{Some, None}

def mean(xs: Seq[Double]): Option[Double] =
  if xs.isEmpty then None
  else Some(xs.sum / xs.length)
```

The return type now reflects the possibility that the result may not always be defined. We still always return a result of the declared type (now Option[Double]) from our function, so mean is now a *total function*, meaning it takes each value of the input type to exactly one value of the output type. Figure 4.1 contrasts using sentinel values with using the Option type.

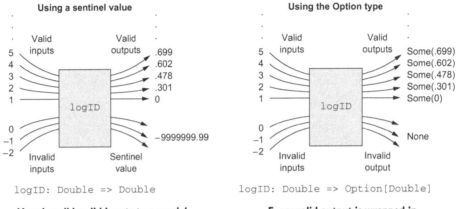

Responding to invalid inputs

logID: Double => Double

Mapping all invalid inputs to a special value of the same type as the valid outputs. The choice of the special value is ambiguous, and the compiler can't check that the caller handles it correctly.

logID: Double => Option[Double]

Every valid output is wrapped in Some. Invalid inputs are mapped to None. The compiler forces the caller to deal explicitly with the possibility of failure.

Figure 4.1   Techniques for making a function total while responding to invalid inputs

4.3.1   *Usage patterns for Option*

Partial functions abound in programming, and Option (and the Either data type that we'll discuss shortly) is typically how this partiality is dealt with in FP. You'll see Option used throughout the Scala standard library in the following cases, for instance:

- Map lookup for a given key (http://mng.bz/g1qv) returns Option.
- headOption and lastOption defined for lists and other iterables (http://mng.bz/ePqV) return an Option containing the first or last elements of a sequence if it's nonempty.

These examples aren't comprehensive; we'll see Option come up in many different situations. What makes Option convenient is that we can factor out common patterns of error handling via higher-order functions, freeing us from writing the usual boilerplate that comes with exception-handling code. In this section, we'll cover some of the basic functions for working with Option. Our goal here is not attaining fluency with all these functions but getting familiar enough that you can revisit this chapter and make progress on your own when you have to write some functional code to deal with errors.

BASIC FUNCTIONS ON OPTION

Option can be thought of like a List that can contain at most one element, and many of the List functions we saw earlier have analogous functions on Option. Let's look at some of these functions.

Like we did with the functions on Tree in chapter 3, we'll place our functions inside the body of the Option type so they can be called with the obj.fn(arg) syntax. This choice raises one additional complication with regard to variance that we'll discuss in a moment. Let's take a look.

Listing 4.2 The Option data type

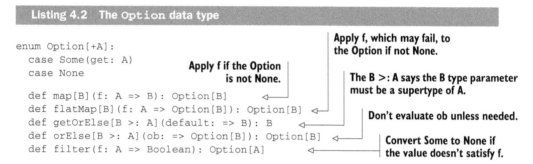

```
enum Option[+A]:
  case Some(get: A)
  case None

  def map[B](f: A => B): Option[B]
  def flatMap[B](f: A => Option[B]): Option[B]
  def getOrElse[B >: A](default: => B): B
  def orElse[B >: A](ob: => Option[B]): Option[B]
  def filter(f: A => Boolean): Option[A]
```

Apply f if the Option is not None.

Apply f, which may fail, to the Option if not None.

The B >: A says the B type parameter must be a supertype of A.

Don't evaluate ob unless needed.

Convert Some to None if the value doesn't satisfy f.

There is some new syntax here. The default: => B type annotation in getOrElse (and the similar annotation in orElse) indicates that the argument is of type B, but it won't be evaluated until it's needed by the function. Don't worry about this for now; we'll talk much more about this concept of *nonstrictness* in the next chapter. Also, the B >: A type parameter on the getOrElse and orElse functions indicates that B must be equal to or a *supertype* of A. It's needed to convince Scala that it's still safe to declare Option[+A] as covariant in A. See the chapter notes (https://github.com/fpinscala/fpinscala/wiki) for more details. It's unfortunately somewhat complicated but a necessary complication in Scala; fortunately, fully understanding subtyping and variance isn't essential for our purposes.

EXERCISE 4.1

Implement all of the preceding functions on Option. As you implement each function, try to think about what it means and in what situations you'd use it. We'll explore when to use each of these functions next. Here are a few hints for solving this exercise:

- It's fine to use pattern matching, though you should be able to implement all the functions besides map and getOrElse without resorting to pattern matching. Try implementing flatMap, orElse, and filter in terms of map and getOrElse.
- For map and flatMap, the type signature should be enough to determine the implementation.
- getOrElse returns the result inside the Some case of the Option, or if the Option is None, it returns the given default value.

- orElse returns the first `Option` if it's defined; otherwise, it returns the second `Option`.

USAGE SCENARIOS FOR THE BASIC OPTION FUNCTIONS

Although we can explicitly pattern match on an `Option`, we'll almost always use the preceding higher-order functions. Here we'll try to provide some guidance for when to use each one. Fluency with these functions will come with practice, but the objective here is to get some basic familiarity. Next time you try writing some functional code that uses `Option`, see if you can recognize the patterns these functions encapsulate before you resort to pattern matching.

Let's start with map. The `map` function can be used to transform the result inside an `Option`, if it exists. We can think of it as proceeding with a computation on the assumption that an error hasn't occurred; it's also a way of deferring the error handling to later code:

```
case class Employee(
  name: String,
  department: String,
  manager: Option[Employee])

def lookupByName(name: String): Option[Employee] = ...

val joeDepartment: Option[String] =
  lookupByName("Joe").map(_.department)
```

Here `lookupByName("Joe")` returns an `Option[Employee]`, which we transform to an `Option[String]` using `map` to pull out the department. Note that we don't need to explicitly check the result of `lookupByName("Joe")`; we simply continue the computation as if no error occurred inside the argument to map. If `lookupByName("Joe")` returns `None`, this will abort the rest of the computation, and map will not call the `_.department` function at all. Figure 4.2 shows additional chained computations. `flatMap` is similar, except the function we provide to transform the result can itself fail.

■ **EXERCISE 4.2** ────────────────────────────────────

Implement the `variance` function in terms of `flatMap`. If the mean of a sequence is m, the variance is the mean of `math.pow(x - m, 2)` for each element x in the sequence. See the definition of variance on Wolfram MathWorld (https://mng.bz/7ZgQ):

```
def mean(xs: Seq[Double]): Option[Double] =
  if xs.isEmpty then None
  else Some(xs.sum / xs.length)

def variance(xs: Seq[Double]): Option[Double]
```

Figure 4.2   Chaining computations that work with Option

As the implementation of variance demonstrates, with `flatMap` we can construct a computation with multiple stages, any of which may fail, and the computation will abort as soon as the first failure is encountered, since `None.flatMap(f)` will immediately return `None`, without running `f`.

We can use `filter` to convert successes into failures if the successful values don't match the given predicate. A common pattern is transforming an `Option` via calls to `map`, `flatMap`, and/or `filter` and then using `getOrElse` to do error handling at the end:

```
val dept: String =
  lookupByName("Joe").
  map(_.department).
  filter(_ != "Accounting").
  getOrElse("Default Dept")
```

`getOrElse` is used here to convert from an `Option[String]` to a `String` by providing a default department in case the key `"Joe"` didn't exist in the `Map` or Joe's department was `"Accounting"`. `orElse` is similar to `getOrElse`, except that we return another `Option` if the first is undefined. This is often useful when we need to chain together possibly failing computations, trying the second if the first hasn't succeeded.

A common idiom is using `o.getOrElse(throw Exception("FAIL"))` to convert the `None` case of an `Option` back to an exception. The general rule is using exceptions only if no reasonable program would ever catch the exception; if for some callers the exception might be a recoverable error, we use `Option` (or `Either`, as discussed later) to give them flexibility. When in doubt, avoid the use of exceptions, especially when getting started—what may seem like a good use case for exceptions often ends up better expressed with values due to unfamiliarity.

As you can see, returning errors as ordinary values can be convenient, and the use of higher-order functions lets us achieve the same sort of consolidation of error-handling logic that we would get from using exceptions. Note that we don't have to check for None at each stage of the computation; we can apply several transformations and then check for and handle None when we're ready. But we also get additional safety, since Option[A] is a different type than A, and the compiler won't let us forget to explicitly defer or handle the possibility of None.

4.3.2   *Option composition, lifting, and wrapping exception-oriented APIs*

It may be easy to jump to the conclusion that once we start using Option, it spreads throughout our entire code base. One can imagine how any callers of methods that take or return Option will have to be modified to handle either Some or None, but this doesn't happen because we can *lift* ordinary functions to become functions that operate on Option.

For example, the map function lets us operate on values of the Option[A] type using a function of the A => B type, which returns Option[B]. Another way of looking at this is that map turns a function f of type A => B into a function of type Option[A] => Option[B]. Let's make this explicit:

```
def lift[A, B](f: A => B): Option[A] => Option[B] =
  _.map(f)
```

> Recall _.map(f) is equivalent to an anonymous function oa => oa.map(f).

This tells us that any function we already have lying around can be transformed (via lift) to operate within the context of a single Option value. Let's look at an example:

```
val absO: Option[Double] => Option[Double] =
  lift(math.abs)

scala> val ex1 = absO(Some(-1.0))
val ex1: Option[Double] = Some(1.0)
```

Figure 4.3 breaks this example down further.

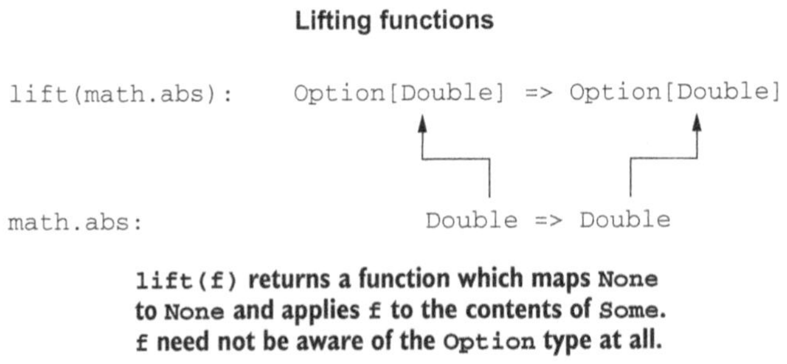

Lifting functions

```
lift(math.abs):    Option[Double] => Option[Double]


math.abs:          Double => Double
```

lift(f) returns a function which maps None to None and applies f to the contents of Some. f need not be aware of the Option type at all.

Figure 4.3   Lifting a function to work with Options

The math object contains various standalone mathematical functions, including abs, sqrt, exp, and so on. We didn't need to rewrite the math.abs function to work with optional values; we just lifted it into the Option context after the fact. We can do this for any function. Let's look at another example.

Suppose we're implementing the logic for a car insurance company's website, which contains a page on which users can submit a form to request an instant online quote. We'd like to parse the information from this form and ultimately call our rate function:

```
/**
 * Top secret formula for computing an annual car
 * insurance premium from two key factors.
 */
def insuranceRateQuote(age: Int, numberOfSpeedingTickets: Int): Double
```

We want to be able to call this function, but if the user is submitting their age and number of speeding tickets in a web form, these fields will arrive as simple strings that we have to (try to) parse into integers. This parsing may fail; given a string, s, we can attempt to parse it into an Int using s.toInt, which throws a NumberFormatException if the string isn't a valid integer:

```
scala> "112".toInt
res0: Int = 112

scala> "hello".toInt
java.lang.NumberFormatException: For input string: "hello"
  at java.lang.NumberFormatException.forInputString(...)
  ...
```

We can write a utility function that converts that exception into a None:

```
def toIntOption(s: String): Option[Int] =
  try Some(s.toInt)
  catch case _: NumberFormatException => None
```

This syntax allows us to catch any exception of type NumberFormat-Exception. Since we don't need to reference the caught exception, we don't give it a name and instead use _.

Let's use toIntOption to implement a function parseInsuranceRateQuote, which takes the age and number of speeding tickets as strings and attempts calling the insuranceRateQuote function if parsing both values is successful.

Listing 4.3   Using Option

```
def parseInsuranceRateQuote(
    age: String,
    numberOfSpeedingTickets: String): Option[Double] =
  val optAge: Option[Int] = toIntOption(age)
  val optTickets: Option[Int] = toIntOption(numberOfSpeedingTickets)
  insuranceRateQuote(optAge, optTickets)
```

Convert the age of type String to an Option[Int].

It doesn't type check!

But there's a problem—after we parse `optAge` and `optTickets` into `Option[Int]`, how do we call `insuranceRateQuote`, which currently takes two `Int` values? Do we have to rewrite `insuranceRateQuote` to take `Option[Int]` values instead? No, and changing `insuranceRateQuote` would be entangling concerns, forcing it to be aware that a prior computation may have failed, not to mention that we may not have the ability to modify `insuranceRateQuote`—perhaps it's defined in a separate module we don't have access to. Instead, we'd like to lift `insuranceRateQuote` to operate in the context of two optional values. We could do this by using explicit pattern matching in the body of `parseInsuranceRateQuote`, but that's going to be tedious.

■ EXERCISE 4.3

Write a generic function `map2` that combines two `Option` values using a binary function. If either `Option` value is `None`, then the return value is too. Here is its signature:

```
def map2[A, B, C](a: Option[A], b: Option[B])(f: (A, B) => C): Option[C]
```

Note that we have two parameter lists here; the first parameter list takes an `Option[A]` and an `Option[B]`, and the second parameter list takes a function `(A, B) => C`. To call this function, we supply values for each parameter list—for example, `map2(oa, ob)` `(_ + _)`. We could have defined this with a single parameter list instead, though it's common style to use two parameter lists when a function takes multiple parameters and the last parameter is itself a function.[3] Doing so allows a syntax variation when passing multiline anonymous functions, where the final parameter list is replaced with either an indented block or a brace delimited block:

```
map2(oa, ob): (a, b) =>          ◁─┐  Indented block following a
  a + b                             │  colon and parameter list

map2(oa, ob) { (a, b) =>         ◁─┐
  a + b                             │  Brace delimited block
}
```

We'll use indented blocks in this book, but feel free to experiment with both styles.

---

[3] There was another benefit of multiple parameter lists in Scala 2: better type inference. Scala 2 inferred type parameters on each parameter list in succession. If Scala 2 was able to infer a concrete type in the first parameter list, then any appearance of that type in subsequent parameter lists would be fixed (i.e., not further inferred or generalized). For example, `map(List(1, 2, 3), _ + 1)` from chapter 3 would fail to compile with a type inference error, but had we defined `map` with two parameter lists, resulting in usage like `map(List(1, 2, 3))(_ + 1)`, compilation would have succeeded. Scala 3 can infer type parameters from all parameter lists simultaneously, so there are no longer type inference advantages to using multiple parameter lists.

With map2 we can now implement parseInsuranceRateQuote:

```
def parseInsuranceRateQuote(
    age: String,
    numberOfSpeedingTickets: String): Option[Double] =
  val optAge: Option[Int] = toIntOption(age)
  val optTickets: Option[Int] = toIntOption(numberOfSpeedingTickets)
  map2(optAge, optTickets)(insuranceRateQuote)
```

> **If either parse fails, this will immediately return None.**

The map2 function means we never need to modify any existing functions of two arguments to make them Option-aware. We can lift them to operate in the context of Option after the fact. Can you already see how you might define map3, map4, and map5? Let's look at a few other similar cases.

■ EXERCISE 4.4

Write a function sequence that combines a list of Options into one Option containing a list of all the Some values in the original list. If the original list contains None even once, the result of the function should be None; otherwise, the result should be Some, with a list of all the values. Here is its signature:[4]

```
def sequence[A](as: List[Option[A]]): Option[List[A]]
```

Sometimes we'll want to map over a list using a function that might fail, returning None if applying it to any element of the list returns None. For example, what if we have a whole list of String values that we wish to parse to Option[Int]? In that case, we can simply sequence the results of the map:

```
def parseInts(as: List[String]): Option[List[Int]] =
  sequence(as.map(a => toIntOption(s)))
```

Unfortunately, this is inefficient since it traverses the list twice—first to convert each String to an Option[Int] and second to combine these Option[Int] values into an Option[List[Int]]. Wanting to sequence the results of a map this way is a common enough occurrence to warrant a new generic function, traverse, with the following signature:

```
def traverse[A, B](as: List[A])(f: A => Option[B]): Option[List[B]]
```

---

[4] This is a clear instance in which it's not appropriate to define the function in the OO style. This shouldn't be a method on List (which shouldn't need to know anything about Option), and it can't be a method on Option, so it goes in the Option companion object.

Implement this function. It's straightforward to do using map and sequence, but try for a more efficient implementation that only looks at the list once. In fact, implement sequence in terms of traverse.

For-comprehensions

Since lifting functions is so common in Scala, Scala provides a syntactic construct called the *for-comprehension*, which it expands automatically to a series of flatMap and map calls. Let's look at how map2 could be implemented with for-comprehensions. Here's our original version:

```
def map2[A, B, C](a: Option[A], b: Option[B])(f: (A, B) => C): Option[C] =
  a.flatMap: aa =>
    b.map: bb =>
      f(aa, bb)
```

And here's the exact same code written as a for-comprehension:

```
def map2[A, B, C](a: Option[A], b: Option[B])(f: (A, B) => C): Option[C] =
  for
    aa <- a
    bb <- b
  yield f(aa, bb)
```

A for-comprehension consists of a sequence of bindings, like aa <- a, followed by a yield, where the yield may make use of any of the values on the left side of any previous <- binding. The compiler desugars the bindings to flatMap calls, with the final binding and yield being converted to a call to map.[5]

You should feel free to use for-comprehensions in place of explicit calls to flatMap and map. Likewise, feel free to rewrite a for-comprehension as a sequence of flat-Map calls followed by a final map if doing so helps you understand the expression. For-comprehensions are purely a syntax convenience.

Adapting functions to options

Between map, lift, sequence, traverse, map2, map3, and so on, you should never have to modify any existing functions to work with optional values.

---

[5] For-comprehensions support additional features that aren't relevant to our purposes, such as filtering via guards and performing side effects. See http://mng.bz/v444 for more details.

4.4   *The Either data type*

The big idea in this chapter is that we can represent failures and exceptions with ordinary values and write functions that abstract out common patterns of error handling and recovery. Option isn't the only data type we could use for this purpose, and although it gets used frequently, it's rather simple. You may have noticed that Option doesn't tell us anything about what went wrong in the case of an exceptional condition. All it can do is give us None, indicating there's no value to be had. But sometimes we want to know more. For example, we might want a String that provides more information, or if an exception was raised, we might want to know what that error actually was.

We can craft a data type that encodes whatever information we want about failures. Sometimes just knowing whether a failure occurred is sufficient, and in that case, we can use Option; other times, we want more information. In this section, we'll walk through a simple extension to Option: the Either data type, which lets us track a reason for the failure. Let's look at its definition:

```
enum Either[+E, +A]:
  case Left(value: E)
  case Right(value: A)
```

Either has only two cases, just like Option. The essential difference is that both cases carry a value. The Either data type represents, in a very general way, values that can be one of two things. We can say that it's a *disjoint union* of two types. When we use it to indicate success or failure, by convention. the Right constructor is reserved for the success case (a pun on *right*, meaning correct), and Left is used for failure. We've given the left type parameter the suggestive name E (for error).[6]

Let's look at the mean example again—this time returning a String in case of failure:

```
import Either.{Left, Right}

def mean(xs: Seq[Double]): Either[String, Double] =
  if xs.isEmpty then
    Left("mean of empty list!")
  else
    Right(xs.sum / xs.length)
```

Sometimes we might want to include more information about the error—for example, a stack trace showing the location of the error in the source code. In such cases, we can simply return the exception in the Left side of an Either:

```
import scala.util.control.NonFatal

def safeDiv(x: Int, y: Int): Either[Throwable, Int] =
  try Right(x / y)
  catch case NonFatal(t) => Left(t)         ◄─────────
```

The NonFatal pattern match ensures we do not catch fatal errors, like OutOfMemoryException.

---

[6] Either is also often used more generally to encode one of two possibilities in cases where it isn't worth defining a fresh data type. We'll see some examples of this throughout the book.

We can extract a more general function, `catchNonFatal`, which factors out this common pattern of converting thrown exceptions to values:

```
def catchNonFatal[A](a: => A): Either[Throwable, A] =
  try Right(a)
  catch case NonFatal(t) => Left(t)
```

This function is general enough to be defined on the `Either` companion object since it's not tied to a single use case.

EXERCISE 4.6

Implement versions of `map`, `flatMap`, `orElse`, and `map2` on `Either` that operate on the Right value:

> **When flat mapping over the right side, we must promote the left type parameter to some supertype to satisfy the +E variance annotation.**
>
> **It is similar for orElse.**

```
enum Either[+E, +A]:
  case Left(value: E)
  case Right(value: A)

  def map[B](f: A => B): Either[E, B]
  def flatMap[EE >: E, B](f: A => Either[EE, B]): Either[EE, B]  <─┐
  def orElse[EE >: E,B >: A](b: => Either[EE, B]): Either[EE, B]  <─┘
  def map2[EE >: E, B, C](that: Either[EE, B])(f: (A, B) => C): Either[EE, C]
```

Note that with these definitions, `Either` can now be used in for-comprehensions (recall that for-comprehensions are syntactic sugar for calls to `flatMap`, `map`, and so on). Take the following, for instance:

```
def parseInsuranceRateQuote(
    age: String,
    numberOfSpeedingTickets: String): Either[Throwable,Double] =
  for
    a <- Either.catchNonFatal(age.toInt)
    tickets <- Either.catchNonFatal(numberOfSpeedingTickes.toInt)
  yield insuranceRateQuote(a, tickets)
```

Now we get information about the actual exception that occurred, rather than just getting back `None` in the event of a failure.

EXERCISE 4.7

Implement `sequence` and `traverse` for `Either`. These should return the first error that's encountered if there is one:

```
def sequence[E, A](as: List[Either[E, A]]): Either[E, List[A]]

def traverse[E, A, B](as: List[A])(
                      f: A => Either[E, B]): Either[E, List[B]]
```

As a final example, here's an application of map2 where the function Person.make validates both the given name and the given age before constructing a valid Person.

Listing 4.4 Using Either to validate data

```
case class Name private (value: String)          ◄─────────────────────┐
object Name:                                                           │
  def apply(name: String): Either[String, Name] =                      │
    if name == "" || name == null then Left("Name is empty.")          │
    else Right(new Name(name))                                         │
                                                  Name and Age are      │
case class Age private (value: Int)             case classes with private
object Age:                                     constructors, resulting in
  def apply(age: Int): Either[String, Age] =      construction only being
    if age < 0 then Left("Age is out of range.")  allowed in their companion
    else Right(new Age(age))                      objects. The apply method
                                                  in each companion
case class Person(name: Name, age: Age)         validates the input before
object Person:                                    constructing a value.
  def make(name: String, age: Int): Either[String, Person] =
    Name(name).map2(Age(age))(Person(_, _))
```

4.4.1 Accumulating errors

The implementation of map2 is only able to report one error, even if both arguments are invalid (that is, both arguments are Lefts). It would be more useful if we could report both errors. For example, when creating a Person from a name and age, and both the name and age have failed validation, we might want to present both errors to the user of our program.

Let's create a function similar to map2 that reports both errors. We'll need to adjust the return type of the function to return a List[E]:

```
def map2Both[E, A, B, C](
  a: Either[E, A],
  b: Either[E, B],
  f: (A, B) => C
): Either[List[E], C] =
  (a, b) match
    case (Right(aa), Right(bb)) => Right(f(aa, bb))
    case (Left(e), Right(_)) => Left(List(e))
    case (Right(_), Left(e)) => Left(List(e))
    case (Left(e1), Left(e2)) => Left(List(e1, e2))
```

With this new function, we can write an alternative to `Person.make` that returns both errors:

```
object Person:
  def makeBoth(name: String, age: Int): Either[List[String], Person] =
    map2Both(Name(name), Age(age), Person(_, _))
```

When both inputs are invalid, we get both errors returned in a list wrapped in a `Left`:

```
scala> val p = Person.makeBoth("", -1)
val p: Either[List[String], Person] =
  Left(List(Name is empty., Age is out of range.))
```

Unfortunately, the usefulness of `map2Both` is rather limited. Consider what happens when we want to combine the result of two calls to `Person.makeBoth`:

```
scala> val p1 = Person.makeBoth("Curry", 34)
val p1: Either[List[String], Person] = Right(Person(Name(Curry),Age(34)))

scala> val p2 = Person.makeBoth("Howard", 44)
val p2: Either[List[String], Person] = Right(Person(Name(Howard),Age(44)))

scala> val pair = map2Both(p1, p2, (_, _))
val pair: Either[List[List[String]], (Person, Person)] =
  Right((Person(Name(Curry),Age(34)),Person(Name(Howard),Age(44))))
```

This compiles fine, but take a close look at the inferred type of `pair`—the left side of the `Either` now has nested lists! Each successive use of `map2Both` adds another layer of `List` to the error type. We can fix this by changing `map2Both` slightly. We'll require the input values to already have a `List[E]` on the left side. Let's call this new variant `map2All`:

```
def map2All[E, A, B, C](
  a: Either[List[E], A],
  b: Either[List[E], B],
  f: (A, B) => C
): Either[List[E], C] =
  (a, b) match
    case (Right(aa), Right(bb)) => Right(f(aa, bb))
    case (Left(es), Right(_)) => Left(es)
    case (Right(_), Left(es)) => Left(es)
    case (Left(es1), Left(es2)) => Left(es1 ++ es2)
```

Besides the change to the type of the a and b parameters, the only other differences are in the cases where `Left` values appear. If there's a single `Left` value, we can return it unmodified (instead of wrapping it in a singleton `List` like in `map2Both`). If both inputs are `Left` values, we return their concatenation wrapped in a `Left`. With `map2All` we can preserve the correct type while combining any number of `Either` values:

```
scala> val pair = map2All(p1, p2, (_, _))
val pair: Either[List[String], (Person, Person)] =
  Right((Person(Name(Curry),Age(81)),Person(Name(Howard),Age(96))))
```

Now let's try implementing a variant of traverse that returns all errors. Changing just the return type gives us a signature like the following:

```
def traverseAll[E, A, B](
  as: List[A],
  f: A => Either[E, B]
): Either[List[E], List[B]]
```

We can implement this in the same way that we've implemented traverse previously—with a foldRight that uses map2 on each element to build the final list but substituting map2All for map2:

```
def traverseAll[E, A, B](
  as: List[A],
  f: A => Either[List[E], B]
): Either[List[E], List[B]] =
  as.foldRight(Right(Nil): Either[List[E], List[B]])((a, acc) =>
    map2All(f(a), acc, _ :: _)
  )
```

Note that we also changed the type of f from A => Either[E, B] to A => Either[List[E], B]. We could have used the original type instead of (A => Either[E, B]) and converted the result of calling f prior to calling map2All, but doing so reduces our ability to build new functions out of this definition. For example, with the new signature, defining sequenceAll in terms of traverseAll is straightforward; we can pass the identity function for f:

```
def sequenceAll[E, A](
  as: List[Either[List[E], A]]
): Either[List[E], List[A]] =
  traverseAll(as, identity)
```

4.4.2 *Extracting a Validated type*

Either[List[E], A], along with functions like map2All, traverseAll, and sequence-All, gives us the ability to accumulate errors. Instead of defining these related functions in this ad hoc way, we can *name* this accumulation behavior—that is, we can give this behavior its own type:

```
enum Validated[+E, +A]:
  case Valid(get: A)
  case Invalid(errors: List[E])
```

A value of Validated[E, A] can be converted to an Either[List[E], A] and vice versa. By introducing a new type, we have a place to define map2All, traverseAll, and sequenceAll—and in fact, we no longer need the All suffix, since we can define this Validated type to inherently support the accumulation of errors:

```scala
enum Validated[+E, +A]:
  case Valid(get: A)
  case Invalid(errors: List[E])

  def toEither: Either[List[E], A] =
    this match
      case Valid(a) => Either.Right(a)
      case Invalid(es) => Either.Left(es)

  def map[B](f: A => B): Validated[E, B] =
    this match
      case Valid(a) => Valid(f(a))
      case Invalid(es) => Invalid(es)

  def map2[EE >: E, B, C](
    b: Validated[EE, B])(
    f: (A, B) => C
  ): Validated[EE, C] =
    (this, b) match
      case (Valid(aa), Valid(bb)) => Valid(f(aa, bb))
      case (Invalid(es), Valid(_)) => Invalid(es)
      case (Valid(_), Invalid(es)) => Invalid(es)
      case (Invalid(es1), Invalid(es2)) => Invalid(es1 ++ es2)

object Validated:
  def fromEither[E, A](e: Either[List[E], A]): Validated[E, A] =
    e match
      case Either.Right(a) => Valid(a)
      case Either.Left(es) => Invalid(es)

  def traverse[E, A, B](
    as: List[A], f: A => Validated[E, B]
  ): Validated[E, List[B]] =
    as.foldRight(Valid(Nil): Validated[E, List[B]])((a, acc) =>
      f(a).map2(acc)(_ :: _))

  def sequence[E, A](vs: List[Validated[E, A]]): Validated[E, List[A]] =
    traverse(vs, identity)
```

Is the introduction of Validated overkill given that it's no more expressive than using Either[List[E], A] and the various -All methods? On one hand, introducing a new type means there's something new to learn, but on the other hand, introducing a new type gives a name to a concept which can then be used to reference, discuss, and ultimately internalize the concept. We encounter this choice often when functional programming as a result of our heavy use of composition. When does the result of composing some types together deserve a new type?[7] Balancing the cognitive load of new names against that of composed types is a judgement call.

---

[7] Or even just a type name? In later chapters, we'll encounter different ways of assigning names to composed types.

Let's make one further generalization: our `Validated` type accumulates a `List[E]` of errors. Why `List`, though? What if we want to use some other type, like a `Vector`? Or a collection type that requires at least one entry, since an `Invalid(Nil)` doesn't make much sense? Or maybe a type with some additional structure, like some form of `Tree`? In fact, if we carefully look through the definition of `Validated`, there's only one place that depends on errors being modeled as a list: in the definition of `map2` when we concatenate the errors from two `Invalid` values. Let's redefine `Validated` to avoid the direct dependency on `List` for error accumulation:

```
enum Validated[+E, +A]:
  case Valid(get: A)
  case Invalid(error: E)
```

> The error case is now a single E instead of a List[E].

At first glance, it appears we've taken a step backward by defining `Validated` very much like `Either` is defined. The key difference between this version of `Validated` and `Either` is in the signature of `map2`. In particular, we need a way to combine two invalid values into a single invalid value. In the previous definition of `Validated`, where `Invalid` wrapped a `List[E]`, our combining action was list concatenation. But with this new definition, we need a way to combine two `E` values into a single `E` value, and we know nothing about `E`. It seems like we're stuck, but we can modify the signature of `map2` and simply ask for such a combining action:

```
enum Validated[+E, +A]:
  case Valid(get: A)
  case Invalid(error: E)

  def map2[EE >: E, B, C](
    b: Validated[EE, B])(
    f: (A, B) => C)(
    combineErrors: (EE, EE) => EE
  ): Validated[EE, C] =
    (this, b) match
      case (Valid(aa), Valid(bb)) => Valid(f(aa, bb))
      case (Invalid(e), Valid(_)) => Invalid(e)
      case (Valid(_), Invalid(e)) => Invalid(e)
      case (Invalid(e1), Invalid(e2)) =>
        Invalid(combineErrors(e1, e2))
```

> We ask the caller to provide a function that combines two errors into one error.

> In a case in which both inputs are invalid, we use the caller-supplied combining action to merge the errors.

With this version of `Validated`, creating a `Person` would return `Validated[List[String], Person]`, and since we're using `List[String]` for the error type, we'd have to pass list concatenation as the value of `combineErrors` when calling `map2`. For example, assuming `Name` and `Age` are also modified to return a `Validated` with `List[String]` as the error type, we could create a `Person` via `Name(name).map2(Age(age))(Person(_, _))(_ ++ _)`.

Because `traverse` calls `map2`, it must pass a value for `combineErrors`, but `traverse` doesn't know anything about the error type. Hence, we'll need to change the signature of `traverse` to take `combineErrors` as a parameter as well. And by a similar argument, `sequence` needs a `combineErrors` parameter:

```
def traverse[E, A, B](
  as: List[A], f: A => Validated[E, B],
  combineErrors: (E, E) => E
): Validated[E, List[B]] =
  as.foldRight(Valid(Nil): Validated[E, List[B]])((a, acc) =>
    f(a).map2(acc)(_ :: _)(combineErrors))

def sequence[E, A](
  vs: List[Validated[E, A]],
  combineErrors: (E, E) => E
): Validated[E, List[A]] =
  traverse(vs, identity, combineErrors)
```

Passing around the `combineErrors` function is pretty inconvenient, and we'll see how to deal with such boilerplate in part 3 of this book.[8] For now, the key idea is that `Validated[E, A]` is convertible to and from `Either[E, A]`, with the only difference being the behavior of `map2`.[9]

Option and Either in the standard library

As mentioned earlier in this chapter, both `Option` and `Either` exist in the Scala standard library (the `Option` API is at http://mng.bz/EVKq; the `Either` API is at http://mng.bz/N8oE), and most of the functions we've defined in this chapter exist for the standard library versions. You're encouraged to read through the API for `Option` and `Either` to understand the differences. There are a few missing functions though—notably `sequence`, `traverse`, and `map2`. The Typelevel Cats functional programming library (https://typelevel.org/cats/) defines those missing functions.

The `toIntOption` function we wrote has an equivalent on `String`, which returns a standard library `Option[Int]`. For example, `"asdf".toIntOption` returns a `None`, whereas `"42".toIntOption` returns a `Some(42)`.

The standard library also defines the data type `Try[A]` (the API is at http://mng.bz/D10y), which is basically equivalent to `Either[Throwable, A]`. The `Try` API has some operations that are specialized for working with exceptions. For example, the `apply` method on the `Try` companion object is equivalent to the `catchNonFatal` method we defined earlier. `Either` is to `Try` as Java's checked exceptions are to unchecked exceptions. That is, `Either` lets us track a precise error type (e.g., `Either[NumberFormatException, Int]`), whereas `Try` tracks `Throwable`.

---

[8] A reader familiar with typeclasses may recognize that we can avoid explicitly passing `combineErrors` by using a `Monoid[E]`, covered in chapter 10, or the weaker `Semigroup[E]` (the latter of which is not covered in this book).

[9] A reader familiar with monadic functional programming may recognize that `Validated` provides an alternative applicative functor to the one implied by the `Either` monad.

Finally, the general version of the `Validated` data type is provided by the Typelevel Cats library (the API is at http://mng.bz/9NXj). The version of `Validated` in Cats uses a concept we'll cover in chapter 10 to avoid the need for manually passing `combineErrors` to various functions.

4.5 Conclusion

In this chapter, we noted some of the problems with using exceptions and introduced the basic principles of purely functional error handling. Although we focused on the algebraic data types `Option` and `Either`, the bigger idea is that we can represent exceptions as ordinary values and use higher-order functions to encapsulate common patterns of handling and propagating errors. This general idea, of representing effects as values, is something we'll see again and again throughout this book in various guises.

We don't expect you to be fluent with all the higher-order functions we wrote in this chapter, but you should now have enough familiarity to get started writing your own functional code complete with error handling. With these new tools in hand, exceptions should be reserved only for truly unrecoverable conditions.

Lastly, in this chapter we touched briefly on the notion of a nonstrict function (recall the functions `orElse`, `getOrElse`, and `catchNonFatal`). In the next chapter, we'll look more closely at why nonstrictness is important and how it can buy us greater modularity and efficiency in our functional programs.

Summary

- Throwing exceptions is a side effect because doing so breaks referential transparency.
- Throwing exceptions inhibits local reasoning because program meaning changes depending on which `try` block a throw is nested in.
- Exceptions are not type safe; the potential for an error occurring is not communicated in the type of the function, leading to unhandled exceptions becoming runtime errors.
- Instead of exceptions, we can model errors as values.
- Rather than modeling error values as return codes, we use various ADTs that describe success and failure.
- The `Option` type has two data constructors, `Some(a)` and `None`, which are used to model a successful result and an error. No details are provided about the error.
- The `Either` type has two data constructors, `Left(e)` and `Right(a)`, which are used to model an error and a successful result. The `Either` type is similar to `Option`, except it provides details about the error.

- The `Try` type is like `Either`, except errors are represented as `Throwable` values instead of arbitrary types. By constraining errors to be subtypes of `Throwable`, the `Try` type is able to provide various convenience operations for code that throws exceptions.
- The `Validated` type is like `Either`, except errors are accumulated when combining multiple failed computations.
- Higher-order functions, like `map` and `flatMap`, let us work with potentially failed computations without explicitly handling an error from every function call. These higher-order functions are defined for each of the various error-handling data types.

4.6   Exercise answers

ANSWER 4.1

```
enum Option[+A]:
  case Some(get: A)
  case None

  def map[B](f: A => B): Option[B] = this match
    case None => None
    case Some(a) => Some(f(a))

  def getOrElse[B>:A](default: => B): B = this match
    case None => default
    case Some(a) => a

  def flatMap[B](f: A => Option[B]): Option[B] =
    map(f).getOrElse(None)

  def orElse[B>:A](ob: => Option[B]): Option[B] =
    map(Some(_)).getOrElse(ob)

  def filter(f: A => Boolean): Option[A] =
    flatMap(a => if f(a) then Some(a) else None)
```

The `map` and `getOrElse` methods are each implemented by pattern matching on `this` and defining behavior for each data constructor. The `flatMap` and `orElse` methods are both implemented by creating nested options and then using `getOrElse` to remove the outer layer. Finally, `filter` is implemented via `flatMap` in the same way we implemented it for `List`.

ANSWER 4.2

```
def variance(xs: Seq[Double]): Option[Double] =
  mean(xs).flatMap(m => mean(xs.map(x => math.pow(x - m, 2))))
```

We first take the mean of the original samples, which results in an `Option[Double]`. We call `flatMap` on that, passing an anonymous function of type `Double =>` `Option[Double]`. In the definition of this anonymous function, we map over the original samples, transforming each element x to `math.pow(x - m, 2)`, and we then take the mean of that transformed sequence. Note that the inner call to `mean` returns an `Option[Double]`, which is why we needed to `flatMap` the result of the outer `mean`. Had we used `map` instead, we'd have ended up with an `Option[Option[Double]]`.

■ ANSWER 4.3 ──

```
def map2[A, B, C](a: Option[A], b: Option[B])(f: (A, B) => C): Option[C] =
  a.flatMap(aa => b.map(bb => f(aa, bb)))
```

This implementation uses `flatMap` on the first option and `map` on the second option. If we had used `map` on both options, we would have ended up with an `Option[Option[C]]`, which we'd then need to reduce via `getOrElse(None)`, but `map(g).getOrElse(None)` is the definition of `flatMap`. Alternatively, we could have used pattern matching:

```
def map2[A, B, C](a: Option[A], b: Option[B])(f: (A, B) => C): Option[C] =
  (a, b) match
    case (Some(aa), Some(bb)) => Some(f(aa, bb))
    case _ => None
```

■ ANSWER 4.4 ──

```
def sequence[A](as: List[Option[A]]): Option[List[A]] =
  as.foldRight[Option[List[A]]](Some(Nil))((a, acc) => map2(a, acc)(_ :: _))
```

We right fold the list of options, using `map2`, with list cons as our combining function. Note we're using the standard library version of `List` here, which uses different names than the data type we previously created. In particular, `::` takes the place of `Cons`; `h :: t` is the standard library equivalent of `Cons(h, t)` from chapter 3.

■ ANSWER 4.5 ──

```
def traverse[A, B](as: List[A])(f: A => Option[B]): Option[List[B]] =
  as.foldRight(Some(Nil): Option[List[B]])((a, acc) =>
    map2(f(a), acc)(_ :: _))
```

We use the same strategy for `traverse` as we did for our initial implementation of `sequence`: a right fold over the list elements, with `map2` and `::` as the combining function. The only difference is that we apply each element to f before calling map2. To implement sequence, we pass the identity function to traverse since each element in our input list is already an option:

```
def sequence[A](as: List[Option[A]]): Option[List[A]] =
  traverse(as)(a => a)
```

ANSWER 4.6

```
enum Either[+E, +A]:
  case Left(value: E)
  case Right(value: A)

  def map[B](f: A => B): Either[E, B] = this match
    case Right(value) => Right(f(value))
    case Left(value) => Left(value)

  def flatMap[EE >: E, B](f: A => Either[EE, B]): Either[EE, B] =
    this match
      case Right(value) => f(value)
      case Left(value) => Left(value)

  def orElse[EE >: E,B >: A](b: => Either[EE, B]): Either[EE, B] =
    this match
      case Right(value) => Right(value)
      case Left(_) => b

  def map2[EE >: E, B, C](that: Either[EE, B])(
    f: (A, B) => C
  ): Either[EE, C] =
    for
      a <- this
      b <- that
    yield f(a, b)
```

The map, flatMap, and orElse operations are implemented using pattern matching. The map2 operation is implemented using a for-comprehension, which expands to flatMap(a => that.map(b => f(a, b))).

ANSWER 4.7

We can apply our experience with sequencing and traversing with lists of options, changing the definitions slightly:

```
def sequence[E, A](as: List[Either[E, A]]): Either[E, List[A]] =
  traverse(as)(x => x)

def traverse[E, A, B](as: List[A])(f: A => Either[E, B]): Either[E, List[B]] =
  as.foldRight[Either[E, List[B]]](Right(Nil))((a, b) => f(a).map2(b)(_ :: _))
```

Besides type signatures, the only change is our choice of an initial accumulator:
Right(Nil) instead of Some(Nil).

Strictness and laziness

This chapter covers

- Contrasting strictness and nonstrictness
- Introducing lazy lists
- Separating program description from evaluation

In chapter 3, we talked about purely functional data structures, using singly linked lists as an example. We covered a number of bulk operations on lists: map, filter, foldLeft, foldRight, zipWith, and so on. We noted that each of these operations makes its own pass over the input and constructs a fresh list for the output.

Imagine you had a deck of cards and were asked to remove the odd-numbered cards and then flip over all the queens. Ideally, you'd make a single pass through the deck, looking for queens and odd-numbered cards at the same time. This is more efficient than removing the odd cards and then looking for queens in the remainder—and yet the latter is what Scala is doing. Consider the following code:[1]

```scala
scala> List(1,2,3,4).map(_ + 10).filter(_ % 2 == 0).map(_ * 3)
List(36,42)
```

---

[1] We're now using the Scala standard library's List type here, where map and filter are methods on List rather than standalone functions like the ones we wrote in chapter 3.

In this expression, `map(_ + 10)` will produce an intermediate list that then gets passed to `filter(_ % 2 == 0)`, which in turn constructs a list that gets passed to `map(_ * 3)`, which then produces the final list. In other words, each transformation will produce a temporary list that only ever gets used as input to the next transformation and is then immediately discarded.

Think about how this program will be evaluated. If we manually produce a trace of its evaluation, the steps would look something like this.

Listing 5.1 Program trace for `List`

```
List(1,2,3,4).map(_ + 10).filter(_ % 2 == 0).map(_ * 3)
List(11,12,13,14).filter(_ % 2 == 0).map(_ * 3)
List(12,14).map(_ * 3)
List(36,42)
```

Here we're showing the result of each substitution performed to evaluate our expression. For example, to go from the first line to the second, we've replaced `List(1,2,3,4).map(_ + 10)` with `List(11,12,13,14)`, based on the definition of map.[2] This view makes it clear how the calls to map and filter each perform their own traversal of the input and allocate lists for the output. Wouldn't it be nice if we could somehow fuse sequences of transformations like this into a single pass and avoid creating temporary data structures? We could rewrite the code into a while loop by hand, but ideally, we'd like to have this done automatically while retaining the same high-level compositional style. We want to compose our programs using higher-order functions, like map and filter, instead of writing monolithic loops.

It turns out that we can accomplish this kind of automatic loop fusion by using *non-strictness* (or, less formally, *laziness*). In this chapter, we'll explain exactly what this means, and we'll work through the implementation of a lazy list type that fuses sequences of transformations. Although building a *better* list is the motivation for this chapter, we'll see that nonstrictness is a fundamental technique for improving on the efficiency and modularity of functional programs in general.

5.1 Strict and nonstrict functions

Before we get to our example of lazy lists, we need to cover some basics. What do the concepts *strictness* and *nonstrictness* refer to, and how are they expressed in Scala?

Nonstrictness is a property of a function. To say that a function is nonstrict just means the function may choose not to evaluate one or more of its arguments. In contrast, a *strict* function always evaluates its arguments. Strict functions are the norm in most programming languages, and indeed, most languages only support functions that expect their arguments fully evaluated. Unless we instruct it otherwise, any function definition

---

[2] With program traces like these, it's often more illustrative to not fully trace the evaluation of every subexpression. In this case, we've omitted the full expansion of `List(1,2,3,4).map(_ + 10)`. We could enter the definition of map and trace its execution, but we chose to omit this level of detail here.

in Scala will be strict (and almost all the functions we've defined so far have been strict). As an example, consider the following function:

```
def square(x: Double): Double = x * x
```

When you invoke square(41.0 + 1.0), the function square will receive the evaluated value of 42.0 because it's strict. If you invoke square(sys.error("failure")), you'll get an exception before square has a chance to do anything since the sys.error ("failure") expression will be evaluated before entering the body of square.

Although we haven't yet learned the syntax for indicating nonstrictness in Scala (though we saw a preview with getOrElse and orElse last chapter), you're almost certainly familiar with the concept. For example, the short-circuiting Boolean functions && and || found in many programming languages, including Scala, are nonstrict. You may be used to thinking of && and || as built-in syntax—part of the language—but you can also think of them as functions that may choose not to evaluate their arguments. The function && takes two Boolean arguments but only evaluates the second argument if the first is true:

```
scala> false && { println("!!"); true } // does not print anything
res0: Boolean = false
```

And || only evaluates its second argument if the first is false:

```
scala> true || { println("!!"); false } // doesn't print anything either
res1: Boolean = true
```

Another example of nonstrictness is the if control construct in Scala:

```
val result = if input.isEmpty then sys.error("empty input") else input
```

Even though if is a built-in language construct in Scala, it can be thought of as a function accepting three parameters: a condition of type Boolean, an expression of some type A to return in case the condition is true, and another expression of the same type A to return if the condition is false. This if function would be nonstrict since it won't evaluate all of its arguments. To be more precise, we'd say the if function is strict in its condition parameter—since it will always evaluate the condition to determine which branch to take—and nonstrict in the two branches for the true and false cases—since it will only evaluate one or the other based on the condition.

In Scala, we can write nonstrict functions by accepting some of our arguments unevaluated. We'll show how this is done explicitly just to illustrate what's happening, and then we'll show some nicer syntax for it that's built into Scala. Here's a nonstrict if function:

```
def if2[A](cond: Boolean, onTrue: () => A, onFalse: () => A): A =
  if cond then onTrue() else onFalse()
```

```
if2(a < 22,
  () => println("a"),
  () => println("b")
)
```

⟵⎯⎯⎤   **The function literal syntax**
        for creating a () => A

The `onTrue` and `onFalse` arguments use some new syntax we have not encountered yet: the type `() => A`. A value of type `() => A` is a function that accepts zero arguments and returns an A.[3] In general, the unevaluated form of an expression is called a *thunk*, and we can force the thunk to evaluate the expression and get a result. We do so by invoking the function and passing an empty argument list, as in `onTrue()` or `onFalse()`. Likewise, callers of `if2` have to explicitly create thunks, and the syntax follows the same conventions as the function-literal syntax we've already seen.

Overall, this syntax makes it very clear what's happening; we're passing a function of no arguments in place of each nonstrict parameter and then explicitly calling this function to obtain a result in the body. We may even choose to call this function multiple times or zero times—but this is such a common case that Scala provides some nicer syntax:

```
def if2[A](cond: Boolean, onTrue: => A, onFalse: => A): A =
  if cond then onTrue else onFalse
```

The `onTrue` and `onFalse` arguments now have the type `=> A`. In the body of the function, we don't need to do anything special to evaluate an argument annotated with `=>`—we just reference the identifier as usual—nor do we need to do anything special to call this function. We just use the normal function call syntax, and Scala takes care of wrapping the expression in a thunk for us:

```
scala> if2(false, sys.error("fail"), 3)
res2: Int = 3
```

With either syntax, an argument that's passed unevaluated to a function will be evaluated once for each place it's referenced in the body of the function. That is, Scala won't (by default) cache the result of evaluating an argument:

```
scala> def maybeTwice(b: Boolean, i: => Int) = if b then i + i else 0
maybeTwice: (b: Boolean, i: => Int)Int

scala> val x = maybeTwice(true, { println("hi"); 1 + 41 })
hi
hi
x: Int = 84
```

Here `i` is referenced twice in the body of `maybeTwice`, and we've made it particularly obvious that it's evaluated each time by passing the block `{println("hi"); 1 + 41}`, which prints `hi` as a side effect before returning a result of 42. The expression 1 + 41

---

[3] In fact, the type `() => A` is a syntactic alias for the type `Function0[A]`.

will be computed twice as well. We can cache the value explicitly if we wish to only evaluate the result once by using the `lazy` keyword:

```scala
scala> def maybeTwice2(b: Boolean, i: => Int) =
     |   lazy val j = i
     |   if b then j + j else 0
maybeTwice: (b: Boolean, i: => Int)Int

scala> val x = maybeTwice2(true, { println("hi"); 1 + 41 })
hi
x: Int = 84
```

Adding the `lazy` keyword to a `val` declaration will cause Scala to delay evaluation of the right-hand side of that `lazy val` declaration until its first reference during evaluation of another expression. It will also cache the result so subsequent references to it don't trigger repeated evaluation.

> **Formal definition of strictness**
>
> If the evaluation of an expression runs forever or throws an error instead of returning a definite value, we say the expression doesn't *terminate* or it evaluates to *bottom*. A function f is *strict* if the expression f(x) evaluates to bottom for all x that evaluate to bottom.

As a final bit of terminology, we say a nonstrict function in Scala takes its arguments by *name* rather than by *value*.

5.2   *Lazy lists: An extended example*

Let's now return to the problem posed at the beginning of this chapter. We'll explore how laziness can be used to improve the efficiency and modularity of functional programs, using *lazy lists* as an example. We'll see how chains of transformations on lazy lists are fused into a single pass by using laziness. There are a few new things in the following simple `LazyList` definition that we'll discuss next.

Listing 5.2   A simple definition for `LazyList`

```scala
enum LazyList[+A]:
  case Empty
  case Cons(h: () => A, t: () => LazyList[A])    ◁── A nonempty lazy list consists of a
                                                      head and a tail, which are both
                                                      nonstrict.

object LazyList:
  def cons[A](
    hd: => A, tl: => LazyList[A]                  A smart constructor for creating
  ): LazyList[A] =                          ◁──    a nonempty lazy list
    lazy val head = hd                      ◁──
    lazy val tail = tl                            We cache the head and tail as lazy
    Cons(() => head, () => tail)                  values to avoid repeated evaluation.
```

```
def empty[A]: LazyList[A] = Empty        ◁─┤
```
A smart constructor for creating an empty LazyList of a particular type

```
def apply[A](as: A*): LazyList[A] =      ◁─
  if as.isEmpty then empty
  else cons(as.head, apply(as.tail*))
```
A convenient variable-argument method for constructing a LazyList from multiple elements

This type looks identical to our List type, except the Cons data constructor takes *explicit* thunks (() => A and () => LazyList[A]), instead of regular strict values. We use explicit thunks here because Scala doesn't allow the parameters of a case class to be by-name parameters (and each data constructor of an enum that takes parameters defines a case class).[4] If we wish to examine or traverse the LazyList, we need to force these thunks as we did earlier in our definition of if2. For instance, here's a function to optionally extract the head of a LazyList, defined as a method on the LazyList type:

```
def headOption: Option[A] = this match
  case Empty => None
  case Cons(h, _) => Some(h())    ◁──────┘
```
Explicit forcing of the h thunk using h()

Note that we have to force h explicitly via h(), but other than that, the code works the same way as it would for List. But this ability of LazyList to evaluate only the portion actually demanded (we don't evaluate the tail of the Cons) is useful, as we'll see.

5.2.1 *Memoizing lazy lists and avoiding recomputation*

We typically want to cache the values of a Cons node once they are forced. If we use the Cons data constructor directly, for instance, this code will actually compute expensive(x) twice:

```
val x = Cons(() => expensive(x), tl)
val h1 = x.headOption
val h2 = x.headOption
```

We typically avoid this problem by defining *smart* constructors, which is what we call functions for constructing data types that ensure some additional invariant or provide a slightly different signature than the real constructors used for pattern matching. By convention, smart constructors typically lowercase the first letter of the corresponding data constructor. Here, our cons smart constructor takes care of memoizing the by-name arguments for the head and tail of the Cons. This is a common trick, and it ensures our thunk will only do its work once when forced for the first time. Subsequent forces will return the cached lazy val:

```
def cons[A](hd: => A, tl: => LazyList[A]): LazyList[A] =
  lazy val head = hd
  lazy val tail = tl
  Cons(() => head, () => tail)
```

---

[4] This limitation is the result of each parameter of a case class getting a corresponding public val.

Each time the head thunk is referenced in the resulting `LazyList`, the value of the `lazy val head` is returned. If that `lazy val` has already been initialized, then its cached value is returned. Otherwise, it's computed, cached, and returned. This smart constructor gives us the best of all worlds; there is no need to manually create thunks at the call site of `Cons` or to cache the result, so it's only computed once, and we retain the features provided by case classes:

```
def empty[A]: LazyList = Empty
```

The `empty` smart constructor just returns `Empty` but annotates `Empty` as a `Lazy-List[A]`, which is better for type inference in some cases:[5]

```
def apply[A](as: A*): LazyList[A] =
  if as.isEmpty then empty
  else cons(as.head, apply(as.tail*))
```

Again, Scala takes care of wrapping the arguments to `cons` in thunks, so the `as.head` and `apply(as.tail*)` expressions won't be evaluated until we force the `LazyList`. The `as` argument to `apply` is strict, however! When `apply` is called, each individual `A` expression is evaluated before the definition of `apply` is evaluated. To defer evaluation of each argument until forced by the resulting `LazyList`, we'd need each `A` to be by-name. It would need to be something like `def apply[A](as: (=> A)*): LazyList[A]`, but Scala doesn't support this syntax. We'll discuss other ways of lazily constructing a `LazyList` later in this chapter.

5.2.2   *Helper functions for inspecting lazy lists*

Before continuing, let's write a few helper functions to make inspecting lazy lists easier.

■ **EXERCISE 5.1**
───

Write a function to convert a `LazyList` to a `List`, which will force its evaluation and let you look at it in the REPL. You can convert to the regular `List` type in the standard library, and you can place this and other functions that operate on a `LazyList` inside the `LazyList` enum:

```
def toList: List[A]
```

---
[5] Recall that Scala uses subtyping to represent data constructors, but we almost always want to infer `LazyList` as the type, not `Cons` or `Empty`. Making smart constructors that return the base type is a common trick, though one that was more important in Scala 2 than Scala 3, as Scala 3 will generally prefer to infer the type of the enum (e.g., `LazyList[A]`) instead of the type of the data constructor (e.g., `Cons[A]`).] We can see how both smart constructors are used in the `LazyList.apply` function.

■ (EXERCISE 5.2)

Write the function `take(n)` for returning the first n elements of a `LazyList` and
`drop(n)` for skipping the first n elements of a `LazyList`. Define these functions inside
the `LazyList` enum:

```
def take(n: Int): LazyList[A]
def drop(n: Int): LazyList[A]
```

■ (EXERCISE 5.3)

Write the function `takeWhile` for returning all starting elements of a `LazyList` that
match the given predicate:

```
def takeWhile(p: A => Boolean): LazyList[A]
```

You can use `take` and `toList` together to inspect lazy lists in the REPL. For example,
try printing `LazyList(1,2,3).take(2).toList`.

5.3   *Separating program description from evaluation*

A major theme in functional programming is *separation of concerns*. We want to separate the description of computations from actually running them; we've already
touched on this theme in previous chapters in different ways. For example, first-class
functions capture some computation in their bodies but only execute it once they
receive their arguments. And we used `Option` to capture the fact that an error
occurred, where the decision of what to do about it became a separate concern. With
`LazyList`, we're able to build up a computation that produces a sequence of elements
without running the steps of that computation until we need those elements.

More generally speaking, laziness lets us separate the description of an expression
from the evaluation of that expression. This gives us a powerful ability: we may choose
to describe a larger expression than we need and then evaluate only a portion of it. As
an example, let's look at the function `exists` that checks whether an element matching a `Boolean` function exists in this `LazyList`:

```
def exists(p: A => Boolean): Boolean = this match
  case Cons(h, t) => p(h()) || t().exists(p)
  case _ => false
```

Note that `||` is nonstrict in its second argument. If `p(h())` returns `true`, then `exists`
terminates the traversal early and returns `true` as well. Remember also that the tail of

the lazy list is a `lazy val`, so not only does the traversal terminate early, but the tail of the lazy list is never evaluated at all! So whatever code would have generated the tail is never actually executed.

The `exists` function here is implemented using explicit recursion. But remember from chapter 3 that with `List` we could implement a general recursion in the form of `foldRight`. We can do the same thing for `LazyList` but lazily:

```
def foldRight[B](acc: => B)(f: (A, => B) => B): B =
  this match
    case Cons(h, t) => f(h(), t().foldRight(acc)(f))
    case _ => acc
```

The arrow `=>` in front of the argument type B means the function f takes its second argument by name and may choose not to evaluate it.

If f doesn't evaluate its second argument, the recursion never occurs.

This looks very similar to the `foldRight` we wrote for `List`, but note how our combining function `f` is nonstrict in its second parameter. If `f` chooses not to evaluate its second parameter, the traversal is terminated early; we can see this by using `foldRight` to implement `exists`:[6]

```
def exists(p: A => Boolean): Boolean =
  foldRight(false)((a, b) => p(a) || b)
```

Here `b` is the unevaluated recursive step that folds the tail of the lazy list. If `p(a)` returns, `trueb` will never be evaluated, and the computation will terminate early.

Since `foldRight` can terminate the traversal early, we can reuse it to implement `exists`, which we can't do with a strict version of `foldRight`; we'd have to write a specialized recursive `exists` function to handle early termination. Laziness makes our code more reusable.

■ **EXERCISE 5.4**

Implement `forAll`, which checks that all elements in the `LazyList` match a given predicate. Your implementation should terminate the traversal as soon as it encounters a nonmatching value:

```
def forAll(p: A => Boolean): Boolean
```

■ **EXERCISE 5.5**

Use `foldRight` to implement `takeWhile`.

---

[6] This definition of `exists`, though illustrative, isn't stack safe if the lazy list is large and all elements test `false`.

■ **EXERCISE 5.6**

Implement headOption using foldRight.

■ **EXERCISE 5.7**

Implement map, filter, append, and flatMap using foldRight. The append method should be nonstrict in its argument.

Note that these implementations are *incremental*—they don't fully generate their answers. It's not until some other computation looks at the elements of the resulting LazyList that the computation to generate that LazyList actually takes place—and then it will do just enough work to generate the requested elements. Because of this incremental nature, we can call these functions one after another without fully instantiating the intermediate results.

Let's look at a simplified program trace for (a fragment of) the motivating example we started this chapter with: LazyList(1, 2, 3, 4).map(_ + 10).filter(_ % 2 == 0). We'll convert this expression to a List to force evaluation. Take a minute to work through this trace to understand what's happening. It's a bit more challenging than the trace we looked at earlier in this chapter. Remember that a trace like this is just the same expression repeated multiple times, evaluated by one more step each time.

Listing 5.3 Program trace for `LazyList`

```
LazyList(1, 2, 3, 4).map(_ + 10).filter(_ % 2 == 0).toList

cons(11, LazyList(2, 3, 4).map(_ + 10)).filter      Apply map to the
⟹ (_ % 2 == 0).toList                                first element.

LazyList(2, 3, 4).map(_ + 10).filter                Apply filter to the
⟹ (_ % 2 == 0).toList                                first element.

cons(12, LazyList(3, 4).map(_ + 10)).filter         Apply map to the
⟹ (_ % 2 == 0).toList                                second element.

12 :: LazyList(3, 4).map(_ + 10).filter             Apply filter to the second element.
⟹ (_ % 2 == 0).toList                                Produce the first element of the result.

12 :: cons(13, LazyList(4).map(_ + 10)).filter(_ % 2 == 0).toList

12 :: LazyList(4).map(_ + 10).filter(_ % 2 == 0).toList

12 :: cons(14, LazyList().map(_ + 10)).filter(_ % 2 == 0).toList
```

```
12 :: 14 :: LazyList().map(_ + 10).filter
  (_ % 2 == 0).toList
```
Apply filter to the fourth element, and produce the final element of the result.

```
12 :: 14 :: List()
```
map and filter have no more work to do, and the empty lazy list becomes the empty list.

The thing to notice in this trace is how the filter and map transformations are interleaved—the computation alternates between generating a single element of the output of map and testing with filter to see if that element is divisible by 2 (adding it to the output list if it is). Note that we don't fully instantiate the intermediate lazy list that results from the map. It's exactly as if we had interleaved the logic using a special-purpose loop. For this reason, people sometimes describe lazy lists as *first-class loops* whose logic can be combined using higher-order functions, like map and filter.

Since intermediate lazy lists aren't instantiated, it's easy to reuse existing operations in novel ways without having to worry that we're doing more processing of the lazy list than necessary. For example, we can reuse filter to define find, a method to return just the first element that matches if it exists. Even though filter transforms the whole lazy list, that transformation is done lazily, so find terminates as soon as a match is found:

```
def find(p: A => Boolean): Option[A] =
  filter(p).headOption
```

The incremental nature of lazy list transformations also has important consequences for memory usage. Because intermediate lazy lists aren't generated, a transformation of the lazy list requires only enough working memory to store and transform the current element. For instance, in the transformation LazyList(1,2,3,4).map(_ + 10) .filter(_ % 2 == 0), the garbage collector can reclaim the space allocated for the values 11 and 13 emitted by map as soon as filter determines they aren't needed. Of course, this is a simple example; in other situations, we might be dealing with larger numbers of elements, and the lazy list elements themselves could be large objects that retain significant amounts of memory. Being able to reclaim this memory as quickly as possible can cut down on the amount of memory required by your program as a whole. We'll have a lot more to say about defining memory-efficient streaming calculations, in particular calculations that require I/O, in part 4 of this book.

5.4   *Infinite lazy lists and corecursion*

Because they're incremental, the functions we've written also work for *infinite lazy lists.* Here's an example of an infinite LazyList of 1s:

```
val ones: LazyList[Int] = LazyList.cons(1, ones)
```

Although ones is infinite, the functions we've written so far only inspect the portion of the lazy list needed to generate the demanded output. For example:

```
scala> ones.take(5).toList
res0: List[Int] = List(1, 1, 1, 1, 1)

scala> ones.exists(_ % 2 != 0)
res1: Boolean = true
```

Try playing with a few other examples:

```
ones.map(_ + 1).exists(_ % 2 == 0)
  ones.takeWhile(_ == 1)
  ones.forAll(_ != 1)
```

In each case, we get back a result immediately. Be careful, though, since it's easy to write expressions that never terminate or aren't stack safe. For example, `ones.forAll(_ == 1)` will forever need to inspect more of the series since it'll never encounter an element that allows it to terminate with a definite answer (this will manifest as a stack overflow rather than an infinite loop).[7]

An infinite lazy list

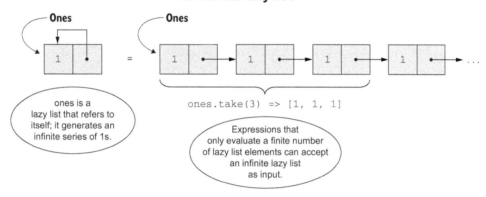

Many functions can be evaluated using finite resources even
if their inputs generate infinite sequences.

Figure 5.1   An infinite lazy list

Let's see what other functions we can discover for generating lazy lists.

EXERCISE 5.8

Generalize `ones` slightly to the function `continually`, which returns an infinite `LazyList` of a given value:

```
def continually[A](a: A): LazyList[A]
```

---

[7] It's possible to define a stack-safe version of `forAll` using an ordinary recursive loop.

■   **EXERCISE 5.9**

Write a function that generates an infinite lazy list of integers starting from n, then n + 1, n + 2, and so on:[8]

```
def from(n: Int): LazyList[Int]
```

■   **EXERCISE 5.10**

Write a function `fibs` that generates the infinite lazy list of Fibonacci numbers: 0, 1, 1, 2, 3, 5, 8, and so on.

■   **EXERCISE 5.11**

Write a more general `LazyList`-building function called `unfold`. It takes an initial state and a function for producing both the next state and the next value in the generated lazy list:

```
def unfold[A, S](state: S)(f: S => Option[(A, S)]): LazyList[A]
```

`Option` is used to indicate when the `LazyList` should be terminated, if at all. The function `unfold` is a very general `LazyList`-building function.

The `unfold` function is an example of what's sometimes called a *corecursive* function. Whereas a recursive function consumes data, a corecursive function produces data. And whereas recursive functions terminate by recursing on smaller inputs, corecursive functions need not terminate so long as they remain *productive*, which just means we can always evaluate more of the result in a finite amount of time. The `unfold` function is productive as long as f terminates since we just need to run the function f one more time to generate the next element of the `LazyList`. Corecursion is also sometimes called guarded *recursion*, and productivity is also sometimes called *cotermination*. These terms aren't very important to our discussion, but you'll hear them used sometimes in the context of functional programming. If you're curious to learn where they come from and understand some of the deeper connections, follow the references in the chapter notes (https://github.com/fpinscala/fpinscala/wiki).

---

[8] In Scala, the Int type is a 32-bit signed integer, so this lazy list will switch from positive to negative values at some point and will repeat itself after about four billion elements.

■   EXERCISE 5.12

Write fibs, from, continually, and ones in terms of unfold.[9]

■   EXERCISE 5.13

Use unfold to implement map, take, takeWhile, zipWith (as in chapter 3), and zipAll. The zipAll function should continue the traversal as long as either lazy list has more elements; it uses Option to indicate whether each lazy list has been exhausted:

```
def zipAll[B](that: LazyList[B]): LazyList[(Option[A], Option[B])]
```

Now that we have some practice writing lazy list functions, let's return to the exercise we covered at the end of chapter 3—a function, hasSubsequence—to check whether a list contains a given subsequence. With strict lists and list-processing functions, we were forced to write a rather tricky monolithic loop to implement this function without doing extra work. Using lazy lists, can you see how you could implement hasSubsequence by combining some other functions we've already written?[10] Try to think about it on your own before continuing.

■   EXERCISE 5.14

Hard: Implement startsWith using functions you've written. It should check if one LazyList is a prefix of another. For instance, LazyList(1,2,3).startsWith(LazyList(1,2)) would be true:

```
def startsWith[A](prefix: LazyList[A]): Boolean
```

---

[9] Using unfold to define continually and ones means we don't get sharing as in the recursive definition val ones: LazyList[Int] = cons(1, ones). The recursive definition consumes constant memory, even if we keep a reference to it around while traversing it, while the unfold-based implementation does not. Preserving sharing isn't something we usually rely on when programming with lazy lists since it's extremely delicate and not tracked by the types. For instance, sharing is destroyed when calling even xs.map(x => x).

[10] This small example of assembling hasSubsequence from simpler functions using laziness was created by Cale Gibbard. See this post: https://mng.bz/aPP9.

■ **EXERCISE 5.15**

Implement `tails` using `unfold`. For a given `LazyList`, `tails` returns the `LazyList` of suffixes of the input sequence, starting with the original `LazyList`. For example, given `LazyList(1, 2, 3)`, it would return `LazyList(LazyList(1, 2, 3), LazyList(2, 3), LazyList(3)`, and `LazyList())`:

```
def tails: LazyList[LazyList[A]]
```

We can now implement `hasSubsequence` using functions we've written:

```
def hasSubsequence[A](l: LazyList[A]): Boolean =
  tails.exists(_.startsWith(l))
```

This implementation performs the same number of steps as a more monolithic implementation using nested loops with logic for breaking out of each loop early. By using laziness, we can compose this function from simpler components and still retain the efficiency of the more specialized (and verbose) implementation.

■ **EXERCISE 5.16**

Hard: Generalize `tails` to the function `scanRight`, which is like a `foldRight` that returns a lazy list of the intermediate results. For example:

```
scala> LazyList(1, 2, 3).scanRight(0)(_ + _).toList
res0: List[Int] = List(6, 5, 3, 0)
```

This example should be equivalent to the expression `List(1 + 2 + 3 + 0, 2 + 3 + 0, 3 + 0, 0)`. Your function should reuse intermediate results, so traversing a `LazyList` with n elements always takes time linear in n. Can it be implemented using `unfold`? How, or why not? Could it be implemented using another function we've written?

LazyList in the standard library

Like many of the other data structures we've seen so far, `LazyList` exists in the Scala standard library (see the API at https://mng.bz/MOOD). Throughout the rest of this book, when we use `LazyList`, we'll use the standard library version instead of the one we've built in this chapter.

5.5 Conclusion

In this chapter, we introduced nonstrictness as a fundamental technique for implementing efficient and modular functional programs. Nonstrictness can be thought of as a technique for recovering some efficiency when writing functional code, but it's also a much bigger idea—nonstrictness can improve modularity by separating the description of an expression from the how-and-when of its evaluation. Keeping these concerns separate lets us reuse a description in multiple contexts, evaluating different portions of our expression to obtain different results. We weren't able to do that when description and evaluation were intertwined as they are in strict code. We saw a number of examples of this principle in action over the course of the chapter, and we'll see many more in the remainder of the book.

We'll switch gears in the next chapter and talk about purely functional approaches to state. This is the last building block needed before we begin exploring the process of functional design.

Summary

- Nonstrictness is a useful technique that allows separation of concerns and improved modularity.
- A function is described as nonstrict when it does not evaluate one or more of its arguments. In contrast, a strict function always evaluates its arguments.
- The short circuiting `&&` and `||` operators are examples of nonstrict functions; each avoids evaluation of its second argument, depending on the value of the first argument.
- In Scala, nonstrict functions are written using by-name parameters, which are indicated by a `=>` in front of the parameter type.
- An unevaluated expression is referred to as a thunk, and we can force a thunk to evaluate the expression to a result.
- `LazyList` allows the definition of infinitely long sequences, and various operations on `LazyList`, like `take`, `foldRight`, and `exists`, allow partial evaluation of those infinite sequences.
- `LazyList` is similar to `List`, except the head and tail of `Cons` are evaluated lazily instead of strictly, like in `List.Cons`.
- Memoization is the process of caching the result of a computation upon first use.
- Smart constructors are functions that create an instance of a data type and provide some additional validation or provide a slightly different type signature than the real data constructors.
- Separating the description of a computation from its evaluation provides opportunities for reuse and efficiency.
- The `foldRight` function on `LazyList` supports early termination and is subsequently safe for use with infinite lazy lists.

- The unfold function, which generates a LazyList from a seed and a function, is an example of a corecursive function. Corecursive functions produce data and continue to run as long as they are productive.

5.6   *Exercise answers*

ANSWER 5.1

The simplest approach is recursing on the structure of the lazy list:

```
def toList: List[A] = this match
  case Cons(h, t) => h() :: t().toList
  case Empty => Nil
```

Like we saw in chapter 3, such recursive definitions are not stack safe since they do additional work with the result of the recursive call. We can write a stack-safe version by using tail recursion:

```
def toList: List[A] =
  @annotation.tailrec
  def go(ll: LazyList[A], acc: List[A]): List[A] =
    ll match
      case Cons(h, t) => go(t(), h() :: acc)
      case Empty => acc.reverse
  go(this, Nil)
```

ANSWER 5.2

First let's implement take:

```
def take(n: Int): LazyList[A] = this match
  case Cons(h, t) if n > 1 => cons(h(), t().take(n - 1))
  case Cons(h, t) if n == 1 => cons(h(), empty)
  case _ => empty
```

If we have a Cons and more than 1 element to take, we return a new Cons with the head set to the original head and the tail set to recursively calling take on the tail n decremented. The case where n is equal to 1 is more interesting—while we could leave out that case entirely and compute the right answer, doing so unnecessarily forces the computation of the tail due to t().take(n - 1). It's wasteful to compute that tail just to immediately throw it away, so we define a special case for taking a single element. Similarly, in the case where n is 0, we do not force the computation of the head or the tail. We'll look at this type of lazy evaluation in greater detail in the next section.

Is this implementation stack safe? At first glance, it appears it isn't due to the recursive call not being in tail position. However, the recursive call is suspended until the tail of the returned Cons is forced, and hence this is stack safe. The drop function can be implemented via tail recursion:

```
@annotation.tailrec
final def drop(n: Int): LazyList[A] = this match
  case Cons(_, t) if n > 0 => t().drop(n - 1)
  case _ => this
```

This is very similar to how we would define drop on a List, but again, note that we do not force the computation of the elements that are dropped.

■   **ANSWER 5.3**

We can implement takeWhile in much the same way as we implemented take:

```
def takeWhile(p: A => Boolean): LazyList[A] = this match
  case Cons(h, t) if p(h()) => cons(h(), t().takeWhile(p))
  case _ => empty
```

■   **ANSWER 5.4**

We'll use foldRight in the same way that we used it to implement exists, ensuring that we only evaluate b if the predicate returns true for the current element:

```
def forAll(p: A => Boolean): Boolean =
  foldRight(true)((a, b) => p(a) && b)
```

■   **ANSWER 5.5**

```
def takeWhile(p: A => Boolean): LazyList[A] =
  foldRight(empty)((a, b) => if p(a) then cons(a, b) else empty)
```

We start the fold with an empty lazy list. For each element, if the predicate evaluates to true, then we build a Cons using that element and the remainder of the computation, represented by the b passed to our folding function.

We need to return `None` when the lazy list is empty, so we start our fold with a `None`. Then, when we receive an element and the accumulator (the lazy part of our computation), we simply return the element wrapped in `Some`, ignoring the accumulator. Because the accumulator is discarded, the rest of the lazy list is never evaluated:

```
def headOption: Option[A] =
  foldRight(None: Option[A])((a, _) => Some(a))
```

To implement `map`, we construct a `Cons` for each element, transforming the element with the supplied function:

```
def map[B](f: A => B): LazyList[B] =
  foldRight(empty[B])((a, acc) => cons(f(a), acc))
```

Similarly, `filter` tests the element with the supplied predicate and builds a `Cons` if it passes and skips it if it doesn't:

```
def filter(p: A => Boolean): LazyList[A] =
  foldRight(empty[A])((a, acc) => if p(a) then cons(a, acc) else acc)
```

The append function is a little more interesting:

```
def append[A2 >: A](that: => LazyList[A2]): LazyList[A2] =
  foldRight(that)((a, acc) => cons(a, acc))
```

We take the argument to append as a by-name parameter, ensuring it is not computed until it is needed. We also need to add a type parameter, `A2`, that's a supertype of `A`; otherwise, the compiler complains about variance. (Note: if we defined this as a standalone function instead of a method on `LazyList`, we wouldn't need to worry about variance.)

We start the fold with the lazy list we're appending, and for each element in the original lazy list, we cons it on to the accumulator. Finally, `flatMap` can be implemented using append:

```
def flatMap[B](f: A => LazyList[B]): LazyList[B] =
  foldRight(empty[B])((a, acc) => f(a).append(acc))
```

◼ ANSWER 5.8

A simple definition is obtained by replacing 1 with a:

```
def continually[A](a: A): LazyList[A] =
  cons(a, continually(a))
```

A more efficient implementation allocates a single Cons cell that references itself:

```
def continually[A](a: A): LazyList[A] =
  lazy val single: LazyList[A] = cons(a, single)
  single
```

◼ ANSWER 5.9

We construct a Cons with the head equal to n and the tail a recursive call to from with n + 1. Like ones and continually, the infinite recursion is totally safe because the tail is not evaluated until forced:

```
def from(n: Int): LazyList[Int] =
  cons(n, from(n + 1))
```

◼ ANSWER 5.10

We'll use a recursive auxiliary function that tracks the current and next Fibonacci numbers. When it's evaluated, it returns a lazy list with the current Fibonacci number as the head and a recursive call as the tail, shifting the next number into the current position and computing a new next by summing current and next:

```
val fibs: LazyList[Int] =
  def go(current: Int, next: Int): LazyList[Int] =
    cons(current, go(next, current + next))
  go(0, 1)
```

Note that we can define this as a val instead of a def—doing so does not generate the entire infinite sequence.

On each invocation of unfold, we apply the state parameter to the function f. If the result is a None, then we're done, so we return the empty lazy list. Otherwise, we return the result of consing the generated value on to the lazy list we get by unfolding with the newly computed state. Once again, the recursion is stack safe because Cons lazily evaluates its arguments:

```
def unfold[A, S](state: S)(f: S => Option[(A, S)]): LazyList[A] =
  f(state) match
    case Some((a, s)) => cons(a, unfold(s)(f))
    case None => empty
```

Our recursive fibs definition passes two parameters to the recursive call: current and next. We can capture those parameters as the state that's used in an unfold by putting them in a tuple:

```
val fibs: LazyList[Int] =
  unfold((0, 1)): case (current, next) =>
    Some((current, (next, current + next)))
```

Likewise, the state used in from is the next integer to emit:

```
def from(n: Int): LazyList[Int] =
  unfold(n)(n => Some((n, n + 1)))
```

The remaining functions need no state, so we can pass any value at all for the unfold state. Normally, we'll pass a unit value in such circumstances to make it clear we do not use it:

```
def continually[A](a: A): LazyList[A] =
  unfold(())(_ => Some((a, ())))

val ones: LazyList[Int] =
  unfold(())(_ => Some((1, ())))
```

Like in the previous exercise, the trick is determining what state to use in conjunction with unfold. To implement map, we use the untransformed list as the state:

```
def mapViaUnfold[B](f: A => B): LazyList[B] =
  unfold(this):
    case Cons(h, t) => Some((f(h()), t()))
    case _ => None
```

For `take`, we use the original list and the number of remaining elements to take:

```
def takeViaUnfold(n: Int): LazyList[A] =
  unfold((this, n)):
    case (Cons(h, t), 1) => Some((h(), (empty, 0)))
    case (Cons(h, t), n) if n > 1 => Some((h(), (t(), n-1)))
    case _ => None
```

And `takeWhile`, like map, just uses the original list as the state:

```
def takeWhileViaUnfold(f: A => Boolean): LazyList[A] =
  unfold(this):
    case Cons(h, t) if f(h()) => Some((h(), t()))
    case _ => None
```

To implement `zipAll`, we use both lazy lists as the state. On each unfold iteration, we pattern match on the structure of our state and define cases for each combination of `Empty` and `Cons`. For example, in the case in which both lazy lists are `Cons` elements, we return a `Some` indicating we produced an element. Inside that `Some`, we provide both heads wrapped in `Some` as the value to emit, and we provide both tails as the new state. In the answer, we used the `=>` method to create a pair to reduce the number of parentheses—`a => b` is equivalent to `(a, b)`:

```
def zipAll[B](that: LazyList[B]): LazyList[(Option[A], Option[B])] =
  unfold((this, that)):
    case (Empty, Empty) => None
    case (Cons(h1, t1), Empty) =>
      Some((Some(h1()) -> None) -> (t1() -> Empty))
    case (Empty, Cons(h2, t2)) =>
      Some((None -> Some(h2())) -> (Empty -> t2()))
    case (Cons(h1, t1), Cons(h2, t2)) =>
      Some((Some(h1()) -> Some(h2())) -> (t1() -> t2()))
```

There are some interesting opportunities for generalization here: we could define a zip variant that terminates upon reaching the end of either lazy list, or we could define the ability to zip the elements with a function instead of returning `(Option[A], Option[B])`. See the answers in the GitHub repository for more details.

We can take advantage of laziness by zipping our input list with the prefix list, aligning each element and stopping upon reaching the end of the prefix list. We can then return true if we are able to ensure that every element pairing is equal:

```
def startsWith[A](prefix: LazyList[A]): Boolean =
  zipAll(prefix).takeWhile(_(1).isDefined).forAll((a1, a2) => a1 == a2)
```

The initial state for unfolding is the initial lazy list. Upon an empty input, we'll stop unfolding. Upon a nonempty input, we'll emit the list and then unfold the tail of that list. Finally, we need to append the final empty lazy list, which we do by calling append on the result of unfold:

```
def tails: LazyList[LazyList[A]] =
  unfold(this):
    case Empty => None
    case Cons(h, t) => Some((Cons(h, t), t()))
  .append(LazyList(empty))
```

In the pattern match, we use a new syntax—case l @ Cons(_, t)—which binds the name l to the pattern matched value—the Cons(_, t). Doing so lets us avoid constructing a new Cons object when returning the value to emit.

We can't implement scanRight via unfold because unfold builds a lazy list from left to right. Instead, we can use foldRight with a slight modification; instead of folding each element to a single B, we fold the elements to a LazyList[B]:

```
def scanRight[B](init: B)(f: (A, => B) => B): LazyList[B] =
  foldRight(init -> LazyList(init)): (a, b0) =>
    lazy val b1 = b0
    val b2 = f(a, b1(0))
    (b2, cons(b2, b1(1)))
  .apply(1)
```

The accumulator of our foldRight has type (B, LazyList[B])—the first element of the tuple is the last computed B (or the initial value if we haven't yet computed a B), and the second element of the tuple is the history of all computed B values. For each element in the original list, we call f with that element and the last computed B. We then output that new B paired with the result of consing that same B onto our accumulated outputs. When the fold completes, we discard the first element of the state and return just the accumulated lazy list. Note that we are careful to avoid forcing b0 until necessary, and since we use b0 twice, we cache it in a lazy val, ensuring it's not evaluated more than once.

Purely functional state

This chapter covers

- Discussing purely functional random number generation
- Working with stateful APIs
- Introducing the `State` data type

In this chapter, we'll see how to write purely functional programs that manipulate state, using the simple domain of *random number generation* as the example. Although by itself it's not the most compelling use case for the techniques in this chapter, the simplicity of random number generation makes it a good first example. We'll see more compelling use cases in parts 3 and 4 of the book, especially part 4, where we'll discuss dealing with state and effects in much greater detail. The goal here is to provide you with the basic pattern for making any stateful API purely functional. As you start writing your own functional APIs, you'll likely run into many of the same questions we explore here.

6.1 Generating random numbers using side effects

If you need to generate random[1] numbers in Scala, there's a class in the standard library, called `scala.util.Random` (Scala API link: https://mng.bz/7W8g), with a pretty typical imperative API that relies on side effects. The following listing shows an example of its use.

---

[1] Actually, pseudo-random, but we'll ignore this distinction.

Listing 6.1   Using `scala.util.Random` to generate random numbers

```
scala> val rng = new scala.util.Random
```
Creates a new random number generator seeded with the current system time

```
scala> rng.nextDouble
val res1: Double = 0.9867076608154569

scala> rng.nextDouble
val res2: Double = 0.8455696498024141

scala> rng.nextInt
val res3: Int = -623297295
```
Gets a random integer between 0 and 9

```
scala> rng.nextInt(10)
val res4: Int = 4
```

Even if we don't know anything about what happens inside `scala.util.Random`, we can assume the object rng has some internal state that gets updated after each invocation, since we'd otherwise get the same value each time we called `nextInt` or `nextDouble`. Because the state updates are performed as a side effect, these methods aren't referentially transparent. And as we know, this implies that they aren't as testable, composable, modular, and easily parallelized as they could be.

Let's take testability as an example. If we want to write a method that makes use of randomness, we need tests to be reproducible. Let's say we had the following side-effecting method, intended to simulate the rolling of a single six-sided die, which should return a value between 1 and 6, inclusive:

```
def rollDie: Int =
  val rng = new scala.util.Random
  rng.nextInt(6)
```
Returns a random number from 0 to 5

This method has an off-by-one error. While it's supposed to return a value between 1 and 6, it actually returns a value from 0 to 5. But even though it doesn't work properly, a test of this method will meet the specification five out of six times! And if a test did fail, it would be ideal if we could reliably reproduce the failure.

Note that what's important here is not this specific example but the general idea. In this case, the bug is obvious and easy to reproduce. But we can easily imagine a situation where the method is much more complicated and the bug far more subtle. The more complex the program and the subtler the bug, the more important it is to be able to reproduce bugs in a reliable way.

One suggestion might be passing in the random number generator. That way, when we want to reproduce a failed test, we can pass the same generator that caused the test to fail:

```
def rollDie(rng: scala.util.Random): Int = rng.nextInt(6)
```

But there's a problem with this solution: the same generator has to be both created with the same seed and be in the same state, which means its methods have been called a certain number of times since it was created. That will be very difficult to guarantee because every time we call nextInt, for example, the previous state of the random number generator is destroyed. Do we now need a separate mechanism to keep track of how many times we've called the methods on Random?

No. The answer to all of this, of course, is that we should eschew side effects on principle.

6.2   *Purely functional random number generation*

The key to recovering referential transparency is making the state updates *explicit*. Don't update the state as a side effect, but simply return the new state along with the value we're generating. Here's one possible interface to a random number generator:

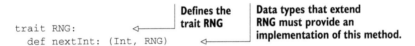

| Defines the trait RNG | Data types that extend RNG must provide an implementation of this method. |

```
trait RNG:
    def nextInt: (Int, RNG)
```

Let's look first at the definition of the data type, which begins with the keyword trait. Like enum, the trait keyword introduces a data type. A trait is an abstract interface that may optionally contain implementations of some methods. Here we're declaring a trait, called RNG, with a single abstract method on it.

The nextInt method should generate a random Int; later, we'll define other functions in terms of nextInt. Rather than returning only the generated random number (as is done in scala.util.Random) and updating some internal state by mutating it in place, we return the random number and the new state, leaving the old state unmodified.[2] In effect, we separate the concern of computing what the next state is from the concern of communicating the new state to the rest of the program. No global mutable memory is being used—we simply return the next state back to the caller. This leaves the caller of nextInt in complete control of what to do with the new state. Note that we're still *encapsulating* the state in the sense that users of this API don't know anything about the implementation of the random number generator itself.

But we do need to have an implementation, so let's pick a simple one. The following is a simple random number generator that uses the same algorithm as scala.util.Random, which happens to be what's called a *linear congruential generator* (http://mng.bz/r046). The details of this implementation aren't important for our purposes, but notice that nextInt returns both the generated value and a new RNG to use for generating the next value.

Listing 6.2   A purely functional random number generator

```
case class SimpleRNG(seed: Long) extends RNG:
    def nextInt: (Int, RNG) =
        val newSeed = (seed * 0x5DEECE66DL + 0xBL) & 0xFFFFFFFFFFFFL
```

& is bitwise AND. We use the current seed to generate a new seed.

---

[2] Recall that (A, B) is the type of two-element tuples, and given p: (A, B), you can use p._1 to extract the A and p._2 to extract the B.

```
        val nextRNG = SimpleRNG(newSeed)
        val n = (newSeed >>> 16).toInt
        (n, nextRNG)
```

The next state, which is an RNG instance created from the new seed

The return value is a tuple containing both a pseudo-random integer and the next RNG state.

> > > is right binary shift with zero fill. The value n is the new pseudo-random integer.

Here's an example of using this API from the interpreter:

```
scala> val rng = SimpleRNG(42)
val rng: SimpleRNG = SimpleRNG(42)

scala> val (n1, rng2) = rng.nextInt
val n1: Int = 16159453
val rng2: RNG = SimpleRNG(1059025964525)

scala> val (n2, rng3) = rng2.nextInt
val n2: Int = -1281479697
val rng3: RNG = SimpleRNG(197491923327988)
```

Let's choose an arbitrary seed value: 42.

Syntax for declaring two values by deconstructing the pair returned by rng.nextInt

We can run this sequence of statements as many times as we want, and we'll always get the same values. When we call `rng.nextInt`, it will always return 16159453 and a new RNG, whose `nextInt` will always return -1281479697. In other words, this API is pure. Figure 6.1 summarizes this approach.

A functional RNG

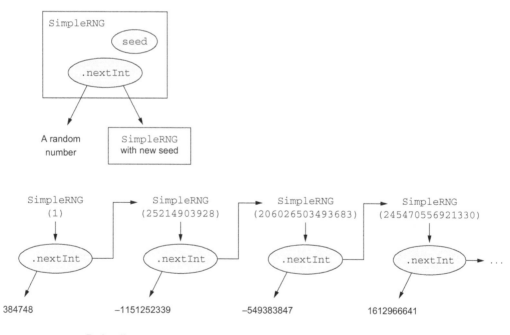

Each call to `SimpleRNG.nextInt` returns the next random number in the sequence and the `SimpleRNG` object needed to continue the sequence.

Figure 6.1   A functional RNG

6.3   *Making stateful APIs pure*

This problem of making seemingly stateful APIs pure and its solution (having the API compute the next state rather than actually mutate anything) aren't unique to random number generation. It comes up frequently, and we can always deal with it in this same way.[3]

For instance, suppose you have a class like this:

```
class Foo:
  private var s: FooState = ...
  def bar: Bar
  def baz: Int
```

Suppose bar and baz each mutate s in some way. We can mechanically translate this to the purely functional API by making the transition from one state to the next explicit:

```
trait Foo:
  def bar: (Bar, Foo)
  def baz: (Int, Foo)
```

Whenever we use this pattern, we make the caller responsible for passing the computed next state through the rest of the program. For the pure RNG interface just shown, if we reuse a previous RNG it will always generate the same value it generated before. For instance:

```
def randomPair(rng: RNG): (Int, Int) =
  val (i1, _) = rng.nextInt
  val (i2, _) = rng.nextInt
  (i1, i2)
```

Here i1 and i2 will be the same! If we want to generate two distinct numbers, we need to use the RNG returned by the first call to nextInt to generate the second Int:

Note the use of rng2 here.

```
def randomPair(rng: RNG): ((Int, Int), RNG) =
  val (i1, rng2) = rng.nextInt
  val (i2, rng3) = rng2.nextInt
  ((i1, i2), rng3)
```

We return the final state after generating the two random numbers. This lets the caller generate more random values using the new state.

You can see the general pattern, and perhaps you can also see how it might get tedious to use this API directly. Let's write a few functions to generate random values and see if we notice any repetition we can factor out.

---

[3] An efficiency loss comes with computing next states using pure functions because it means we can't actually mutate the data in place. (It's not really a problem here since the state is just a single Long that must be copied.) This loss of efficiency can be mitigated by using efficient purely functional data structures. It's also possible in some cases to mutate the data in place without breaking referential transparency, which we'll talk about in part 4.

Write a function that uses `RNG.nextInt` to generate a random integer between `0` and `Int.MaxValue` (inclusive). Make sure to handle the corner case when `nextInt` returns `Int.MinValue`, which doesn't have a nonnegative counterpart:

```
def nonNegativeInt(rng: RNG): (Int, RNG)
```

Dealing with awkwardness in functional programming

As you write more functional programs, you'll sometimes encounter situations like this, where the functional way of expressing a program feels awkward or tedious. Does this imply that purity is the equivalent of trying to write an entire novel without using the letter *E*? Of course not. Awkwardness like this is almost always a sign of some missing abstraction waiting to be discovered.

When you encounter these situations, we encourage you to plow ahead and look for common patterns you can factor out. Most likely, this is a problem others have encountered, and you may even rediscover the standard solution yourself. Even if you get stuck, struggling to puzzle out a clean solution yourself will help you better understand what solutions others have discovered for dealing with similar problems.

With practice, experience, and more familiarity with the idioms contained in this book, expressing a program functionally will become effortless and natural. Of course, good design is still hard, but programming using pure functions greatly simplifies the design space.

Write a function to generate a `Double` between `0` and `1`, not including `1`. Note that you can use `Int.MaxValue` to obtain the maximum positive integer value, and you can use `x.toDouble` to convert an `x: Int` to a `Double`:

```
def double(rng: RNG): (Double, RNG)
```

Write functions to generate an `(Int, Double)` pair, a `(Double, Int)` pair, and a `(Double, Double, Double)` 3-tuple. You should be able to reuse the functions you've already written:

```
def intDouble(rng: RNG): ((Int, Double), RNG)
def doubleInt(rng: RNG): ((Double, Int), RNG)
def double3(rng: RNG): ((Double, Double, Double), RNG)
```

■　EXERCISE 6.4

Write a function to generate a list of random integers:

```
def ints(count: Int)(rng: RNG): (List[Int], RNG)
```

6.4   *A better API for state actions*

Looking back at our implementations, we'll notice a common pattern: each of our functions has a type of the form `RNG => (A, RNG)` for some type A. Functions of this type are called *state actions* or *state transitions* because they transform `RNG` states from one to the next. These state actions can be combined in various ways to generate new state actions. We'll define a number of such combining functions in this section. Since it's pretty tedious and repetitive to pass the state along ourselves, we want our functions to pass the state from one action to the next automatically.

To make the type of actions convenient to talk about and to simplify our thinking about them, let's make a type alias for the `RNG` state action data type:

```
type Rand[+A] = RNG => (A, RNG)
```

We can think of a value of type `Rand[A]` as a *randomly generated* A, although that's not really precise. It's really a state action—a program that depends on some `RNG`, uses it to generate an A, and transitions the `RNG` to a new state that can be used by another action later.

We can now turn methods such as `RNG`'s `nextInt` into values of this new type:

```
val int: Rand[Int] = rng => rng.nextInt    ◁—— We could even use the shortand _.nextInt.
```

We want to write functions that let us combine `Rand` actions, while avoiding explicitly passing along the `RNG` state. We'll end up with a kind of domain-specific language that does all the passing for us. For example, a simple `RNG` state transition is the unit action, which passes the `RNG` state through without using it, always returning a constant value rather than a random value:

```
def unit[A](a: A): Rand[A] =
  rng => (a, rng)
```

There's also `map` for transforming the output of a state action without further modifying the resultant state. Remember that `Rand[A]` is just a type alias for a function type `RNG => (A, RNG)`, so this is just a kind of function composition:

```
def map[A, B](s: Rand[A])(f: A => B): Rand[B] =
  rng =>
    val (a, rng2) = s(rng)
    (f(a), rng2)
```

As an example of how map is used, here's nonNegativeEven, which reuses nonNegative-Int to generate an Int that's greater than or equal to zero and divisible by two:

```
def nonNegativeEven: Rand[Int] =
  map(nonNegativeInt)(i => i - (i % 2))
```

■—— **EXERCISE 6.5** ————————————————————————————

Use map to reimplement double in a more succinct way. See exercise 6.2.

6.4.1 *Combining state actions*

Unfortunately, map isn't powerful enough to implement intDouble and doubleInt from exercise 6.3. Instead, we need a new function, map2, that can combine two RNG actions into one using a binary rather than unary function.

■—— **EXERCISE 6.6** ————————————————————————————

Write the implementation of map2 based on the following signature. This function takes two actions, ra and rb, and a function, f, for combining their results and returns a new action that combines them:

```
def map2[A, B, C](ra: Rand[A], rb: Rand[B])(f: (A, B) => C): Rand[C]
```

We only have to write the map2 function once, and then we can use it to combine arbitrary RNG state actions. For example, if we have an action that generates values of type A and another to generate values of type B, then we can combine them into one action that generates pairs of both A and B:

```
def both[A, B](ra: Rand[A], rb: Rand[B]): Rand[(A, B)] =
  map2(ra, rb)((_, _))
```

We can use this to reimplement intDouble and doubleInt from exercise 6.3 more succinctly:

```
val randIntDouble: Rand[(Int, Double)] =
  both(int, double)

val randDoubleInt: Rand[(Double, Int)] =
  both(double, int)
```

■ — (EXERCISE 6.7) ————————————————————————————————

Hard: If you can combine two RNG actions, you should be able to combine an entire list of them. Implement `sequence` for combining a `List` of actions into a single action. Use it to reimplement the `ints` function you wrote before. For the latter, you can use the standard library function `List.fill(n)(x)` to make a list with x repeated n times:

```
def sequence[A](rs: List[Rand[A]]): Rand[List[A]]
```

6.4.2   *Nesting state actions*

A pattern is beginning to emerge: we're progressing toward implementations that don't explicitly mention or pass along the RNG value. The `map` and `map2` functions allowed us to implement, in a rather succinct and elegant way, functions that were otherwise tedious and error-prone to write. But there are some functions we can't write in terms of `map` and `map2`. One such function is `nonNegativeLessThan`, which generates an integer between 0 (inclusive) and n (exclusive):

```
def nonNegativeLessThan(n: Int): Rand[Int]
```

A first stab at an implementation might be to generate a non-negative integer modulo n:

```
def nonNegativeLessThan(n: Int): Rand[Int] =
  map(nonNegativeInt)(_ % n)
```

This will certainly generate a number in the range, but it'll be skewed because `Int.MaxValue` may not be exactly divisible by n. So numbers less than the remainder of that division will come up more frequently. When `nonNegativeInt` generates numbers higher than the largest multiple of n that fits in a 32-bit integer, we should retry the generator and hope to get a smaller number. We might attempt this:

```
def nonNegativeLessThan(n: Int): Rand[Int] =
  map(nonNegativeInt): i =>
    val mod = i % n
    if i + (n-1) - mod >= 0 then mod else nonNegativeLessThan(n)(???)
```

> Retry recursively if the Int we got is higher than the largest multiple of n that fits in a 32-bit Int.

This is moving in the right direction, but `nonNegativeLessThan(n)` has the wrong type. Remember that it should return a `Rand[Int]`, which is a function that expects an RNG. But we don't have a RNG value to pass to the result of `nonNegativeLessThan(n)` there. What we would like is to chain things together so the RNG that's returned by `nonNegativeInt` is passed along to the recursive call to `nonNegativeLessThan`. We could pass it along explicitly instead of using `map`, like this:

```
def nonNegativeLessThan(n: Int): Rand[Int] =
  rng =>
    val (i, rng2) = nonNegativeInt(rng)
    val mod = i % n
    if i + (n-1) - mod >= 0 then
      (mod, rng2)
    else nonNegativeLessThan(n)(rng2)
```

But it would be better to have a function that does this passing along for us—neither map nor map2 will cut it. We need a more powerful function: flatMap.

■ EXERCISE 6.8

Implement flatMap, and then use it to implement nonNegativeLessThan:

```
def flatMap[A, B](r: Rand[A])(f: A => Rand[B]): Rand[B]
```

flatMap allows us to generate a random A with Rand[A] and then take that A and choose a Rand[B] based on its value. In nonNegativeLessThan we use it to choose whether to retry or not, based on the value generated by nonNegativeInt.

■ EXERCISE 6.9

Reimplement map and map2 in terms of flatMap. The fact that this is possible is what we're referring to when we say that flatMap is more powerful than map and map2.

We can now revisit our example from the beginning of this chapter. Can we make a more testable die roll using our purely functional API? Here's an implementation of rollDie using nonNegativeLessThan, including the off-by-one error we had before:

```
def rollDie: Rand[Int] = nonNegativeLessThan(6)
```

If we test this function with various RNG states, we'll soon find an RNG that causes this function to return 0:

```
scala> val zero = rollDie(SimpleRNG(5))._1
val zero: Int = 0
```

And we can recreate this reliably by using the same SimpleRNG(5) random generator, without having to worry about its state being destroyed after it's been used.
    Fixing the bug is trivial:

```
def rollDie: Rand[Int] = map(nonNegativeLessThan(6))(_ + 1)
```

6.5   *A general state action data type*

The functions we've just written—unit, map, map2, flatMap, and sequence—aren't specific to random number generation at all. They're general-purpose functions for working with state actions and don't care about the type of the state. Note that, for instance, map doesn't care that it's dealing with RNG state actions, and we can give it a more general signature:

```
def map[S, A, B](action: S => (A, S))(f: A => B): S => (B, S)
```

Changing this signature doesn't require modifying the implementation of map. The more general function was there all along; we just didn't see it.

We should then come up with a more general type than Rand for handling any type of state:

```
type State[S, +A] = S => (A, S)
```

Here State is short for *computation that carries some state along, state action, state transition*, or even *statement* (see the next section). We might want to write it as its own type instead of using an alias, allowing us to define methods without worrying about conflicting with the methods on the function type. We could do so by simply wrapping the underlying function value like this:

```
case class State[S, +A](run: S => (A, S))
```

Alternatively, we can use a feature of the Scala 3 type system called *opaque types*. An opaque type behaves like a type alias inside the defining scope. Outside of the defining scope, though, the opaque type is unrelated to the representation type. Here *defining scope* refers to the object containing the definition or, if the definition is top level, the package containing it. Here's what State could look like using an opaque type:

```
opaque type State[S, +A] = S => (A, S)

object State:
  extension [S, A](underlying: State[S, A])
    def run(s: S): (A, S) = underlying(s)

  def apply[S, A](f: S => (A, S)): State[S, A] = f
```

Besides the opaque type definition, we provide an extension method run, allowing the invocation of the underlying function as well as an apply method on the companion, which allows a State value to be constructed from a function. In both cases, the fact that State[S, A] is equivalent to S => (A, S) is known, which makes these two operations simple and seemingly redundant. However, outside the defining scope—in a different package, for example—the equivalence of State[S, A] and S => (A, S) is not known, and hence we need such conversions. See the official documentation for more details on opaque type (https://mng.bz/gRR8) and extension methods (https://mng.bz/5mm7).

Like the case class version, the opaque type version introduces a distinct type (from the perspective of callers). Hence, there's no confusing a standalone function with a `State[S, A]` value. And like the type alias version, the opaque type version avoids the runtime overhead of wrapping the function. At the cost of some boilerplate conversions, we get both encapsulation and performance.

The case class wrapper introduces an extra object allocation for each `State` value, while the opaque type version does not. This allocation is almost assuredly meaningless in real programs, since most runtimes are ridiculously good at garbage collecting these types of objects. Don't be afraid of using the simpler case class encoding and only refactoring to opaque types if allocation cost proves to be a bottleneck in your program.

The representation you pick doesn't matter too much—any of the approaches are fine. What's important is that we have a single, general-purpose type, and using this type, we can write general-purpose functions for capturing common patterns of stateful programs.

We can now make `Rand` a type alias for `State`:

```
type Rand[A] = State[RNG, A]
```

■ ─ EXERCISE 6.10 ──

Generalize the functions `unit`, `map`, `map2`, `flatMap`, and `sequence`. Add them as extension methods on the `State` type where possible. Otherwise, you should put them in the `State` companion object.

───

The functions we've written here capture only a few of the most common patterns. As you write more functional code, you'll likely encounter other patterns and discover other functions to capture them.

6.6 *Purely functional imperative programming*

In the preceding sections, we wrote functions that followed a definite pattern. We'd run a state action, assign its result to a `val`, run another state action that used that `val`, assign its result to another `val`, and so on. It looks a lot like *imperative* programming.

In the imperative programming paradigm, a program is a sequence of statements, where each statement may modify the program state. That's exactly what we've been doing, except our statements are really `State` actions, which are really functions. As functions, they read the current program state simply by receiving it in their argument, and they write to the program state by returning a value.

We implemented some functions like `map`, `map2`, and ultimately `flatMap` to handle the propagation of the state from one statement to the next. But in doing so, we seem to have lost a bit of the imperative mood.

Aren't imperative and functional programming opposites?

Imperative and functional programming absolutely aren't opposites. Remember that functional programming is simply programming without side effects. Imperative programming is about programming with statements that modify some program state, and as we've seen, it's entirely reasonable to maintain state without side effects.

Functional programming has excellent support for writing imperative programs, with the added benefit that such programs can be reasoned about equationally because they're referentially transparent. We'll have much more to say about equational reasoning about programs in part 2 and imperative programs in particular in parts 3 and 4.

Consider the following example (which assumes we've made Rand[A] a type alias for State[RNG, A]):

```
val ns: Rand[List[Int]] =
  int.flatMap(x =>
    int.flatMap(y =>
      ints(x).map(xs =>
        xs.map(_ % y))))
```

int is a value of type Rand[Int] that generates a single random integer.

ints(x) generates a list of length x.

Replaces every element in the list with its remainder when divided by y

It's not clear what's going on here, but since we have map and flatMap defined, we can use a for-comprehension[4] to recover the imperative style:

```
val ns: Rand[List[Int]] =
  for
    x <- int
    y <- int
    xs <- ints(x)
  yield xs.map(_ % y)
```

Generates an integer x

Generates another integer y

Generates a list xs of length x

Returns the list xs with each element replaced with its remainder when divided by y

This code is much easier to read (and write), and it looks like what it is: an imperative program that maintains some state. But it's the same code. We get the next Int and assign it to x, get the next Int after that and assign it to y, generate a list of length x, and, finally, return the list with all of its elements modulo y.

To facilitate this kind of imperative programming with for-comprehensions (or flatMaps), we really only need two primitive State constructors: one for reading the state and one for writing the state. If we imagine that we have a constructor get for getting the current state and a constructor set for setting a new state, then we could implement a constructor that could modify the state in arbitrary ways:

---

[4] Remember that for-comprehensions are just syntax sugar for a sequence of calls to flatMap followed by a final map. See the for-comprehensions section in chapter 4 for details.

```
def modify[S](f: S => S): State[S, Unit] =
  for
    s <- get
    _ <- set(f(s))
  yield ()
```

Gets the current state
and assigns it to s

Sets the new state to f applied to s

This constructor[5] returns a State action that modifies the incoming state by the function f. It yields Unit to indicate that it doesn't have a return value other than the state.

What would the get and set actions look like? They're exceedingly simple. The get action simply passes the incoming state along and returns it as the value:

```
def get[S]: State[S, S] = s => (s, s)
```

The set action is constructed with a new state s. The resulting action ignores the incoming state, replaces it with the new state, and returns () instead of a meaningful value:

```
def set[S](s: S): State[S, Unit] = _ => ((), s)
```

These two simple actions along with the State functions we wrote—unit, map, map2, and flatMap—are all the tools we need to implement any kind of state machine or stateful program in a purely functional way. Instead of mutable data structures and side effects, we use immutable data structures and functions that compute the next state from the previous, and we use State to remove the boilerplate.

EXERCISE 6.11

Hard: To get some experience using State, implement a finite state automaton that models a simple candy dispenser. The machine has two types of input: you can insert a coin, or you can turn the knob to dispense candy. It can be in one of two states: locked or unlocked. It also tracks how many candies are left and how many coins it contains:

```
enum Input:
  case Coin, Turn

case class Machine(locked: Boolean, candies: Int, coins: Int)
```

The rules of the machine are as follows:

- Inserting a coin into a locked machine will cause it to unlock if there's any candy left.
- Turning the knob on an unlocked machine will cause it to dispense candy and become locked.

---

[5] Sometimes the term *constructor* is used to refer to a function that creates a value of a type. It's important not to confuse this with the object-oriented notion of a class constructor, which Scala also supports.

- Turning the knob on a locked machine or inserting a coin into an unlocked machine does nothing.
- A machine that's out of candy ignores all inputs.

The `simulateMachine` method should operate the machine based on the list of inputs and return the number of coins and candies left in the machine at the end. For example, if the input `Machine` has 10 coins and five candies, and a total of four candies are successfully bought, the output should be `(14, 1)`:

```
def simulateMachine(inputs: List[Input]): State[Machine, (Int, Int)]
```

6.7   *Conclusion*

In this chapter, we touched on writing purely functional programs that have state. We used random number generation as the motivating example, but the overall pattern comes up in many different domains. The idea is simple: use a pure function that accepts a state as its argument, and it will return the new state alongside its result. Next time you encounter an imperative API that relies on side effects, see if you can provide a purely functional version of it, and then use some of the functions we wrote here to make working with it more convenient.

Summary

- The `scala.util.Random` type provides generation of pseudo-random numbers but performs generation as a side effect.
- Pseudo-random number generation can be modeled as a pure function from an input seed to an output seed and a generated value.
- Making stateful APIs pure by having the API compute the next state from the current state rather than actually mutating anything is a general technique not limited to pseudo-random number generation.
- When the functional approach feels awkward or tedious, look for common patterns that can be factored out.
- The `Rand[A]` type is an alias for a function `Rng => (A, Rng)`. There are a variety of functions that create and transform `Rand` values, like `unit`, `map`, `map2`, `flatMap`, and `sequence`.
- Opaque types behave like type aliases in their defining scope but behave like unrelated types outside their defining scope. An opaque type encapsulates the relationship with the representation type, allowing the definition of new types without runtime overhead.
- Extension methods can be used to add methods to opaque types.
- Case classes can be used instead of opaque types, but they come with the runtime cost of wrapping the underlying value.
- The `State[S, A]` type is an opaque alias for a function `S => (A, S)`.

- State supports the same operations as Rand—unit, map, map2, flatMap, and sequence—since none of these operations had any dependency on Rng being the state type.
- The State data type simplifies working with stateful APIs by removing the need to manually thread input and output states throughout computations.
- State computations can be built with for-comprehensions, which result in imperative-looking code.

6.8 Exercise Answers

 EXERCISE 6.1

```
def nonNegativeInt(rng: RNG): (Int, RNG) =
  val (i, r) = rng.nextInt
  (if i < 0 then -(i + 1) else i, r)
```

We first call rng.nextInt to generate an integer from Int.MinValue to Int.MaxValue. We unpack the resulting tuple into two values: i for the generated random value and r for the next RNG. If i is nonnegative, then we can safely return it. Otherwise, we increment the result by one and flip its sign. Note that this solution doesn't skew random number generation because there are exactly the same number of values in the range [Int.MinValue, -1] as in the range [0, Int.MaxValue]. In both cases, we pair the result with the next RNGr.

 EXERCISE 6.2

We use the nonNegativeInt function we wrote in the previous exercise to generate an integer in the range [0, Int.MaxValue]. We then divide that value by Int.MaxValue + 1 to adjust the result to the desired range. Again, we have to pair the result with the next RNG value:

```
def double(rng: RNG): (Double, RNG) =
  val (i, r) = nonNegativeInt(rng)
  (i / (Int.MaxValue.toDouble + 1), r)
```

EXERCISE 6.3

Let's implement intDouble first:

```
def intDouble(rng: RNG): ((Int, Double), RNG) =
  val (i, r1) = rng.nextInt
  val (d, r2) = double(r1)
  ((i, d), r2)
```

We first use `rng.nextInt` to generate a random integer. We destructure the resulting tuple into the generated integer and the next `RNGr1`. We then generate a random double using the `double` method we wrote in exercise 6.2, again destructuring the resulting tuple into the generated double and a new next `RNG`. Finally, we pair the integer and double as the result and pair that with the `RNG` returned from `double`.

We could implement `doubleInt` in a similar fashion, but instead, let's reuse `intDouble`:

```
def doubleInt(rng: RNG): ((Double, Int), RNG) =
  val ((i, d), r) = intDouble(rng)
  ((d, i), r)
```

Here we destructure two levels of tuples at once: the outer tuple, consisting of the generated `(Int, Double)` and the next `RNG`, as well as the inner tuple `(Int, Double)`. We then build up a nested tuple, swapping the positions of the integer and the double.

Finally, we can implement `double3` via three invocations of `double`:

```
def double3(rng: RNG): ((Double, Double, Double), RNG) =
  val (d1, r1) = double(rng)
  val (d2, r2) = double(r1)
  val (d3, r3) = double(r2)
  ((d1, d2, d3), r3)
```

We call `double`, passing the original `rng` argument to the first invocation and the resulting `RNG` of the previous invocation for each subsequent invocation. If, instead, we passed the `rng` argument to every invocation, we'd end up with a triple consisting of the same three doubles.

■ EXERCISE 6.4

We can implement this via a tail-recursive auxiliary function:

```
def ints(count: Int)(rng: RNG): (List[Int], RNG)
  def go(count: Int, r: RNG, xs: List[Int]): (List[Int], RNG) =
    if count <= 0 then
      (xs, r)
    else
      val (x, r2) = r.nextInt
      go(count - 1, r2, x :: xs)
  go(count, rng, Nil)
```

The go auxiliary function keeps track of the remaining count, the next `RNG` value to use, and the accumulated list of integers. When invoked, if the remaining count is less than or equal to zero, then we return the accumulated list of integers and the last `RNG` value. Otherwise, we use the last `RNG` value to generate a new random integer, destructing the result into the generated integer and a new RNG. We then recursively invoke go, decrementing the count, and pass the most recently generated RNG and the generated integer consed on to the accumulated integers.

Note that the list of numbers output by this implementation is in the reverse order as the numbers generated by the original (not tail recursive) implementation. If we want to address that, we could reverse the output list in the main body of ints after go has returned.

■ **EXERCISE 6.5**

In the original definition of double, there were two main concerns: converting the computed nonnegative integer to a double and manipulating the RNG values—passing the RNG to nonNegativeInt, pattern matching on the result, and building back up a final result tuple. By using map with nonNegativeInt, we can focus only on the int-to-double conversion and let the implementation of map manage all the RNG manipulation:

```
val double: Rand[Double] =
  map(nonNegativeInt)(i => i / (Int.MaxValue.toDouble + 1))
```

■ **EXERCISE 6.6**

Recall that Rand[C] is a type alias for RNG => (C, RNG). We take advantage of this and return an anonymous function of that type. We then invoke ra using the received rng0, giving us back a value of type A as well as a new RNG. Likewise, we invoke rb, being careful to use the RNG returned from invoking ra and not the original rng0 parameter of the anonymous function. Finally, we can invoke f with the generated values of type A and B and pair the result with the RNG returned from invoking rb:

```
def map2[A, B, C](ra: Rand[A], rb: Rand[B])(f: (A, B) => C): Rand[C] =
  rng0 =>
    val (a, rng1) = ra(rng0)
    val (b, rng2) = rb(rng1)
    (f(a, b), rng2)
```

In the definition of map2, there are three different values of type RNG: rng0, rng1, and rng2. We had to be careful to ensure we used the right value in each expression or risk losing randomness. When writing Rand values in terms of anonymous functions, this error-prone bookkeeping is common. Hence, we prefer to put this type of manipulation into generic functions, like map2, making our logic easier to understand and verify.

We use a foldRight over the supplied list of RNG actions, starting with a unit(Nil: List[A])—an RNG action that passes through the RNG parameter without using it, returning an empty list. For each action in the original list, we compute an output of type Rand[List[A]], using an input element of type Rand[A] and an accumulated Rand[List[A]]. We use map2 to combine those actions into a new action, consing the output value of the first action onto the output list of the accumulated action:

```
def sequence[A](rs: List[Rand[A]]): Rand[List[A]] =
  rs.foldRight(unit(Nil: List[A]))((r, acc) => map2(r, acc)(_ :: _))
```

This is eerily similar to the definition of sequence for Option from exercise 4.4:

```
def sequence[A](as: List[Option[A]]): Option[List[A]] =
  as.foldRight(Some(Nil): Option[List[A]])((a, acc) => map2(a, acc)(_ :: _))
```

This similarity hints at an undiscovered abstraction—something that lets us write sequence once for a variety of data types. We'll return to this idea in chapter 12. Finally, we can define ints in terms of sequence by creating a list of the requested size and setting each element to the int value we defined earlier:

```
def ints(count: Int): Rand[List[Int]] =
  sequence(List.fill(count)(int))
```

Like when we implemented map2, we return an anonymous function, giving us access to the starting RNG. We apply this initial RNG to the supplied action, resulting in a value of type A and a new RNG. We then apply that A value to the supplied function f, giving us a Rand[B]. Finally, we apply our earlier output RNG to that Rand[B], yielding a (B, RNG). If we hadn't invoked the function returned from f(a), which is a value of type Rand[B], then we'd have gotten a compilation error:

```
def flatMap[A, B](r: Rand[A])(f: A => Rand[B]): Rand[B] =
  rng0 =>
    val (a, rng1) = r(rng0)
    f(a)(rng1)
```

nonNegativeLessThan can be implemented by calling flatMap on nonNegativeInt and passing an anonymous function that returns a Rand[Int]. If we find a value that meets our criteria, we return it, but we must convert it from an Int to a Rand[Int] first. We do so via unit; otherwise, if our output value doesn't meet our criteria, then we recursively call nonNegativeLessThan(n) to generate a new output value:

```
def nonNegativeLessThan(n: Int): Rand[Int] =
  flatMap(nonNegativeInt): i =>
    val mod = i % n
    if i + (n-1) - mod >= 0 then unit(mod) else nonNegativeLessThan(n)
```

■ **EXERCISE 6.9**

First let's implement `map`:

```
def map[A, B](r: Rand[A])(f: A => B): Rand[B] =
  flatMap(r)(a => unit(f(a)))
```

We call `flatMap`, passing the initial action and an anonymous function that receives the generated value of type A. The anonymous function must have the `A => Rand[B]` type, and we have a `f` of type `A => B`, so we first apply our received A to `f`, yielding a value of type B. We then convert that result to a `Rand[B]` via `unit`.

Now `map2`:

```
def map2[A, B, C](ra: Rand[A], rb: Rand[B])(f: (A, B) => C): Rand[C] =
  flatMap(ra)(a => map(rb)(b => f(a, b)))
```

Like in the definition of `map`, we call `flatMap`, passing the first action and a function that receives the generated value of type A. In our anonymous function, we call `map` on the second action, passing another function that applies the A and B to the supplied function `f`, yielding a C.

We cannot use a for-comprehension in this case, despite the call sequence being a `flatMap` followed by a `map`. Recall that for-comprehensions require the type of the expression on the right-hand side of a binding to define the `flatMap` and `map` methods. Our definitions of `flatMap` and `map` are defined as standalone functions, though, not methods on `Rand[A]` values; notice how we pass the target value as the first parameter to each function. We could address this by defining `flatMap` and `map` as extension methods on a `Rand[A]` value, but since `Rand[A]` is a type alias, we'd be defining `flatMap` and `map` for all functions of the shape `RNG => (A, RNG)`. We'll see how to address this better later in this chapter.

■ **EXERCISE 6.10**

Let's start with `unit`, which we define on the companion object:

```
def unit[S, A](a: A): State[S, A] =
  s => (a, s)
```

This is almost identical to the earlier definition of unit defined specifically for Rand. The only significant difference is in the type signature, where we added a type parameter S instead of hardcoding Rand.[6]

In exercise 6.9, we saw that map and map2 can be implemented in terms of flatMap, so we can directly port their implementations to extension methods. Similarly, we can directly port flatMap, adjusting only type parameters and names. And now that we have methods for map and flatMap, in lieu of standalone functions, we can use a for-comprehension to define map2:

```
extension [S, A](underlying: State[S, A])
  def run(s: S): (A, S) = underlying(s)

  def map[B](f: A => B): State[S, B] =
    flatMap(a => unit(f(a)))

  def map2[B, C](sb: State[S, B])(f: (A, B) => C): State[S, C] =
    for
      a <- underlying
      b <- sb
    yield f(a, b)

  def flatMap[B](f: A => State[S, B]): State[S, B] =
    s =>
      val (a, s1) = underlying(s)
      f(a)(s1)
```

Lastly, we can define sequence on the companion object of State, making only minimal changes to pass the S type parameter throughout:

```
def sequence[S, A](states: List[State[S, A]]): State[S, List[A]] =
  states.foldRight(unit[S, List[A]](Nil))((s, acc) => s.map2(acc)(_ :: _))
```

___

█ **EXERCISE 6.11**

___

We start by writing the state transition rules as a function of an Input and a Machine that returns a new Machine. Each rule is implemented via a pattern match on the input and current machine state:

```
def update(i: Input, s: Machine): Machine =
  (i, s) match
    case (_, Machine(_, 0, _)) => s
    case (Input.Coin, Machine(false, _, _)) => s
    case (Input.Turn, Machine(true, _, _)) => s
    case (Input.Coin, Machine(true, candy, coin)) =>
      Machine(false, candy, coin + 1)
    case (Input.Turn, Machine(false, candy, coin)) =>
      Machine(true, candy - 1, coin)
```

___

[6] If using the case class encoding, we need to wrap the anonymous function like so: State(s => (a, s)).

With this definition of update, simulateMachine can be implemented by first converting each input to a state action that modifies the machine state and then sequencing all of the state actions together:

```
State.sequence(inputs.map(i => State.modify[Machine](update(i, _))))
```

This expression has the State[Machine, List[Unit]] type; the List[Unit] has an element for each processed input, so we can just discard that result, get the current Machine state via State.get, and then return the number of coins and candies, calling the right accessors on Machine:

```
def simulateMachine(inputs: List[Input]): State[Machine, (Int, Int)] =
  for
    _ <- State.sequence(inputs.map(i => State.modify(update(i, _))))
    s <- State.get
  yield (s.coins, s.candies)
```

But wait! We're mapping over a list and then subsequently sequencing the result. Recall from earlier chapters that mapping followed by sequencing is equivalent to traversing. Let's extract out a traverse operation for State:

```
def traverse[S, A, B](as: List[A])(f: A => State[S, B]): State[S, List[B]] =
  as.foldRight(unit[S, List[B]](Nil))((a, acc) => f(a).map2(acc)(_ :: _))
```

And then let's refactor simulateMachine to use traverse:

```
def simulateMachine(inputs: List[Input]): State[Machine, (Int, Int)] =
  for
    _ <- State.traverse(inputs)(i => State.modify(update(i, _))))
    s <- State.get
  yield (s.coins, s.candies)
```

Finally, notice that every time we called update, we curried it by passing a placeholder for the second parameter; by calling update(i, _), we got back a Machine => Machine suitable for passing to modify. Let's make that explicit by moving the currying to the definition of update instead of doing it at each call site:

```
def simulateMachine(inputs: List[Input]): State[Machine, (Int, Int)] =
  for
    _ <- State.traverse(inputs)(i => State.modify(update(i)))
    s <- State.get
  yield (s.coins, s.candies)
val update = (i: Input) => (s: Machine) =>
  (i, s) match
    case (_, Machine(_, 0, _)) => s
    case (Input.Coin, Machine(false, _, _)) => s
    case (Input.Turn, Machine(true, _, _)) => s
    case (Input.Coin, Machine(true, candy, coin)) =>
      Machine(false, candy, coin + 1)
    case (Input.Turn, Machine(false, candy, coin)) =>
      Machine(true, candy - 1, coin)
```

Part 2

Functional design and combinator libraries

We said in chapter 1 that FP is a radical premise that affects how we write and organize programs at every level. In part 1, we covered the fundamentals of FP and saw how the commitment to using only pure functions affects the basic building blocks of programs: loops, data structures, exceptions, and so on. In part 2, we'll see how the assumptions of FP affect *library design*.

We'll create three useful libraries in part 2—one for parallel and asynchronous computation, another for testing programs, and a third for parsing text. There won't be much in the way of new syntax or language features, but we'll make heavy use of the material already covered. Our primary goal isn't teaching you about parallelism, testing, and parsing; instead, it is helping you develop skill in designing functional libraries, even for domains that look nothing like the ones here.

This part of the book will be a somewhat meandering journey, as functional design can be a messy, iterative process. We hope to show at least a stylized view of how functional design proceeds in the real world. Don't worry if you don't follow every part of discussion. These chapters should be like peering over the shoulder of someone as they think through possible designs. And because no two people approach this process the same way, the path we walk in each case might not strike you as the most natural one—perhaps it considers issues in what seems like an odd order, skips too fast, or goes too slow. Keep in mind that when you design your own functional libraries, you get to do it at your own pace, taking whatever path you want, and whenever questions come up about design choices, you get to think through the consequences in whatever way makes sense for you, which could include running little experiments, creating prototypes, and so on.

There are no right answers in functional library design. Instead, we have a collection of design choices, each with different trade-offs. Our goal is that you start to understand these trade-offs and what different choices mean. Sometimes when designing a library, we'll come to a fork in the road. In this text we may, for pedagogical purposes, deliberately make a choice with undesirable consequences that we'll uncover later. We want you to see this process firsthand because it's part of what actually occurs when designing functional programs. We're less interested in the particular libraries covered in this part and more interested in giving you insight into how functional design proceeds and how to navigate situations you will likely encounter. Library design is not something only a select few people get to do; it's part of the day-to-day work of ordinary functional programming. In these chapters and beyond, you should absolutely feel free to experiment, play with different design choices, and develop your own aesthetic.

As a final note, while you work through part 2, you may notice repeated patterns of similar-looking code. Keep this in the back of your mind. When we get to part 3, we'll discuss how to remove this duplication, and we'll discover an entire world of fundamental abstractions common to all libraries.

7

Purely functional parallelism

This chapter covers

- Developing a functional API for parallel computations
- Approaching APIs algebraically
- Defining generic combinators

Because modern computers have multiple cores per CPU, and often multiple CPUs, it's more important than ever to design programs in such a way that they can take advantage of this parallel processing power. But the interaction of programs that run with parallelism is complex, and the traditional mechanism for communication among execution threads—shared mutable memory—is notoriously difficult to reason about. This can all too easily result in programs that have race conditions and deadlocks, aren't readily testable, and don't scale well.

In this chapter, we'll build a purely functional library for creating parallel and asynchronous computations. We'll rein in the complexity inherent in parallel programs by describing them using only pure functions. This will let us use the substitution

143

model to simplify our reasoning and hopefully make working with concurrent computations both easy and enjoyable.

After reading this chapter, you should take away not only how to write a library for purely functional parallelism but how to approach the problem of designing a purely functional library. Our main concern will be making our library highly composable and modular. To this end, we'll keep to our theme of separating the concern of describing a computation from actually running it. We want to allow users of our library to write programs at a very high level, insulating them from the nitty-gritty of how their programs will be executed. For example, toward the end of the chapter, we'll develop an operation, parMap, that will let us easily apply a function, f, to every element in a collection simultaneously:

```
val outputList = parMap(inputList)(f)
```

To get there, we'll work iteratively. We'll begin with a simple use case we'd like our library to handle and then develop an interface that facilitates this use case; only then will we consider what our implementation of this interface should be. As we keep refining our design, we'll oscillate between the interface and implementation while gaining a better understanding of the domain and design space through progressively more complex use cases. We'll emphasize *algebraic reasoning* and introduce the idea that an API can be described by an *algebra* that obeys specific laws.

Why design our own library? Why not just use the concurrency primitives that come with Scala's standard library in the scala.concurrent package? This is partially for pedagogical purposes—we want to show you how easy it is to design your own practical libraries. But there's another reason: we want to encourage the view that no existing library is authoritative or beyond reexamination, even if designed by experts and labeled standard. There's a certain safety in doing what everybody else does, but what's conventional isn't necessarily the most practical. Most libraries contain a lot of arbitrary design choices, many made unintentionally. When you start from scratch, you get to revisit all the fundamental assumptions that went into designing the library, take a different path, and discover things about the problem space that others may not have even considered. As a result, you might arrive at your own design that suits your purposes better. In this case, our fundamental assumption will be that our library admits absolutely no side effects.

We'll write a lot of code in this chapter, largely posed as exercises for you, the reader. As always, you can find the answers in the downloadable content that goes along with the book.

7.1 *Choosing data types and functions*

When you begin designing a functional library, you usually have some general ideas about what you want to be able to do, and the difficulty in the design process is in refining these ideas and finding a data type that enables the functionality you want. In our case, we'd like to be able to create parallel computations, but what does that mean exactly? Let's try to refine this into something we can implement by examining a simple, parallelizable computation: summing a list of integers. The usual left fold for this would be as follows:

```
def sum(ints: Seq[Int]): Int =
  ints.foldLeft(0)((a, b) => a + b)
```

Here `Seq` is a superclass of lists and other sequences in the standard library. Importantly, it has a `foldLeft` method. Instead of folding sequentially, we could use a divide-and-conquer algorithm (see the following listing).

Listing 7.1 Summing a list using a divide-and-conquer algorithm

```
def sum(ints: IndexedSeq[Int]): Int =          ◁──  IndexedSeq is a superclass of random-access
  if ints.size <= 1 then                              sequences, like Vector, in the standard library.
    ints.headOption.getOrElse(0)        ◁──           Unlike lists, these sequences provide an efficient
  else                                                splitAt method for dividing them into two parts
    val (l, r) = ints.splitAt(ints.size / 2)  ◁──     at a particular index.
    sum(l) + sum(r)
```

IndexedSeq is a superclass of random-access sequences, like Vector, in the standard library. Unlike lists, these sequences provide an efficient splitAt method for dividing them into two parts at a particular index.

headOption is a method defined on all collections in Scala. We saw this function in chapter 4.

Recursively sums both halves and adds the results together

Divides the sequence in half using the splitAt function

We divide the sequence in half using the `splitAt` function, recursively sum both halves, and then combine their results. And unlike the `foldLeft`-based implementation, this implementation can be parallelized; the two halves can be summed in parallel.

The importance of simple examples

Summing integers is, in practice, probably so fast that parallelization imposes more overhead than it saves. But simple examples like this are exactly the kind that are most helpful to consider when designing a functional library. Complicated examples include all sorts of incidental structure and extraneous detail that can confuse the initial design process. We're trying to explain the essence of the problem domain, and a good way of doing this is by starting with trivial examples, factoring out common concerns across these examples, and gradually adding complexity. In functional design, our goal is achieving expressiveness not with mountains of special cases but by building a simple and composable set of core data types and functions.

As we think about what sort of data types and functions could enable parallelizing this computation, we can shift our perspective. Rather than focusing on how this parallelism will ultimately be implemented and forcing ourselves to work with the implementation APIs directly (likely related to `java.lang.Thread` and the `java.util.concurrent` library), we'll instead design our own ideal API, as illuminated by our examples, and work backward from there to an implementation.

7.1.1   *A data type for parallel computations*

Look at the line sum(1) + sum(r), which invokes sum on the two halves recursively. Just from looking at this single line, we can see that any data type we might choose to represent our parallel computations needs to be able to contain a result. That result will have some meaningful type (in this case Int), and we require some way of extracting this result. Let's apply this newfound knowledge to our design. For now, we can just invent a container type for our result, Par[A] (for *parallel*), and legislate the existence of the functions we need:

- def unit[A](a: => A): Par[A]—Takes an unevaluated A, returning a computation that might evaluate it in a separate thread. We call it unit because, in a sense, it creates a unit of parallelism that just wraps a single value.
- def get[A](a: Par[A]): A—Extracts the resulting value from a parallel computation.

Can we really do this? Yes, of course! For now, we don't need to worry about what other functions we require, what the internal representation of Par might be, or how these functions are implemented. We're simply reading off the necessary data types and functions by inspecting our simple example. Let's update this example now.

Listing 7.2   Updating sum with our custom data type

```
def sum(ints: IndexedSeq[Int]): Int =
  if ints.size <= 1 then
    ints.headOption.getOrElse(0)
  else
    val (l, r) = ints.splitAt(ints.size / 2)
    val sumL: Par[Int] = Par.unit(sum(l))     Computes the left half in parallel
    val sumR: Par[Int] = Par.unit(sum(r))     Computes the right half in parallel
    Par.get(sumL) + Par.get(sumR)             Extracts both results
                                              and sums them
```

We've wrapped the two recursive calls to sum in calls to unit, and we're calling get to extract the two results from the two subcomputations.

The problem with using concurrency primitives directly

What of java.lang.Thread and Runnable? Let's take a look at these classes. Here's a partial excerpt of their API, transcribed into Scala:

```
trait Runnable:
  def run: Unit                Begins running r in a separate thread

class Thread(r: Runnable):
  def start: Unit              Blocks the calling thread
  def join: Unit               until r finishes running
```

We can already see a problem with both of these types: none of the methods return a meaningful value. Therefore, if we want to get any information out of a Runnable it has to have some side effect, like mutating some state we can inspect.

This is bad for compositionality; we can't manipulate Runnable objects generically since we always need to know something about their internal behavior. Thread also has the disadvantage that it maps directly onto operating system threads, which are a scarce resource. It would be preferable to create as many logical threads as is natural for our problem and deal with mapping these onto actual OS threads later.

This kind of thing can be handled by something like java.util.concurrent .Future, ExecutorService or similar. Why don't we use them directly? Here's a portion of their API:

```
class ExecutorService:
  def submit[A](a: Callable[A]): Future[A]

trait Future[A]:
  def get: A
```

While they are a tremendous help in abstracting over physical threads, these primitives are still at a much lower level of abstraction than the library we want to create in this chapter. A call to Future.get, for example, blocks the calling thread until the ExecutorService has finished executing it, and its API provides no means of composing futures. Of course, we can build the implementation of our library on top of these tools (and this is, in fact, what we end up doing later in the chapter), but they don't present a modular and compositional API that we'd want to use directly from functional programs.

We now have a choice about the meaning of unit and get; unit could begin evaluating its argument immediately in a separate (logical) thread,[1] or it could simply hold onto its argument until get is called and begin evaluation then. But note that in this example, if we want to obtain any degree of parallelism, we require unit to begin evaluating its argument concurrently and return immediately. Can you see why?[2]

But if unit begins evaluating its argument concurrently, then calling get arguably breaks referential transparency. We can see this by replacing sumL and sumR with their definitions; if we do so, we still get the same result, but our program is no longer parallel:

```
Par.get(Par.unit(sum(l))) + Par.get(Par.unit(sum(r)))
```

If unit starts evaluating its argument right away, get will wait for that evaluation to complete. This means the two sides of the + sign won't run in parallel if we simply inline the sumL and sumR variables. We can see that unit has a definite side effect but only with regard to get. That is, unit simply returns a Par[Int] in this case, representing an

---

[1] We'll use the term *logical thread* somewhat informally throughout this chapter to mean a computation that runs concurrently with the main execution thread of our program. There need not be a one-to-one correspondence between logical threads and OS threads; we may have a large number of logical threads mapped onto a smaller number of OS threads via thread pooling, for instance.

[2] Function arguments in Scala are strictly evaluated from left to right, so if unit delays execution until get is called, then we will both spawn the parallel computation and wait for it to finish before spawning the second parallel computation. This means the computation is effectively sequential!

asynchronous computation. But as soon as we pass that Par to get, we explicitly wait for it, exposing the side effect. So it seems we want to avoid calling get—or at least delay calling it until the very end. We want to be able to combine asynchronous computations without waiting for them to finish.

Before we continue, take a moment to examine what we've done. First, we conjured up a simple, almost trivial, example. We next explored this example a bit to uncover a design choice. Then, via some experimentation, we discovered an interesting consequence of one option and, in the process, learned something fundamental about the nature of our problem domain! The overall design process is a series of these little adventures. You don't need any special license to do this sort of exploration, and you don't need to be an expert in functional programming either. Just dive in, and see what you find.

7.1.2   *Combining parallel computations*

Let's see if we can avoid the aforementioned pitfall of combining unit and get. If we don't call get, that implies that our sum function must return a Par[Int]. What consequences does this change reveal? Again, let's invent functions with the required signatures:

```
def sum(ints: IndexedSeq[Int]): Par[Int] =
  if ints.size <= 1 then
    Par.unit(ints.headOption.getOrElse(0))
  else
    val (l, r) = ints.splitAt(ints.size / 2)
    Par.map2(sum(l), sum(r))(_ + _)
```

■ EXERCISE 7.1

Par.map2 is a new higher-order function for combining the result of two parallel computations. What is its signature? Give the most general signature possible (without assuming it works only for Int).

Observe that we're no longer calling unit in the recursive case, and it isn't clear whether unit should accept its argument lazily anymore. In this example, accepting the argument lazily doesn't seem to provide any benefit, but perhaps this isn't always the case. Let's come back to this question later.

What about map2—should it take its arguments lazily? It would make sense for map2 to run both sides of the computation in parallel, giving each side equal opportunity to run (it would seem arbitrary for the order of the map2 arguments to matter, since we simply want map2 to indicate that the two computations being combined are independent and can be run in parallel). What choice lets us implement this meaning? As a simple test case, consider what happens if map2 is strict in both arguments and we're evaluating sum(IndexedSeq(1,2,3,4)). Take a minute to work through and understand the following (somewhat stylized) program trace.

Listing 7.3 Program trace for `sum`

```
sum(IndexedSeq(1,2,3,4))
map2(
  sum(IndexedSeq(1,2)),
  sum(IndexedSeq(3,4)))(_ + _)
map2(
  map2(
    sum(IndexedSeq(1)),
    sum(IndexedSeq(2)))(_ + _),
  sum(IndexedSeq(3,4)))(_ + _)
map2(
  map2(
    unit(1),
    unit(2))(_ + _),
  sum(IndexedSeq(3,4)))(_ + _)
map2(
  map2(
    unit(1),
    unit(2))(_ + _),
  map2(
    sum(IndexedSeq(3)),
    sum(IndexedSeq(4)))(_ + _))(_ + _)
...
```

In this trace, to evaluate sum(x), we substitute x into the definition of sum, as we've done in previous chapters. Because map2 is strict and Scala evaluates arguments left to right, whenever we encounter map2(sum(x), sum(y))(_+_), we must evaluate sum(x) and so on recursively. This has the rather unfortunate consequence of requiring us to strictly construct the entire left half of the tree of summations first before moving on to (strictly) constructing the right half. Here sum(IndexedSeq(1,2)) gets fully expanded before we consider sum(IndexedSeq(3,4)). And if map2 evaluates its arguments in parallel (using whatever resource is being used to implement the parallelism, like a thread pool), that implies the left half of our computation will start executing before we even begin constructing the right half of our computation.

What if we keep map2 strict but don't have it begin execution immediately? Does this help? If map2 doesn't begin evaluation immediately, this implies a Par value is merely constructing a description of what needs to be computed in parallel. Nothing actually occurs until we evaluate this description, perhaps using a get-like function. The problem is that if we construct our descriptions strictly, they'll be rather heavyweight objects. Looking back at our trace, our description will have to contain the full tree of operations to be performed:

```
map2(
  map2(
    unit(1),
    unit(2))(_ + _),
  map2(
    unit(3),
    unit(4))(_ + _))(_ + _)
```

No matter what data structure we use to store this description, it'll likely occupy more space than the original list itself. It would be nice if our descriptions were more lightweight.

It seems we should make map2 lazy and have it begin immediate execution of both sides in parallel. This also addresses the problem of giving neither side priority over the other.

7.1.3   *Explicit forking*

Something still doesn't feel right about our latest choice. Is it always the case that we want to evaluate the two arguments to map2 in parallel? Probably not. Consider this simple hypothetical example:

```
Par.map2(Par.unit(1), Par.unit(1))(_ + _)
```

In this case, we happen to know that the two computations we're combining will execute so quickly that there isn't much point in spawning off a separate logical thread to evaluate them, but our API doesn't give us any way of providing this sort of information. That is, our current API is very *inexplicit* about when computations get forked off the main thread; the programmer doesn't get to specify where this forking should occur. What if we make the forking more explicit? We can do that by inventing another function, def fork[A](a: => Par[A]): Par[A], which we can take to mean that the given Par should be run in a separate logical thread:

```
def sum(ints: IndexedSeq[Int]): Par[Int] =
  if ints.size <= 1 then
    Par.unit(ints.headOption.getOrElse(0))
  else
    val (l, r) = ints.splitAt(ints.size / 2)
    Par.map2(Par.fork(sum(l)), Par.fork(sum(r)))(_ + _)
```

With fork we can now make map2 strict, leaving it up to the programmer to wrap arguments if they wish. A function like fork solves the problem of instantiating our parallel computations too strictly, but more fundamentally, it puts the parallelism explicitly under programmer control. We're addressing two concerns here: The first is that we need some way to indicate that the results of the two parallel tasks should be combined. Separate from this, we have the choice of whether a particular task should be performed asynchronously. By keeping these concerns separate, we avoid having any sort of global policy for parallelism attached to map2 and other operations we write, which would mean making tough (and ultimately arbitrary) choices about what global policy is best.

Let's now return to the question of whether unit should be strict or lazy. With fork we can now make unit strict without any loss of expressiveness. A nonstrict version of it—let's call it lazyUnit—can be implemented using unit and fork:

```
def unit[A](a: A): Par[A]
def lazyUnit[A](a: => A): Par[A] = fork(unit(a))
```

The function lazyUnit is a simple example of a *derived combinator*, as opposed to a *primitive combinator*, like unit. We're using the term *combinator* rather informally here to refer to functions and values designed with composition in mind, allowing interesting functionality to be built up incrementally from single-purpose parts. We were able to define lazyUnit in terms of other operations; later, when we pick a representation for Par, lazyUnit won't need to know anything about this representation—its only knowledge of Par will come from the operations fork and unit that are defined on Par.[3]

We know we want fork to signal that its argument gets evaluated in a separate logical thread, but we still have the question of whether it should begin doing so immediately upon being called or hold on to its argument to be evaluated in a logical thread later when the computation is forced, using something like get. In other words, should evaluation be the responsibility of fork or of get? Should evaluation be eager or lazy? When you're unsure about a meaning to assign to some function in your API, you can always continue with the design process; at some point later, the trade-offs of different choices of meaning may become clear. Here we make use of a helpful trick: we'll think about what sort of information is required to implement fork and get with various meanings.

If fork begins evaluating its argument immediately in parallel, the implementation must clearly know something, either directly or indirectly, about how to create threads or submit tasks to some sort of thread pool. Moreover, this implies that the thread pool (or whatever resource we use to implement the parallelism) must be (globally) accessible and properly initialized wherever we want to call fork.[4] This means we lose the ability to control the parallelism strategy used for different parts of our program. And while there's nothing inherently wrong with having a global resource for executing parallel tasks, we can imagine how it would be useful to have more fine-grained control over what implementations are used where (we might want each subsystem of a large application to get its own thread pool with different parameters, for example). It seems much more appropriate to give get the responsibility of creating threads and submitting execution tasks.

Note that coming to these conclusions didn't require knowing exactly how fork and get will be implemented or even what the representation of Par will be. We just

---

[3] This sort of indifference to representation is a hint that the operations are actually more general and can be abstracted to work for types other than just Par. We'll explore this topic in detail in part 3.

[4] This is much like how the credit card processing system was accessible to the buyCoffee method in our Cafe example in chapter 1.

reasoned informally about the sort of information required to actually spawn a parallel task and examined the consequences of having Par values know this information.

In contrast, if fork simply holds onto its unevaluated argument until later, it requires no access to the mechanism for implementing parallelism; it just takes an unevaluated Par and marks it for concurrent evaluation. Let's now assume this meaning for fork. With this model, Par itself doesn't need to know how to actually implement the parallelism. It's more a description of a parallel computation that gets interpreted at a later time by something like the get function. This is a shift from before, where we were considering Par to be a container of a value that we could simply get when it becomes available. Now it's more of a first-class program we can run. So let's rename our get function to run and dictate that this is where the parallelism actually gets implemented:

```
extension [A](pa: Par[A]) def run: A
```

Because Par is now just a pure data structure, run needs to have some means of implementing the parallelism, whether it spawns new threads, delegates tasks to a thread pool, or uses some other mechanism.

7.2   *Picking a representation*

Just by exploring this simple example and thinking through the consequences of different choices, we've sketched out the following API.

> **Listing 7.4   Basic sketch for an API for Par**

Creates a computation that immediately results in the value a

Combines the results of two parallel computations with a binary function

```
def unit[A](a: A): Par[A]
extension [A](pa: Par[A])
  def map2[B, C](pb: Par[B])(f: (A, B) => C): Par[C]
def fork[A](a: => Par[A]): Par[A]
def lazyUnit[A](a: => A): Par[A] = fork(unit(a))
extension [A](pa: Par[A]) def run: A
```

Marks a computation for concurrent evaluation by run

Wraps the expression a for concurrent evaluation by run

Fully evaluates a given Par, spawning parallel computations as requested by fork and extracting the resulting value

We've also loosely assigned meaning to these various functions:

- unit—Promotes a constant value to a parallel computation
- map2—Combines the results of two parallel computations with a binary function
- fork—Marks a computation for concurrent evaluation—the evaluation won't occur until forced by run
- lazyUnit—Wraps its unevaluated argument in a Par and marks it for concurrent evaluation
- run—Extracts a value from a Par by performing the computation

At any point while sketching out an API, you can start thinking about possible representations for the abstract types that appear.

■   EXERCISE 7.2

Before continuing, try to come up with representations for `Par` that make it possible
to implement the functions of our API.

Let's see if we can come up with a representation. We know `run` needs to execute asynchronous tasks somehow. We could write our own low-level API, but there's already a class
we can use in the Java Standard Library: `java.util.concurrent.ExecutorService`.
Here is its API, excerpted and transcribed to Scala:

```scala
class ExecutorService:
  def submit[A](a: Callable[A]): Future[A]

trait Callable[A]:
  def call: A   ⟵——— Essentially just a lazy A

trait Future[A]:
  def get: A
  def get(timeout: Long, unit: TimeUnit): A
  def cancel(evenIfRunning: Boolean): Boolean
  def isDone: Boolean
  def isCancelled: Boolean
```

So `ExecutorService` lets us submit a `Callable` value (in Scala we'd probably just use a
lazy argument to `submit`) and get back a corresponding `Future` that's a handle to a
computation that's potentially running in a separate thread. We can obtain a value
from a `Future` with its `get` method (which blocks the current thread until the value is
available), and it has some extra features for cancellation (throwing an exception
after blocking for a certain amount of time and so on).

Let's try assuming our `run` function has access to an `ExecutorService` and see if
that suggests anything about the representation for `Par`:

```scala
extension [A](pa: Par[A]) def run(s: ExecutorService): A
```

The simplest possible model for `Par[A]` might be `ExecutorService => A`. This would
make `run` trivial to implement. But it might be nice to defer the decision of how long
to wait for a computation, or whether to cancel it, to the caller of `run`. So `Par[A]`
becomes `ExecutorService => Future[A]`, and `run` simply returns the `Future`:

```scala
opaque type Par[A] = ExecutorService => Future[A]

extension [A](pa: Par[A]) def run(s: ExecutorService): Future[A] = pa(s)
```

**Par is defined as an opaque type, though we could have used a regular type alias or a case class
that wraps a function, like with State in the previous chapter. Using an opaque type provides
encapsulation of the internal representation, while avoiding unnecessary allocations.**

Note that since Par is represented by a function that needs an ExecutorService, the creation of the Future doesn't actually happen until this ExecutorService is provided. Is it really that simple? Let's assume it is for now and revise our model if we find it doesn't allow some functionality we'd like.

7.2.1   Refining the API

The way we've worked so far is a bit artificial. In practice, there aren't such clear boundaries between designing the API and choosing a representation, and one doesn't necessarily precede the other. Ideas for a representation can inform the API, the API can inform the choice of representation, and it's natural to shift fluidly between these two perspectives, run experiments as questions arise, build prototypes, and so on.

We'll devote this section to exploring our API. Though we got a lot of mileage out of considering a simple example, before we add any new primitive operations, let's learn more about what's expressible using those we already have. With our primitives and choices of meaning for them, we've carved out a little universe for ourselves. We now get to discover what ideas are expressible in this universe. This can and should be a fluid process; we can change the rules of our universe at any time, make a fundamental change to our representation or introduce a new primitive, and explore how our creation then behaves.

Let's begin by implementing the functions of the API that we've developed so far. Now that we have a representation for Par, a first crack at it should be straightforward. What follows is a simple implementation using the representation of Par we've chosen.

Listing 7.5   Basic implementation for `Par`

unit is represented as a function that returns a UnitFuture, which is a simple implementation of Future that just wraps a constant value. It doesn't use the ExecutorService at all; it's always done and can't be cancelled. Its get method simply returns the value we gave it.

```scala
object Par:
  def unit[A](a: A): Par[A] = es => UnitFuture(a)          ◁────

  private case class UnitFuture[A](get: A) extends Future[A]:
    def isDone = true
    def get(timeout: Long, units: TimeUnit) = get
    def isCancelled = false
    def cancel(evenIfRunning: Boolean): Boolean = false

  extension [A](pa: Par[A])
    def map2[B, C](pb: Par[B])(f: (A,B) => C): Par[C] =     ◁──
      (es: ExecutorService) =>
        val futureA = a(es)
        val futureB = b(es)
```

We return a function from ExecutorService to Future[C]. The type ascription on es is optional here; Scala can infer it from the definition of Par.

map2 doesn't evaluate the call to f in a separate logical thread, in accord with our design choice of having fork be the sole function in the API for controlling parallelism. We can always do fork(pa.map2(pb)(f)) if we want the evaluation of f to occur in a separate thread.

```
                  UnitFuture(f(futureA.get, futureB.get))
```

```
  ┌──▷ def fork[A](a: => Par[A]): Par[A] =
             es => es.submit(new Callable[A] {
               def call = a(es).get
             })
```

This implementation of map2 does not respect timeouts. It simply passes the ExecutorService on to both Par values, waits for the results of the Futures af and bf, applies f to them, and wraps them in a UnitFuture. To respect timeouts, we'd need a new Future implementation that records the amount of time spent evaluating af and then subtracts that time from the available time allocated for evaluating bf.

This is the simplest and most natural implementation of fork, but there are some problems with it; for one, the outer Callable will block waiting for the inner task to complete. Since this blocking occupies a thread in our thread pool, or whatever resource backs the ExecutorService, this implies we're losing out on some potential parallelism. Essentially, we're using two threads when one should suffice. This is a symptom of a more serious problem with the implementation that we'll discuss later in the chapter.

We should note that Future doesn't have a purely functional interface. This is part of the reason we don't want users of our library to deal with Future directly. But importantly, even though methods on Future rely on side effects, our entire Par API remains pure. It's only after the user calls run and the implementation receives an ExecutorService that we expose the Future machinery. Our users, therefore, program to a pure interface whose implementation nevertheless relies on effects at the end of the day. But since our API remains pure, these effects aren't side effects. In part 4, we'll discuss this distinction in detail.

EXERCISE 7.3

Hard: Fix the implementation of map2 so it respects the contract of timeouts on Future.

EXERCISE 7.4

This API already enables a rich set of operations. Here's a simple example. Using lazyUnit, write a function to convert any function A => B to one that evaluates its result asynchronously:

```
def asyncF[A, B](f: A => B): A => Par[B]
```

What else can we express with our existing combinators? Let's look at a more concrete example.

Suppose we have a `Par[List[Int]]` representing a parallel computation that produces a `List[Int]`, and we'd like to convert this to a `Par[List[Int]]` whose result is sorted:

```
def sortPar(parList: Par[List[Int]]): Par[List[Int]]
```

We could, of course, run the `Par`, sort the resulting list, and repackage it in a `Par` with unit—but we want to avoid calling run. The only other combinator we have that allows us to manipulate the value of a `Par` in any way is map2. So if we passed parList to one side of map2, we'd be able to gain access to the `List` inside and sort it, and we can pass whatever we want to the other side of map2, so let's just pass a no-op:

```
def sortPar(parList: Par[List[Int]]): Par[List[Int]] =
  parList.map2(unit(()))((a, _) => a.sorted)
```

We can now tell a `Par[List[Int]]` that we'd like that list sorted, but we might as well generalize this further. We can lift any function of type `A => B` to become a function that takes `Par[A]` and returns `Par[B]`, and we can map any function over a `Par`:

```
extension [A](pa: Par[A]) def map[B](f: A => B): Par[B] =
  pa.map2(unit(()))((a, _) => f(a))
```

For instance, sortPar is now simply this:

```
def sortPar(parList: Par[List[Int]]) =
  parList.map(_.sorted)
```

That's terse and clear. We just combined the operations to make the types line up. Yet if you look at the implementations of map2 and unit, it should be clear that this implementation of map means something sensible.

Was it cheating to pass a bogus value, unit(()), as an argument to map2 only to ignore its value? Not at all! The fact that we can implement map in terms of map2, but not the other way around, just shows that map2 is strictly more powerful than map. This sort of thing happens a lot when we're designing libraries; a function that seems to be primitive often turns out to be expressible using some more powerful primitive.

What else can we implement using our API? Could we map over a list in parallel? Unlike map2, which combines two parallel computations, parMap (let's call it) needs to combine *N* parallel computations. It seems like this should somehow be expressible:

```
def parMap[A, B](ps: List[A])(f: A => B): Par[List[B]]
```

We could always just write parMap as a new primitive. Remember that `Par[A]` is simply an alias for `ExecutorService => Future[A]`.

There's nothing wrong with implementing operations as new primitives. In some cases, we can even implement the operations more efficiently by assuming something about the underlying representation of the data types we're working with. But right now, we're interested in exploring what operations are expressible using our existing API and grasping the relationships between the various operations we've defined. Understanding what combinators are truly primitive will become more important in part 3 when we show how to abstract over common patterns across libraries.[5]

Let's see how far we can get implementing parMap in terms of existing combinators:

```
def parMap[A, B](ps: List[A])(f: A => B): Par[List[B]] =
  val fbs: List[Par[B]] = ps.map(asyncF(f))
  ...
```

Remember that asyncF converts an A => B to an A => Par[B] by forking a parallel computation to produce the result. So we can fork off our *N* parallel computations pretty easily, but we need some way of collecting their results. Are we stuck? Well, just from inspecting the types, we can see that we need some way of converting our List[Par[B]] to the Par[List[B]] required by the return type of parMap.

■ EXERCISE 7.5

Write this function, called sequence. No additional primitives are required; do not call run:

```
def sequence[A](ps: List[Par[A]]): Par[List[A]]
```

Once we have sequence, we can complete our implementation of parMap:

```
def parMap[A, B](ps: List[A])(f: A => B): Par[List[B]] =
  fork:
    val fbs: List[Par[B]] = ps.map(asyncF(f))
    sequence(fbs)
```

Note that we've wrapped our implementation in a call to fork. With this implementation, parMap will return immediately, even for a huge input list. When we later call run, it will fork a single asynchronous computation, which itself spawns *N* parallel computations and then waits for these computations to finish, collecting their results into a list. If, instead, we left out the call to fork, calling parMap would first create the fbs list before calling sequence, resulting in performing some of the computation on the calling thread.

---

[5] In this case, there's another good reason not to implement parMap as a new primitive: it's challenging to do so correctly, particularly if we want to properly respect timeouts. It's frequently the case that primitive combinators encapsulate some rather tricky logic, and reusing them means we don't have to duplicate this logic.

■ **EXERCISE 7.6**

Implement `parFilter`, which filters elements of a list in parallel:

```
def parFilter[A](as: List[A])(f: A => Boolean): Par[List[A]]
```

Can you think of any other useful functions to write? Experiment with writing a few parallel computations of your own to see which ones can be expressed without additional primitives. Here are some ideas to try:

- Is there a more general version of the parallel summation function we wrote at the beginning of this chapter? Try using it to find the maximum value of an `IndexedSeq` in parallel.
- Write a function that takes a list of paragraphs (a `List[String]`) and returns the total number of words across all paragraphs in parallel. Look for ways to generalize this function.
- Implement `map3`, `map4`, and `map5` in terms of `map2`.

7.3   *The algebra of an API*

As the previous section demonstrates, we often get far just by writing down the type signature for an operation we want and then following the types to an implementation. When working this way, we can almost forget the concrete domain (for instance, when we implemented `map` in terms of `map2` and `unit`) and just focus on lining up types. This isn't cheating; it's a natural style of reasoning, analogous to the reasoning one does when simplifying an algebraic equation. We're treating the API as an *algebra*[6] or an abstract set of operations, along with a set of *laws* or properties we assume to be true, and simply doing formal symbol manipulation following the rules specified by this algebra.

Up until now, we've been reasoning somewhat informally about our API. There's nothing wrong with this, but it can be helpful to take a step back and formalize what laws you expect to hold (or would like to hold) for your API.[7] Without realizing it, you've probably mentally built up a model of what properties or laws you expect. Actually writing these down and making them precise can highlight design choices that wouldn't be otherwise apparent when reasoning informally.

---

[6] We do mean *algebra* in the mathematical sense of one or more sets, together with a collection of functions operating on objects of these sets, and a set of *axioms*. Axioms are statements assumed to be true from which we can derive other theorems that must also be true. In our case, the sets are particular types like `Par[A]` and `List[Par[A]]`, and the functions are operations like `map2`, `unit`, and `sequence`.

[7] We'll have much more to say about this throughout the rest of the book. In the next chapter, we'll design a declarative testing library that lets us define properties we expect functions to satisfy and automatically generates test cases to check these properties. In part 3, we'll introduce abstract interfaces specified only by sets of laws.

7.3.1 The law of mapping

Like any design choice, choosing laws has consequences; it places constraints on what the operations can mean, determines what implementation choices are possible, and affects what other properties can be true. Let's look at an example in which we'll make up a possible law that seems reasonable. This might be used as a test case if we were writing tests for our library:

```
unit(1).map(_ + 1) == unit(2)
```

We're saying that mapping over unit(1) with the _ + 1 function is in some sense equivalent to unit(2). (Laws often start out this way—as concrete examples of *identities*[8] we expect to hold.) In what sense are they equivalent? This is an interesting question. For now, let's say two Par objects are equivalent if for any valid ExecutorService argument, their Future results have the same value.

We can check that this holds for a particular ExecutorService with a function like this:

```
def equal[A](e: ExecutorService)(p: Par[A], p2: Par[A]): Boolean =
  p(e).get == p2(e).get
```

Laws and functions share much in common. Just as we can generalize functions, we can generalize laws. For instance, the preceding could be generalized this way:

```
unit(x).map(f) == unit(f(x))
```

Here we're saying that this equality should hold for any choice of x and f, not just 1 and the _ + 1 function. This equality places some constraints on our implementation; our implementation of unit can't, say, inspect the value it receives and decide to return a parallel computation with a result of 42 when the input is 1—it can only pass along whatever it receives. Similarly, for our ExecutorService, when we submit Callable objects to it for execution, it can't make any assumptions or change behavior based on the values it receives. More concretely, this law disallows downcasting or isInstanceOf checks (often grouped under the term *typecasing*) in the implementations of map and unit.

Much like we strive to define functions in terms of simpler functions, each of which do just one thing, we can define laws in terms of simpler laws that each say just one thing. Let's see if we can simplify this law further. We said we wanted this law to hold for any choice of x and f. Something interesting happens if we substitute the identity function for f.[9] We can simplify both sides of the equation and get a new law that's considerably simpler:[10]

---

[8] Here we mean *identity* in the mathematical sense of a statement that two expressions are identical or equivalent.
[9] The identity function is defined as def id[A](a: A): A = a.
[10]This is the same sort of substitution and simplification one might do when solving an algebraic equation.

```
unit(x).map(f) == unit(f(x))   ◄──── Initial law
unit(x).map(id) == unit(id(x)) ◄─────┐
unit(x).map(id) == unit(x)     ◄───┐ │  Substitute the identity function for f.
┌─► y.map(id) == y                 │
│                                  │   Simplify.
Substitute y for unit(x) on both sides.
```

Fascinating! Our new, simpler law talks only about map; apparently, the mention of unit was an extraneous detail. To get some insight into what this new law is saying, let's think about what map can't do. It can't, say, throw an exception and crash the computation before applying the function to the result (can you see why this violates the law?). All it can do is apply the function f to the result of y, which, of course, leaves y unaffected when that function is id.[11] Even more interestingly, given y.map(id) == y, we can perform the substitutions in the other direction to get back our original, more complex law. (Try it!) Logically, we have the freedom to do so because map can't possibly behave differently for different function types it receives. Thus, given y.map(id) == y, it must be true that unit(x).map(f) == unit(f(x)). Since we get this second law or theorem for free, simply because of the parametricity of map, it's sometimes called a *free theorem*.[12]

■ EXERCISE 7.7

Hard: Given y.map(id) == y, y.map(g).map(f) == y.map(f compose g) is a free theorem. (This is sometimes called *map fusion*, and it can be used as an optimization; rather than spawning a separate parallel computation to compute the second mapping, we can fold it into the first mapping.)[13] Can you prove it?

7.3.2   The law of forking

As interesting as all this is, this particular law doesn't do much to constrain our implementation. You've probably been assuming these properties without even realizing it (it would be strange to have any special cases in the implementations of map, unit, or ExecutorService.submit or have map randomly throwing exceptions). Let's consider a stronger property—fork should not affect the result of a parallel computation:

```
fork(x) == x,
```

---

[11] We say that map is required to be *structure-preserving* in that it doesn't alter the structure of the parallel computation, only the value inside the computation.

[12] The idea of free theorems was introduced by Philip Wadler in his classic paper "Theorems for Free!" (http://mng.bz/Z9f1).

[13] Our representation of Par doesn't give us the ability to implement this optimization, since it's an opaque function. For example, y.map(g) returns a new Par that's a black box—when we then call .map(f) on that result, we've lost the knowledge of the parts that were used to construct y.map(g): namely, y, map, and g. All we see is the opaque function and, hence, cannot extract out g to compose with f. If Par were reified as a data type (e.g., an enumeration of various operations), then we could pattern match and discover opportunities to apply this rule. You may want to try experimenting with this idea on your own.

This seems like it should obviously be true of our implementation, and it is clearly a desirable property, consistent with our expectation of how `fork` should work. `fork(x)` should do the same thing as x but asynchronously—in a logical thread separate from the main thread. If this law didn't always hold, then we'd have to somehow know when it was safe to call without changing meaning, without any help from the type system.

Surprisingly, this simple property places strong constraints on our implementation of `fork`. After you've written down a law like this, take off your implementer hat, put on your debugger hat, and try to break your law. Think through any possible corner cases, try to come up with counterexamples, and even construct an informal proof that the law holds—at least thoroughly enough to convince a skeptical fellow programmer.

7.3.3 *Breaking the law: A subtle bug*

Let's try this mode of thinking. We're expecting `fork(x) == x` for all choices of x and any choice of `ExecutorService`. We have a good sense of what x could be; it's some expression making use of `fork`, `unit`, and `map2` (and other combinators derived from these). What about `ExecutorService`? What are some possible implementations of it? There's a good listing of different implementations in the class `java.util.concurrent.Executors` (see the API for more information: http://mng.bz/urQd).

EXERCISE 7.8

Hard: Look through the various static methods in `Executors` to get a feel for the different implementations of `ExecutorService` that exist. Then, before continuing, go back and revisit your implementation of `fork`, and try to find a counterexample or convince yourself that the law holds for your implementation.

Why laws about code and proofs are important

It may seem unusual to state and prove properties about an API. This certainly isn't something typically done in ordinary programming. Why is it important in FP?

In functional programming, it's easy and expected to factor out common functionality into generic, reusable components that can be composed. Side effects hurt compositionality, but more generally, any hidden or out-of-band assumption or behavior that prevents us from treating our components (be they functions or anything else) as *black boxes* makes composition difficult or impossible.

In our example of the law for `fork`, we can see that if the law we posited didn't hold, many of our general-purpose combinators, like `parMap`, would no longer be sound (and their usage might be dangerous, since they could, depending on the broader parallel computation they were used in, result in deadlocks).

Giving our APIs an algebra with laws that are meaningful and aid reasoning makes the APIs more usable for clients but also means we can treat the objects of our APIs as black boxes. As we'll see in part 3, this is crucial for our ability to factor out common patterns across the different libraries we've written.

There's actually a rather subtle problem that will occur in most implementations of fork. When using an ExecutorService backed by a thread pool of bounded size (see Executors.newFixedThreadPool), it's very easy to run into a deadlock.[14] Suppose we have an ExecutorService backed by a thread pool, where the maximum number of threads is 1. Try running the following example using our current implementation:

```
val a = lazyUnit(42 + 1)
val es = Executors.newFixedThreadPool(1)
println(Par.equal(es)(a, fork(a)))
```

Most implementations of fork will result in this code deadlocking. Can you see why? Let's look again at our implementation of fork:

```
def fork[A](a: => Par[A]): Par[A] =
  es => es.submit(new Callable[A] { def call = a(es).get })
```

Waits for the result of one Callable inside another Callable

Note that we're submitting the Callable first, and within that Callable we're submitting another Callable to the ExecutorService and blocking on its result (recall that a(es) will submit a Callable to the ExecutorService and get back a Future). This is a problem if our thread pool has size 1. The outer Callable gets submitted and picked up by the sole thread; within that thread, before it will complete, we submit and block waiting for the result of another Callable, but there are no threads available to run this Callable. They're waiting on each other, and therefore our code deadlocks.

■ **EXERCISE 7.9**

Hard: Show that any fixed-size thread pool can be made to deadlock given this implementation of fork.

When you find counterexamples like this, you have two choices: you can try to fix your implementation such that the law holds, or you can refine your law a bit to state more explicitly the conditions under which it holds (you could simply stipulate that you require thread pools that can grow unbounded). Even this is a good exercise; it forces you to document invariants or assumptions that were previously implicit.

Can we fix fork to work on fixed-size thread pools? Let's look at a different implementation:

```
def fork[A](fa: => Par[A]): Par[A] =
  es => fa(es)
```

---

[14]In the next chapter, we'll write a combinator library for testing that can help discover problems like these automatically.

This certainly avoids deadlock. The only problem is that we aren't actually forking a separate logical thread to evaluate `fa`. So `fork(hugeComputation)(es)` for some `ExecutorService es` would run `hugeComputation` in the main thread, which is exactly what we wanted to avoid by calling `fork`. This is still a useful combinator, though, since it lets us delay instantiation of a computation until it's actually needed. Let's give it the name `delay`:

```
def delay[A](fa: => Par[A]): Par[A] =
  es => fa(es)
```

But we'd really like to be able to run arbitrary computations over fixed-size thread pools. To do that, we'll need to pick a different representation of `Par`.

7.3.4   A fully non-blocking Par implementation using actors

In this section, we'll develop a fully non-blocking implementation of `Par` that works for fixed-size thread pools. Since this isn't essential to our overall goals of discussing various aspects of functional design, you may skip to the next section if you prefer. Otherwise, read on.

The essential problem with the current representation is that we can't get a value out of a `Future` without the current thread blocking on its `get` method. A representation of `Par` that doesn't leak resources this way has to be *non-blocking* in the sense that the implementations of `fork` and `map2` must never call a method that blocks the current thread like `Future.get`. Writing such an implementation correctly can be challenging. Fortunately, we have our laws with which to test our implementation, and we only need to get it right *once*. After that, the users of our library can enjoy a composable and abstract API that does the right thing every time.

In the code that follows, you don't need to understand exactly what's going on with every part of it. We just want to show you, using real code, what a correct representation of `Par` that respects the laws might look like.

THE BASIC IDEA

How can we implement a non-blocking representation of `Par`? The idea is simple. Instead of turning a `Par` into a `java.util.concurrent.Future` we can get a value out of (which requires blocking), we'll introduce our own version of `Future`, with which we can register a callback that will be invoked when the result is ready. This is a slight shift in perspective:

```
opaque type Future[+A] = (A => Unit) => Unit
opaque type Par[+A] = ExecutorService => Future[A]
```

A function that takes a function of type A => Unit as an argument and returns Unit

Par looks the same, but we're using our new non-blocking Future instead of the one in java.util.concurrent.

Our `Par` type looks identical, except we're now using our new version of `Future`, which has a different API than the one in `java.util.concurrent`. Rather than calling `get` to obtain the result from our `Future`, our `Future` is an opaque type encapsulating a function that receives another function—one that expects an A and returns a Unit. The A => Unit function is sometimes called a *continuation* or a *callback*.

With this encoding, when we apply an ExecutorService to the function representing a Par[A], we get back a new function: (A => Unit) => Unit. We can then call that by passing a callback that handles the produced A value. Our callback will get invoked whenever the A is computed—not immediately.

> ### Using local side effects for a pure API
>
> The Future type we defined here is rather imperative—an A => Unit. Such a function can only be useful for executing some side effect using the given A, as we certainly aren't using the returned result. Are we still doing functional programming when using a type like Future? Yes, but we're making use of the common technique of using side effects as an implementation detail for a purely functional API. We can get away with this because the side effects we use are not observable to code that uses Par. Note that the function representation of Future is opaque and can't be called by outside code.
>
> As we go through the rest of our implementation of the non-blocking Par, you may want to convince yourself that the side effects employed can't be observed by outside code. The notion of local effects, observability, and subtleties of our definitions of purity and referential transparency are discussed in much greater detail in chapter 14, but for now, an informal understanding is fine.

With this representation of Par, let's look at how we might implement the run function first, which we'll change to just return an A. Since it goes from Par[A] to A, it will have to construct a continuation and pass it to the Future.

Listing 7.6   Implementing `run` for `Par`

A mutable, thread-safe reference to use for storing the result (see the java.util.concurrent.atomic package for more information about these classes)

```
extension [A](pa: Par[A]) def run(es: ExecutorService): A =
  val ref = new AtomicReference[A]
  val latch = new CountDownLatch(1)
  pa(es) { a => ref.set(a); latch.countDown }
  latch.await
  ref.get
```

When we receive the value, it sets the result and releases the latch.

A java.util.concurrent.CountDownLatch allows threads to wait until its countDown method is called a certain number of times. Here the countDown method will be called once when we've received the value of type A from p, and we want the run implementation to block until that happens.

Waits until the result becomes available and the latch is released

Once we've passed the latch, we know ref has been set, and we return its value

It should be noted that run blocks the calling thread while waiting for the latch. It's not possible to write an implementation of run that doesn't block. Since it needs to return a value of type A, it needs to wait for that value to become available before it can return. For this reason, we want users of our API to avoid calling run until they want to wait for a result. We could even go so far as to remove run from our API altogether and expose the apply method on Par instead so users can register asynchronous callbacks. That would certainly be a valid design choice, but we'll leave our API as it is for now.

Let's look at an example of creating a Par. The simplest one is unit:

```
def unit[A](a: A): Par[A] =          It simply passes the value to the continuation.
  es => cb => cb(a)                   Note that the ExecutorService isn't needed.
```

Since unit already has a value of type A available, all it needs to do is call the continuation cb, passing it this value. If that continuation is the one from our run implementation, for example, this will release the latch and make the result available immediately.

What about fork? This is where we introduce the actual parallelism:

```
def fork[A](a: => Par[A]): Par[A] =     eval forks off the evaluation of a and returns
  es => cb => eval(es)(a(es)(cb))        immediately. The callback will be invoked
                                         asynchronously on another thread.

def eval(es: ExecutorService)(r: => Unit): Unit =     A helper function to evaluate
  es.submit(new Callable[Unit] { def call = r })      an action asynchronously using
                                                        some ExecutorService
```

When the Future returned by fork receives its continuation cb, it will fork off a task to evaluate the by-name argument a. Once the argument has been evaluated and called to produce a Future[A] we register cb to be invoked when that Future has its resulting A.

What about map2? Recall the signature:

```
extension [A](pa: Par[A]) def map2[B, C](pb: Par[B])(f: (A, B) => C): Par[C]
```

Here a non-blocking implementation is considerably trickier. Conceptually, we'd like map2 to run both Par arguments in parallel. When both results have arrived, we want to invoke f and then pass the resulting C to the continuation. But there are several race conditions to worry about here, and a correct non-blocking implementation is difficult using only the low-level primitives of java.util.concurrent.

A BRIEF INTRODUCTION TO ACTORS

To implement map2, we'll use a non-blocking concurrency primitive, called an *actor*. An Actor is essentially a concurrent process that doesn't constantly occupy a thread. Instead, it only occupies a thread when it receives a message. Importantly, although multiple threads may be concurrently sending messages to an actor, the actor processes only one message at a time, queueing other messages for subsequent processing. This makes them useful as a concurrency primitive when writing tricky code that must be accessed by multiple threads and which would otherwise be prone to race conditions or deadlocks.

It's best to illustrate this with an example. Many implementations of actors would suit our purposes just fine, including the one in the popular Akka library (see https://github.com/akka/akka), but in the interest of simplicity, we'll use our own minimal actor implementation included with the chapter code in the Actor.scala file:

```
scala> import fpinscala.parallelism.*
```
An actor uses an ExecutorService to process messages when they arrive, so we create one here.

```
scala> val s = Executors.newFixedThreadPool(4)
s: java.util.concurrent.ExecutorService = ...
```

```
scala> val echoer = Actor[String](s):
     |   msg => println(s"Got message: '$msg'")
echoer: fpinscala.parallelism.Actor[String] = ...
```
This is a very simple actor that just echoes the String messages it receives. Note that we supply s, an ExecutorService, for processing messages.

Let's try out this Actor:

It sends the "hello" message to the actor.

```
scala> echoer ! "hello"
Got message: 'hello'
```

Note that echoer doesn't occupy a thread at this point since it has no further messages to process.

```
scala>
```

It sends the "goodbye" message to the actor. The actor reacts by submitting a task to its ExecutorService to process that message.

```
scala> echoer ! "goodbye"
Got message: 'goodbye'
```

```
scala> echoer ! "You're just repeating everything I say, aren't you?"
Got message: 'You're just repeating everything I say, aren't you?'
```

It's not at all essential to understand the Actor implementation. A correct, efficient implementation is rather subtle, but if you're curious, see the Actor.scala file in the chapter code. The implementation is just under 100 lines of ordinary Scala code.[15]

IMPLEMENTING MAP2 VIA ACTORS

We can now implement map2 using an Actor to collect the result from both arguments. The code is straightforward, and there are no race conditions to worry about since we know the Actor will only process one message at a time.

Listing 7.7   Implementing map2 with Actor

```
extension [A](p: Par[A]) def map2[B, C](p2: Par[B])(f: (A, B) => C): Par[C] =
  es => cb =>
    var ar: Option[A] = None
    var br: Option[B] = None
    // this implementation is a little too liberal in forking of threads -
    // it forks a new logical thread for the actor and for stack-safety,
    // forks evaluation of the callback `cb`
```
Two mutable vars are used to store the two results.

---

[15] The main trickiness in an actor implementation has to do with the fact that multiple threads may be messaging the actor simultaneously. The implementation needs to ensure messages are processed one at a time as well as that all messages sent to the actor are processed eventually, rather than queued indefinitely. Even so, the code ends up being short.

```
        val combiner = Actor[Either[A,B]](es):
          case Left(a) =>
            if br.isDefined then eval(es)(cb(f(a, br.get)))
            else ar = Some(a)
          case Right(b) =>
            if ar.isDefined then eval(es)(cb(f(ar.get, b)))
            else br = Some(b)
        p(es)(a => combiner ! Left(a))
        p2(es)(b => combiner ! Right(b))
```

An actor that awaits both results, combines them with f, and passes the result to cb

If the A result came in first, it stores it in ar and waits for the B. If the A result came last, and we already have our B, it calls f with both results and passes the resulting C to the callback, cb.

It passes the actor as a continuation to both sides. On the A side, we wrap the result in Left, and on the B side, we wrap it in Right. These are the constructors of the Either data type, and they serve to indicate to the actor where the result came from.

Analogously, if the B result came in first, it stores it in br and waits for the A. If the B result came last and we already have our A, it calls f with both results and passes the resulting C to the callback, cb.

Given these implementations, we should now be able to run Par values of arbitrary complexity, without having to worry about running out of threads, even if the actors only have access to a single JVM thread.

Let's try this out in the REPL:

```
scala> import java.util.concurrent.Executors, fpinscala
     .parallelism.Nonblocking.Par

scala> val p = Par.parMap(List.range(1, 100000))(math.sqrt(_))
p: fpinscala.parallelism.Nonblocking.Par[List[Double]] = < function >

scala> val x = p.run(Executors.newFixedThreadPool(2))
x: List[Double] = List(1.0, 1.4142135623730951, 1.7320508075688772,
2.0, 2.23606797749979, 2.449489742783178, 2.6457513110645907, 2.828
4271247461903, 3.0, 3.1622776601683795, 3.3166247903554, 3.46410...
```

That will call fork about 100,000 times, starting about 100,000 actors and combining the results two at a time. Thanks to our non-blocking Actor implementation, we don't need 100,000 JVM threads.

Fantastic. Our law of forking now holds for fixed-size thread pools.

EXERCISE 7.10

Hard: Our non-blocking representation doesn't currently handle errors at all. If at any point our computation throws an exception, the run implementation's latch never counts down, and the exception is simply swallowed. Can you fix that?

Taking a step back, the purpose of this section hasn't necessarily been to figure out the best non-blocking implementation of fork but rather to show that laws are important. They give us another angle to consider when thinking about the design of a library. If we hadn't tried writing out some of the laws of our API, we might not have discovered the thread resource leak in our first implementation until much later.

In general, there are multiple approaches you can consider when choosing laws for your API. You can think about your conceptual model and reason from there to postulate laws that should hold. You can also just invent laws that you think might be useful or instructive (like we did with our `fork` law) and see if it's possible and sensible to ensure they hold for your model. And lastly, you can look at your implementation and come up with laws you expect to hold based on that.[16]

7.4   *Refining combinators to their most general form*

Functional design is an iterative process. After you write down your API and have at least a prototype implementation, try using it for progressively more complex or realistic scenarios; sometimes you'll find that these scenarios require new combinators. Before jumping right to implementation, it's a good idea to see if you can refine the combinator you need to its most general form. It may be that you just need a specific case of some more general combinator.

About the exercises in this section

The exercises and answers in this section use our original simpler (blocking) representation of `Par[A]`. If you'd like to work through the exercises and answers using the non-blocking implementation we developed in the previous section instead, see the Nonblocking.scala file in both the `exercises` and `answers` projects.

Let's look at an example of this. Suppose we want a function to choose between two forking computations based on the result of an initial computation:

```
def choice[A](cond: Par[Boolean])(t: Par[A], f: Par[A]): Par[A]
```

This constructs a computation that proceeds with `t` if `cond` results in `true` or `f` if `cond` results in `false`. We can certainly implement this by blocking on the result of the `cond` and then using this result to determine whether to run `t` or `f`. Here's a simple blocking implementation:[17]

```
def choice[A](cond: Par[Boolean])(t: Par[A], f: Par[A]): Par[A] =
  es =>
    if cond.run(es).get then t(es)          Notice we are blocking
    else f(es)                              on the result of cond.
```

---

[16]This last way of generating laws is probably the weakest since it can be too easy to just have the laws reflect the implementation, even if the implementation is buggy or requires all sorts of unusual side conditions that make composition difficult.

[17]See `Nonblocking.scala` in the chapter code for the non-blocking implementation.

But before we move on, let's think about this combinator a bit. What is it doing? It's running cond, and then when the result is available, it runs either t or f. This seems reasonable, but let's see if we can think of some variations to understand the essence of this combinator. There's something rather arbitrary about the fact that we are using Boolean and only selecting among *two* possible parallel computations, t and f, here. Why just two? If it's useful to be able to choose between two parallel computations based on the results of a first, it should be useful to choose between *N* computations:

```
def choiceN[A](n: Par[Int])(choices: List[Par[A]]): Par[A]
```

Let's say that choiceN runs n and then uses that to select a parallel computation from choices. This is a bit more general than choice.

EXERCISE 7.11

Implement choiceN and then choice in terms of choiceN.

Note what we've done so far; we've refined our original combinator, choice, to choiceN, which turns out to be more general and is capable of expressing choice as well as other use cases not supported by choice. But let's keep going to see if we can refine choice to an even more general combinator.

EXERCISE 7.12

There's still something rather arbitrary about choiceN: the choice of List seems overly specific. Why does it matter what sort of container we have? For instance, what if instead of a list of computations we have a Map of them?[18]

```
def choiceMap[K, V](key: Par[K])(choices: Map[K, Par[V]]): Par[V]
```

The Map encoding of the set of possible choices feels overly specific, just like List. If we look at our implementation of choiceMap, we can see we aren't really using much of the API of Map. Really, the Map[A,Par[B]] is used to provide a function: A => Par[B]. And now that we've spotted that, looking back at choice and choiceN, we can see that for choice, the pair of arguments was being used as a function of type Boolean => Par[A] (where the Boolean selects one of the two Par[A] arguments), and for

---

[18]Map[K,V] (see the API: http://mng.bz/eZ4l) is a purely functional data structure in the Scala standard library. It associates keys of type K with values of type V in a one-to-one relationship and allows us to look up the value by the associated key.

choiceN, the list was being used as a function of type `Int => Par[A]`! Let's make a more general signature that unifies them all:

```
extension [A](pa: Par[A]) def chooser[B](choices: A => Par[B]): Par[B]
```

EXERCISE 7.13

Implement this new primitive chooser, and then use it to implement choice and choiceN.

Whenever you generalize functions like this, take a critical look at your generalized function when you're finished. Although the function may have been motivated by some specific use case, the signature and implementation may have a more general meaning. In this case, chooser is perhaps no longer the most appropriate name for this operation, which is actually quite general—it's a parallel computation that, when run, will run an initial computation whose result is used to determine a second computation. This second computation is not even required to exist before the first computation's result is available. It doesn't need to be stored in a container, like List or Map. Perhaps it's being generated from whole cloth using the result of the first computation. This function, which comes up often in functional libraries, is usually called bind or flatMap:

```
extension [A](pa: Par[A]) def flatMap[B](f: A => Par[B]): Par[B]
```

Is flatMap really the most primitive possible function, or can we generalize further? Let's play around with it a bit more. The name flatMap is suggestive of the fact that this operation could be decomposed into two steps: *mapping* f: A => Par[B] over our Par[A], which generates a Par[Par[B]], and then *flattening* this nested Par[Par[B]] to a Par[B]. But this is interesting; it suggests all we needed to do was add an even simpler combinator—let's call it join—for converting a Par[Par[X]] to Par[X] for any choice of X:

```
def join[A](ppa: Par[Par[A]]): Par[A]
```

Again, we're just following the types. We have an example that demands a function with the given signature, so we bring it into existence. Now that it exists, we can think about what the signature means. We call it join, since conceptually, it's a parallel computation that, when run, will execute the inner computation, wait for it to finish (much like Thread.join), and then return its result.

Implement `join`. Can you see how to implement `flatMap` using `join`? And can you implement `join` using `flatMap`?

We'll stop here, but you're encouraged to explore this algebra further. Try more complicated examples, discover new combinators, and see what you find! Here are some questions to consider:

- Can you implement a function with the same signature as `map2` but using `flatMap` and `unit`? How is its meaning different than that of `map2`?
- Can you think of laws relating `join` to the other primitives of the algebra?
- Are there parallel computations that can't be expressed using this algebra? Can you think of any computations that can't even be expressed by adding new primitives to the algebra?

Recognizing the expressiveness and limitations of an algebra

As you practice more functional programming, one of the skills you'll develop is the ability to recognize which functions are expressible from an algebra and what the limitations of that algebra are. For instance, in the preceding example, it may not have been obvious at first that a function like `choice` couldn't be expressed purely in terms of `map`, `map2`, and `unit`, and it may not have been obvious that `choice` was just a special case of `flatMap`. Over time, observations like this will come quickly, and you'll also get better at spotting how to modify your algebra to make some needed combinator expressible. These skills will be helpful for all of your API design work.

As a practical consideration, being able to reduce an API to a minimal set of primitive functions is extremely useful. As we noted earlier when we implemented `parMap` in terms of existing combinators, it's frequently the case that primitive combinators encapsulate some rather tricky logic, and reusing them means we don't have to duplicate this logic.

7.5   Conclusion

We've now completed the design of a library for defining parallel and asynchronous computations in a purely functional way. Although this domain is interesting, the primary goal of this chapter was to provide you with a window into the process of functional design, a sense of the sorts of problems you're likely to encounter, and ideas about handling those problems.

Chapters 4–6 had a strong theme of separation of concerns, specifically related to the idea of separating the description of a computation from the interpreter that then runs it. In this chapter, we saw that principle in action in the design of a library that describes parallel computations as values of a data type `Par`, with a separate interpreter `run` to actually spawn the threads to execute them.

In the next chapter, we'll look at a completely different domain, take another meandering journey toward an API for that domain, and draw further lessons about functional design.

Summary

- No existing library is beyond reexamination. Most libraries contain arbitrary design choices. Experimenting with building alternative libraries may result in discovering new things about the problem space.
- Simple examples let us focus on the essence of the problem domain instead of getting lost in incidental detail.
- Parallel and asynchronous computations can be modeled in a purely functional way.
- Building a description of a computation along with a separate interpreter that runs the computations allows computations to be treated as values, which can then be combined with other computations.
- An effective technique for API design is conjuring types and implementations, trying to implement those types and implementations, adjusting, and iterating.
- The `Par[A]` type describes a computation that may evaluate some or all of the computation on multiple threads.
- `Par` values can be transformed and combined with many familiar operations, such as `map`, `flatMap`, and `sequence`.
- Treating an API as an algebra and defining laws that constrain implementations are both valuable design tools and an effective testing technique.
- Partitioning an API into a minimal set of primitive functions and a set of combinator functions promotes reuse and understanding.
- An actor is a non-blocking concurrency primitive based on message passing. Actors are not purely functional but can be used to implement purely functional APIs, as demonstrated with the implementation of `map2` for the non-blocking `Par`.

7.6   Exercise answers

Let's introduce a type parameter for each of the parallel computations as well as the output of the function that combines the results of each parallel computation:

```
def map2[A, B, C](pa: Par[A], pb: Par[B])(f: (A, B) => C): Par[C]
```

Alternatively, we can define `map2` as an extension method on a `Par[A]`:

```
extension [A](pa: Par[A]) def map2[B, C](pb: Par[B])(f: (A, B) => C): Par[C]
```

◼ **ANSWER 7.2**

The answer is discussed immediately after exercise 7.2.

◼ **ANSWER 7.3**

Our original implementation of `map2` waited for both futures to complete before returning a `UnitFuture` with the final result. Before the caller ever sees a `Future`, we've waited for both of the constituent computations to complete!

Instead of using `UnitFuture`, we'll need to start the constituent computations and immediately return a composite `Future` that references them. The caller can then use the `get` overload with a timeout or any of the other methods on `Future`.

To implement the timeout variant of `get`, we'll need to call it on each of the futures we've started. We can await the first result using the supplied timeout and measure the amount of time it takes to complete. We can then await the second result, decrementing the timeout by the amount of time we waited for the first result:

```
extension [A](pa: Par[A])
  def map2Timeouts[B, C](pb: Par[B])(f: (A, B) => C): Par[C] =
    es => new Future[C]:
      private val futureA = pa(es)           ◁───   When the future is
      private val futureB = pb(es)                  created, we immediately
      @volatile private var cache: Option[C] = None  start the constituent
                                                    computations.
      def isDone = cache.isDefined

      def get() = get(Long.MaxValue, TimeUnit.NANOSECONDS)

      def get(timeout: Long, units: TimeUnit) =
        val timeoutNs = TimeUnit.NANOSECONDS.convert(timeout, units)
        val started = System.nanoTime
  ──▷   val a = futureA.get(timeoutNs, TimeUnit.NANOSECONDS)
        val elapsed = System.nanoTime - started
        val b = futureB.get(timeoutNs - elapsed,      Wait for futureB to complete,
          ➧ TimeUnit.NANOSECONDS)            ◁───     but only wait for the difference
        val c = f(a, b)                               between the requested timeout
        cache = Some(c)                               and the elapsed time waiting on
        c                                             futureA completion.

      def isCancelled = futureA.isCancelled || futureB.isCancelled

      def cancel(evenIfRunning: Boolean) =
        futureA.cancel(evenIfRunning) || futureB.cancel(evenIfRunning)
```

Wait for futureA to complete, timing out if it doesn't complete in the requested time.

We return an anonymous function that upon receiving a value of type A, immediately calls lazyUnit, passing f(a):

```
def asyncF[A, B](f: A => B): A => Par[B] =
  a => lazyUnit(f(a))
```

Because the lazyUnit takes a by-name parameter, f(a) is not evaluated yet. To see why lazyUnit(f(a)) implements the desired functionality, let's incrementally substitute definitions:

```
a => lazyUnit(f(a))
a => fork(unit(f(a)))        ◁──── Substitute lazyUnit.
a => es => es.submit(
  new Callable[B] { def run = unit(f(a))(es).get })   ◁──── Substitute fork.
a => es => es.submit(
  new Callable[B] { def run = (es => UnitFuture(f(a)))(es).get })  ◁─┤ Substitute
                                                                     │ unit.
a => es => es.submit(
  new Callable[B] { def run = UnitFuture(f(a)).get })  ◁─┐
a => es => es.submit(                                   │ Apply es to es =>
  new Callable[B] { def run = f(a) })  ◁─┤ Substitute    │ UnitFuture(f(a)).
                                         │ UnitFuture#get.
```

We're left with a function that receives an A and returns a Par, which submits a job to the executor that computes f(a) when run on an OS thread.

We've implemented sequence many times by now—a foldRight that uses map2. So let's just copy, paste, and adjust the types a bit:

```
def sequence[A](pas: List[Par[A]]): Par[List[A]] =
  pas.foldRight(unit(List.empty[A]))((pa, acc) => pa.map2(acc)(_ :: _))
```

We can do a bit better in this case, though, using a similar technique to the one we used in sums. Let's divide the computation into two halves and compute each in parallel. Since we'll again need efficient random access to the elements in our collection, we'll first write a version that works with an IndexedSeq[Par[A]]:

```
def sequenceBalanced[A](pas: IndexedSeq[Par[A]]): Par[IndexedSeq[A]] =
  if pas.isEmpty then unit(IndexedSeq.empty)
  else if pas.size == 1 then pas.head.map(a => IndexedSeq(a))
  else
    val (l, r) = pas.splitAt(pas.size / 2)
    sequenceBalanced(l).map2(sequenceBalanced(r))(_ ++ _)
```

We can then implement sequence in terms of sequenceBalanced:

```
def sequence[A](pas: List[Par[A]]): Par[List[A]] =
  sequenceBalanced(pas.toIndexedSeq).map(_.toList)
```

■ **ANSWER 7.6**

We could first filter the list with the supplied predicate and lift the resulting list into Par:

```
def parFilter[A](as: List[A])(f: A => Boolean): Par[List[A]] =
  unit(as.filter(f))
```

This solution doesn't have any parallelism, though. We could try to fix that by using lazyUnit instead of unit:

```
def parFilter[A](as: List[A])(f: A => Boolean): Par[List[A]] =
  lazyUnit(as.filter(f))
```

This is a little better, as the filtering is done on a different logical thread, but all filtering is done on the same logical thread. We really want each invocation of the predicate to get its own logical thread. Like in parMap, we can use asyncF, but this time, instead of passing f directly, we pass an anonymous function that converts an A into a List[A]—a single element list if the predicate passes or an empty list otherwise:

> Like in parMap, we fork immediately, so the mapping over the original list is done on a separate logical thread rather than the caller's thread.

```
def parFilter[A](as: List[A])(f: A => Boolean): Par[List[A]] =
  fork:                          ◄──────────────────────────
    val pars: List[Par[List[A]]] =
      as.map(asyncF(a =>
        if f(a) then List(a) else Nil))  ◄──┐
    sequence(pars).map(_.flatten)   ◄──┐
```

> We use asyncF to convert our A => List[A] function to an A => Par[List[A]] function.

> sequence(pars) returns a Par[List[List[A]]], so we map over that and flatten the inner nested lists.

□ **ANSWER 7.7**

We'll start with the equality we're seeking to prove and then make algebraic substitutions until we've shown both sides of the equation simplify to the same value:

Initial law
```
  ┌─► y.map(g).map(f) == y.map(f compose g)
  │    y.map(id).map(f compose g) == y.map((f compose g)compose id)   ◄──
  │    y.map(id).map(f compose g) == y.map(f compose g)   ◄───────┐
  └─► y.map(f compose g) == y.map(f compose g)   Simplify (f compose g)
┌─
│ Simplify y.map(id) to y on the left-hand side.          compose id on the right-
                                                          hand side to f compose g.
```

> Substitute the identity function for g and f compose g for f on both sides.

ANSWER 7.8

Consider what happens when using a fixed thread pool with only a single thread. This is explored in greater detail in the next section.

ANSWER 7.9

Any fixed-size thread pool can be deadlocked by running an expression of the form `fork(fork(fork(x)))`, where there's at least one more `fork` than there are threads in the pool. Each thread in the pool blocks on the call to `.get`, resulting in all threads being blocked, while one more logical thread is waiting to run and, hence, resolve all the waiting.

ANSWER 7.10

We'll return to this in chapter 13.

ANSWER 7.11

We compute the index of the choice by running n and awaiting the result. We then look up the Par in the choices at that index and run it:

```
def choiceN[A](n: Par[Int])(choices: List[Par[A]]): Par[A] =
  es =>
    val index = n.run(es).get % choices.size
    choices(index).run(es)
```

Implementing choice in terms of choiceN involves converting the conditional to an index, which we can do via map. Here we've chosen to make the true case index 0 and the false case index 1:

```
def choice[A](cond: Par[Boolean])(t: Par[A], f: Par[A]): Par[A] =
  choiceN(cond.map(b => if b then 0 else 1))(List(t, f))
```

■ **ANSWER 7.12**

The implementation of `choiceMap` is almost identical to the implementation of `choiceN`; instead of looking up a `Par` in a `List` using an index, we're doing the lookup in a `Map` using a key:

```
def choiceMap[K, V](key: Par[K])(choices: Map[K, Par[V]]): Par[V] =
  es =>
    val k = key.run(es).get
    choices(k).run
```

If you want, stop reading here, and see if you can come up with a new and more general combinator in terms of which you can implement choice, choiceN, and choiceMap.

■ **ANSWER 7.13**

The implementation is almost identical to both `choiceN` and `choiceMap`, with the only difference being how the choice lookup is done:

```
extension [A](pa: Par[A]) def chooser[B](choices: A => Par[B]): Par[B] =
  es =>
    val a = pa.run(es).get
    choices(a).run
```

choice can now be implemented via chooser by passing a function that selects t when cond returns a true and f otherwise:

```
def choice[A](cond: Par[Boolean])(t: Par[A], f: Par[A]): Par[A] =
  cond.chooser(b => if b then t else f)
```

Similarly, choiceN can be implemented by passing a function that does a lookup in the choices list.

```
def choiceN[A](n: Par[Int])(choices: List[Par[A]]): Par[A] =
  n.chooser(i => choices(i % choices.size))
```

■ **ANSWER 7.14**

We first run the outer Par and wait for it to complete. We then run the resulting inner Par:

```
def join[A](ppa: Par[Par[A]]): Par[A] =
  es => ppa.run(es).get.run(es)
```

To implement `flatMap` via `join`, we first map `f` over the initial `pa`, giving us a `Par[Par[B]]`. We then join that:

```
extension [A](pa: Par[A]) def flatMap[B](f: A => Par[B]): Par[B] =
  join(pa.map(f))
```

Implementing `join` in terms of `flatMap` is a little bit trickier. `flatMap` lets us convert a `Par[X]` to a `Par[Y]`, given a function `X => Par[Y]`. The trick is taking `X = Par[A]` and `Y = A`. Hence, we need a function `Par[A] => Par[A]`, which is the identity function:

```
def join[A](ppa: Par[Par[A]]): Par[A] =
  ppa.flatMap(identity)
```

Property-based testing 8

This chapter covers

- Verifying properties of APIs
- Developing a property-based testing library

In chapter 7, we worked through the design of a functional library for expressing parallel computations. There we introduced the idea that an API should form an algebra—that is, a collection of data types, functions over these data types, and, importantly, laws or properties that express relationships between these functions. We also hinted at the idea that it might be possible to somehow check these laws automatically.

This chapter takes us toward a simple but powerful library for *property-based testing*. The general idea of such a library is decoupling the specification of program behavior from the creation of test cases. The programmer focuses on specifying the behavior of programs and giving high-level constraints on the test cases; the framework then automatically generates test cases that satisfy these constraints and runs tests to ensure programs behave as specified.

Although a library for testing has a very different purpose than a library for parallel computations, we'll discover that these libraries have a lot of surprisingly similar combinators. This similarity is something we'll return to in part 3.

8.1   *A brief tour of property-based testing*

As an example, in ScalaCheck (http://mng.bz/n2j9), a property-based testing library for Scala, a property looks something like the following listing.

Listing 8.1   ScalaCheck properties

```
import org.scalacheck.{Gen, Prop}
val intList = Gen.listOf(Gen.choose(0, 100))
val prop =
  Prop.forAll(intList)(ns =>
    ns.reverse.reverse == ns) &&
  Prop.forAll(intList)(ns =>
    ns.headOption == ns.reverse.lastOption)
val failingProp =
  Prop.forAll(intList)(ns => ns.reverse == ns)
```

A generator of lists of integers between 0 and 100

A property that specifies the behavior of the List.reverse method

Check that reversing a list twice gives back the original list.

Check that the first element becomes the last element after reversal.

A property that is obviously false

And we can check properties as follows:

```
scala> prop.check
+ OK, passed 100 tests.

scala> failingProp.check
! Falsified after 6 passed tests.
> ARG_0: List(0, 1)
```

Here, intList is not a List[Int] but a Gen[List[Int]], which is something that knows how to generate test data of the List[Int] type. We can sample from this generator, and it will produce lists of different lengths, filled with random numbers between 0 and 100. Generators in a property-based testing library have a rich API. We can combine and compose generators in different ways, reuse them, and so on.

The function Prop.forAll creates a property by combining a generator of type Gen[A] with some predicate of type A => Boolean. The property asserts that all values produced by the generator should satisfy the predicate. Figure 8.1 shows the relationship between the intList generator and one of the properties that uses it. Like generators, properties can also have a rich API. In this simple example, we've used && to combine two properties. The resulting property will hold only if neither property can be falsified by any of the generated test cases. Together, the two properties form a partial specification of the correct behavior of the reverse method.[1]

When we invoke prop.check, ScalaCheck will randomly generate List[Int] values to try to find a case that falsifies the predicates we've supplied. The output indicates that ScalaCheck has generated 100 test cases (of type List[Int]) and that they all satisfied

---

[1] The goal of this sort of testing is not necessarily fully specifying program behavior but providing greater confidence in the code. Like testing in general, we can always make our properties more complete, but we should do the usual cost–benefit analysis to determine whether the additional work is worth doing.

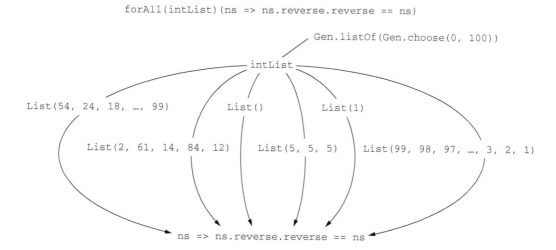

**A Gen object generates a variety of different objects to pass to
a Boolean expression, searching for one that will make it false.**

Figure 8.1   **Generators and properties**

the predicates. Properties can, of course, fail; the output of `failingProp.check` indicates that the predicate tested false for some input, which is helpfully printed out to
facilitate further testing or debugging.

■ EXERCISE 8.1

To get used to thinking about testing in this way, come up with properties that specify
the implementation of a `sum: List[Int] => Int` function. You don't have to write your
properties down as executable ScalaCheck code—an informal description is fine.
Here are some ideas to get you started:

- Reversing a list and summing it should provide the same result as summing the
  original, nonreversed list.
- What should the sum be if all elements of the list are of the same value?
- Can you think of other properties?

■ EXERCISE 8.2

What properties specify a function that finds the maximum of a `List[Int]`?

Property-based testing libraries often come equipped with other useful features. We'll talk more about some of these features later, but the following should provide an idea of what's possible:

- *Test case minimization*—In the event of a failing test, the framework tries smaller sizes until it finds the smallest test case that also fails, which is more illuminating for debugging purposes. For instance, if a property fails for a list of size 10, then the framework tries smaller lists and reports the smallest list that fails the test.
- *Exhaustive test case generation*—We call the set of values that could be produced by some Gen[A] the *domain*.[2] When the domain is small enough (for instance, if it's all even integers less than 100), we may exhaustively test all its values, rather than generate sample values. If the property holds for all values in a domain, then we have an actual proof, rather than just the absence of evidence to the contrary.

ScalaCheck is just one property-based testing library, and we'll derive our own library in this chapter, starting from scratch. Like in chapter 7, this is mostly for pedagogical purposes but also partly because we should consider no library to be the final word on any subject. There's certainly nothing wrong with using an existing library, like Scala-Check, and existing libraries can be a good source of ideas. But even if you decide you like the existing library's solution, spending an hour or two playing with designs and writing down some type signatures is a great way to learn more about the domain and understand the design trade-offs.

8.1.1   *Choosing data types and functions*

This section will be another messy and iterative process of discovering data types and functions for our library. This time around, we're designing a library for property-based testing. As before, this is a chance to peer over the shoulder of someone working through possible designs.

The particular path we take and the library we arrive at aren't necessarily the same as what you would come up with on your own. If property-based testing is unfamiliar to you, even better; this is a chance to explore a new domain and its design space and make your own discoveries about it. If at any point you're feeling inspired or have ideas of your own about how to design a library like this, don't wait for an exercise to prompt you; put the book down, and go off to play with your ideas. You can always come back to the chapter if you run out of ideas or get stuck.

---

[2] This is the same usage of *domain* as the domain of a function (http://mng.bz/ZP8q); generators describe possible inputs to functions we'd like to test. Note that we'll also still sometimes use *domain* in the more colloquial sense to refer to a subject or area of interest—for example, *the domain of functional parallelism* or *the error-handling domain.*

8.1.2 Initial snippets of an API

With that said, let's get started. What data types should we use for our testing library? What primitives should we define, and what might they mean? What laws should our functions satisfy? As before, we can look at a simple example, read off the needed data types and functions, and see what we find. For inspiration, let's look at the ScalaCheck example we showed earlier:

```
val intList = Gen.listOf(Gen.choose(0, 100))
val prop =
  Prop.forAll(intList)(ns => ns.reverse.reverse == ns) &&
  Prop.forAll(intList)(ns => ns.headOption == ns.reverse.lastOption)
```

Without knowing anything about the implementation of `Gen.choose` or `Gen.listOf`, we can guess that whatever data type they return (let's call it Gen—short for *generator*) must be parametric in some type. That is, `Gen.choose(0, 100)` probably returns a `Gen[Int]`, and `Gen.listOf` is then a function with the signature `Gen[Int] => Gen[List[Int]]`. But since it doesn't seem like `Gen.listOf` should care about the type of the Gen it receives as input (it would be odd to require separate combinators for creating lists of `Int`, `Double`, `String`, and so on), let's make it polymorphic:

```
def listOf[A](a: Gen[A]): Gen[List[A]]
```

We can learn many things by looking at this signature. Notice what we're not specifying—the size of the list to generate. For this to be implementable, our generator must therefore either assume or be told the size. Assuming a size seems a bit inflexible since any assumption is unlikely to be appropriate in all contexts. Therefore, it seems generators must be told the size of test cases to generate. We can imagine an API where this is made explicit:

```
def listOfN[A](n: Int, a: Gen[A]): Gen[List[A]]
```

This would certainly be a useful combinator, but not having to explicitly specify sizes is powerful as well. It means that whatever function runs the tests has the freedom to choose test case sizes, which opens up the possibility of doing the test case minimization we mentioned earlier. If the sizes are always fixed and specified by the programmer, then the test runner won't have this flexibility. Keep this concern in mind as we get further along in our design.

What about the rest of this example? The `Prop.forAll` function looks interesting; we can see that it accepts a `Gen[List[Int]]` and what looks to be a corresponding predicate: `List[Int] => Boolean`. But again, it doesn't seem like `forAll` should care about the types of the generator and the predicate, as long as they match up. We can express this with the type:

```
def forAll[A](a: Gen[A])(f: A => Boolean): Prop
```

Here we've simply invented a new type, Prop (short for *property*, following the Scala-Check naming), for the result of binding a Gen to a predicate. We might not know the internal representation of Prop or what other functions it supports, but based on this example, we can see it has an && operator, so let's introduce that:

```
trait Prop:
   def &&(that: Prop): Prop
```

8.1.3   *The meaning and API of properties*

Now that we have a few fragments of an API, let's discuss what we want our types and functions to mean. First consider Prop. We know there exist functions forAll (for creating a property), && (for composing properties), and check (for running a property). In ScalaCheck this check method has a side effect of printing to the console. It's fine to expose this as a convenience function, but it's not a basis for composition. For instance, we couldn't implement && for Prop if its representation were just the check method:[3]

```
trait Prop:
   def check: Unit
   def &&(that: Prop): Prop = ???
```

Since check has a side effect, the only option for implementing && in this case would be running the check method on both Prop values. So if check prints out a test report, then we would get two of them, and they would print failures and successes independently of each other. That's likely not a correct implementation; the problem is not so much that check has a side effect but, more generally, that it throws away information.

To combine Prop values using combinators like &&, we need check (or whatever function runs properties) to return some meaningful value. What type should that value have? Let's consider what sort of information we'd like to get out of checking our properties. At a minimum, we need to know whether the property succeeded or failed, which lets us implement &&.

■   **EXERCISE 8.3**

Assuming the following representation of Prop, implement && as a method of Prop:

```
trait Prop:
   def check: Boolean
```

---

[3] This might remind you of similar problems we discussed in chapter 7 when we looked at using Thread and Runnable for parallelism.

In this representation, `Prop` is equivalent[4] to a non-strict `Boolean`, and any of the usual `Boolean` functions (AND, OR, NOT, XOR, and so on) can be defined for `Prop`—but a `Boolean` alone is probably insufficient. If a property fails, we might want to know how many tests succeeded first and what arguments produced the failure, and if a property succeeds, it would be useful to know how many tests it ran. Let's try returning an `Either` to indicate success or failure:

```
object Prop:
  opaque type SuccessCount = Int  ⟵——— Opaque type aliases like this
  ...                                    can improve the readability
trait Prop:                            and type safety of an API.
  def check: Either[???, SuccessCount]
```

What type shall we return in the failure case? We don't know anything about the types of test cases being generated. Should we add a type parameter to `Prop` and make it `Prop[A]`? Then `check` could return `Either[A, Int]`. Before going too far down this path, let's ask ourselves whether we really care about the type of the value that caused the property to fail. We don't really; we would only care about the type if we were going to do further computation with the failure. Most likely we're just going to end up printing it to the screen for inspection by the person running the tests. After all, the goal here is to find bugs and indicate to someone what test cases trigger those bugs so they can fix them. As a general rule, we shouldn't use `String` to represent data we want to compute with. But for values, we're just going to show to human beings that a `String` is absolutely appropriate. This suggests we can get away with the following representation for `Prop`:

```
object Prop:
  opaque type FailedCase = String
  opaque type SuccessCount = Int

trait Prop:
  def check: Either[(FailedCase, SuccessCount), SuccessCount]
```

In case of failure, `check` returns a `Left((s, n))`, where s is some `String` that represents the value that caused the property to fail, and n is the number of cases that succeeded before the failure occurred. That takes care of the return value of `check`—at least for now—but what about the arguments to `check`? Right now, the `check` method takes no arguments. Is this sufficient? We can think about what information `Prop` will have access to just by inspecting the way `Prop` values are created. In particular, let's look at `forAll`:

```
def forAll[A](a: Gen[A])(f: A => Boolean): Prop
```

---

[4] It is equivalent in the sense that we could model a `Prop` as `() => Boolean`, instead of a trait with a single method, without losing any expressivity.

Without knowing more about the representation of Gen, it's hard to say whether there's enough information here to be able to generate values of type A (which is what we need to implement check). So for now, let's turn our attention to Gen to get a better idea of what it means and what its dependencies might be.

8.1.4   *The meaning and API of generators*

We determined earlier that a Gen[A] is something that knows how to generate values of type A. What are some ways it could do that? Well, it could randomly generate these values. Look back at the example from chapter 6; in that chapter, we gave an interface for a purely functional random number generator, RNG, and showed how to make it convenient to combine computations that made use of it. We could just make Gen a type that wraps a State transition over a random number generator:[5]

```
opaque type Gen[+A] = State[RNG, A]
```

EXERCISE 8.4

Implement Gen.choose using this representation of Gen. It should generate integers in the range start to stopExclusive. Feel free to use functions you've already written:

```
def choose(start: Int, stopExclusive: Int): Gen[Int]
```

EXERCISE 8.5

Let's see what else we can implement using this representation of Gen. Try implementing unit, boolean, and listOfN.

```
def unit[A](a: => A): Gen[A]          Always generates
def boolean: Gen[Boolean]              the value a
extension [A](self: Gen[A])
  def listOfN[A](n: Int): Gen[List[A]]    Generates lists of length n
                                          using the generator g
```

As we discussed in chapter 7, we're interested in understanding what operations are primitive and what operations are derived as well as finding a small yet expressive set of primitives. A good way to explore what is expressible with a given set of primitives is picking some concrete examples you'd like to express and seeing if you can assemble the functionality you want. As you do so, look for patterns, try factoring out these patterns into combinators, and refine your set of primitives. We encourage you to stop reading here and simply play with the primitives and combinators we've written so far. If you want some concrete examples to inspire you, here are some ideas:

---

[5] Recall the following definition: opaque type State[S, +A] = S => (A, S).

- If we can generate a single `Int` in some range, do we need a new primitive to generate an `(Int, Int)` pair in some range?
- Can we produce a `Gen[Option[A]]` from a `Gen[A]`? What about a `Gen[A]` from a `Gen[Option[A]]`?
- Can we generate strings somehow using our existing primitives?

The importance of play

You don't have to wait around for a concrete example to force exploration of the design space. In fact, if you rely exclusively on concrete, obviously useful, or important examples to design your API, you'll often miss out on aspects of the design space and generate APIs with ad hoc, overly specific features. We don't want to overfit our design to the examples we happen to think of right now. We want to reduce the problem to its essence, and sometimes the best way of doing this is play. Don't try solving important problems or producing useful functionality—not right away. Just experiment with different representations, primitives, and operations; let questions naturally arise; and explore whatever piques your curiosity. (You might think, *These two functions seem similar. I wonder if there's some more general operation hiding inside; Would it make sense to make this data type polymorphic?*; or *What would it mean to change this aspect of the representation from a single value to a* `List` *of values?*) There's no right or wrong way of doing this, but there are so many different design choices that it's impossible *not* to run headlong into fascinating questions to play with. It doesn't matter where you begin—if you keep playing the domain will inexorably guide you to make all the design choices required.

8.1.5   *Generators that depend on generated values*

Suppose we'd like a `Gen[(String, String)]` that generates pairs, where the second string contains only characters from the first. Or suppose we had a `Gen[Int]` that chooses an integer between 0 and 11, and we'd like to make a `Gen[List[Double]]` that then generates lists of whatever length is chosen. In both of these cases, there's a *dependency*: we generate a value, and then we use that value to determine what generator to use next. For this, we need `flatMap`, which lets one generator depend on another.

■ **EXERCISE 8.6**

Implement `flatMap`, and then use it to implement this more dynamic version of `listOfN`. Put `flatMap` and `listOfN` in the `Gen` class:

```
extension [A](self: Gen[A]) def flatMap[B](f: A => Gen[B]): Gen[B]
extension [A](self: Gen[A]) def listOfN(size: Gen[Int]): Gen[List[A]]
```

Implement union, for combining two generators of the same type into one, by pulling values from each generator with equal likelihood:

```
def union[A](g1: Gen[A], g2: Gen[A]): Gen[A]
```

Implement weighted, a version of union that accepts a weight for each Gen and generates values from each Gen with probability proportional to its weight:

```
def weighted[A](g1: (Gen[A], Double), g2: (Gen[A], Double)): Gen[A]
```

8.1.6   *Refining the Prop data type*

Now that we know more about our representation of generators, let's return to our definition of Prop. Our Gen representation has revealed information about the requirements for Prop, and our current definition of Prop looks like this:

```
trait Prop:
  def check: Either[(FailedCase, SuccessCount), SuccessCount]
```

Prop is equivalent[6] to a non-strict Either, but it's missing some information. We have the number of successful test cases in SuccessCount, but we haven't specified how many test cases to examine before considering the property to have passed the test. We could certainly hardcode something, but it would be better to abstract over this dependency:

```
opaque type TestCases = Int
object TestCases:
  extension (x: TestCases) def toInt: Int = x
  def fromInt(x: Int): TestCases = x

opaque type Prop = TestCases =>
                      Either[(FailedCase, SuccessCount), SuccessCount]
```

Also, we're recording the number of successful tests on both sides of that Either. But when a property passes, it's implied that the number of passed tests will be equal to the argument to check, so the caller of check learns nothing new by being told the

---

[6] This is in the sense that we could replace the trait with a thunk that returns an Either.

success count. Since we don't currently need any information in the Right case of that Either, we can turn it into an Option:

```
opaque type Prop = TestCases => Option[(FailedCase, SuccessCount)]
```

This seems a little weird, since None will mean all tests succeeded and the property passed, and Some will indicate a failure. Until now, we've only used the None case of Option to indicate failure, but in this case, we're using it to represent the absence of a failure. That's a perfectly legitimate use for Option, but its intent isn't very clear. So let's make a new data type, equivalent to Option[(FailedCase, SuccessCount)], that shows our intent very clearly.

Listing 8.2   Creating a Result data type

```
enum Result:                                        Indicates one of
  case Passed        <———— Indicates all tests passed rows ×   the test cases
  case Falsified(                                    falsified the
    failure: FailedCase, successes: SuccessCount)  <———— property

  def isFalsified: Boolean = this match
    case Passed => false
    case Falsified(_, _) => true
```

Is this now a sufficient representation of Prop? Let's take another look at forAll. Can it be implemented? Why, or why not?

```
def forAll[A](a: Gen[A])(f: A => Boolean): Prop
```

We can see that forAll doesn't have enough information to return a Prop. Besides the number of test cases to try, running a Prop must have all the information needed to generate test cases. If it needs to generate random test cases using our current representation of Gen, it's going to need an RNG. Let's propagate that dependency to Prop:

```
opaque type Prop = (TestCases, RNG) => Result
```

If we think of other dependencies it might need, besides the number of test cases and the source of randomness, we can just add these as extra parameters to check later.

We now have enough information to implement forAll. The following listing shows a simple implementation.

Listing 8.3   Implementing forAll

```
def forAll[A](as: Gen[A])(f: A => Boolean): Prop =
  (n, rng) =>
    randomLazyList(as)(rng)
      .zip(LazyList.from(0))
      .take(n)                    A lazy list of pairs, (a, i), where a is a random
      .map:          <———————     value and i is its index in the list
        case (a, i) =>
          try
```

```
                    if f(a) then Passed
If a test case        else Falsified(a.toString, i)  ◄——
generates an        catch
exception,            case e: Exception =>
record it in  ——▷       Falsified(buildMsg(a, e), i)
the result.   |.find(_.isFalsified)
                 .getOrElse(Passed)
      }

    def randomLazyList[A](g: Gen[A])(rng: RNG): LazyList[A] =
      LazyList.unfold(rng)(rng => Some(g.run(rng)))   ◄——

    def buildMsg[A](s: A, e: Exception): String =
      s"test case: $s\n" +
      s"generated an exception: ${e.getMessage}\n" +   ◄——
      s"stack trace:\n ${e.getStackTrace.mkString("\n")}"
```

> **When a test fails, record the failed case and its index so we know how many tests succeeded before it.**

> **This generates an infinite lazy list of A values by repeatedly sampling a generator. Recall that run on a State evaluates the state action.**

> **This is string interpolation syntax. A string starting with s" can refer to a Scala value v as $v or ${v} in the string. The Scala compiler will expand this to v.toString.**

Notice that we're catching exceptions and reporting them as test failures rather than letting the run throw the error (which would lose information about what argument triggered the failure).

EXERCISE 8.9

Now that we have a representation of Prop, implement && and || for composing Prop values. Notice that in the case of failure, we don't know which property was responsible—the left or right. Can you devise a way of handling this, perhaps by allowing Prop values to be assigned a tag or label that gets displayed in the event of a failure?

```
extension (self: Prop) def &&(that: Prop): Prop
extension (self: Prop) def ||(that: Prop): Prop
```

8.2   *Test case minimization*

Earlier we mentioned the idea of test case minimization, meaning we'd ideally like our framework to find the smallest or simplest failing test case to better illustrate the problem and facilitate debugging. Let's see if we can tweak our representations to support this outcome. There are two general approaches we could take:

- *Shrinking*—After we've found a failing test case, we can run a separate procedure to minimize the test case by successively decreasing its size until it no longer fails. This is called *shrinking*, and it usually requires writing separate code for each data type to implement this minimization process.
- *Sized generation*—Rather than shrinking test cases after the fact, we simply generate our test cases in order of increasing size and complexity, meaning we start small and increase the size until we find a failure. This idea can be extended in various ways to allow the test runner to make larger jumps in the space of possible sizes while still making it possible to find the smallest failing test.

ScalaCheck, incidentally, takes the first approach: shrinking. There's nothing wrong with this approach (it's also used by the Haskell Free Library QuickCheck, which Scala-Check is based on: http://mng.bz/E24n), but we'll see what we can do with sized generation. It's a bit simpler and, in some ways, more modular because our generators only need to know how to generate a test case of a given size. They don't need to be aware of the schedule used to search the space of test cases, and the function that runs the tests therefore has the freedom to choose this schedule. We'll see how this plays out shortly.

Instead of modifying our Gen data type, for which we've already written a number of useful combinators, let's introduce sized generation as a separate layer in our library. A simple representation of a sized generator is just a function that takes a size and produces a generator:

```
opaque type SGen[+A] = Int => Gen[A]
```

■ **EXERCISE 8.10**

Implement a helper function for converting a Gen to an SGen, which ignores the size parameter. You can add this as an extension method on Gen:

```
extension [A](self: Gen[A]) def unsized: SGen[A]
```

☐ **EXERCISE 8.11**

Not surprisingly, SGen, at a minimum, supports many of the same operations as Gen, and the implementations are rather mechanical. Define some convenience functions on SGen that simply delegate to the corresponding functions on Gen.[7]

■ **EXERCISE 8.12**

Implement a list combinator that doesn't accept an explicit size. It should return an SGen instead of a Gen. The implementation should generate lists of the requested size:

```
extension [A](self: Gen[A]) def list: SGen[List[A]]
```

Let's see how SGen affects the definition of Prop and Prop.forAll. The SGen equivalent of forAll looks like this:

```
@annotation.targetName("forAllSized")          ◁————
def forAll[A](g: SGen[A])(f: A => Boolean): Prop
```

> **Without this annotation, forAll for an SGen conflicts with forAll for a Gen (assuming both are defined in the Prop companion). With this annotation, we disambiguate the compiled name, avoiding the conflict.**

---

[7] In part 3, we'll discuss ways of factoring out this sort of duplication.

Can you see why it's not possible to implement this function? SGen is expecting to be told a size, but Prop doesn't receive any size information. Much like we did with the source of randomness and number of test cases, we simply need to add this as a dependency to Prop. But since we want to put Prop in charge of invoking the underlying generators with various sizes, we'll have Prop accept a maximum size. Prop will then generate test cases up to and including the maximum specified size—this will also allow it to search for the smallest failing test case. Let's see how this works out.[8]

Listing 8.4   Generating test cases up to a given maximum size

```
opaque type MaxSize = Int
object MaxSize:
  extension (x: MaxSize) def toInt: Int = x
  def fromInt(x: Int): MaxSize = x

opaque type Prop = (MaxSize, TestCases, RNG) => Result

object Prop:
  def forAll[A](g: SGen[A])(f: A => Boolean): Prop =
    (max, n, rng) =>
      val casesPerSize = (n.toInt - 1) / max.toInt + 1      ◁──┐ For each size, generate
      val props: LazyList[Prop] =                                │ many random cases.
        LazyList.from(0)
          .take((n.toInt min max.toInt) + 1)    ◁──┐ Make one property per size but
          .map(i => forAll(g(i))(f))                 │ no more than n properties.
      val prop: Prop =
        props.map[Prop](p => (max, n, rng) =>
          p(max, casesPerSize, rng))
          .toList                          ┐ Combine them all
          .reduce(_ && _)        ◁─────────┘ into one property.
      prop(max, n, rng)
```

8.2.1   *Using the library and improving its usability*

We've converged on what seems like a reasonable API. We could keep tinkering with it, but at this point, let's try using the library to construct tests and see if we notice any deficiencies, either in what it can express or in its general usability. *Usability* is somewhat subjective, but we generally like to have convenient syntax and appropriate helper functions for common usage patterns. We aren't necessarily aiming to make the library more expressive, but we want to make it pleasant to use.

8.2.2   *Some simple examples*

Let's revisit an example we mentioned at the start of this chapter: specifying the behavior of the function max, available as a method on List (see the API docs:

---

[8] This rather simple implementation gives an equal number of test cases to each size being generated and increases the size by 1, starting from 0. We could imagine a more sophisticated implementation that does something more like a binary search for a failing test case size—starting with sizes 0,1,2,4,8,16… and then narrowing the search space in the event of a failure.

http://mng.bz/Pz86). The maximum of a list should be greater than or equal to every other element in the list. Let's specify this:

```
val smallInt = Gen.choose(-10, 10)

val maxProp = Prop.forAll(smallInt.list): l =>
  val max = l.max
  l.forall(_ <= max)    <———— No value greater than max should exist in ns.
```

With this opaque type representation of Prop, we need a way to check our properties. Let's define a check extension method that evaluates a Prop and returns a Result.

Listing 8.5 A check helper function for Prop

```
extension (self: Prop)
  def check(                        A default
    maxSize: MaxSize = 100,    <——┘ argument of I00
    testCases: TestCases = 100,
    rng: RNG = RNG.Simple(System.currentTimeMillis)
  ): Result =
    self(maxSize, testCases, rng)
```

And to make experimenting in the REPL easier, we can introduce a helper function for running our Prop values and printing their results to the console in a useful format.

Listing 8.6 A run helper function for Prop

```
extension (self: Prop)
  def run(maxSize: MaxSize = 100,
          testCases: TestCases = 100,
          rng: RNG = RNG.Simple(System.currentTimeMillis)): Unit =
    self(maxSize, testCases, rng) match
      case Falsified(msg, n) =>
        println(s"! Falsified after $n passed tests:\n $msg")
      case Passed =>
        println(s"+ OK, passed $testCases tests.")
```

We're taking advantage of default arguments here, which makes the methods more convenient to call. We want a default of enough tests to get good coverage, but we don't want so many that they'll take too long to run.

If we try running check or run on maxProp, we notice that the property fails! Property-based testing has a way of revealing hidden assumptions we have about our code and forcing us to be more explicit about these assumptions. The standard library's implementation of max crashes when given the empty list. We need to fix our property to take this into account.

Define nonEmptyList for generating nonempty lists, and then update your specification of max to use this generator.

Let's try a few more examples.

Write a property to verify the behavior of List.sorted (see the API docs: http://mng
.bz/N4En), which you can use to sort (among other things) a List[Int].[9] For
instance, List(2, 1, 3).sorted is equal to List(1, 2, 3).

8.2.3   *Writing a test suite for parallel computations*

Recall that in chapter 7 we discovered laws that should hold for our parallel computations. Can we express these laws with our library? The first law we looked at was actually a particular test case:

```
unit(1).map(_ + 1) == unit(2)
```

We certainly can express this law for Par, but the result is somewhat complicated:[10]

```
val executor: ExecutorService = Executors.newCachedThreadPool
val p1 = Prop.forAll(Gen.unit(Par.unit(1)))(pi =>
  pi.map(_ + 1).run(executor).get == Par.unit(2).run(executor).get)
```

We've expressed the test, but it's verbose and cluttered, and the idea of the test is obscured by details that aren't relevant here. Notice that this isn't a question of the API being expressive enough—yes, we can express what we want, but a combination of missing helper functions and poor syntax obscures the intent.

PROVING PROPERTIES

Let's improve on this. Our first observation is that forAll is a bit too general for this test case. We aren't varying the input to this test; we just have a hardcoded example. Hardcoded examples should be just as convenient to write as in a traditional unit testing library. Let's introduce a combinator for it (on the Prop companion object):

```
def verify(p: => Boolean): Prop
```

----

[9] sorted takes an implicit Ordering for the elements of the list to control the sorting strategy.
[10] This is using our initial encoding of Par[A] that returns a java.util.concurrent.Future[A] when run.

How would we implement this? One possible way is using `forAll`:

```
def verify(p: => Boolean): Prop =        ◁──── We are nonstrict here.
  lazy val result = p           ◁─────────┐
  forAll(unit(()))(_ => result)           │  The result is memoized
                                             to avoid recomputation.
```

This doesn't seem quite right. We're providing a unit generator that only generates a single value, and then we're proceeding to ignore that value just to drive the evaluation of the given `Boolean`.

Even though we memoize the result so it's not evaluated more than once, the test runner will still generate multiple test cases and test the `Boolean` multiple times. For example, if we say `verify(true).run()`, this will test the property 100 times and print `OK, passed 100 tests`. But checking a property that is always `true` 100 times is a terrible waste of effort. What we need is a new primitive.

Remember that the representation of `Prop` we have so far is just a function of type `(MaxSize, TestCases, RNG) => Result`, where `Result` is either `Passed` or `Falsified`. A simple implementation of a `verify` primitive is constructing a `Prop` that ignores the number of test cases:

```
def verify(p: => Boolean): Prop =
  (_, _, _) => if p then Passed else Falsified("()", 0)
```

This is certainly better than using `forAll`, but `verify(true).run()` will still print `passed 100 tests`, even though it only tests the property once. It's not really true that such a property has passed, in the sense that it remains unfalsified after a number of tests. It is proved after just one test. It seems we want a new kind of `Result`:

```
enum Result:
  case Passed
  case Falsified(failure: FailedCase, successes: SuccessCount)
  case Proved
```

Then we can just return `Proved` instead of `Passed` in a property created by `verify`. We'll need to modify the test runner to take this case into account.

Listing 8.7   Using `run` to handle a `Proved` object

```
extension (self: Prop)
  def run(maxSize: MaxSize = 100,
          testCases: TestCases = 100,
          rng: RNG = RNG.Simple(System.currentTimeMillis)): Unit =
    self(maxSize, testCases, rng) match
      case Falsified(msg, n) =>
        println(s"! Falsified after $n passed tests:\n $msg")
      case Passed =>
        println(s"+ OK, passed $testCases tests.")
      case Proved =>
        println(s"+ OK, proved property.")
```

We also need to modify our implementations of Prop combinators like &&. These changes are quite trivial, since such combinators don't need to distinguish between Passed and Proved results.

EXERCISE 8.15

Hard: A verify property is easy to prove conclusively because the test just involves evaluating the Boolean argument, but some forAll properties can be proved as well. For instance, if the domain of the property is Boolean, then there are really only two cases to test. If a property, forAll(p), passes for both p(true) and p(false), then it is proved. Some domains (e.g., Boolean and Byte) are so small that they can be exhaustively checked, and with sized generators, even infinite domains can be exhaustively checked up to the maximum size. Automated testing is very useful, but it's even better if we can automatically prove our code correct. Modify our library to incorporate this kind of exhaustive checking of finite domains and sized generators. This is less of an exercise and more of an extensive, open-ended design project.

TESTING PAR

Getting back to proving the property that Par.unit(1).map(_ + 1) is equal to Par.unit(2), we can use our new Prop.verify primitive to express this in a way that doesn't obscure the intent:

```
val p2 = Prop.verify:
  val p = Par.unit(1).map(_ + 1)
  val p2 = Par.unit(2)
  p.run(executor).get == p2.run(executor).get
```

This is now pretty clear, but can we do something about the p.run(executor).get and p2.run(executor).get noise? There's something rather unsatisfying about it. For one, we're forcing this code to be aware of the internal implementation details of Par simply to compare two Par values for equality. One improvement is lifting the equality comparison into Par using map2, which means we only need to run a single Par at the end to get our result:

```
def equal[A](p: Par[A], p2: Par[A]): Par[Boolean] =
  p.map2(p2)(_ == _)

val p3 = Prop.verify:
  equal(
    Par.unit(1).map(_ + 1),
    Par.unit(2)
  ).run(executor).get
```

This is a bit nicer than having to run each side separately. We could even use equal in conjunction with forAll:

```
val p4 = Prop.forAll(Gen.smallInt): i =>
  equal(
    Par.unit(i).map(_ + 1),
    Par.unit(i + 1)
  ).run(executor).get
```

But while we're at it, let's move the running of Par out into a separate function: forAllPar. This also gives us a good place to insert variation across different parallel strategies, without it cluttering up the property we're specifying:

```
val executors: Gen[ExecutorService] = weighted(          ◁——————
  choose(1, 4).map(Executors.newFixedThreadPool) -> .75,
  unit(Executors.newCachedThreadPool) -> .25)
——▷

def forAllPar[A](g: Gen[A])(f: A => Par[Boolean]): Prop =
  forAll(executors.map2(g)((_, _)))((s, a) => f(a).run(s).get)
a -> b is syntactic sugar for (a, b).
```

This generator creates a fixed thread pool executor 75% of the time and an unbounded one 25% of the time.

executors.map2(g)((_, _)) is a rather noisy way of combining two generators to produce a pair of their outputs. Let's quickly introduce a combinator to clean that up:[11]

```
extension [A](self: Gen[A])
  @annotation.targetName("product")          ◁——
  def **[B](gb: Gen[B]): Gen[(A, B)] =
    map2(gb)((_, _))
```

The targetName annotation provides an alternative, alphanumeric name for a symbolic operator. It's generally considered good practice to always provide an alphanumeric equivalent for each symbolic operator.

This is much nicer:

```
def forAllPar[A](g: Gen[A])(f: A => Par[Boolean]): Prop =
  forAll(executors ** g)((s, a) => f(a)(s).get)
```

We can even introduce ** as a pattern using a custom extractor, which lets us write this:

```
def forAllPar[A](g: Gen[A])(f: A => Par[Boolean]): Prop =
  forAll(executors ** g):
    case s ** a =>
      f(a)(s).get
```

This syntax works nicely when tupling up multiple generators; when pattern matching, we don't have to nest parentheses like using the tuple pattern directly would require. To enable ** as a pattern, we define an object called ** with an unapply function:

```
object `**`:                        ◁——
  def unapply[A, B](p: (A, B)) = Some(p)
```

The backticks around ** are escapes, not part of the object name.

---

[11] Calling this ** is actually appropriate since this function is taking the *product* of two generators, in the sense we discussed in chapter 3.

See the custom extractors documentation (http://mng.bz/4pUc) for more details on this technique. So executors is a Gen[ExecutorService] that will vary over fixed-size thread pools from 1–4 threads and consider an unbounded thread pool. Now our property looks a lot cleaner:[12]

```
def verifyPar(p: Par[Boolean]): Prop =
  forAllPar(Gen.unit(()))(_ => p)

val p2 = verifyPar:
  equal(
    Par.unit(1).map(_ + 1),
    Par.unit(2)
  )
```

A variant of verify, which takes a Par[Boolean] and uses various executors to evaluate the property

These might seem like minor changes, but this sort of factoring and cleanup can greatly improve the usability of our library, and the helper functions we've written make the properties easier to read and more pleasant to write. You may want to add a forAllPar version for sized generators as well.

Let's look at some other properties from chapter 7. Recall that we generalized our test case:

```
unit(x).map(f) == unit(f(x))
```

We then simplified it to the law that mapping the identity function over a computation should have no effect:

```
y.map(x => x) == y
```

Can we express this? Not exactly. This property implicitly states that equality holds for all choices of y as well as for all types. We're forced to pick particular values for y:

```
val gpy: Gen[Par[Int]] = Gen.choose(0,10).map(Par.unit(_))
val p5 = Prop.forAllPar(gpy)(py => equal(py.map(y => y), py))
```

We can certainly range over more choices of y, but what we have here is probably good enough. The implementation of map can't care about the values of our parallel computation, so there isn't much point in constructing the same test for Double, String, and so on. The structure of the parallel computation could affect map. If we wanted greater assurance that our property held, we could provide richer generators for the structure. Here we're only supplying Par expressions with one level of nesting.

---

[12] We can't use the standard Java/Scala equals method or == method in Scala (which delegates to the equals method) since that method returns a Boolean directly, and we need to return a Par[Boolean].

■ **EXERCISE 8.16**

Hard: Write a richer generator for `Par[Int]` that builds more deeply nested parallel computations than the simple ones we gave previously.

■ **EXERCISE 8.17**

Express the property about `fork` from chapter 7—that `fork(x) == x`.

8.3   *Testing higher-order functions and future directions*

So far, our library seems quite expressive, but there's one area where it's lacking: we don't currently have a good way to test higher-order functions. While we have lots of ways of generating data using our generators, we don't really have a good way of generating functions.

For instance, let's consider the `takeWhile` function defined for `List` and `LazyList`. Recall that this function returns the longest prefix of its input whose elements all satisfy a predicate—for instance, `List(1, 2, 3).takeWhile(_ < 3)` results in `List(1, 2)`. A simple property we'd like to check is that for any list, as: `List[A]`, and any `f: A => Boolean`, the expression `as.takeWhile(f).forall(f)` evaluates to `true`. That is, every element in the returned list satisfies the predicate.[13]

■ **EXERCISE 8.18**

Come up with some other properties that `takeWhile` should satisfy. Can you think of a good property expressing the relationship between `takeWhile` and `dropWhile`?

☐ **EXERCISE 8.19**

Hard: We want to generate a function that uses its argument in some way to select which `Int` to return. Can you think of a good way of expressing this? This is a very open-ended and challenging design exercise. See what you can discover about this problem and if there's a nice general solution you can incorporate into the library we've developed so far.

---

[13] In the Scala standard library, `forall` is a method on `List` and `LazyList` with the signature `def forall [A](f: A => Boolean): Boolean`.

Try venturing out and using the library we've developed! See what else you can test with it, and see if you discover any new idioms for its use or perhaps ways it could be extended further or made more convenient. Here are a few ideas to get you started:

- Write properties to specify the behavior of some of the other functions we wrote for List and LazyList—for instance, take, drop, filter, and unfold.
- Write a sized generator for producing the Tree data type defined in chapter 3, and then use this to specify the behavior of the fold function we defined for Tree. Can you think of any ways of improving the API to make this easier?
- Write properties specifying the behavior of the sequence function we defined for Option and Either.

8.4   *The laws of generators*

Isn't it interesting that many of the functions we've implemented for our Gen type look quite similar to other functions we defined on Par, List, LazyList, and Option? As an example, for Par we defined this:

```
extension [A](pa: Par[A]) def map[B](f: A => B): Par[B]
```

And in this chapter, we defined map for Gen:

```
extension [A](ga: Gen[A]) def map[B](f: A => B): Gen[B]
```

We've also defined similar-looking functions for Option, List, LazyList, and State. We have to wonder whether our functions merely share similar-looking signatures, or they also satisfy the same laws. Let's look at a law we introduced for Par in chapter 7:

```
y.map(id) == y
```

Does this law hold for our implementation of Gen.map? What about for LazyList, List, Option, and State? Yes, it does! Try it and see. This indicates that not only do these functions share similar-looking signatures, but they also, in some sense, have analogous meanings in their respective domains. It appears there are deeper forces at work! We're uncovering some fundamental patterns that cut across domains. In part 3, we'll learn the names of these patterns, discover the laws that govern them, and understand what it all means.

8.5 Conclusion

In this chapter, we worked through another extended exercise in functional library design, using the domain of property-based testing as inspiration. We reiterate that our goal is not necessarily learning about property-based testing but highlighting particular aspects of functional design.

First, we saw that oscillating between the abstract algebra and the concrete representation lets the two inform each other. This avoids overfitting the library to a particular representation and prevents us from ending up with a floating abstraction disconnected from the end goal. Second, we noticed that this domain led us to discover many of the same combinators we've now seen a few times before: map, flatMap, and so on. Not only are the signatures of these functions analogous, but the laws satisfied by the implementations are analogous too. There are a great many seemingly distinct problems being solved in the world of software, but the space of functional solutions is much smaller. Many libraries are just simple combinations of certain fundamental structures that appear repeatedly across a variety of different domains. This provides an opportunity for code reuse that we'll exploit in part 3 when we learn both the names of some of these structures and how to spot more general abstractions.

In the next and final chapter of part 2, we'll look at another domain, *parsing*, which has its own unique challenges. We'll take a slightly different approach in that chapter, but once again, familiar patterns will emerge.

Summary

- Properties of our APIs can be automatically tested and, in some cases, proven using property-based testing.
- A property can be expressed as a function that takes arbitrary input values and asserts a desired outcome based on those inputs.
- In the library developed in this chapter, the Prop type is used to model these properties.
- Properties defined in this way assert various invariants about the functionality being tested—things that should be true for all possible input values. An example of such a property is that reversing a list and then summing the elements should be the same as summing the original list.
- Defining properties for arbitrary input values requires a way of generating such values.
- In the library developed in this chapter, the Gen and SGen types are used for arbitrary value generation.
- Test case minimization is the ability of a property-based testing library to find the smallest input values that fail a property.
- Exhaustive test case generation is the ability to generate all possible inputs to a property. This is only possible for finite domains and only practically possible when the size of the domain is small.

- If every possible input to a property is tested and all pass, then the property is proved true. If instead, the property simply does not fail for any of the generated inputs, then the property is passed. There might still be some input that wasn't generated but fails the property.
- Combinators like map and flatMap continue to appear in data types we create, and their implementations satisfy the same laws.

8.6   Exercise answers

ANSWER 8.1

- The sum of the empty list is 0—sum(Nil) == 0.
- The sum of a list whose elements are all equal to x is the list's size multiplied by x—sum(List.fill(n)(x)) == n * x.
- For any list xs, its sum is equal to the sum of xs.reverse; that is, sum(xs) == sum(xs.reverse). This follows from the fact that addition is commutative.
- For any list xs, partitioning it into two lists, summing each partitioning, and then adding the sums yields the same result as summing xs. This follows from the fact that addition is associative.
- The sum of the list with elements 1, 2, 3…n is n*(n+1)/2.

ANSWER 8.2

- The max of an empty list is an error.
- The max of a single element list is that element.
- The max of a list whose elements are all equal to x is x.
- The max of a list is an element in the list.
- The max of a list is greater than or equal to every element in the list.

ANSWER 8.3

Now that check returns a Boolean, we can implement && to call check on the first property and, if that passes, call check on the argument:

```
trait Prop:
  self =>                    ◁─────────┐  This syntax introduces an alias for
  def check: Boolean                   │  this, which we need later to refer
  def &&(that: Prop): Prop =           │  to the outer Prop instance.
    new Prop:
      def check = self.check && that.check
```

We can implement choose by first generating a random nonnegative integer and then shifting that integer into the requested range. Since Gen[A] is an opaque type for a State[RNG, A], we must return a state action, where RNG is the state type.

Recall the nonNegativeInt function we wrote in chapter 6, which has the signature def nonNegativeInt(rng: RNG): (Int, RNG). We can wrap that function with State to get a state action that generates a nonnegative integer. Then we can map over that with a function that shifts the integer to the right range:

```
def choose(start: Int, stopExclusive: Int): Gen[Int] =
  State(RNG.nonNegativeInt).map(n => start + n % (stopExclusive - start))
```

The implementation of unit can directly reuse State.unit, given that Gen[A] is equivalent to State[RNG, A]:

```
def unit[A](a: => A): Gen[A] =
  State.unit(a)
```

Likewise, boolean can reuse the definition of RNG.boolean, which has the signature def boolean(rng: RNG): (Boolean, RNG). As with nonNegativeInt, we simply need to wrap it into a state action:

```
def boolean: Gen[Boolean] =
  State(RNG.boolean)
```

The trickiest is listOfN. We first create a list of n elements, where each element is the supplied generator. Doing so gives us a List[Gen[A]], but since Gen[A] = State[RNG, A], this is really a List[State[RNG, A]]. With that knowledge, we can use State.sequence to flip the position of the Gen and List, giving us the needed Gen[List[A]]:

```
extension [A](self: Gen[A]) def listOfN(n: Int): Gen[List[A]] =
  State.sequence(List.fill(n)(self))
```

We can directly reuse the flatMap operation on State—with a catch. The flatMap extension method we are defining takes precedence over the flatMap extension method on State. Hence, the natural expression ga.flatMap(f) does not call the flatMap on State but rather results in infinite recursion. We can indicate that we really want the method defined on State by directly calling the extension method:

```
extension [A](self: Gen[A]) def flatMap[B](f: A => Gen[B]): Gen[B] =
  State.flatMap(self)(f)
```

Using flatMap, we can then implement the variant of listOfN, which takes a size as a Gen[Int] in terms of the listOfN method we defined earlier, which takes an integer size parameter:

```
extension [A](self: Gen[A]) def listOfN(size: Gen[Int]): Gen[List[A]] =
  size.flatMap(listOfN)
```

ANSWER 8.7

Since we want equal likelihood, we can use the boolean generator we defined earlier as a coin flip, selecting g1 when getting a true and g2 when false. We use flatMap on boolean to be able to access the coin flip result when selecting the subsequent generator:

```
def union[A](g1: Gen[A], g2: Gen[A]): Gen[A] =
  boolean.flatMap(b => if b then g1 else g2)
```

ANSWER 8.8

weighted can be implemented in a similar fashion to union, except instead of a coin flip, we compute the probability [0, 1). We then select g1 when the generated probability is less than the normalized weighting:

```
def weighted[A](g1: (Gen[A], Double), g2: (Gen[A], Double)): Gen[A]
  val g1Threshold = g1(1).abs / (g1(1).abs + g2(1).abs)
  State(RNG.double).flatMap(d => if d < g1Threshold then g1(0) else g2(0))
```

ANSWER 8.9

To implement &&, we can return a function that first runs the property on the left-hand side of && and, if that is successful, then runs the property on the right-hand side:

```
extension (self: Prop) def &&(that: Prop): Prop =
  (n, rng) => self(n, rng) match
    case Passed => that(n, rng)
    case x => x
```

We can implement || in a similar fashion, running the left property first and then only running the right property if the left fails:

```
extension (self: Prop) def ||(that: Prop): Prop =
  (n, rng) => self(n, rng) match
    case Falsified(_, _) => that(n, rng)
    case x => x
```

Let's also define a way of running our properties so we can experiment with them in the REPL (we'll expand on this notion of checking and running properties later in the chapter; for now, we just want a way of invoking the underlying function and printing the result):

```
extension (self: Prop)
  def run(): Unit =
    self(100, RNG.Simple(System.currentTimeMillis)) match
      case Falsified(msg, n) =>
        println(s"! Falsified after $n passed tests:\n $msg")
      case Passed =>
        println(s"+ OK, passed $testCases tests.")
```

The run() method evaluates the property with 100 test cases and an RNG initialized with the current time. It then prints the results to the console.

The implementations of && and || work but don't provide enough information when a failure occurs. Consider the following examples, where p is a property that always passes and q is a property that randomly fails:

```
val p: Prop = Prop.forAll(Gen.boolean)(x => x == x)
val q: Prop = Prop.forAll(Gen.boolean)(x => x)
```

When running composite properties built with && and ||, we don't get any information about which constituent property caused the failure:

```
scala> (p && q).run()
! Falsified after 4 passed tests:
 false

scala> (q && p).run()
! Falsified after 1 passed tests:
 false

scala> (q || q).run()
! Falsified after 2 passed tests:
 false
```

We can address this by adding a tag combinator to Prop, which decorates the error message returned in the Falsified case:

```
extension (self: Prop) def tag(msg: String): Prop =
  (n, rng) => self(n, rng) match
    case Falsified(e, c) => Falsified(FailedCase.fromString(s"$msg($e)"), c)
    case x => x
```

This implementation wraps the original error message with the message passed to tag, though a more sophisticated implementation could change the Falsified type to store a richer data structure, like a stack or tree of expressions. We also need to remember to use tag in the implementation of && and ||:

```
extension (self: Prop) def &&(that: Prop): Prop =
  (n, rng) => self.tag("and-left")(n, rng) match
    case Passed => that.tag("and-right")(n, rng)
    case x => x

extension (self: Prop) def ||(that: Prop): Prop =
  (n, rng) => self.tag("or-left")(n, rng) match
    case Falsified(msg, _) =>
      that.tag("or-right").tag(msg.string)(n, rng)
    case x => x
```

Our error messages now give a hint about which parts of our properties are failing:

```
scala> (p && q).run()
! Falsified after 4 passed tests:
 and-right(false)

scala> (q && p).run()
! Falsified after 1 passed tests:
 and-left(false)

scala> (q || q).run()
! Falsified after 2 passed tests:
 or-left(false)(or-right(false))
```

■ ANSWER 8.10

Since SGen is just a function from a size to a Gen, we can return an anonymous function that ignores the size parameter:

```
extension [A](self: Gen[A]) def unsized: SGen[A] =
  _ => self
```

□ ANSWER 8.11

Let's first implement map:

```
extension [A](self: SGen[A]) def map[B](f: A => B): SGen[B] =
  n => self(n).map(f)
```

The implementation can be determined solely by following the types. We need to return an SGen[B], so we build an anonymous function from a size (n) to a Gen[B]. To get a Gen[B] we apply the size parameter to the original SGen[A], giving us a Gen[A]. Finally, we use our map function on Gen to convert that Gen[A] to a Gen[B]. This type-guided implementation is what we mean by *mechanical*.

Let's do one more—flatMap:

```
extension [A](self: SGen[A]) def flatMap[B](f: A => SGen[B]): SGen[B] =
  n => self(n).flatMap(a => f(a)(n))
```

Using the same technique, we return an anonymous function that takes a size and returns a Gen[B]. We apply the size to our original SGen[A], giving us a Gen[A]. We call flatMap on that Gen[A], but we can't just pass f to flatMap like we did with map; flatMap wants a function A => Gen[B]. So we pass a function that first applies a to f, returning an SGen[B] and then applying the size parameter to that SGen[B] to convert it to a Gen[B].

■ ANSWER 8.12

We can return an anonymous function that takes a size as an argument and applies it to the listOfN method we wrote earlier:

```
extension [A](self: Gen[A]) def list: SGen[List[A]] =
  n => self.listOfN(n)
```

■ ANSWER 8.13

We can use the same implementation as we used for listOf but with a check to ensure the size passed to listOfN is at least 1:

```
extension [A](self: Gen[A]) def nonEmptyList: SGen[List[A]] =
  n => listOfN(n.max(1))

val maxProp = Prop.forAll(smallInt.nonEmptyList): ns =>
  val max = ns.max
  !ns.exists(_ > max)

scala> maxProp.run()
+ OK, passed 100 tests.
```

The output of sorting an arbitrary list should be a list for which each element is less than or equal to the next element. We can write this as a property by zipping the elements of a list with its tail and then verifying that every pair adheres to this ordering requirement. We also need to verify that the sorted list has all the elements in the original list and no other elements:

```
val sortedProp = Prop.forAll(smallInt.list): l =>
  val ls = l.sorted
  val ordered = l.isEmpty || ls.zip(ls.tail).forall((a, b) => a <= b)
  ordered && l.forall(ls.contains) && ls.forall(l.contains)
```

We can augment Gen[A] with the ability to exhaustively list the members of the domain, while retaining the ability to select random samples and describe infinite domains. One such encoding is pairing a random generator with an exhaustive list of elements:

```
case class Gen[+A](sample: State[RNG, A], exhaustive: LazyList[Option[A]])
```

Here we've chosen to model a finite, exhaustive list of domain elements as a lazy list of options. The list provides each value of the domain wrapped in a Some, until we've enumerated every element, and then returns an empty list. For infinite domains, we set exhaustive to a list of a single None, indicating that the domain was not exhaustively enumerated.

Can we implement map2 for this new version of Gen? Yes! Let's take a look:

```
case class Gen[+A](sample: State[RNG, A], exhaustive: LazyList[Option[A]]):
  def map2[B, C](g: Gen[B])(f: (A, B) => C): Gen[C] =
    Gen(sample.map2(g.sample)(f),
        map2LazyList(exhaustive, g.exhaustive)(map2Option(_,_)(f)))
```

Here we use map2 on LazyList and Option to combine the exhaustive values.[14] This is pretty powerful! We can generate the Cartesian product of two or more exhaustive generators.

Next we need to modify forAll to use this new Gen type. Remember that a Prop is a function from (MaxSize, TestCases, RNG) to Result. Of particular interest is the TestCases argument, which may be smaller than the number of elements in the domain. We should respect the specified number of test cases when running a property.

---

[14] The definitions of map2LazyList and map2Option are elided here (see Exhaustive.scala in the answer source code accompanying this chapter).

If the size of the domain is less than the specified number of test cases, we can definitively prove our property. Otherwise, we can only claim we did not find a failing test case, given the test cases we ran. Hence, we'll slightly change the way we model the result of a property test to provide us this expressiveness:

```
enum Status:
  case Proven, Unfalsified

enum Result:
  case Falsified(failure: FailedCase)
  case Passed(status: Status, testCases: TestCases)
```

Property results are now represented as either having been falsified or having passed after a certain number of test cases, along with an indicator showing whether the property was proven or simply not falsified.

Returning to `forAll`, we need to decide on a strategy for test cases. One option is first running all the samples in the exhausted list, up to the specified number of test cases. If we reach the end of that list without encountering a `None` or a failure when evaluating a sample, then we've proven the property, since we've tested against every element of the domain. If instead we encounter a `None`, we can generate the necessary additional test cases randomly using `sample`.

There's a problem with this approach, though. If the `TestCases` argument is smaller than the size of the domain, then we'll run the same test cases every time we run the property. We can address this by limiting how many elements we use from the exhaustive list before switching to random samples. In the following implementation of `forAll`, we've decided to take a third of the test cases from the exhaustive list and the remainder as random samples:

```
def forAll[A](a: Gen[A])(f: A => Boolean): Prop =
  (max, n, rng) =>
    def go(i: Int, j: Int, l: LazyList[Option[A]],
           onEnd: Int => Result
    ): Result =
      if i == j then Passed(Unfalsified, i)
      else l match
        case Some(h) #:: t =>
          try
            if f(h) then go(i+1, j, t, onEnd)
            else Falsified(h.toString)
          catch
            case e: Exception => Falsified(buildMsg(h, e))
        case None #:: _ => Passed(Unfalsified, i)
        case _ => onEnd(i)
    val numFromExhaustiveList = TestCases.fromInt(n.toInt / 3)
    go(0, numFromExhaustiveList, a.exhaustive, i => Passed(Proven, i)) match
      case Passed(Unfalsified, _) =>
        val rands = randomLazyList(a)(rng).map(Some(_))
        go(numFromExhaustiveList, n, rands, i => Passed(Unfalsified, i))
      case s => s // If proven or failed, stop immediately
```

Here's a sample usage:

```
scala> val andCommutative =
          Prop.forAll(Gen.boolean.map2(Gen.boolean)((_, _))):
            (p, q) => (p && q) == (q && p))

scala> andCommutative.run()
+ OK, property proven, ran 4 tests.
```

The source code in the accompanying GitHub repository extends this solution to cover sized generators.

___

ANSWER 8.16

One technique is generating a `List[Int]` and then folding that list into a single `Par[Int]`, where each combination forks the computation:

```
val gpy2: Gen[Par[Int]] =
  choose(-100, 100).listOfN(choose(0, 20)).map(ys =>
    ys.foldLeft(Par.unit(0))((p, y) =>
      Par.fork(p.map2(Par.unit(y))(_ + _))))
```

We create a `Gen[List[Int]]` via `choose(-100, 100).listOfN(choose(0, 20))`. We then map over that generator and reduce the list to a single `Par[Unit]` by using `fork` and `map2`. We could extract a new generic function on lists, `parTraverse`, and use it to implement our generator:

```
extension [A](self: List[A])
  def parTraverse[B](f: A => Par[B]): Par[List[B]] =
    self.foldRight(Par.unit(Nil: List[B]))((a, pacc) =>
      Par.fork(f(a).map2(pacc)(_ :: _)))

val gpy3: Gen[Par[Int]] =
  choose(-100, 100).listOfN(choose(0, 20)).map(ys =>
    ys.parTraverse(Par.unit).map(_.sum))
```

___

ANSWER 8.17

We can express this directly via `forAllPar` and the `Gen[Par[Int]]` that we've previously written:

```
val forkProp = Prop.forAllPar(gpy2)(y => equal(Par.fork(y), y))
```

■ **ANSWER 8.18**

Requiring `as.takeWhile(f).forall(f) == true` doesn't enforce `takeWhile` returning the longest possible prefix for which the property holds. To verify that, we could introduce another property that says that the head of the remaining list, if not empty, must fail the predicate—something like `!f(as(as.takeWhile(f).size))`, but handling the case where `as.size == as.takeWhile(f).size`. Another property describes how `takeWhile` and `dropWhile` relate: concatenating the result of calling `takeWhile` with the result of calling `dropWhile` on the same list should result in that same list.

If we try writing any of these properties using our library, we'll run into a problem. Each of these properties requires a `Gen[Int => Boolean]`, but we don't have a way of generating functions.

We could certainly take the approach of only examining particular arguments when testing higher-order functions. For instance, here's a more specific property for `takeWhile`:

```
def isEven(i: Int) = i % 2 == 0
val takeWhileProp =
  Prop.forAll(Gen.int.list)(ys => ys.takeWhile(isEven).forall(isEven))
```

This works, but is there a way we could let the testing framework handle generating functions to use with `takeWhile`?[15] Let's consider our options. To make this concrete, let's suppose we have a `Gen[Int]` and would like to produce a `Gen[String => Int]`. What are some ways we could do that? One option is by producing `String => Int` functions that simply ignore their input string and delegate to the underlying `Gen[Int]`:

```
def genStringIntFn(g: Gen[Int]): Gen[String => Int] =
  g.map(i => (s => i))
```

This approach isn't sufficient, though; we're simply generating constant functions that ignore their input. In the case of `takeWhile`, where we need a function that returns a `Boolean`, this will be a function that always returns `true` or always returns `false`—which is clearly not very interesting for testing the behavior of our function.

---

[15] Recall that in chapter 7 we introduced the idea of free theorems and discussed how parametricity frees us from having to inspect the behavior of a function for every type of argument. Still, there are many situations where being able to generate functions for testing is useful.

Let's start by looking at the signature of our motivating example, generating a function from `String => Int`, given a `Gen[Int]`:

```
def genStringIntFn(g: Gen[Int]): Gen[String => Int]
```

Now let's generalize this a bit so it isn't specialized to `Int`, because that would let us cheat (by, say, returning the `hashCode` of the input `String`, which just so happens to be an `Int`):

```
def genStringFn[A](g: Gen[A]): Gen[String => A]
```

We've already ruled out just returning a function that ignores the input `String`, since that's not very interesting! Instead, we want to make sure we use information from the input `String` to influence which `A` we generate. How can we do that? The only way we can have any influence on what value a `Gen` produces is by modifying the `RNG` value it receives as input.

Recall our definition of `Gen`:

```
opaque type Gen[+A] = State[RNG, A]
```

Just by following the types, we can start writing the following:

```
def genStringFn[A](g: Gen[A]): Gen[String => A] =
  State[RNG, String => A]: rng => ???
```

`???` has to be of type `(String => A, RNG)`, and moreover, we want `String` to somehow affect which `A` is generated. We do that by modifying the seed of the `RNG` before passing it to the `Gen[A]` sample function. A simple way of doing this is computing the hash of the input string and mixing this into the `RNG` state before using it to produce an `A`:

```
def genStringFn[A](g: Gen[A]): Gen[String => A] =
  State[RNG, String => A]: rng =>
    val (seed, rng2) = rng.nextInt         ◄——————  We still use rng to produce a
    val f = (s: String) =>                           seed, so we get a new function
      g.run(RNG.Simple(seed.toLong ^ s.hashCode.toLong))(0)   each time.
    (f, rng2)
```

More generally, any function that takes a `String` and an `RNG` and produces a new `RNG` could be used. Here we're computing the `hashCode` of the `String` and then using exclusive or (XOR) with a seed value to produce a new `RNG`. We could just as easily take the length of the `String` and use this value to perturb our `RNG` state or take the first three characters of the string. The choices affect what type of function we are producing:

- If we use hashCode to perturb the RNG state, the function we are generating uses all the information of the String to influence the A value generated. Only input strings that share the same hashCode are guaranteed to produce the same A.
- If we use the length, the function we are generating is only using some of the information of the String to influence the A being generated. For all input strings that have the same length, we are guaranteed to get the same A.

The strategy we pick depends on what functions we think are realistic for our tests. Do we want functions that use all available information to produce a result, or are we more interested in functions that use only bits and pieces of their input? We can wrap the policy up in a type:

```
opaque type Cogen[-A] = (A, RNG) => RNG
```

With this new type, we can generalize genStringFn to work for any input type:

```
def fn[A, B](in: Cogen[A], out: Gen[B]): Gen[A => B] =
  State[RNG, A => B]: rng =>
    val (seed, rng2) = rng.nextInt
    val f = (a: A) => out.run(in(a, rng2))(0)
    (f, rng2)
```

One problem with this approach is reporting test case failures back to the user. In the event of a failure, all the user will see is that for some opaque function, the property failed, which isn't very enlightening. There's been work in the Haskell Free Library QuickCheck (http://mng.bz/MvYW) to be able to report back to the user and even shrink down the generated functions to the simplest form that still falsifies the property. See Malcolm Wallace's talk on shrinking and showing functions from the Haskell Symposium 2012 for more information: http://mng.bz/aZq7.

ANSWER 8.20

The source code in the accompanying GitHub repository uses the library developed in this chapter to unit test the exercises that appear throughout this book. Take a look at how various properties are tested.

Parser combinators 9

This chapter covers

- Introducing parser combinators
- Designing and using APIs without implementations

In this chapter, we'll work through the design of a combinator library for creating *parsers*. We'll use JSON parsing (http://mng.bz/DpNA) as a motivating use case. Like chapters 7 and 8, this chapter is not so much about parsing as it is about providing further insight into the process of functional design.

What is a parser?
A parser is a specialized program that takes unstructured data (e.g., text or any kind of stream of symbols, numbers, or tokens) as input, and outputs a structured representation of that data. For example, we can write a parser to turn a comma-separated file into a list of lists, where the elements of the outer list represent the records, and the elements of each inner list represent the comma-separated fields of each record. Another example is a parser that takes an XML or JSON document and turns it into a tree-like data structure.

In a parser combinator library like the one we'll build in this chapter, a parser doesn't have to be anything quite that complicated, and it doesn't have to parse entire documents. It can do something as elementary as recognize a single character in the input. We then use combinators to assemble composite parsers from elementary ones and still more complex parsers from those.

This chapter will introduce a design approach we'll call *algebraic design*. This is just a natural evolution of what we've already done to different degrees in past chapters— designing our interface first, along with associated laws, and letting this guide our choice of data type representations.

At a few key points during this chapter, we'll provide more open-ended exercises intended to mimic the scenarios you might encounter when writing your own libraries from scratch. You'll get the most out of this chapter if you use these opportunities to put the book down and spend some time investigating possible approaches. When you design your own libraries, you won't be handed a nicely chosen sequence of type signatures to fill in with implementations. You'll have to make the decisions about what types and combinators you need, and a goal of part 2 of this book has been preparing you to do this on your own. As always, if you get stuck on one of the exercises or want some more ideas, you can keep reading or consult the answers. It may also be a good idea to do these exercises with another person or compare notes with other readers online.

Parser combinators versus parser generators

You might be familiar with *parser generator* libraries, like Yacc (http://mng.bz/w3zZ), or similar libraries in other languages (e.g., ANTLR in Java: http://mng.bz/aj8K). These libraries generate code for a parser based on a specification of the grammar. This approach works fine and can be quite efficient, but it comes with all the usual problems of code generation: the libraries produce as their output a monolithic chunk of code that's difficult to debug. It's also difficult to reuse fragments of logic since we can't introduce new combinators or helper functions to abstract over common patterns in our parsers.

In a parser combinator library, parsers are just ordinary first-class values. The resulting parsers tend to be slower than those generated by tools like Yacc and ANTLR, and we need to reimplement the grammar in terms of the parser combinators. Reusing parsing logic is trivial, though, and we don't need any sort of external tool separate from our programming language.

9.1 Designing an algebra first

Recall that we defined an *algebra* as a collection of functions operating over some data type(s), along with a set of laws specifying relationships between these functions. In past chapters, we moved rather fluidly between inventing functions in our algebra, refining the set of functions, and tweaking our data type representations. Laws were somewhat of an afterthought; we worked out the laws only after we had a representation and an API fleshed out. There's nothing wrong with this style of design,[1] but here we'll take a different approach. We'll start with the algebra (including its laws) and decide on a representation later. This approach—let's call it *algebraic design*—can be used for any design problem but works particularly well for parsing because it's easy to imagine what combinators are required for parsing different kinds of inputs.[2] This lets us keep an eye on the concrete goal even as we defer deciding on a representation.

There are many different kinds of parsing libraries.[3] Ours will be designed for expressiveness (we'd like to be able to parse arbitrary grammars), speed, and good error reporting—this last point is important. Whenever we run a parser on input that it doesn't expect, which can happen if the input is malformed, it should generate a parse error. If there are parse errors, we want to be able to point out exactly where the error is in the input and accurately indicate its cause. Error reporting is often an afterthought in parsing libraries, but we'll make sure we give it careful attention.

OK, let's begin. For simplicity and for speed, our library will create parsers that operate on strings as input.[4] We need to pick some parsing tasks to help us discover a good algebra for our parsers. What should we look at first? Something practical like parsing an email address, JSON, or HTML? No! These tasks can come later. A good and simple domain to start with is parsing various combinations of repeated letters and gibberish words like "abracadabra" and "abba". As silly as this sounds, we've seen before how simple examples like this help us ignore extraneous details and focus on the essence of the problem.

So let's start with the simplest of parsers: one that recognizes the single character input 'a'. As in past chapters, we can just invent a combinator for the task—char:

```
def char(c: Char): Parser[Char]
```

What have we done here? We've conjured up a type, Parser, which is parameterized on a single parameter, indicating the *result type* of the Parser. That is, running a parser shouldn't simply yield a yes/no response; if it succeeds, we want to get a result that has some useful type, and if it fails, we expect information about the failure. The

---

[1] For more about different functional design approaches, see the chapter notes (https://github.com/fpinscala/fpinscala/wiki) for this chapter.

[2] As we'll see, there's a connection between algebras for parsers and the classes of languages (i.e., regular, context-free, and context-sensitive) studied by computer science.

[3] The Scala standard library used to include a parser combinator library, though it was moved to its own repository and is now community maintained. There are many other popular open source parser combinator libraries, offering a wide range of features, including cats-parse and FastParse. As in the previous chapter, we're deriving our own library from first principles, partially for pedagogical purposes as well as to further encourage the idea that no library is authoritative.

[4] This is certainly a simplifying design choice. We can make the parsing library more generic at some cost. See the chapter notes (https://github.com/fpinscala/fpinscala/wiki) for more discussion.

char('a') parser will succeed only if the input is exactly the character 'a', and it will return that same character 'a' as its result.

This talk of *running a parser* makes it clear that our algebra needs to be extended somehow to support that. Let's invent another function for it:

```
extension [A](p: Parser[A]) def run(input: String): Either[ParseError, A]
```

Wait a minute; what is ParseError? It's another type we just conjured into existence! At this point, we don't care about the representation of ParseError—or Parser, for that matter. We're in the process of specifying an interface that happens to make use of two types, whose representation or implementation details we choose to remain ignorant of for now. Let's make this explicit with a trait:

```
trait Parsers[ParseError, Parser[+_]]:      ←———————⎤ Parser is a type parameter
                                                     ⎟ that itself is a covariant
                                                     ⎦ type constructor.
  extension [A](p: Parser[A]) def run(input: String): Either[ParseError, A]

  def char(c: Char): Parser[Char]      ←———⎤ Here the Parser type constructor
                                            ⎦ is applied to Char.
```

What's with the funny Parser[+_] type argument? It's not too important for now, but that's Scala's syntax for a type parameter that is itself a type constructor.[5] Making Parse-Error a type argument lets the Parsers interface work for any representation of ParseError, and making Parser[+_] a type parameter means the interface works for any representation of Parser. The underscore just means that whatever Parser is, it expects one type argument to represent the type of the result, as in Parser[Char]. This code will compile as is. We don't need to pick a representation for ParseError or Parser, and we can continue placing additional combinators in the body of this trait.

Our char function should satisfy an obvious law: for any Char, c

```
char(c).run(c.toString) == Right(c)
```

Let's continue. We can recognize the single character 'a', but what if we want to recognize the string "abracadabra"? We don't have a way of recognizing entire strings right now, so let's add that:

```
def string(s: String): Parser[String]
```

Likewise, this should satisfy an obvious law: for any String, s

```
string(s).run(s) == Right(s)
```

What if we want to recognize either the string "abra" or the string "cadabra"? We could add a very specialized combinator for it:

```
def orString(s1: String, s2: String): Parser[String]
```

---

[5] We'll say much more about this in the next few chapters.

But choosing between two parsers seems like something that would be more generally useful, regardless of their result type, so let's make this polymorphic:

```
extension [A](p: Parser[A]) def or(p2: Parser[A]): Parser[A]
```

We expect that `string("abra").or(string("cadabra"))` will succeed whenever either `string` parser succeeds:

```
string("abra").or(string("cadabra")).run("abra") == Right("abra")
string("abra").or(string("cadabra")).run("cadabra") == Right("cadabra")
```

Incidentally, we can give this `or` combinator nice infix syntax, like `s1 | s2` or, alternately, `s1 or s2`.

Listing 9.1 Adding infix syntax to parsers

```
trait Parsers[ParseError, Parser[+_]]:
  def char(c: Char): Parser[Char]
  def string(s: String): Parser[String]

  extension [A](p: Parser[A])
    def run(input: String): Either[ParseError, A]

    infix def or(p2: Parser[A]): Parser[A]
    def |(p2: Parser[A]): Parser[A] = p.or(p2)
```

The infix modifier allows or to be used as an operator.

The | operator is an alias for or. There's no need for an infix modifier because all symbolic names are operators.

We haven't yet picked a representation of `Parser`, but given a value `P` of type `Parsers`, writing `import P.*` lets us write expressions like `string("abra") | string("cadabra")` to create parsers. This will work for all implementations of `Parsers`. We'll use the `a | b` syntax liberally throughout the rest of this chapter.

We can now recognize various strings, but we don't have a way of talking about repetition. For instance, how would we recognize three repetitions of our `string("abra")` | `string("cadabra")` parser? Once again, let's add a combinator for it:[6]

```
extension [A](p: Parser[A]) def listOfN(n: Int): Parser[List[A]]
```

We made `listOfN` parametric in the choice of `A` since it doesn't seem like it should care whether we have a `Parser[String]`, a `Parser[Char]`, or some other type of parser. Here are some examples of what we expect from `listOfN`:

```
val p = (string("ab") | string("cad")).listOfN(3)
p.run("ababcad") == Right(List("ab", "ab", "cad"))
p.run("cadabab") == Right(List("cad", "ab", "ab"))
p.run("ababab") == Right(List("ab", "ab", "ab"))
```

---

[6] This should remind you of a similar function we wrote in the previous chapter.

At this point, we've just been collecting required combinators, but we haven't tried to refine our algebra into a minimal set of primitives, and we haven't talked much about more general laws. We'll start doing this next, but rather than give the game away, we'll ask you to examine a few more simple use cases yourself and try designing a minimal algebra with associated laws. This should be a challenging exercise, but enjoy struggling with it, and see what you can come up with.

Here are additional parsing tasks to consider, along with some guiding questions:

- *A* Parser[Int] *that recognizes zero or more* 'a' *characters and whose result value is the number of* 'a' *characters it has seen*—For instance, given "aa", the parser results in 2; given "" or "b123" (a string not starting with 'a'), it results in 0; and so on.

- *A* Parser[Int] *that recognizes one or more* 'a' *characters and whose result value is the number of 'a' characters it has seen*—(Is this defined somehow in terms of the same combinators as the parser for 'a' repeated zero or more times?) The parser should fail when given a string without a starting 'a'. How would you like to handle error reporting in this case? Could the API support giving an explicit message like "Expected one or more 'a'" in the case of failure?

- *A parser that recognizes zero or more* 'a' *followed by one or more* 'b' *and which results in the pair of counts of characters seen*—For instance, given "bbb", we get (0, 3), given "aaaab" we get (4, 1), and so on.

There are a few more considerations:

- If we're trying to parse a sequence of zero or more "a" characters and are only interested in the number of characters seen, it seems inefficient to have to build up, say, a List[Char] only to throw it away and extract the length. Could something be done about this?

- Are the various forms of repetition primitive in our algebra, or could they be defined in terms of something simpler?

- We introduced a type ParseError earlier, but so far we haven't chosen any functions for the API of ParseError, and our algebra doesn't have any way of letting the programmer control which errors are reported. This seems like a limitation, given we'd like meaningful error messages from our parsers. Can you do something about it?

- Does a | b mean the same thing as b | a? This is a choice you get to make. What are the consequences if the answer is yes? What about if the answer is no?

- Does a | (b | c) mean the same thing as (a | b) | c? If yes, is this a primitive law for your algebra, or is it implied by something simpler?

- Try to come up with a set of laws to specify your algebra. You don't necessarily need the laws to be complete; just write down some laws you expect should hold for any Parsers implementation.

Spend some time coming up with combinators and possible laws based on this guidance. When you feel stuck or at a good stopping point, continue by reading the next section, which walks through one possible design.

> **The advantages of algebraic design**
>
> When you design the algebra of a library first, representations for the data types of the algebra don't matter as much. As long as they support the required laws and functions, you don't even need to make your representations public.
>
> There's an idea here that a type is given meaning based on its relationship to other types (which are specified by the set of functions and their laws), rather than its internal representation.[7] This viewpoint is often associated with category theory, a branch of mathematics. See the chapter notes (https://github.com/fpinscala/fpinscala/wiki) for more on this connection if you're interested.

9.2 *A possible algebra*

We'll walk through the discovery of a set of combinators for the parsing tasks mentioned earlier. If you worked through this design task yourself, you likely took a different path and may have ended up with a different set of combinators, which is fine.

First, let's consider the parser that recognizes zero or more repetitions of the character `'a'` and returns the number of characters it has seen. We can start by adding a primitive combinator for it; let's call it many:

```
extension [A](p: Parser[A]) def many: Parser[List[A]]
```

This isn't exactly what we're after; we need a `Parser[Int]` that counts the number of elements. We could change the many combinator to return a `Parser[Int]`, but that feels too specific—undoubtedly, there will be occasions when we care about more than just the list length. It is better to introduce another combinator that should be familiar by now—map:

```
extension [A](p: Parser[A]) def map[B](f: A => B): Parser[B]
```

We can now define our parser like this:

```
val numA: Parser[Int] = char('a').many.map(_.size)
```

We expect that, for instance, numA.run("aaa") gives Right(3) and numA.run("b") gives Right(0).

---

[7] This viewpoint might also be associated with object-oriented (OO) design, although OO hasn't traditionally placed much emphasis on algebraic laws. Furthermore, an important reason for encapsulation in OO is that objects often have some mutable state, and making this public would allow client code to violate invariants. That concern isn't relevant in FP.

We have a strong expectation for the behavior of `map`: it should merely transform the result value if the `Parser` was successful. No additional input characters should be examined by `map`, and a failing parser can't become a successful one via `map`, or vice versa. In general, we expect `map` to be *structure preserving*, much like we required for Par and Gen. Let's formalize this by stipulating the now-familiar law:

```
p.map(a => a) == p
```

How should we document this law? We could put it in a documentation comment, but in the preceding chapter, we developed a way of making our laws *executable*. Let's use that library here.

Listing 9.2 Combining `Parser` with `map`

```
import fpinscala.testing.*

trait Parsers[ParseError, Parser[+_]]:
  ...
  object Laws:
    def equal[A](p1: Parser[A], p2: Parser[A])(in: Gen[String]): Prop =
      Prop.forAll(in)(s => p1.run(s) == p2.run(s))

    def mapLaw[A](p: Parser[A])(in: Gen[String]): Prop =
      equal(p, p.map(a => a))(in)
```

This will come in handy later when we test that our implementation of Parsers behaves as we expect. When we discover more laws later on, you're encouraged to write them out as actual properties inside the Laws object.[8]

Incidentally, now that we have `map`, we can implement `char` in terms of `string`:

```
def char(c: Char): Parser[Char] =
  string(c.toString).map(_.charAt(0))
```

Similarly, another combinator, `succeed`, can be defined in terms of `string` and `map`:

```
def succeed[A](a: A): Parser[A] =
  string("").map(_ => a)
```

This parser always succeeds with the value a, regardless of the input string (since `string("")` will always succeed, even if the input is empty). Does this combinator seem familiar to you? We can specify its behavior with a law:

```
succeed(a).run(s) == Right(a)
```

---

[8] Again, see the chapter code for more examples. In the interest of keeping this chapter shorter, we won't give Prop implementations of all the laws, but that doesn't mean you shouldn't write them yourself!

9.2.1   *Slicing and nonempty repetition*

The combination of many and map certainly lets us express the parsing task of counting the number of 'a' characters, but it seems inefficient to construct a List[Char] only to discard its values and extract its length. It would be nice if we could run a Parser purely to see what portion of the input string it examines. Let's conjure up a combinator for that purpose:

```
extension [A](p: Parser[A]) def slice: Parser[String]
```

We call this combinator slice, since we intend for it to return the portion of the input string examined by the parser if successful. As an example, (char('a') | char('b')).many.slice.run("aaba") results in Right("aaba"); we ignore the list accumulated by many and simply return the portion of the input string matched by the parser.

With slice, our parser that counts 'a' characters can now be written as char('a').many.slice.map(_.size). The _.size function here is now referencing the size method on String, which takes constant time, rather than the size method on List, which takes time proportional to the length of the list (and requires us to actually construct the list).

Note that there's no implementation here yet; we're still just coming up with our desired interface. But slice does put a constraint on the implementation—namely, that even if the parser p.many.map(_.size) will generate an intermediate list when run, p.many.slice.map(_.size) will not. This is a strong hint that slice is primitive, since it will have to have access to the internal representation of the parser.

Let's consider the next use case. What if we want to recognize one or more 'a' characters? First we introduce a new combinator for it—many1:

```
extension [A](p: Parser[A]) def many1: Parser[List[A]]
```

It feels like many1 shouldn't have to be primitive, but it should be defined somehow in terms of many. Really, p.many1 is just p followed by p.many. So it seems we need some way of running one parser followed by another, assuming the first is successful, and returning the product of their results. Let's add that:

```
extension [A](p: Parser[A])
  def product[B](p2: Parser[B]): Parser[(A, B)]
  def **[B](p2: Parser[B]): Parser[(A, B)] = product(p2)
```

> Operator alias for product, where a ** b delegates to a.product(b)

■ EXERCISE 9.1

Using product, implement the now-familiar combinator map2, and then use this to implement many1 in terms of many. Note that we could have chosen to make map2 primitive and defined product in terms of map2, as we've done in previous chapters. The choice is up to you:

```
extension [A](p: Parser[A])
  def map2[B, C](p2: Parser[B])(f: (A, B) => C): Parser[C]
```

With many1, we can now implement the parser for zero or more 'a' followed by one or more 'b', as follows:

```
char('a').many.slice.map(_.size) ** char('b').many1.slice.map(_.size)
```

EXERCISE 9.2

Hard: Try coming up with laws to specify the behavior of product.

Now that we have map2, is many really primitive? Let's think about what p.many will do. It tries running p, followed by p.many again, then again, and so on, until the attempt to parse p fails. It'll accumulate the results of all successful runs of p into a list. As soon as p fails, the parser returns the empty List.

EXERCISE 9.3

Hard: Before continuing, see if you can define many in terms of |, map2, and succeed.

EXERCISE 9.4

Hard: Using map2 and succeed, implement the listOfN combinator from earlier:

```
extension [A](p: Parser[A]) def listOfN(n: Int): Parser[List[A]]
```

Now let's try to implement many. Here's an implementation in terms of |, map2, and succeed:

```
extension [A](p: Parser[A]) def many: Parser[List[A]] =
  p.map2(p.many)(_ :: _) | succeed(Nil)
```

This code looks nice and tidy. We're using map2 to say we want p followed by p.many again and that we want to combine their results with :: to construct a list of results. Or if that fails, we want to succeed with the empty list—but there's a problem with this implementation. Can you spot what it is? We're calling many recursively in the second argument to map2, which is strict in evaluating its second argument. Consider a simplified program trace of the evaluation of p.many for some parser p. We're only showing the expansion of the left side of the | here:

```
p.many
p.map2(p.many)(_ :: _)
p.map2(p.map2(p.many)(_ :: _))(_ :: _)
p.map2(p.map2(p.map2(p.many)(_ :: _))(_ :: _))(_ :: _)
...
```

Because a call to map2 always evaluates its second argument, our many function will never terminate! That's no good. This indicates we need to make product and map2 nonstrict in their second argument:

```
extension [A](p: Parser[A])
  def product[B](p2: => Parser[B]): Parser[(A, B)]

  def map2[B,C](p2: => Parser[B])(f: (A, B) => C): Parser[C] =
    p.product(p2).map((a, b) => f(a, b))
```

EXERCISE 9.5

We could also deal with nonstrictness with a separate combinator, like we did in chapter 7. Try this here, and make the necessary changes to your existing combinators. What do you think of that approach in this instance?

Now our implementation of many should work fine. Conceptually, product should have been nonstrict in its second argument anyway, since if the first Parser fails, the second won't even be consulted.

We now have good combinators for parsing one thing followed by another or multiple things of the same kind in succession. But since we're considering whether combinators should be nonstrict, let's revisit the or combinator from earlier:

```
extension [A](p: Parser[A]) def or(p2: Parser[A]): Parser[A]
```

We'll assume or is left biased, meaning it tries p1 on the input and then tries p2 only if p fails.[9] In this case, we ought to make it nonstrict in its second argument, which may never even be consulted:

```
extension [A](p: Parser[A]) infix def or(p2: => Parser[A]): Parser[A]
```

We'll need to make the same change to the | operator.

---

[9] This is a design choice. You may wish to think about the consequences of having a version of or that always runs both p and p2.

9.3   *Handling context sensitivity*

Let's take a step back and look at the primitives we have so far:

- string(s)—Recognizes and returns a single String
- p.slice—Returns the portion of input inspected by p if successful
- succeed(a)—Always succeeds with the value a
- p.map(f)—Applies the function f to the result of p, if successful
- p1.product(p2)—Sequences two parsers, running p1 and then p2, and returns the pair of their results if both succeed
- p1 or p2—Chooses between two parsers, first attempting p1 and then p2 if p1 fails

Using these primitives, we can express repetition and nonempty repetition (many, listOfN, and many1), as well as combinators like char and map2. Would it surprise you if these primitives were sufficient for parsing any context-free grammar, including JSON? Well, they are! We'll start writing that JSON parser soon, but what can't we express yet?

Suppose we want to parse a single digit, like '4', followed by many 'a' characters (this sort of problem should feel familiar from previous chapters). Examples of valid inputs include "0", "1a", "2aa", "4aaaa", and so on. This is an example of a context-sensitive grammar. It can't be expressed with product because our choice of the second parser depends on the result of the first (the second parser depends on its context). We want to run the first parser and then do a listOfN using the number extracted from the first parser's result. Can you see why product can't express this?

This progression might feel familiar to you. In past chapters, we encountered similar expressiveness limitations and dealt with them by introducing a new primitive: flatMap. Let's introduce that here:

```
extension [A](p: Parser[A]) def flatMap[B](f: A => Parser[B]): Parser[B]
```

Can you see how this signature implies an ability to sequence parsers, where each parser in the chain depends on the output of the previous one?

■ **EXERCISE 9.6**

Using flatMap and any other combinators, write the context-sensitive parser we couldn't express earlier. To parse the digits, you can make use of a new primitive, regex, which promotes a regular expression to a Parser.[10] In Scala, a string s can be promoted to a Regex object (which has methods for matching) using s.r—for instance, "[a-zA-Z_][a-zA-Z0-9_]*".r:

```
def regex(r: Regex): Parser[String]
```

---

[10]In theory, this isn't necessary; we could write out string("0") | string("1") | ... string("9") to recognize a single digit, but this isn't likely to be very efficient.

Implement `product` and `map2` in terms of `flatMap`.

`map` is no longer primitive. Express it in terms of `flatMap` and/or other combinators.

It appears we have a new primitive, `flatMap`, which enables context-sensitive parsing and allows us to implement `map` and `map2`. This is not the first time `flatMap` has made an appearance.

We now have an even smaller set of just six primitives: `string`, `regex`, `slice`, `succeed`, `or`, and `flatMap`. But we also have more power than before. With `flatMap`, instead of the less-general `map` and `product`, we can parse not just arbitrary context-free grammars, like JSON, but context-sensitive grammars as well, including extremely complicated ones, like C++ and PERL.

9.4 *Writing a JSON parser*

Let's write that JSON parser now, shall we? We don't have an implementation of our algebra yet, and we've yet to add any combinators for good error reporting, but we can deal with these things later. Our JSON parser doesn't need to know the internal details of how parsers are represented. We can simply write a function that produces a JSON parser using only the set of primitives we've defined and any derived combinators. That is, for some JSON parse result type (we'll explain the JSON format and the parse result type shortly), we'll write a function like this:

```
def jsonParser[Err, Parser[+_]](          Err and Parser are type parameters, and P
  P: Parsers[Err, Parser]      ◄───────   is a value of type Parsers[Err, Parser].
): Parser[JSON] =
  import P.*                    ◄────────  This imports all members of P, giving us access
  val spaces = char(' ').many.slice        to the combinators we've written so far.
  ...
  
char, many, and slice are imported from P.
```

This might seem like a peculiar thing to do, since we won't be able to run our parser until we have a concrete implementation of the `Parsers` interface. However, we'll proceed because in FP it's common to define an algebra and explore its expressiveness without having a concrete implementation. A concrete implementation can tie us down and makes changes to the API more difficult. Especially during the design phase of a library, it can be much easier to refine an algebra without having to commit to any particular implementation, and part of our goal here is getting you comfortable with this style of working.

After this section, we'll return to the question of adding better error reporting to our parsing API. We can do this without disturbing the overall structure of the API or changing our JSON parser very much. We'll also come up with a concrete, runnable representation of our `Parser` type. Importantly, the JSON parser we'll implement in the next section will be completely independent of that representation.

9.4.1 The JSON format

If you aren't already familiar with all the details of the JSON format, you may want to read the grammar specification (http://json.org). Here's an example JSON document:

```
{
  "Company name" : "Microsoft Corporation",
  "Ticker"  : "MSFT",
  "Active"  : true,
  "Price"   : 30.66,
  "Shares outstanding" : 8.38e9,
  "Related companies" :
    [ "HPQ", "IBM", "YHOO", "DELL", "GOOG" ]
}
```

A *value* in JSON can be one of several types. An *object* in JSON is a comma-separated sequence of key-value pairs wrapped in curly braces (`{}`). The keys must be strings like `"Ticker"` or `"Price"`, and the values can be either another object; an *array*, like `["HPQ", "IBM" … ]`, that contains further values; or a *literal*, like `"MSFT"`, `true`, `null`, or `30.66`.

We'll write a rather dumb parser that simply parses a syntax tree from the document, without doing any further processing.[11] We'll need a representation for a parsed JSON document. Let's introduce a data type for this:

```
enum JSON:
  case JNull
  case JNumber(get: Double)
  case JString(get: String)
  case JBool(get: Boolean)
  case JArray(get: IndexedSeq[JSON])
  case JObject(get: Map[String, JSON])
```

9.4.2 A JSON parser

Recall that we've built up the following set of primitives:

- `string(s)`—Recognizes and returns a single `String`
- `regex(s)`—Recognizes a regular expression `s`
- `p.slice`—Returns the portion of input inspected by `p` if successful

---

[11]See the chapter notes (https://github.com/fpinscala/fpinscala/wiki) for discussion of alternate approaches.

- `succeed(a)`—Always succeeds with the value a
- `p.flatMap(f)`—Runs a parser then uses its result to select a second parser to run in sequence
- `p1 | p2`—Chooses between two parsers, first attempting p1 and then p2 if p1 fails

We used these primitives to define a number of combinators, like `map`, `map2`, `many`, and `many1`.

■ **EXERCISE 9.9**

Hard: At this point, you will be taking over the process. You'll be creating a `Parser[JSON]` from scratch using the primitives we've defined. You don't need to worry (yet) about the representation of `Parser`. As you go, you'll undoubtedly discover additional combinators and idioms, notice and factor out common patterns, and so on. Use the skills you've been developing throughout this book, and have fun! If you get stuck, you can always consult the answers.

Here's some minimal guidance:

- Any general-purpose combinators you discover can be added to the `Parsers` trait directly.
- You'll probably want to introduce combinators that make it easier to parse the tokens of the JSON format (like string literals and numbers). For this you could use the `regex` primitive we introduced earlier. You could also add a few primitives, like `letter`, `digit`, `whitespace`, and so on, for building up your token parsers.

Consult the hints if you'd like more guidance. A full JSON parser is given in the JSON.scala file in the answers.

9.5   *Error reporting*

So far, we haven't discussed error reporting at all. We've focused exclusively on discovering a set of primitives that let us express parsers for different grammars, but besides just parsing a grammar, we want to be able to determine how the parser should respond when given unexpected input.

Even without knowing what an implementation of `Parsers` will look like, we can reason abstractly about what information is being specified by a set of combinators. None of the combinators we've introduced so far say anything about what error message should be reported in the event of failure or what other information a `ParseError` should contain. Our existing combinators only specify what the grammar is and what to do with the result if successful. If we were to declare ourselves done and move to implementation at this point, we'd have to make some arbitrary decisions about error reporting and error messages that are unlikely to be universally appropriate.

■   EXERCISE 9.10

Hard: If you haven't already done so, spend some time discovering a nice set of combinators for expressing what errors get reported by a Parser. For each combinator, try to come up with laws specifying what its behavior should be. This is a very open-ended design task; here are some guiding questions:

- Given the parser string("abra") ** string(" ").many ** string("cadabra"), what sort of error would you like to report, given the input "abra cAdabra" (note the capital 'A')—something like Expected 'a' or Expected "cadabra"? What if you wanted to choose a different error message, like "Magic word incorrect, try again!"?
- Given a or b, if a fails on the input, do we always want to run b, or are there cases when we might not want to? If there are such cases, can you think of additional combinators that would allow the programmer to specify when or should consider the second parser?
- How do you want to handle reporting the location of errors?
- Given a | b, if a and b both fail on the input, might we want to support reporting both errors? And do we always want to report both errors, or do we want to give the programmer a way to specify which of the two errors is reported?

We suggest you continue reading once you're satisfied with your design. The next section works through a possible design in detail.

Combinators specify information

In a typical library design scenario, where we have at least some idea of a concrete representation, we often think of functions in terms of how they will affect this representation. By starting with the algebra, we're forced to think differently—we must think of functions in terms of what information they specify to a possible implementation. The signatures determine what information is given to the implementation, and the implementation is free to use this information however it wants, as long as it respects any specified laws.

9.5.1 *A possible design*

Now that you've spent some time coming up with some good error-reporting combinators, we'll work through one possible design. Again, you may have arrived at a different design, and that's totally fine. This is just another opportunity to see a worked design process.

We'll progressively introduce our error-reporting combinators. To start, let's introduce an obvious one. None of the primitives so far let us assign an error message to a parser. We can introduce a primitive combinator for this—`label`:

```
extension [A](p: Parser[A]) def label(msg: String): Parser[A]
```

The intended meaning of `label` is that if `p` fails, its `ParseError` will somehow incorporate `msg`. What does this mean exactly? Well, we could just assume `type ParseError = String` and that the returned `ParseError` will equal the label, but we'd like our parse error to also tell us where the problem occurred. Let's tentatively add this to our algebra:

```
case class Location(input: String, offset: Int = 0):
  lazy val line = input.slice(0, offset + 1).count(_ == '\n') + 1
  lazy val col = input.slice(0, offset + 1).lastIndexOf('\n') match
    case -1 => offset + 1
    case lineStart => offset - lineStart

def errorLocation(e: ParseError): Location
def errorMessage(e: ParseError): String
```

Extracts a concrete Location from an abstract ParseError

Extracts a concrete message from an abstract ParseError

We've picked a concrete representation for `Location` here that includes the full input, an offset into this input, and the line and column numbers, which can be computed lazily from the full input and offset. We can now say more precisely what we expect from `label`. In the event of failure with `Left(e)`, `errorMessage(e)` will equal the message set by `label`. This can be specified with a `Prop`:

```
def labelLaw[A](p: Parser[A], inputs: SGen[String]): Prop =
  forAll(inputs ** Gen.string):
    case (input, msg) =>
      p.label(msg).run(input) match
        case Left(e) => errorMessage(e) == msg
        case _ => true
```

What about the `Location`? We'd like this to be filled in by the `Parsers` implementation with the location where the error occurred. This notion is still a bit fuzzy; if we have a `a | b`, and both parsers fail on the input, which location and label(s) are reported? We'll discuss this in the next section.

9.5.2 *Error nesting*

Is the `label` combinator sufficient for all our error-reporting needs? Not quite. Let's look at an example:

```
val p = string("abra").label("first magic word") **
        string(" ").many **                            ← Skip the whitespace.
        string("cadabra").label("second magic word")
```

What sort of `ParseError` would we like to get back from `p.run("abra cAdabra")`? (Note the capital A in cAdabra.) The immediate cause is that capital `'A'`, instead of the expected lowercase `'a'`. That error will have a location, and it might be nice to report it somehow. But reporting only that low-level error wouldn't be very informative, especially if this were part of a large grammar and we were running the parser on a larger input. We have some more context that would be useful to know—the immediate error occurred in the `Parser` labeled `"second magic word"`. This is certainly helpful information. Ideally, the error message should tell us that while parsing `"second magic word"`, there was an unexpected capital `'A'`. That pinpoints the error and gives us the context needed to understand it. Perhaps the top-level parser (p, in this case) might be able to provide an even higher-level description of what the parser was doing when it failed (`"parsing magic spell"`, say), which could also be informative.

So it seems wrong to assume that one level of error reporting will always be sufficient. Let's therefore provide a way to nest labels:

```
extension [A](p: Parser[A]) def scope(msg: String): Parser[A]
```

Unlike `label`, `scope` doesn't throw away the label(s) attached to p—it merely adds additional information in the event that p fails. Let's specify what this means exactly. First, we modify the functions that pull information out of a `ParseError`. Rather than containing just a single `Location` and `String` message, we should get a `List[(Location, String)]`:

```
case class ParseError(stack: List[(Location, String)])
```

`ParseError` is a stack of error messages indicating what the `Parser` was doing when it failed. We can now specify what `scope` does—if `p.run(s)` is `Left(e1)`, then `p.scope(msg)`.`run(s)` is `Left(e2)`, where `e2.stack.head` will be `msg` and `e2.stack.tail` will be `e1`.

We can write helper functions later to make constructing and manipulating `Parse-Error` values more convenient as well as to format them nicely for human consumption. For now, we just want to make sure it contains all the relevant information for error reporting, and it seems like `ParseError` will be sufficient for most purposes. Let's pick this as our concrete representation and remove the abstract type parameter from Parsers:

```
trait Parsers[Parser[+_]]:
  extension [A](p: Parser[A])
    def run(input: String): Either[ParseError, A]
  ...
```

Now we're giving the `Parsers` implementation all the information it needs to construct nice, hierarchical errors, if it chooses. As users of the `Parsers` library, we'll judiciously sprinkle our grammar with `label` and `scope` calls that the `Parsers` implementation can use when constructing parse errors. Note that it would be perfectly reasonable for implementations of `Parsers` to not use the full power of `ParseError` and retain only basic information about the cause and location of errors.

9.5.3   *Controlling branching and backtracking*

There's one last concern regarding error reporting that we need to address. As we just discussed, when we have an error that occurs inside an or combinator, we need some way of determining which error(s) to report. We don't want to only have a global convention for this; we sometimes want to allow the programmer to control this choice. Let's look at a more concrete motivating example:

```
val spaces = string(" ").many
val p1 =
  (string("abra") ** spaces ** string("cadabra")).scope("magic spell")
val p2 =
  (string("abba") ** spaces ** string("babba")).scope("gibberish")
val p = p1 | p2
```

What ParseError would we like to get back from p.run("abra cAdabra")? (Again, note the capital A in cAdabra.) Both branches of the or will produce errors on the input. The "gibberish"-labeled parser will report an error due to expecting the first word to be "abba", and the "magic spell" parser will report an error due to the accidental capitalization in "cAdabra". Which of these errors do we want to report back to the user?

In this instance, we happen to want the "magic spell" parse error; after successfully parsing the "abra" word, we're committed to the "magic spell" branch of the or, which means if we encounter a parse error, we don't examine the next branch of the or. In other instances, we may want to allow the parser to consider the next branch of the or.

So it appears we need a primitive to let the programmer indicate when to commit to a particular parsing branch. Recall that we loosely assigned p1 | p2 to mean *try running p1 on the input, and then try running p2 on the same input if p1 fails.* We can change its meaning to *try running p1 on the input, and if it fails in an uncommitted state, try running p2 on the same input; otherwise, report the failure.* This is useful for more than just providing good error messages—it also improves efficiency by letting the implementation avoid examining lots of possible parsing branches.

One common solution to this problem is having all parsers commit by default if they examine at least one character to produce a result.[12] We then introduce a combinator, attempt, which delays committing to a parse:

```
extension [A](p: Parser[A]) def attempt: Parser[A]
```

The attempt combinator should satisfy something like this:[13]

```
def fail(msg: String): Parser[Nothing]
```

New parser that always fails with the supplied error message

```
p.flatMap(_ => fail("")).attempt | p2 == p2
```

---

[12]See the chapter notes (https://github.com/fpinscala/fpinscala/wiki) for more discussion of this.

[13]This is not quite an equality. Even though we want to run p2 if the attempted parser fails, we may want p2 to somehow incorporate the errors from both branches if it fails.

Here `fail` is a parser that always fails. That is, even if p fails midway through examining the input, `attempt` reverts the commit to that parse and allows p2 to be run. The `attempt` combinator can be used whenever there's ambiguity in the grammar, and multiple tokens may have to be examined before the ambiguity can be resolved and parsing can commit to a single branch. As an example, we might write this:

```
((string("abra") ** spaces ** string("abra")).attempt **
  string("cadabra")) | ("abra" ** spaces ** "cadabra!")
```

Suppose this parser is run on `"abra cadabra!"`—after parsing the first `"abra"`, we don't know whether to expect another `"abra"` (the first branch) or `"cadabra!"` (the second branch). By wrapping an `attempt` around `"abra" ** spaces ** "abra"`, we allow the second branch to be considered up until we've finished parsing the second `"abra"`, at which point we commit to that branch.

■ **EXERCISE 9.11**

Can you think of any other primitives that might be useful for letting the programmer specify what error(s) in an `or` chain get reported?

We still haven't written an implementation of our algebra! But this exercise has been more about making sure our combinators provide a way for users of our library to convey the right information to the implementation. It's up to the implementation to figure out how to use this information in a way that satisfies the laws we've stipulated.

9.6   *Implementing the algebra*

By this point, we've fleshed out our algebra and defined a `Parser[JSON]` in terms of it.[14] Aren't you curious to try running it?

Let's again recall our set of primitives:

- `string(s)`—Recognizes and returns a single `String`
- `regex(s)`—Recognizes a regular expression s
- `p.slice`—Returns the portion of input inspected by p, if successful
- `p.label(e)`—In the event of failure, replaces the assigned message with e
- `p.scope(e)`—In the event of failure, adds e to the error stack returned by p
- `f.flatMap(p)`—Runs a parser and then uses its result to select a second parser to run in sequence
- `p.attempt`—Delays committing to p until after it succeeds
- `p1 | p2`—Chooses between two parsers, first attempting p1 and then p2 if p1 fails in an uncommitted state on the input

---

[14] You may want to revisit your parser to make use of some of the error-reporting combinators we discussed in the previous section.

■ EXERCISE 9.12

Hard: In the next section, we'll work through a representation for `Parser` and implement the `Parsers` interface using this representation. But before we do that, try to
come up with some ideas on your own. This is a very open-ended design task, but the
algebra we've designed places strong constraints on possible representations. You
should be able to come up with a simple, purely functional representation of `Parser`
that can be used to implement the `Parsers` interface.[15]

Your code will likely look something like this:

```
class MyParser[+A](...):
  ...

object MyParsers extends Parsers[MyParser]:
  // implementations of primitives go here
```

Replace `MyParser` with whatever data type you use for representing your parsers.
When you have something you're satisfied with, get stuck, or want some more ideas,
keep reading.

9.6.1   *One possible implementation*

We're now going to discuss an implementation of `Parsers`. Our parsing algebra supports many features. Rather than jumping right to the final representation of `Parser`,
we'll build it up gradually by inspecting the primitives of the algebra and reasoning
about the information that will be required to support each one.

Let's begin with the `string` combinator:

```
def string(s: String): Parser[A]
```

We know we need to support the function run:

```
extension [A](p: Parser[A]) def run(input: String): Either[ParseError, A]
```

As a first guess, we can assume our `Parser` is simply the implementation of the run
function:

```
opaque type Parser[+A] = String => Either[ParseError,A]
```

---

[15]Note that if you try running your JSON parser once you have an implementation of `Parsers`, you may get a
stack overflow error. See the end of the next section for a discussion of this.

We could use this to implement the `string` primitive:

```
def string(s: String): Parser[A] =
  input =>
    if input.startsWith(s) then
      Right(s)
    else
      Left(Location(input).toError("Expected: " + s))
```

Uses toError, defined later, to construct a ParseError

The `else` branch has to build up a `ParseError`. These are a little inconvenient to construct right now, so we've introduced a helper function, `toError`, on `Location`:

```
case class Location(input: String, offset: Int = 0):
  def toError(msg: String): ParseError =
    ParseError(List((this, msg)))
```

9.6.2 Sequencing parsers

So far, so good. We have a representation for `Parser` that at least supports `string`. Let's move on to sequencing parsers. Unfortunately, to represent a parser like `string("abra") ** string("cadabra")`, our existing representation isn't going to suffice. If the parse of `"abra"` is successful, then we want to consider those characters consumed and run the `"cadabra"` parser on the remaining characters. So to support sequencing, we require a way of letting a `Parser` indicate how many characters it consumed. Capturing this is pretty easy:[16]

A parser now returns a Result that's either a success or a failure.

```
opaque type Parser[+A] = Location => Result[A]
```

```
enum Result[+A]:
  case Success(get: A, charsConsumed: Int)
  case Failure(get: ParseError) extends Result[Nothing]
```

In the success case, we return the number of characters consumed by the parser.

Failure does not reference the type parameter A, so we explicitly extend Result[Nothing], which means we don't need to copy failures when changing the type param.

We introduced a new type here, `Result`, rather than just using `Either`.

In the event of success, we return a value of type `A` as well as the number of characters of input consumed, which the caller can use to update the `Location` state.[17] This type is starting to get at the essence of what a `Parser` is—it's a kind of state action that can fail, similar to what we built in chapter 6. It receives an input state, and if successful, it returns a value as well as enough information to control how the state should be updated.

This understanding—that a `Parser` is just a state action—gives us a way of framing a representation that supports all the fancy combinators and laws we've stipulated. We simply consider what each primitive requires our state type to track (just a `Location`

---

[16]Recall that `Location` contains the full input string and an offset into this string.

[17]Note that returning an `(A, Location)` would give `Parser` the ability to change the input stored in the `Location`. That's granting it too much power!

may not be sufficient) and work through the details of how each combinator transforms this state.

Implement string, regex, succeed, and slice for this initial representation of Parser. Note that slice is less efficient than it could be, since it must still construct a value only to discard it. We'll return to this later.

9.6.3   *Labeling parsers*

Moving down our list of primitives, let's look at scope next. In the event of failure, we want to push a new message onto the ParseError stack. Let's introduce a helper function for this on ParseError; we'll call it push:[18]

```
case class ParseError(stack: List[(Location, String)] = Nil):
  def push(loc: Location, msg: String): ParseError =
    copy(stack = (loc, msg) :: stack)
```

With this we can implement scope:

```
extension [A](p: Parser[A]) def scope(msg: String): Parser[A] =
  l => p(l).mapError(_.push(l, msg))
```
> In the event of failure, push msg onto the error stack.

The function mapError is defined on Result—it just applies a function to the failing case:

```
def mapError(f: ParseError => ParseError): Result[A] = this match
  case Failure(e) => Failure(f(e))
  case _ => this
```

Because we push onto the stack after the inner parser has returned, the bottom of the stack will have more detailed messages that occurred later in parsing. For example, if (a ** b.scope(msg2)).scope(msg1) fails while parsing b, then the first error on the stack will be msg1, followed by whatever errors were generated by a, then msg2, and, finally, errors generated by b.

We can implement label similarly, but instead of pushing onto the error stack, it replaces what's already there. We can write this again using mapError:

```
extension [A](p: Parser[A]) def label(msg: String): Parser[A] =
  l => p(l).mapError(_.label(msg))
```
> Calls a helper method on ParseError, which is also named label

---

[18] The copy method comes for free with any case class. It returns a copy of the object but with one or more attributes modified. If no new value is specified for a field, it will have the same value as in the original object. Behind the scenes, this uses the ordinary mechanism for default arguments in Scala.

We added a helper function to `ParseError`, also named `label`. We'll make a design decision that `label` trims the error stack, cutting off more detailed messages from inner scopes, using only the most recent location from the bottom of the stack:

```
case class ParseError(stack: List[(Location, String)] = Nil):
  def label(s: String): ParseError =
    ParseError(latestLoc.map((_, s)).toList)

  def latestLoc: Option[Location] =
    latest.map(_(0))

  def latest: Option[(Location, String)] =
    stack.lastOption
```

Gets the last element of the stack
or None if the stack is empty

EXERCISE 9.14

Consider this parser of a nonnegative integer:

```
val nonNegativeInt: Parser[Int] =
  for
    nString <- regex("[0-9]+".r)
    n <- nString.toIntOption match
      case Some(n) => succeed(n)
      case None => fail("expected an integer")
  yield n
```

Revise this implementation to use `scope` or `label` to provide a more meaningful error message in the event of an error.

9.6.4 *Failover and backtracking*

Let's now consider `or` and `attempt`. Recall what we specified for the expected behavior of `or`: it should run the first parser, and if that fails in an uncommitted state, then it should run the second parser on the same input. We said consuming at least one character should result in a committed parse, and that `p.attempt` converts committed failures of `p` to uncommitted failures.

We can support the behavior we want by adding one more piece of information to the `Failure` case of `Result`—a `Boolean` value indicating whether the parser failed in a committed state:

```
case Failure(get: ParseError, isCommitted: Boolean)
```

The implementation of `attempt` just cancels the commitment of any failures that occur. It uses a helper function, `uncommit`, which we can define on `Result`:

```
extension [A](p: Parser[A]) def attempt: Parser[A] =
  l => p(l).uncommit

enum Result[+A]:
```

```
...
def uncommit: Result[A] = this match
  case Failure(e, true) => Failure(e, false)
  case _ => this
```

Now the implementation of or can simply check the isCommitted flag before running the second parser. In the parser p or p2 if p succeeds, then the whole thing succeeds. If p fails in a committed state, we fail early and skip running p2. Otherwise, if p fails in an uncommitted state, then we run p2 and ignore the result of p:

```
extension [A](p: Parser[A]) def or(p2: => Parser[A]): Parser[A] =
  l => p(l) match
    case Failure(e, false) => p2(s)          Committed failure or
    case r => r                        ◁——————  success skips running p2
```

9.6.5 *Context-sensitive parsing*

Now for the final primitive in our list: flatMap. Recall that flatMap enables context-sensitive parsers by allowing the selection of a second parser to depend on the result of the first parser. The implementation is simple: we advance the location before calling the second parser. Again, we use a helper function, advanceBy, on Location. There is one subtlety—if the first parser consumes any characters, we ensure the second parser is committed, using a helper function, addCommit, on ParseError.

> **Listing 9.3 Using addCommit to make sure our parser is committed**

Advance the source location before calling the second parser.

```
extension [A](p: Parser[A]) def flatMap[B](f: A => Parser[B]): Parser[B] =
  l => p(l) match
    case Success(a, n) => f(a)(l.advanceBy(n))        ◁——————
                           .addCommit(n != 0)   ◁——| Commit if the first parser has
                           .advanceSuccess(n)   ◁——| consumed any characters.
    ▷ case f @ Failure(_, _) => f
```

Because Failure extends Result[Nothing] and Result is covariant in its only type parameter, we can return f directly here.

If successful, we increment the number of characters consumed by n to account for characters already consumed by p.

advanceBy has the obvious implementation. We simply increment the offset:

```
def advanceBy(n: Int): Location =
  copy(offset = offset + n)
```

Likewise, addCommit, defined on ParseError, is straightforward:

```
def addCommit(isCommitted: Boolean): Result[A] = this match
  case Failure(e, c) => Failure(e, c || isCommitted)
  case _ => this
```

And finally, advanceSuccess increments the number of consumed characters of a successful result. We want the total number of characters consumed by flatMap to be the sum of the consumed characters of the parser p and the parser produced by f. We use advanceSuccess on the result of f to ensure this:

```
def advanceSuccess(n: Int): Result[A] = this match
  case Success(a, m) => Success(a, n + m)
  case _ => this
```

If unsuccessful, leave the result alone.

EXERCISE 9.15

Implement the rest of the primitives, including run, using this representation of Parser, and try running your JSON parser on various inputs. You'll find, unfortunately, that this representation causes stack overflow for large inputs (e.g., [1,2,3,...10000]). One simple solution to this is providing a specialized implementation of many that avoids using a stack frame for each element of the list being built up. So long as any combinators that do repetition are defined in terms of many (which they all can be), this solves the problem.

EXERCISE 9.16

Come up with a nice way of formatting a ParseError for human consumption. There are many choices to make, but a key insight is that we typically want to combine or group labels attached to the same location when presenting the error as a String for display.

EXERCISE 9.17

Hard: The slice combinator is still less efficient than it could be. For instance, char('a').many.slice will still build up a List[Char], only to discard it. Can you think of a way of modifying the Parser representation to make slicing more efficient?

EXERCISE 9.18

Some information is lost when we combine parsers with the or combinator. If both parsers fail, we're only keeping the errors from the second parser. But we might want to show both error messages or choose the error from whichever branch got furthest without failing. Change the representation of ParseError to keep track of errors that occurred in other branches of the parser.

9.7   *Conclusion*

In this chapter, we introduced algebraic design, an approach to writing combinator libraries, and we used it to design a parser library and implement a JSON parser. Along the way, we discovered a number of combinators similar to what we saw in previous chapters, and these were again related by familiar laws. In part 3, we'll finally understand the nature of the connection between these libraries and learn how to abstract over their common structure.

This is the final chapter in part 2. We hope you've come away from these chapters with a basic sense of how functional design can proceed, and more importantly, we hope these chapters have motivated you to try your hand at designing your own functional libraries for whatever domains interest you. Functional design isn't something reserved only for experts—it should be part of the day-to-day work done by functional programmers at all levels of experience. Before you start on part 3, we encourage you to venture beyond this book, write some more functional code, and design some of your own libraries. Have fun, enjoy struggling with design problems that come up, and see what you discover. When you come back, a universe of patterns and abstractions awaits in part 3.

Summary

- A parser converts a sequence of unstructured data into a structured representation.
- A parser combinator library allows the construction of a parser by combining simple primitive parsers and generic combinators.
- In contrast, a parser generator library constructs a parser based on the specification of a grammar.
- Algebraic design is the process in which an interface and associated laws are designed first and then used to guide the choice of data type representations.
- Judicious use of infix operators, either defined with symbols as in | or with the `infix` keyword as in `or`, can make combinator libraries easier to use.
- The `many` combinator creates a parser that parses zero or more repetitions of the input parser and returns a list of parsed values.
- The `many1` combinator is like `many` but parses one or more repetitions.
- The `product` combinator (or `**` operator) creates a parser from two input parsers, which runs the first parser and, if successful, runs the second parser on the remaining input. The resulting value of each input parser is returned in a tuple.
- The `map`, `map2`, and `flatMap` operations are useful for building composite parsers. In particular, `flatMap` allows the creation of context-sensitive parsers.
- The `label` and `scope` combinators allow better error messages to be generated with parsing fails.
- APIs can be designed by choosing primitive operations, building combinators, and deciding how those operations and combinators should interact.
- API design is an iterative process, where interactions amongst operations, sample usages, and implementation difficulties all contribute to the process.

9.8 Exercise answers

■ **ANSWER 9.1**

Taking the product of p and p2 gives us a `Parser[(A, B)]`. We then map over that with the supplied function f to get a `Parser[C]`:

```
extension [A](p: Parser[A])
  def map2[B, C](p2: Parser[B])(f: (A, B) => C): Parser[C] =
    p.product(p2).map((a, b) => f(a, b))
```

To implement `many1`, we use `map2` to combine the results of p and p.many into a single list by consing the result of p onto the result of p.many:

```
extension [A](p: Parser[A])
  def many1: Parser[List[A]] =
    p.map2(p.many)(_ :: _)
```

■ **ANSWER 9.2**

The `product` operation is associative. These two expressions are roughly equal:

```
(a ** b) ** c
a ** (b ** c)
```

The only difference is how the pairs are nested. The `(a ** b) ** c` parser returns an `((A, B), C)`, whereas the `a ** (b ** c)` returns an `(A, (B, C))`. We can define the functions `unbiasL` and `unbiasR` to convert these nested tuples to flat 3-tuples:

```
def unbiasL[A, B, C](p: ((A, B), C)): (A, B, C) = (p(0)(0), p(0)(1), p(1))
def unbiasR[A, B, C](p: (A, (B, C))): (A, B, C) = (p(0), p(1)(0), p(1)(1))
```

With these, we can now state the associativity property:

```
((a ** b) ** c).map(unbiasL) == (a ** (b ** c)).map(unbiasR)
```

We'll sometimes just use ~= when there is an obvious bijection between the two sides:

```
(a ** b) ** c ~= a ** (b ** c)
```

map and product also have an interesting relationship; we can map either before or after taking the product of two parsers, without affecting the behavior:

```
a.map(f) ** b.map(g) == (a ** b).map((a,b) => (f(a), g(b)))
```

For instance, if a and b were both `Parser[String]` and f and g both computed the length of a string, then it wouldn't matter if we mapped over the result of a to compute its length or whether we did that after the product. See chapter 12 for more discussion of these laws.

ANSWER 9.3

We use the same approach we used for `many1` in exercise 9.1, using `map2` with cons to build a list. When that fails, due to exhausting the input or otherwise, we succeed with an empty list:

```
extension [A](p: Parser[A])
  def many: Parser[List[A]] =
    p.map2(p.many)(_ :: _) | succeed(Nil)
```

This implementation has a problem, though: we recursively call `p.many`, and our `map2` implementation takes its argument strictly, resulting in a stack overflow. To correct this, we need to change `map2` to take the parser argument nonstrictly. We'll look at this in greater depth in the next section of the chapter.

ANSWER 9.4

`listOfN` is very similar to `many`—the only difference being the limit on the number of elements to parse. Hence, we can implement it via a similar technique of a `map2` with a recursive call to `listOfN(n - 1)` on each iteration. When n reaches zero, we succeed with the empty list:

```
extension [A](p: Parser[A])
  def listOfN(n: Int): Parser[List[A]] =
    if n <= 0 then succeed(Nil)
    else p.map2(p.listOfN(n - 1))(_ :: _)
```

ANSWER 9.5

We need a way to defer creation of a parser. We can do this via a new constructor that takes a by-name parser argument and delays evaluation of that argument until it attempts to parse something:

```
def defer[A](p: => Parser[A]): Parser[A]
```

Note that we don't need an implementation of `defer`. We assume it's a primitive to be supplied by implementations of the `Parsers` trait.[19]

```
extension [A](p: Parser[A])
  def many: Parser[List[A]] =
    p.map2(defer(p.many))(_ :: _) | succeed(Nil)
```

In the parallelism chapter, we were particularly interested in avoiding having `Par` objects that took as much time and space to build as the corresponding serial computation, and the `delay` combinator let us control this more carefully. This isn't much of a concern here, and having to think carefully each time we `map2` to decide whether we need to call `defer` seems like unnecessary friction for users of the API.

■ **ANSWER 9.6**

Let's break this problem up into two pieces—parsing a nonnegative integer and then parsing a specified number of `'a'` characters:

```
val nonNegativeInt: Parser[Int] =
  for
    nString <- regex("[0-9]+".r)          ◁——— Parse one or more digit characters using a regular expression.
    n <- nString.toIntOption match        ◁——— Convert the parsed digit string to an integer.
      case Some(n) => succeed(n)           ◁——— If integer conversion succeeded, return the parsed value as a parser via succeed.
      case None => fail("expected an integer")
    yield n
```

Otherwise, return a parser, which fails with an error message.

We used `flatMap` on the regex parser to further validation and transform the parsed string—in this case, converting the string to an integer. We had to create a new primitive, `fail`, which constructs a parser that always fails with the supplied error message.

With `nonNegativeInt` we can use `flatMap` to implement `nConsecutiveAs` using various combinators we've already defined:

```
val nConsecutiveAs: Parser[Int] =
  for
    n <- nonNegativeInt
    _ <- char('a').listOfN(n)              ◁——— We've chosen to return the number of parsed 'a' characters instead of returning the parsed string
  yield n
```

---

[19]Alternatively, we could implement `defer` in terms of `succeed` and `flatMap`, though we don't define `flatMap` until later in this chapter.

Both `product` and `map2` can be implemented with for-comprehensions, which bind the results of p and p2 and then combine those results:

```
extension [A](p: Parser[A])
  def product[B](p2: => B): Parser[(A, B)] =
    for
      a <- p
      b <- p2
    yield (a, b)

  def map2[B, C](p2: => B)(f: (A, B) => C): Parser[C] =
    for
      a <- p
      b <- p2
    yield f(a, b)
```

We can implement `map` using `flatMap` and `succeed`:

```
extension [A](p: Parser[A])
  def map[B](f: A => B): Parser[B] =
    p.flatMap(a => succeed(f(a)))
```

A JSON document starts with either an array or an object. Let's start by sketching that, inventing new parsers as necessary:

```
def document: Parser[JSON] = array | obj
def array: Parser[JSON] = ???
def obj: Parser[JSON] = ???
```

Let's also discard any whitespace at the start of a document. We can do so by writing a parser for whitespace and combining it with array | obj:

```
def whitespace: Parser[String] = Parser.regex("\\s*".r)
def document: Parser[JSON] = whitespace.map2(array | obj)((_, doc) => doc)
```

We used `map2` and discarded the parsed whitespace. We can extract a more general combinator, which combines two parsers and discards the results of the first parser. Likewise, we can discard the results of the right parser:

```
extension [A](p: Parser[A])
  def *>[B](p2: => Parser[B]): Parser[B] = p.map2(p2)((_, b) => b)
  def <*[B](p2: => Parser[B]): Parser[A] = p.map2(p2)((a, _) => a)

def document: Parser[JSON] = whitespace *> (array | obj)
```

We named these combinators `<*` and `*>`—the arrow points in the direction of the result that's kept. Finally, let's ensure there's no remaining input after a parsed array or object:

```
def eof: Parser[String] =
  regex("\\z".r).label("unexpected trailing characters")

def document: Parser[JSON] = whitespace *> (array | obj) <* eof
```

Here we've defined an `eof` parser that only succeeds when given an empty input string. We used a regex parser along with the `\z` pattern, though we could have written it out manually instead.

Now let's implement some of the parsers we left undefined. A JSON array is a list of comma-separated values (CSVs) surrounded by square brackets. We'll need a parser for a JSON value and a way to express a list of elements separated by some other parser. Let's sketch that:

```
val value: Parser[JSON] = ???

extension [A](p: Parser[A])
  def sep(separator: Parser[Any]): Parser[List[A]] = ???

def array: Parser[JSON] =
  string("[") *> value.sep(string(",")).map(vs =>
    JArray(vs.toIndexedSeq)) <* string("]")
```

The `sep` method is similar to `many`, but before repeating the original parser, it parses a separator, which is then discarded (hence the parameter to `sep` has the `Parser[Any]` type). We can implement `sep` in a similar manner as `many`—with a variant that parses one or more values:

```
extension [A](p: Parser[A])
  def sep(separator: Parser[Any]): Parser[List[A]] =
    p.sep1(separator) | succeed(Nil)

  def sep1(separator: Parser[Any]): Parser[List[A]] =
    p.map2((separator *> p).many)(_ :: _)
```

The `sep1` operation is interesting because it combines `p` with the result of many `separator *> p` iterations.

One problem with this version of array is that we aren't handling whitespace. Further, our token parsers (e.g., [,], and ,) are committed, meaning if they fail to match, then they fail the overall parse, instead of allowing alternation via or. Let's create a new constructor to address both of these problems:

```
def token(s: String): Parser[String] =
  string(s).attempt <* whitespace

def array: Parser[JSON] =
  token("[") *> value.sep(token(",")).map(vs =>
    JArray(vs.toIndexedSeq)) <* token("]")
```

Finally, let's use the scope combinator to provide more error information when failing to parse an array:

```
def array: Parser[JSON] = (
  token("[") *> value.sep(token(",")).map(vs =>
    JArray(vs.toIndexedSeq)) <* token("]")
).scope("array")
```

Now let's implement the value parser. A JSON value can be a literal, an array, or an object. A literal is one of the following: * null * a number * a quoted string * true or false.

We can directly convert this to a parser:

```
def value: Parser[JSON] = lit | obj | array

def lit: Parser[JSON] = (
  token("null").as(JNull) |
  double.map(JNumber(_)) |
  escapedQuoted.map(JString(_)) |
  token("true").as(JBool(true)) |
  token("false").as(JBool(false))
).scope("literal")

def double: Parser[Double] = ???
def escapedQuoted: Parser[String] = ???
```

The double and escapedQuoted parsers are left undefined here, but see the answers in the GitHub repository for the full definition.

Finally, let's implement the obj parser from earlier. A JSON object is a comma-separated list of key-value pairs surrounded by curly braces, where each key is a quoted string, and values are separated from keys via a : token:

```
def obj: Parser[JSON] = (
  token("{") *> keyval.sep(token(",")).map(kvs =>
    JObject(kvs.toMap)) <* token("}")
).scope("object")

def keyval: Parser[(String, JSON)] = escapedQuoted ** (token(":") *> value)
```

■ **ANSWER 9.10** ───

The following section walks through one possible design in detail.

■ **ANSWER 9.11** ───

Return the error that occurred after consuming the greatest number of characters, and return the most recently encountered error.

■ **ANSWER 9.12** ───

The following section walks through one possible design in detail.

■ **ANSWER 9.13** ───

To implement `string`, we need to check whether the input starts with the supplied string, and if it does not, report an error indicating which character did not match. We'll use a helper function, `firstNonmatchingIndex`, to do so. The details of `firstNonmatchingIndex` are elided here, but see the Github repository for a full implementation:

```
def firstNonmatchingIndex(s1: String, s2: String, offset: Int): Int = ...

def string(w: String): Parser[String] =
  l =>
    val i = firstNonmatchingIndex(l.input, w, l.offset)
    if i == -1 then
      Success(w, w.length)
    else
      Failure(l.advanceBy(i).toError(s"'$w'"))
```

> We've added an advanceBy method to Location, which increments the offset by the specified amount.

To implement `regex`, we can use the built-in `findPrefixOf` method on `Regex`, passing the remaining input. The remaining input is available via `l.input.substring(l.offset)`:

```
def regex(r: Regex): Parser[String] =
  l => r.findPrefixOf(l.input.substring(l.offset)) match
    case Some(m) => Success(m, m.length)
    case None => Failure(l.toError(s"regex $r"))
```

The implementation of succeed is simple—we ignore the input entirely and return a Success with the specified value and an indication that no input was consumed:

```
def succeed[A](a: A): Parser[A] =
  _ => Success(a, 0)
```

Finally, slice; here we run the wrapped parser and, upon success, return a substring of the original input, with length equal to the number of characters consumed by the wrapped parser, starting from the current offset:

```
extension [A](p: Parser[A])
  def slice: Parser[String] =
    l => p(l) match
      case Success(_, n) =>
        Success(l.input.substring(l.offset, l.offset + n), n)
      case f @ Failure(e) => f
```

ANSWER 9.14

We can wrap the entire parser with label. Doing so replaces any raised error with a simpler error message, indicating that a nonnegative integer was expected. We could alternatively use scope if we wanted to preserve the original error details:

```
val nonNegativeIntOpaque: Parser[Int] =
  nonNegativeInt.label("non-negative integer")
```

ANSWER 9.15

See the full implementation in the GitHub repository: https://mng.bz/QWoj.

ANSWER 9.16

Let's first write a function that collapses errors that occurred at the same location into a single error message:

```
def collapseStack(s: List[(Location, String)]): List[(Location, String)] =
  s.groupBy(_(0)).
    view.
    mapValues(_.map(_(1)).mkString("; ")).
    toList.sortBy(_(0).offset)
```

We used the `groupBy` function to create a `Map[Location, List[(Location, String)]]`. We then transform each inner list by discarding the redundant `Location` and concatenating the error messages, separated by a semicolon. Finally, we convert the result to a list and sort by the location, ensuring errors are reported in the order in which they occurred in the input string.

Now let's use this function in the implementation of `toString` on `ParseError`:

```
override def toString: String =
  if stack.isEmpty then "no error message"
  else
    val collapsed = collapseStack(stack)
    val context =
      collapsed.lastOption.map("\n\n" + _(0).currentLine).getOrElse("") +
      collapsed.lastOption.map("\n" + _(0).columnCaret).getOrElse("")
    collapsed.map((loc, msg) =>
      s"${formatLoc(loc)} $msg").mkString("\n") + context
```

This implementation prints each error in the collapsed list along with the line and column at which that error occurred. For the final error in the stack, we've included the line of input that failed to parse along with a caret pointing to the character in that line where the error occurred. This makes use of a couple of utility functions; see the full implementation in the GitHub repository for details: http://mng.bz/4jPV.

ANSWER 9.17

The key idea is the introduction of a new piece of state: a Boolean flag indicating if the parser is surrounded by a `slice`, indicating its result will be discarded. To do so, we'll need to introduce a new type representing our state:

```
case class ParseState(loc: Location, isSliced: Boolean)
```

Then modify our definition of a parser to use this new state type:

```
opaque type Parser[+A] = ParseState => Result[A]
```

We also need to introduce a new case to our result type, indicating the result is a slice of the input instead of either a successfully parsed value of type A or a failure. To do so, we'll need to convert `Result` from an enum to a `sealed trait`, with subtypes for each case:

```
sealed trait Result[+A]
case class Success[+A](get: A, length: Int) extends Result[A]
case class Failure(
  get: ParseError, isCommitted: Boolean) extends Result[Nothing]
case class Slice(length: Int) extends Result[String]
```

The Slice type takes a single parameter—the number of characters of the input that were sliced. Note that Slice extends Result[String]; this is an example of a generalized algebraic data type (GADT). A GADT is like a regular algebraic data type, except one or more cases refine one or more type parameters. In this case, Slice fixes the type A to String. When we pattern match on a Result[A] and match against a Slice case, Scala knows A is a String and can use that information in further type checking. For example, consider this override of map defined for Parser:

```
override def map[B](f: A => B): Parser[B] =
  s => p(s) match
    case Success(a, n) => Success(f(a), n)
    case Slice(n) => Success(f(s.slice(n)), n)
    case f @ Failure(_, _) => f
```

In the body of the case for Slice, Scala can infer that our parser, p, must be of type Parser[String], or else parsing would not have returned us a Slice value. Hence, it knows that the function f must be a function from String to B and subsequently allows s.slice(n), which returns a String, to be applied to f.

With these definitions, we can modify the slice combinator to set the isSliced flag on the parser state:

```
extension [A](p: Parser[A])
  def slice: Parser[String] =
    s => p(s.copy(isSliced = true)) match
      case s @ Slice(_) => s
      case Success(_, length) => Slice(length)
      case f @ Failure(_, _) => f
```

The slice combinator also transforms the output result, ensuring we replace any Success case with a Slice case.

Finally, we need to use isSliced in various combinators, optimizing them to skip computation of the result when isSliced is true. Here's how we do this for many:

```
override def many: Parser[List[A]] =
  s =>
    var nConsumed: Int = 0
    if s.isSliced then
      def go(p: Parser[String], offset: Int): Result[String] =
        p(s.advanceBy(offset)) match
          case f @ Failure(e, true) => f
          case Failure(e, _) => Slice(offset)
          case Slice(n) => go(p, offset + n)
          case Success(_, _) =>
            sys.error("sliced parser should not return success, only slice")
      go(p.slice, 0).asInstanceOf[Result[List[A]]]
    else
      val buf = new collection.mutable.ListBuffer[A]
      def go(p: Parser[A], offset: Int): Result[List[A]] =
        p(s.advanceBy(offset)) match
```

```
        case Success(a, n) =>
          buf += a
          go(p, offset + n)
        case f @ Failure(e, true) => f
        case Failure(e, _) => Success(buf.toList, offset)
        case Slice(n) =>
          buf += s.input.substring(offset, offset + n)
          go(p, offset + n)
    go(p, 0)
```

There's a lot here! If the state indicates we're sliced, then we use a recursive function that parses until failure—but critically, not accumulating the result of each iteration! Upon encountering an uncommitted failure, a `Slice` is returned, indicating the number of characters that have been consumed. The cast looks a bit worrisome here, but it's completely safe. We know the result is sliced, and hence the output `List[A]` will never be inspected. If instead the state indicates we're not sliced, then we use a similar recursive function, but this time we accumulate each parsed value into a buffer.

Various other combinators will need to be aware of slices (e.g., `map2` and `flatMap`). See the GitHub repository for full details: http://mng.bz/vovM.

ANSWER 9.18

Let's modify `ParserError` to store other errors that occurred when parsing:

```
case class ParseError(stack: List[(Location,String)] = Nil,
                      otherFailures: List[ParseError] = Nil):

  def addFailure(e: ParseError): ParseError =
    copy(otherFailures = e :: otherFailures)
```

We can then implement `or` in a way that keeps track of errors from both branches:

```
extension [A](p: Parser[A])
  infix def or(p2: => Parser[A]): Parser[A] =
    s => p(s) match
      case Failure(e, false) => p2(s).mapError(_.addFailure(e))
      case r => r
```

This change demands additional changes, though. We'll need to update the `toString` of `ParseError` to render these other failures in a way that's useful and intuitive. We should also introduce some combinators for pruning parse errors or otherwise filtering the failures to the most relevant.

Part 3

Common structures
in functional design

We've now written a number of libraries using the principles of functional design. In part 2, we saw these principles applied to a few concrete problem domains. By now you should have a good grasp of how to approach a programming problem in your own work, while striving for compositionality and algebraic reasoning.

Part 3 takes a much wider perspective. We'll look at the common patterns that arise in functional programming. In part 2, we experimented with various libraries that provided concrete solutions to real-world problems, and now we want to integrate what we've learned from our experiments into abstract theories that describe the common structure among those libraries.

This kind of abstraction has a direct practical benefit: it eliminates duplicate code. We can capture abstractions as classes, interfaces, and functions that we can refer to in our actual programs. Its primary benefit, however, is *conceptual integration*. When we recognize common structure among different solutions in different contexts, we unite all of those instances of the structure under a single definition and give it a name. As you gain experience with this, you can look at the general shape of a problem and say, for example, "That looks like a monad!" You're then already far along in finding the shape of the solution. A secondary benefit is that if other people have developed the same kind of vocabulary, you can communicate your designs to them with extraordinary efficiency.

Part 3 won't be a sequence of meandering journeys in the style of part 2. Instead, we'll begin each chapter by introducing an abstract concept, providing its definition, and then tying it back to what we've seen already. The primary goal will be training you to recognize patterns when designing your own libraries and to write code that takes advantage of such patterns.

Monoids

This chapter covers

- Introducing purely algebraic structures
- Discussing monoids
- Introducing typeclasses

By the end of part 2, we were getting comfortable with considering data types in terms of their algebras—that is, the operations they support and the laws that govern those operations. Hopefully, you will have noticed that the algebras of very different data types tend to share certain patterns in common. In this chapter, we'll begin identifying these patterns and taking advantage of them.

This chapter will be our first introduction to *purely algebraic* structures. We'll consider a simple structure, the *monoid*,[1] which is defined only by its algebra. Aside from satisfying the same laws, instances of the monoid interface may have little or nothing to do with one another. Nonetheless, we'll see how this algebraic structure is often all we need to write useful, polymorphic functions.

---

[1] The name *monoid* comes from mathematics. In abstract algebra, a monoid is an associative binary operation closed on a set with an identity element. In category theory, it means a category with one object. These mathematical connections aren't important for our purposes, but see the chapter notes (https://github.com/fpinscala/fpinscala/wiki) for more information.

We choose to start with monoids because they're simple, ubiquitous, and useful. Monoids come up all the time in everyday programming, whether we're aware of them or not. Working with lists, concatenating strings, and accumulating the results of a loop are often phrased in terms of monoids. We'll see how monoids are useful in two ways: they facilitate parallel computation by giving us the freedom to break our problem into chunks that can be computed in parallel, and they can be composed to assemble complex calculations from simpler pieces.

10.1   *What is a monoid?*

Let's consider the algebra of string concatenation. We can add `"foo"` + `"bar"` to get `"foobar"`, and the empty string is an *identity element* for that operation. That is, if we say `(s + "")` or `("" + s)`, then the result is always `s`. Furthermore, if we combine three strings by saying `(r + s + t)`, then the operation is *associative*, it doesn't matter whether we parenthesize it: `((r + s) + t)` or `(r + (s + t))`.

The exact same rules govern integer addition. It's associative, since `(x + y) + z` is always equal to `x + (y + z)`, and it has an identity element, `0`, which does nothing when added to another integer. The same applies for multiplication, whose identity element is `1`. The Boolean operators `&&` and `||` are likewise associative, and they have identity elements `true` and `false`, respectively.

These are just a few simple examples, but algebras like this are virtually everywhere. The term for this kind of algebra is *monoid*, and the laws of associativity and identity are collectively called the *monoid laws*. A monoid consists of the following:

- Some type `A`
- An associative binary operation, `combine`, that takes two values of type `A` and combines them into one: `combine(combine(x, y), z) == combine(x, combine(y, z))` for any choice of `x: A, y: A, z: A`
- A value, `empty: A`, that is an identity for that operation: `combine(x, empty) == x` and `combine(empty, x) == x` for any `x: A`

We can express this with a Scala trait:

> **Satisfies combine(combine(x, y), z) == combine(x, combine(y, z))**

```
trait Monoid[A]:
  def combine(a1: A, a2: A): A   ◄──┐
  def empty: A                  ◄──┘
```

> **Satisfies combine(x, empty) == x and combine(empty, x) == x**

An example instance of this trait is the `String` monoid:

> **Scala can infer we're instantiating a new anonymous subtype of Monoid[String] here, allowing us to write new: instead of new Monoid[String].**

```
val stringMonoid: Monoid[String] = new:   ◄──
  def combine(a1: String, a2: String) = a1 + a2
  val empty = ""
```

List concatenation also forms a monoid:

```
def listMonoid[A]: Monoid[List[A]] = new:
  def combine(a1: List[A], a2: List[A]) = a1 ++ a2
  val empty = Nil
```

> ### The purely abstract nature of an algebraic structure
> Notice that aside from satisfying the monoid laws, the various Monoid instances don't have much to do with each other. The answer to the question *What is a monoid?* is simply that a monoid is a type, together with the monoid operations and a set of laws. A monoid is the algebra—and nothing more. Of course, you may build some other intuition by considering the various concrete instances, but this intuition is necessarily imprecise, and nothing guarantees all monoids you encounter will match your intuition!

■ **EXERCISE 10.1**

Give Monoid instances for integer addition and multiplication as well as the Boolean operators:

```
val intAddition: Monoid[Int]
val intMultiplication: Monoid[Int]
val booleanOr: Monoid[Boolean]
val booleanAnd: Monoid[Boolean]
```

■ **EXERCISE 10.2**

Give a Monoid instance for combining Option values:

```
def optionMonoid[A]: Monoid[Option[A]]
```

■ **EXERCISE 10.3**

A function having the same argument and return type is sometimes called an endofunction.[2] Write a monoid for endofunctions:

```
def endoMonoid[A]: Monoid[A => A]
```

■ **EXERCISE 10.4**

Use the property-based testing framework we developed in part 2 to implement a property for the monoid laws. Use your property to test the monoids we've written:

```
def monoidLaws[A](m: Monoid[A], gen: Gen[A]): Prop
```

---

[2] The Greek prefix *endo-* means *within*, in the sense that an endofunction's codomain is within its domain.

> **Having versus being a monoid**
>
> There is a slight terminology mismatch between programmers and mathematicians
> when they talk about a type *being* a monoid versus *having* a monoid instance. As a
> programmer, it's tempting to think of the instance of type Monoid[A] as being a
> monoid, but that's not accurate terminology. The monoid is actually both things—the
> type together with the instance satisfying the laws. It's more accurate to say that type
> A *forms* a monoid under the operations defined by the Monoid[A] instance. Less pre-
> cisely, we might say *type* A *is a monoid* or even *type* A *is monoidal*. In any case, the
> Monoid[A] instance is simply evidence of this fact.
>
> This is much the same as saying that the page or screen you're reading forms a *rect-
> angle* or is rectangular. It's less accurate to say it is a rectangle (although that still
> makes sense), but to say that it has a rectangle would be strange.

Just what is a monoid, then? It's simply a type A and an implementation of Monoid[A]
that satisfies the laws. Stated tersely, a monoid is a type together with a binary operation
(combine) over that type, satisfying associativity and having an identity element *(empty)*.

What does this buy us? Just like any abstraction, a monoid is useful to the extent we
can write useful generic code assuming only the capabilities provided by the abstraction. Can we write any interesting programs, knowing nothing about a type other than
that it forms a monoid? Absolutely! Let's look at some examples.

10.2   *Folding lists with monoids*

Monoids have an intimate connection with lists. If you look at the signatures of fold-
Left and foldRight on List, you might notice something about the argument types:

```
def foldRight[B](acc: B)(f: (A, B) => B): B
def foldLeft[B](acc: B)(f: (B, A) => B): B
```

What happens when A and B are the same type?

```
def foldRight(acc: A)(f: (A, A) => A): A
def foldLeft(acc: A)(f: (A, A) => A): A
```

The components of a monoid fit these argument types like a glove. So if we had a list
of strings, then we could simply pass the combine and empty functions of the string-
Monoid to reduce the list with the monoid and concatenate all the strings:

```
scala> val words = List("Hic", "Est", "Index")
words: List[String] = List(Hic, Est, Index)

scala> val s = words.foldRight(stringMonoid.empty)(stringMonoid.combine)
s: String = "HicEstIndex"

scala> val t = words.foldLeft(stringMonoid.empty)(stringMonoid.combine)
t: String = "HicEstIndex"
```

Note that it doesn't matter if we choose `foldLeft` or `foldRight` when folding with a monoid;[3] we should get the same result. This is precisely because the laws of associativity and identity hold. A left fold associates operations to the left, whereas a right fold associates to the right, with the identity element on the left and right, respectively:

```
words.foldLeft("")(_ + _)   == ((("" + "Hic") + "Est") + "Index"

words.foldRight("")(_ + _) == "Hic" + ("Est" + ("Index" + ""))
```

We can write a general function `combineAll` that folds a list with a monoid:

```
def combineAll[A](as: List[A], m: Monoid[A]): A =
  as.foldLeft(m.empty)(m.combine)
```

But what if our list has an element type that doesn't have a `Monoid` instance? Well, we can always `map` over the list to turn it into a type that does:

```
def foldMap[A, B](as: List[A], m: Monoid[B])(f: A => B): B
```

■ **EXERCISE 10.5** ───

Implement `foldMap`.

──

■ **EXERCISE 10.6** ───

Hard: The `foldMap` function can be implemented using either `foldLeft` or `foldRight`, but you can also write `foldLeft` and `foldRight` using `foldMap`. Try it!

──

10.3 Associativity and parallelism

The fact that a monoid's operation is associative means we can choose how we fold a data structure like a list. We've already seen that operations can be associated to the left or right to reduce a list sequentially with `foldLeft` or `foldRight`. But if we have a monoid, we can reduce a list using a *balanced fold*, which can be more efficient for some operations as well as allow for parallelism.

As an example, suppose we have a sequence a, b, c, d that we'd like to reduce using some monoid. Folding to the right, the combination of a, b, c, and d would look like this:

```
combine(a, combine(b, combine(c, d)))
```

─────────────────────────────────

[3] Given that both `foldLeft` and `foldRight` have tail-recursive implementations.

Folding to the left would look like this:

```
combine(combine(combine(a, b), c), d)
```

But a balanced fold looks like this:

```
combine(combine(a, b), combine(c, d))
```

The balanced fold allows for parallelism because the two inner combine calls are independent and can be run simultaneously. But beyond that, the more balanced tree structure can be more efficient in cases where the cost of each combine is proportional to the size of its arguments. For instance, consider the runtime performance of this expression:

```
List("lorem", "ipsum", "dolor", "sit").foldLeft("")(_ + _)
```

At every step of the fold, we're allocating the full intermediate String only to discard it and allocate a larger string in the next step. Recall that String values are immutable and that evaluating a + b for strings a and b requires allocating a fresh character array and copying both a and b into this new array. It takes time proportional to a.length + b.length.

Here's a trace of the preceding expression being evaluated:

```
List("lorem", "ipsum", "dolor", "sit").foldLeft("")(_ + _)
List("ipsum", "dolor", "sit").foldLeft("lorem")(_ + _)
List("dolor", "sit").foldLeft("loremipsum")(_ + _)
List("sit").foldLeft("loremipsumdolor")(_ + _)
List().foldLeft("loremipsumdolorsit")(_ + _)
"loremipsumdolorsit"
```

Note that the intermediate strings are being created and then immediately discarded. A more efficient strategy would be combining the sequence by halves, which we call a balanced fold—we first construct "loremipsum" and "dolorsit" and then add those together.

■ **EXERCISE 10.7** ──

Implement a foldMap for IndexedSeq.[4] Your implementation should use the strategy of splitting the sequence in two, recursively processing each half, and then adding the answers together with the monoid:

```
def foldMapV[A,B](as: IndexedSeq[A], m: Monoid[B])(f: A => B): B
```

──

[4] Recall that IndexedSeq is the interface for immutable data structures supporting efficient random access. It also has efficient splitAt and length methods.

◻—— EXERCISE 10.8 ————————————————————————————————

Hard: Implement a parallel version of `foldMap` using the library we developed in chapter 7. Hint: Implement `par`, a combinator to promote `Monoid[A]` to a `Monoid [Par[A]]`,[5] and then use this to implement `parFoldMap`:

```
import fpinscala.parallelism.Nonblocking.*

def par[A](m: Monoid[A]): Monoid[Par[A]]
def parFoldMap[A, B](as: IndexedSeq[A], m: Monoid[B])(f: A => B): Par[B]
```

◼—— EXERCISE 10.9 ————————————————————————————————

Hard: Use `foldMap` to detect whether a given `IndexedSeq[Int]` is ordered. You'll need to come up with a creative `Monoid`.

10.4 Example: Parallel parsing

As a nontrivial use case, let's say we wanted to count the number of words in a `String`. This is a fairly simple parsing problem. We could scan the string character by character, looking for whitespace and counting up the number of runs of consecutive non-whitespace characters. Parsing sequentially like that, the parser state could be as simple as tracking whether the last character seen was a whitespace.

But imagine doing this not for just a short string but for an enormous text file, possibly too big to fit in memory on a single machine. It would be nice if we could work with chunks of the file in parallel. The strategy would be splitting the file into manageable chunks, processing several chunks in parallel, and then combining the results. In that case, the parser state would need to be slightly more complicated, and we would need to be able to combine intermediate results, regardless of whether the section we were looking at was at the beginning, middle, or end of the file. In other words, we would want the combining operation to be associative.

To keep things simple and concrete, let's consider a short string and pretend it's a large file:

```
"lorem ipsum dolor sit amet, "
```

If we split this string roughly in half, we might split it in the middle of a word. In the case of our string, that would yield `"lorem ipsum do"` and `"lor sit amet, "`. When we add up the results of counting the words in these strings, we want to avoid double counting the word `dolor`. Clearly, just counting the words as an `Int` isn't sufficient. We

---

[5] The ability to lift a `Monoid` into the `Par` context is something we'll discuss more generally in chapters 11 and 12.

need to find a data structure that can handle partial results like the half-words `do` and `lor` and track the complete words seen so far, like `ipsum`, `sit`, and `amet`.

The partial result of the word count could be represented by an algebraic data type:

```
enum WC:
  case Stub(chars: String)
  case Part(lStub: String, words: Int, rStub: String)
```

A `Stub` is the simplest case, where we haven't seen any complete words yet. But a `Part` keeps the number of complete words we've seen so far in `words`. The value `lStub` holds any partial word we've seen to the left of those words, and `rStub` holds any partial word on the right.

For example, counting over the string `"lorem ipsum do"` would result in `Part("lorem", 1, "do")`, since there's one word that's certainly complete: `"ipsum"`. And since there's no whitespace to the left of `lorem` or the right of `do`, we can't be sure if they're complete words, so we don't count them yet. Counting over `"lor sit amet, "` would result in `Part("lor", 2, "")`.

■ **EXERCISE 10.10**

Write a monoid instance for `WC`, and make sure it meets the monoid laws:

```
val wcMonoid: Monoid[WC]
```

■ **EXERCISE 10.11**

Use the WC monoid to implement a function that counts words in a `String` by recursively splitting it into substrings and counting the words in those substrings.

Monoid homomorphisms

If you have your law-discovering cap on while reading this chapter, you may notice there's a law that holds for some functions between monoids. Take the `String` concatenation monoid and the integer addition monoid. If you take the lengths of two strings and add them up, it's the same as taking the length of the concatenation of those two strings:

```
"foo".length + "bar".length == ("foo" + "bar").length
```

Here `length` is a function from `String` to `Int` that preserves the monoid structure. Such a function is called a *monoid homomorphism*.[6] A monoid homomorphism `f` between monoids `M` and `N` obeys the following general law for all values `x` and `y`:

```
M.combine(f(x), f(y)) == f(N.combine(x, y))
```

The same law should hold for the homomorphism from `String` to `WC` in the present exercise.

This property can be useful when designing your own libraries. If two types that your library uses are monoids and there exist functions between them, it's a good idea to think about whether those functions are expected to preserve the monoid structure and check the monoid homomorphism law with automated tests.

Sometimes there will be a homomorphism in both directions between two monoids. If they satisfy a *monoid isomorphism* (with *iso-* meaning *equal*), we say the two monoids are isomorphic. A monoid isomorphism between `M` and `N` has two homomorphisms, `f` and `g`, where both `f` andThen `g` and `g` andThen `f` are an identity function.

For example, the `String` and `List[Char]` monoids with concatenation are isomorphic. The Boolean monoids (`false`, `||`) and (`true`, `&&`) are also isomorphic via the `!` (negation) function.

10.5 Typeclasses

The various monoids we've looked at so far have all been defined as simple values and functions. Generic functions like `foldMap`, which made use of monoids, have been defined to take those monoids as arguments. Consider this example:

```scala
def foldMap[A, B](as: List[A], m: Monoid[B])(f: A => B): B =
  as.foldRight(m.empty)((a, acc) => m.combine(f(a), acc))
```
A value of type Monoid[B] is passed as an argument to foldMap.

```scala
val intAddition: Monoid[Int] = new:
  def combine(a1: Int, a2: Int) = a1 + a2
  val empty = 0
```
An instance of Monoid[Int] is defined as a value.

```scala
val strings = List("abra", "ca", "dabra")

val charCount = foldMap(strings, intAddition)(_.length)
```
When we use foldMap, we pass the monoid to use.

Instead of passing monoid values, we can have Scala pass them automatically by slightly altering the definition of `foldMap`:

```scala
def foldMap[A, B](as: List[A])(f: A => B)(using m: Monoid[B]): B =
  as.foldRight(m.empty)((a, acc) => m.combine(f(a), acc))
```

---

[6] *Homomorphism* comes from the Greek *homo*, meaning *same*, and *morphe*, meaning *shape*.

We've moved the `Monoid[B]` parameter to its own parameter list and added the `using` keyword. Parameter lists that start with the `using` keyword define *context parameters.*[7] Context parameters are not explicitly passed to a function; instead, Scala searches for a *given instance* for each context parameter at the call site of the function. Given instances, also known as givens, are defined with the `given` keyword. Let's define `intAddition` as a given instance for `Monoid[Int]`:

```
given intAddition: Monoid[Int] with
  def combine(a1: Int, a2: Int) = a1 + a2
  val empty = 0
```

The name for the given instance is optional,[8] so we could optionally write this instead:

```
given Monoid[Int] with
  def combine(a1: Int, a2: Int) = a1 + a2
  val empty = 0
```

With either definition, we can use `foldMap`, without explicitly naming the monoid to use:

```
val strings = List("abra", "ca", "dabra")
val charCount = foldMap(strings)(_.length)
```

Scala infers that the function passed to `foldMap` returns an `Int` and subsequently searches for a given instance of `Monoid[Int]`. The search succeeds, finding the `intAddition` given instance.

Where does Scala search? The full algorithm is complicated, but as a first approximation, it looks

- In the current lexical scope, looking for defined given instances or imported given instances or
- In the companion objects of the types that appear in the context parameter

The second rule is particularly useful. When searching for a `Monoid[Int]` and failing to find a defined or imported instance in lexical scope, Scala will look in the companion object of both `Monoid` and `Int` for the necessary instance. We can take advantage of this and define all our canonical instances in the `Monoid` companion, but note that we must pick just one instance as the canonical one. Let's redefine some of the instances we defined earlier:

```
object Monoid:
  given intAddition: Monoid[Int] with
    def combine(a1: Int, a2: Int) = a1 + a2
    val empty = 0
```

---

[7] Context parameters are a Scala-3-specific feature. In Scala 2, implicit parameters were used instead.

[8] Scala will generate a name for unnamed givens. We'll generally use named instances throughout the remainder of this book.

```
val intMultiplication: Monoid[Int] = new:
  def combine(a1: Int, a2: Int) = a1 * a2
  val empty = 1

given string: Monoid[String] with
  def combine(a1: String, a2: String) = a1 + a2
  val empty = ""

val booleanOr: Monoid[Boolean] = new:
  def combine(x: Boolean, y: Boolean) = x || y
  val empty = false

val booleanAnd: Monoid[Boolean] = new:
  def combine(x: Boolean, y: Boolean) = x && y
  val empty = true
```

Here we've defined `intAddition` as the canonical `Monoid[Int]`, while providing `intMultiplication` as a regular value. Likewise, we've defined a canonical instance for `Monoid[String]`. We provided `booleanOr` and `booleanAnd` as regular values since neither are good default values. When we call a function that uses context parameters, we can supply our own instances instead of given instances via the `using` keyword. For example

```
val allPositive = foldMap(List(1, 2, 3))(_ > 0)(using Monoid.booleanAnd)
val existsNegative = foldMap(List(1, 2, 3))(_ < 0)(using Monoid.booleanOr)
```

See the official documentation for more details about givens (https://mng.bz/Bx02) and context parameters (https://mng.bz/do7w).

Let's review what we've done here. We have a parameterized trait—`Monoid[A]`—and default, or canonical, instances of that trait for various types. We also have generic functions that take instances of our trait as context parameters. This is the essence of the *typeclass* pattern—a trait with a single type parameter and some number of given instances. The typeclass pattern provides a form of ad hoc polymorphism—that is, the ability to define an interface independent from the definition of a type and then adapt such types to the interface. For the remainder of this chapter, we'll use `Monoid` as a typeclass instead of as a plain value; we'll pass monoids as context parameters and define instances as givens instead of values.

10.6   *Foldable data structures*

In chapter 3, we implemented the data structures `List` and `Tree`, both of which could be folded. In chapter 5, we wrote `LazyList`, a lazy structure that can be folded much like a `List` can, and now we've just written a fold for `IndexedSeq`.

When we're writing code that needs to process data contained in one of these structures, we often don't care about the shape of the structure (i.e., whether it's a tree or a list), whether it's lazy, whether it provides efficient random access, and so forth. For example, if we have a structure full of integers and want to calculate their sum, we can use foldRight:

```
ints.foldRight(0)(_ + _)
```

Looking at just this code snippet, we shouldn't have to care about the type of ints. It could be a Vector, Stream, List, or anything at all with a foldRight method. We can capture this commonality in a typeclass:

```
trait Foldable[F[_]]:
  extension [A](as: F[A])
    def foldRight[B](acc: B)(f: (A, B) => B): B
    def foldLeft[B](acc: B)(f: (B, A) => B): B
    def foldMap[B](f: A => B)(using m: Monoid[B]): B
    def combineAll(using m: Monoid[A]): A =
      as.foldLeft(m.empty)(m.combine)
```

Here we're abstracting over a type constructor F, much like we did with the Parser type in the previous chapter. We write it as F[_], where the underscore indicates F is not a proper type but a type constructor that takes one type argument. Just like functions that take other functions as arguments are called *higher-order functions*, something like Foldable is a *higher-order type constructor* or a *higher-kinded type*.[9]

■ EXERCISE 10.12

Implement Foldable[List], Foldable[IndexedSeq], and Foldable[LazyList]. Remember that foldRight, foldLeft, and foldMap can all be implemented in terms of each other, but that might not be the most efficient implementation.

■ EXERCISE 10.13

Recall the binary Tree data type from chapter 3. Implement a Foldable instance for it:

```
enum Tree[+A]:
  case Leaf[A](value: A)
  case Branch[A](left: Tree[A], right: Tree[A])
```

---

[9] Just like values and functions have types, types and type constructors have *kinds*. Scala uses kinds to track how many type arguments a type constructor takes, whether it's co- or contravariant in those arguments, and what kinds of arguments those are.

EXERCISE 10.14

Write a `Foldable[Option]` instance.

EXERCISE 10.15

Any `Foldable` structure can be turned into a `List`. Add a `toList` extension method to the `Foldable` trait, and provide a concrete implementation in terms of the other methods on `Foldable`:

```
trait Foldable[F[_]]:
  extension [A](as: F[A])
    def toList: List[A] = ???
```

10.7 Composing monoids

The `Monoid` abstraction in itself is not all that compelling, and with the generalized `foldMap`, it's only slightly more interesting. The real power of monoids comes from the fact that they *compose*. This means, for example, that if types A and B are monoids, then the tuple type (A, B) is also a monoid (called their *product*).

EXERCISE 10.16

Implement `productMonoid` using a ma: `Monoid[A]` and mb: `Monoid[B]`. Notice that your implementation of `combine` is associative so long as ma.`combine` and mb.`combine` are both associative:

```
given productMonoid[A, B](
  using ma: Monoid[A], mb: Monoid[B]
): Monoid[(A, B)] with
  def combine(x: (A, B), y: (A, B)) = ???
  val empty = ???
```

10.7.1 Assembling more complex monoids

Some data structures form interesting monoids as long as the types of elements they contain also form monoids. For instance, there's a monoid for merging key-value `Map`s, as long as the value type is a monoid.

Listing 10.1   Merging key-value Maps

```
given mapMergeMonoid[K, V](using mv: Monoid[V]): Monoid[Map[K, V]] with
  def combine(a: Map[K, V], b: Map[K, V]) =
    (a.keySet ++ b.keySet).foldLeft(empty): (acc, k) =>
      acc.updated(k, mv.combine(a.getOrElse(k, mv.empty),
                                b.getOrElse(k, mv.empty)))
  val empty = Map()
```

Using this simple combinator, we can synthesize more complex monoids fairly easily simply by telling the compiler the type of monoid we want and letting it derive an appropriate instance from the various givens available:

```
scala> val m = summon[Monoid[Map[String, Map[String, Int]]]]
m: Monoid[Map[String, Map[String, Int]]] = Monoid$mapMergeMonoid@1d1484fd
```

The summon method searches all of the given instances in scope for a value of the specified type or fails to compile if such an instance is not available. The search can recurse if it finds an instance that takes its own context parameters. In this case, summon searches for a Monoid[Map[String, Map[String, Int]]] and finds our mapMergeMonoid with type parameter K = String and V = Map[String, Int]. But mapMergeMonoid requires a Monoid[V], so Scala searches for a Monoid[Map[String, Int]] and finds mapMergeMonoid again—this time with K = String, V = Int. Again, mapMergeMonoid requires a Monoid[V], so Scala searches for a Monoid[Int] and finds intAddition. Through this search process, Scala has assembled mapMergeMonoid (using mapMergeMonoid(using intAddition)).

This search algorithm isn't unique to the summon method—it's built into Scala's logic for finding given instances. In fact, we could define our own version of summon that has the same behavior by using a context parameter:

```
def mySummon[A](using a: A): A = a
```

This power to automatically synthesize monoids allows us to combine nested expressions with no additional programming and with no explicit references to monoids:

```
scala> val a = Map("o1" -> Map("i1" -> 1, "i2" -> 2))
a: Map[String,Map[String,Int]] = Map(o1 -> Map(i1 -> 1, i2 -> 2))

scala> val b = Map("o1" -> Map("i2" -> 3))
b: Map[String,Map[String,Int]] = Map(o1 -> Map(i2 -> 3))

scala> val c = m.combine(a, b)
c: Map[String,Map[String,Int]] = Map(o1 -> Map(i1 -> 1, i2 -> 5))
```

■──(EXERCISE 10.17)──

Write a monoid instance for functions whose results are monoids:

```
given functionMonoid[A, B](using mb: Monoid[B]): Monoid[A => B] with
  def combine(f: A => B, g: A => B): A => B = ???
  val empty: A => B = ???
```

■──(EXERCISE 10.18)──

A bag is like a set, except it's represented by a map that contains one entry per element, with that element as the key and the value under that key as the number of times the element appears in the bag. For example:

```
scala> bag(Vector("a", "rose", "is", "a", "rose"))
res0: Map[String,Int] = Map(a -> 2, rose -> 2, is -> 1)
```

Use monoids to compute a bag from an `IndexedSeq`:

```
def bag[A](as: IndexedSeq[A]): Map[A, Int]
```

10.7.2 *Using composed monoids to fuse traversals*

The fact that multiple monoids can be composed into one means we can perform multiple calculations simultaneously when folding a data structure. For example, we can take the length and sum of a list at the same time to calculate the mean:

```
scala> import Foldable.given          ◁───────────┐   This imports the
                                                   │   foldMap extension
scala> val p = List(1, 2, 3, 4).foldMap(a => (1, a))│   method. If we forget
p: (Int, Int) = (4, 10)                            │   this import, the
                                                   │   compiler helpfully
scala> val mean = p(1) / p(0).toDouble             │   suggests it.
mean: Double = 2.5
```

We're folding with a product monoid with two additive int monoids. This instance would be tedious to assemble by hand, but Scala derives it for us, thanks to our given instances (in this case, `productMonoid` and `intAddition` defined in the `Monoid` companion).

10.8   *Conclusion*

Our goal in part 3 is to get you accustomed to working with more abstract structures and develop the ability to recognize them. In this chapter, we introduced one of the simplest purely algebraic abstractions: the monoid. When you start looking for it, you'll find ample opportunity to exploit the monoidal structure of your own libraries.

The associative property enables folding any `Foldable` data type and offers the flexibility of doing so in parallel. Monoids are also compositional, and you can use them to assemble folds in a declarative and reusable way.

`Monoid` has been our first purely abstract algebra, defined only in terms of its abstract operations and the laws that govern them. We saw how we can still write useful functions that know nothing about their arguments, except that their type forms a monoid. This more abstract mode of thinking is something we'll develop further in the rest of part 3. We'll consider other purely algebraic interfaces and show how they encapsulate common patterns we've repeated throughout this book.

Summary

- A monoid is a purely algebraic structure consisting of an associative binary operation and an identity element for that operation.
- Associativity lets us move the parentheses around in an expression without changing the result.
- Example monoids include string concatenation with the empty string as the identity, integer addition with `0` as the identity, integer multiplication with `1` as the identity, Boolean and with `true` as the identity, Boolean or with `false` as the identity, and list concatenation with `Nil` as the identity.
- Monoids can be modeled as traits with `combine` and `empty` operations.
- Monoids allow us to write useful, generic functions for a wide variety of data types.
- The `combineAll` function folds the elements of a list into a single value using a monoid.
- The `foldMap` function maps each element of a list to a new type and then combines the mapped values with a monoid instance.
- `foldMap` can be implemented with `foldLeft` or `foldRight`, and both `foldLeft` and `foldRight` can be implemented with `foldMap`.
- The various monoids encountered in this chapter had nothing in common besides their monoidal structure.
- Typeclasses allow us to describe an algebraic structure and provide canonical instances of that structure for various types.
- Context parameters are defined by starting a parameter list with the `using` keyword. At the call site, Scala will search for a given instance of each context parameter. Given instances are defined with the `given` keyword.
- Context parameters can be passed explicitly with the `using` keyword at the call site.
- Scala's given instances and context parameters allow us to offload type-driven composition to the compiler.
- The `summon` method returns the given instance in scope for the supplied type parameter. If no such instance is available, compilation fails.

- The `Foldable` typeclass describes type constructors that support computing an output value by folding over their elements—that is, support `foldLeft`, `foldRight`, `foldMap`, and `combineAll`.

10.9 Exercise answers

 ANSWER 10.1

```
val intAddition: Monoid[Int] = new:
  def combine(x: Int, y: Int) = x + y
  val empty = 0

val intMultiplication: Monoid[Int] = new:
  def combine(x: Int, y: Int) = x * y
  val empty = 1

val booleanOr: Monoid[Boolean] = new:
  def combine(x: Boolean, y: Boolean) = x || y
  val empty = false

val booleanAnd: Monoid[Boolean] = new:
  def combine(x: Boolean, y: Boolean) = x && y
  val empty = true
```

ANSWER 10.2

Let's start with a skeletal implementation:

```
def optionMonoid[A]: Monoid[Option[A]] = new:
  def combine(x: Option[A], y: Option[A]) = ???
  val empty = ???
```

This type signature constrains our implementation quite a bit. Consider the information we don't have here:

- We have no way of constructing a value of type `A`.
- We have no way of modifying a value of type `A`.
- We have no way of combining multiple values of type `A` into a new value.

With these constraints in mind, let's implement `empty` and `combine`.

To implement `empty`, we need to return an `Option[A]`, which acts as an identity for our combine operation. We could either return a `None` or a `Some`, but since we have no way of constructing a value of type `A` to wrap in `Some`, we're forced to return `None`.

What possibilities do we have for implementing `combine`? There are three cases to consider: when both inputs are `None`, when both inputs are `Some`, and when one input is `None` while the other is `Some`:

- When both inputs are None, the only thing we can do is return a None (since returning a Some would require the ability to create a value of A).
- When one input is None and the other is Some, we have a choice: we could return either the None or Some. However, if we returned None, our identity law would fail—for example, combine(empty, Some(x)) would return None, but our law requires it to return Some(x). Hence, we don't really have a choice here— we must return the Some value.
- When both inputs are Some, we have another choice: we can return either value. Notably, though, we cannot combine the values into a new value, as we have no information about A, which allows combining values. Either choice passes our monoid laws.

This gives us the following implementation:

```
def firstOptionMonoid[A]: Monoid[Option[A]] = new:
  def combine(x: Option[A], y: Option[A]) = x orElse y
  val empty = None
```

We could define a different monoid value that returns y first and then x:

```
def lastOptionMonoid[A]: Monoid[Option[A]] = new:
  def combine(x: Option[A], y: Option[A]) = y orElse x
  val empty = None
```

We can generalize this notion of changing the order of x and y and generate a combinator that returns the dual monoid for any input monoid:

```
def dual[A](m: Monoid[A]): Monoid[A] = new:
  def combine(x: A, y: A) = m.combine(y, x)
  val empty = m.empty
```

With dual we can rewrite lastOptionMonoid in terms of firstOptionMonoid:

```
def lastOptionMonoid[A]: Monoid[Option[A]] = dual(firstOptionMonoid)
```

Consider the result of computing the dual monoid for various monoids we've looked at so far. The dual of the integer addition monoid turns out to be equal to the integer addition monoid—because the order in which we sum integers doesn't matter, we always get the same result. We say an operation is *commutative* if the order doesn't matter (e.g., if combine(x, y) == combine(y, x)). The integer multiplication and Boolean monoids are also commutative. However, the string concatenation and list monoids are not commutative, and hence their dual monoids are distinct.

Returning to the Monoid[Option[A]], instead of letting the constraints force us into the monoid definitions we came up with, what if we changed the constraints? We still want a lawful monoid, so we can't change the associativity or identity laws, but we could ask for more information—in particular, we could write a combine operation that combines two `Some` values if we had a way of combining two `A` values. Let's ask for that:

> **This assumes we have a map2 extension method on Option, since the standard library does not define map2.**

```
def optionMonoid[A](f: (A, A) => A): Monoid[Option[A]] = new:
  def combine(x: Option[A], y: Option[A]) = x.map2(y)(f)  ⟵
  val empty = None
```

■ **ANSWER 10.3**

Let's start with a skeletal implementation:

```
def endoMonoid[A]: Monoid[A => A] = new:
  def combine(f: A => A, g: A => A): A => A = ???
  val empty: A => A = ???
```

For `empty` we need to return a function from `A` to `A`—given what we know (or rather what we don't know), the only possible implementation is returning the identity function. For `combine` we have two functions from `A` to `A`, and we can compose them in one of two ways—either first `f` and then `g`, or vice versa. Whichever we choose can be combined with `dual` from exercise 10.2 to generate the other:

```
def endoMonoid[A]: Monoid[A => A] = new:
  def combine(f: A => A, g: A => A): A => A = f andThen g
  val empty: A => A = identity
```

■ **ANSWER 10.4**

We need to write two properties—one for the associativity law and one for the identity law. For the associativity property, we need to generate three values and assert that combining them all is associative. We can use the `**` operation on `Gen` to do this.

The identity property can be tested by generating a single value and ensuring the following:

- Combining it with the empty value results in the generated value
- Combining the empty value with the generated value results in the generated value

```
import fpinscala.testing.{Prop, Gen}
import Gen.`**`

def monoidLaws[A](m: Monoid[A], gen: Gen[A]): Prop =
  val associativity = Prop
    .forAll(gen ** gen ** gen):
      case a ** b ** c =>
```

```
      m.combine(a, m.combine(b, c)) == m.combine(m.combine(a, b), c)
    .tag("associativity")
val identity = Prop
  .forAll(gen): a =>
    m.combine(a, m.empty) == a && m.combine(m.empty, a) == a
  .tag("identity")
associativity && identity
```

Note that we tagged each law with a name, so the cause of failure is more evident.

ANSWER 10.5

Fold starting with the empty element of the monoid and combining the accumulated result with the result of applying the current element to the supplied function:

```
def foldMap[A, B](as: List[A], m: Monoid[B])(f: A => B): B =
  as.foldLeft(m.empty)((b, a) => m.combine(b, f(a)))
```

ANSWER 10.6

Let's look at that signature of foldRight:

```
def foldRight[A, B](as: List[A])(acc: B)(f: (A, B) => B): B = ???
```

The key insight is that we can curry f, converting it from (A, B) => B to A => (B => B). We can then foldMap the elements of the list using that curried function and the endo-Monoid from earlier. The result of that is a single function of type B => B, which we can then invoke using the initial acc value:

```
def foldRight[A, B](as: List[A])(acc: B)(f: (A, B) => B): B =
  foldMap(as, endoMonoid)(f.curried)(acc)
```

This implementation compiles but gives incorrect results. Consider this example:

```
scala> Monoid.foldRight(List("a", "b", "c"))("")(_ + _)
val res0: String = cba
```

The problem is that our function composition is occurring in the wrong order. We can fix that by flipping the parameters to the endoMonoid by using its dual:

```
def foldRight[A, B](as: List[A])(acc: B)(f: (A, B) => B): B =
  foldMap(as, dual(endoMonoid))(f.curried)(acc)
```

The implementation of `foldLeft` follows the same strategy, but we have to reverse the order of the parameters to `f`, and we need to use the original order of function composition:

```
def foldLeft[A, B](as: List[A])(acc: B)(f: (B, A) => B): B =
  foldMap(as, endoMonoid)(a => b => f(b, a))(acc)
```

■ ANSWER 10.7 ——

If as has no elements, then we return the identity element of the `Monoid[B]`. If as has one element, we return the result of invoking `f` with that element. Finally, if as has two or more elements, we split as in half and use the `Monoid[B]` to combine the results of recursively calling `foldMapV` on each half:

```
def foldMapV[A, B](as: IndexedSeq[A], m: Monoid[B])(f: A => B): B =
  if as.length == 0 then
    m.empty
  else if as.length == 1 then
    f(as(0))
  else
    val (l, r) = as.splitAt(as.length / 2)
    m.combine(foldMapV(l, m)(f), foldMapV(r, m)(f))
```

□ ANSWER 10.8 ——

First let's implement par:

```
def par[A](m: Monoid[A]): Monoid[Par[A]] = new:
  def combine(a1: Par[A], a2: Par[A]) = a1.map2(a2)(m.combine)
  val empty = Par.unit(m.empty)
```

In the body of `combine`, we have two `Par[A]` values and the `m.combine` function, which has type `(A, A) => A`. We can use map2 on Par to put those pieces together. In the body of `empty`, we get the empty value of the original monoid and lift it in to Par via unit.

Now let's consider `parFoldMap`. We want both the transformation of each element (the *map*) as well as the reduction of results (the *reduce*) to run in parallel. We can accomplish the former via the parMap operation we wrote in chapter 7. We then need to reduce the resulting `Par[IndexedSeq[B]]` to a `Par[B]`, which we can do with `foldMapV`:

```
def parFoldMap[A, B](as: IndexedSeq[A], m: Monoid[B])(f: A => B): Par[B] =
  Par.parMap(as)(f).flatMap(bs =>
    foldMapV(bs, par(m))(b => Par.lazyUnit(b))
  )
```

ANSWER 10.9

One way of approaching this problem is by treating it as a map-reduce problem. Imagine splitting the sequence in half, determining if each half is ordered, and then combining those results into a final answer. How would we combine the result of checking each half? The overall sequence is ordered if both halves are ordered and the maximum value in the left half is less than or equal to the minimum value in the right half. Hence, we're going to need a monoid that tracks whether a sequence is ordered and tracks the minimum and maximum values in that interval. Let's do that with a new case class:

```
case class Interval(ordered: Boolean, min: Int, max: Int)

val orderedMonoid: Monoid[Option[Interval]] = new:
  def combine(oa1: Option[Interval], oa2: Option[Interval]) =
    (oa1, oa2) match
      case (Some(a1), Some(a2)) =>
        Some(Interval(
          a1.ordered && a2.ordered && a1.max <= a2.min,
          a1.min, a2.max))
      case (x, None) => x
      case (None, x) => x
  val empty = None
```

> By defining Monoid[Option[Interval]] instead of Monoid[Interval], we can define empty as None.

> The merged sequence is ordered when both inputs are ordered and the max value on the left is less than or equal to the min value on the right. We also compute a new max for the overall sequence.

Then we can use this monoid with either foldMap, foldMapV, or parFoldMap—all will return the same result but do so with varying levels of efficiency. We'll need to convert each integer into an Option[Interval], and when foldMapV returns, we'll need to unwrap the option and discard the min/max values:

```
def ordered(ints: IndexedSeq[Int]): Boolean =
  foldMapV(ints, orderedMonoid)(i =>
    Some(Interval(true, i, i)))
      .map(_.ordered).getOrElse(true)
```

> A sequence with a single element is ordered and has a max value equal to that element.

ANSWER 10.10

We need to implement empty and combine; let's consider empty first. Since we haven't seen any characters yet, we can use a Stub("") as the empty value:

```
val wcMonoid: Monoid[WC] = new:
  val empty = WC.Stub("")
```

Now let's consider combine. Since our algebraic data type has two cases, Stub and Part, we'll need combine to handle four total cases: combining a stub with a stub, a stub with a part, a part with a stub, and a part with a part. Let's sketch that:

```
def combine(wc1: WC, wc2: WC) = (wc1, wc2) match
  case (WC.Stub(a), WC.Stub(b)) => ???
  case (WC.Stub(a), WC.Part(l, w, r)) => ???
  case (WC.Part(l, w, r), WC.Stub(a)) => ???
  case (WC.Part(l, w, r), WC.Part(l2, w2, r2)) => ???
```

Combining two stubs should result in a new concatenated stub since we still haven't seen a whole word:

```
case (WC.Stub(a), WC.Stub(b)) => WC.Stub(a + b)
```

Combining a stub with a part and a part with a stub is done by creating a new part, with either the lStub or rStub extended to include the stub. We have to take care to keep the overall characters in the correct order (e.g., ensuring a stub with a part results in extending the resultant left stub):

```
case (WC.Stub(a), WC.Part(l, w, r)) => WC.Part(a + l, w, r)
case (WC.Part(l, w, r), WC.Stub(a)) => WC.Part(l, w, r + a)
```

Finally, combining two parts is done by creating a new part with the left stub of the left part, creating a new part with the right stub of the right part, and summing the word count of the two parts. We also need to combine the *inner stubs*—the right stub of the left part and the left stub of the right part—and count that as a word if it's nonempty:

```
case (WC.Part(l, w, r), WC.Part(l2, w2, r2)) =>
  WC.Part(l, w + (if (r + l2).isEmpty then 0 else 1) + w2, r2)
```

Putting this altogether, we have the following:

```
val wcMonoid: Monoid[WC] = new Monoid[WC]:
  val empty = WC.Stub("")

  def combine(wc1: WC, wc2: WC) = (wc1, wc2) match
    case (WC.Stub(a), WC.Stub(b)) => WC.Stub(a + b)
    case (WC.Stub(a), WC.Part(l, w, r)) => WC.Part(a + l, w, r)
    case (WC.Part(l, w, r), WC.Stub(a)) => WC.Part(l, w, r + a)
    case (WC.Part(l, w, r), WC.Part(l2, w2, r2)) =>
      WC.Part(l, w + (if (r + l2).isEmpty then 0 else 1) + w2, r2)
```

How do we know we got it right? Let's use the monoid laws we implemented in exercise 10.4. To do so, we'll need to create a Gen[WC]:

```
def wcGen: Gen[WC] =
  val smallString = Gen.choose(0, 10).flatMap(Gen.stringN)
  val genStub = smallString.map(s => WC.Stub(s))
  val genPart = for
    lStub <- smallString
    words <- Gen.choose(0, 10)
    rStub <- smallString
  yield WC.Part(lStub, words, rStub)
  Gen.union(genStub, genPart)
```

We can then test our implementation:

```
scala> monoidLaws(wcMonoid, wcGen).run()
+ OK, passed 100 tests.
```

Let's look back at our implementation of `empty`, though. Instead of defining empty as a stub, could we define it as a part that's seen no words? Let's try it:

```
val wcMonoid: Monoid[WC] = new Monoid[WC]:
  val empty = WC.Part("", 0, "")
  ...
```

Then let's run the tests:

```
scala> monoidLaws(wcMonoid, wcGen).run()
! Falsified after 0 passed tests:
 and-right(identity(Part(07A,1,S)))
```

The identity law fails with this implementation. Why? Recall that the identity law says that combining any value with the empty value must result in the original value. What happens when we combine a `Stub("a")` with a `Part("", 0, "")`? We get a `Part("a", 0, "")`, which is not equal to `Stub("a")`.

■ ANSWER 10.11

Let's use `wcMonoid` to fold the characters of the input string. To do so, we'll need a function that converts a character to a `WC`:

```
def wc(c: Char): WC =
  if c.isWhitespace then
    WC.Part("", 0, "")
  else
    WC.Stub(c.toString)
```

This is a bit tricky. If the character is a whitespace character, then we construct a part initialized to zero words. This ensures that the whitespace character separates the non-whitespace characters when reducing.

Using this function, we can fold the characters in the string, resulting in a single output `WC` value. We then need to count the words in that `WC` value:

```
def count(s: String): Int =
  def wc(c: Char): WC =
    if c.isWhitespace then
      WC.Part("", 0, "")
    else
      WC.Stub(c.toString)
  def unstub(s: String) = if s.isEmpty then 0 else 1
```

```
foldMapV(s.toIndexedSeq, wcMonoid)(wc) match
  case WC.Stub(s) => unstub(s)
  case WC.Part(l, w, r) => unstub(l) + w + unstub(r)
```

Here we created an unstub function that returns 0 if the input string is empty and 1 otherwise. If the fold finishes in a single stub, we return either 0 or 1, depending on whether that string is empty. Note that if it's nonempty, it necessarily does not contain whitespace characters, due to our definition of wc. Similarly, if the fold finishes in a part, then we unstub the left and right stubs and add the result to the part's word count.

■ **ANSWER 10.12**

First we can add concrete definitions to the Foldable trait for each of the abstract methods:

```
trait Foldable[F[_]]:
  import Monoid.{endoMonoid, dual}

  extension [A](as: F[A])
    def foldRight[B](acc: B)(f: (A, B) => B): B =
      as.foldMap(f.curried)(using dual(endoMonoid[B]))(acc)

    def foldLeft[B](acc: B)(f: (B, A) => B): B =
      as.foldMap(a => b => f(b, a))(using endoMonoid[B])(acc)

    def foldMap[B](f: A => B)(using mb: Monoid[B]): B =
      as.foldRight(mb.empty)((a, b) => mb.combine(f(a), b))

    def combineAll(using ma: Monoid[A]): A =
      as.foldLeft(ma.empty)(ma.combine)
```

Here we've implemented foldLeft and foldRight in terms of foldMap, and we've implemented foldMap in terms of foldRight, using the implementations from exercise 10.6. This leaves us with no abstract operations! However, an instance will have to override either foldRight or foldMap; otherwise, it will result in infinite recursive loops. This technique allows us to choose which operations are fundamental and which are derived in terms of those fundamental operations based on the target type. An alternate design choice would be leaving foldLeft and foldRight abstract, since we know the implementations of those operations defined in terms of foldMap are likely not as performant.

The List implementation overrides foldLeft and foldRight and delegates to the built-in methods on List:

```
given Foldable[List] with
  extension [A](as: List[A])
    override def foldRight[B](acc: B)(f: (A, B) => B) =
```

```
    as.foldRight(acc)(f)
  override def foldLeft[B](acc: B)(f: (B, A) => B) =
    as.foldLeft(acc)(f)
```

The `IndexedSeq` implementation does the same but also overrides `foldMap`, using `foldMapV` to more efficiently evaluate the result:

```
given Foldable[IndexedSeq] with
  extension [A](as: IndexedSeq[A])
    override def foldRight[B](acc: B)(f: (A, B) => B) =
      as.foldRight(acc)(f)
    override def foldLeft[B](acc: B)(f: (B, A) => B) =
      as.foldLeft(acc)(f)
    override def foldMap[B](f: A => B)(using mb: Monoid[B]): B =
      Monoid.foldMapV(as, mb)(f)
```

The `LazyList` implementation is similar to the `List` implementation, delegating `foldLeft` and `foldRight` to the underlying data type:

```
given Foldable[LazyList] with
  extension [A](as: LazyList[A])
    override def foldRight[B](acc: B)(f: (A, B) => B) =
      as.foldRight(acc)(f)
    override def foldLeft[B](acc: B)(f: (B, A) => B) =
      as.foldLeft(acc)(f)
```

ANSWER 10.13

We implement all three operations, using recursive calls on branches:

```
given Foldable[Tree] with
  import Tree.{Leaf, Branch}
  extension [A](as: Tree[A])
    override def foldRight[B](acc: B)(f: (A, B) => B) = as match
      case Leaf(a) => f(a, acc)
      case Branch(l, r) => l.foldRight(r.foldRight(acc)(f))(f)
    override def foldLeft[B](acc: B)(f: (B, A) => B) = as match
      case Leaf(a) => f(acc, a)
      case Branch(l, r) => r.foldLeft(l.foldLeft(acc)(f))(f)
    override def foldMap[B](f: A => B)(using mb: Monoid[B]): B = as match
      case Leaf(a) => f(a)
      case Branch(l, r) => mb.combine(l.foldMap(f), r.foldMap(f))
```

ANSWER 10.14

```
given Foldable[Option] with
  extension [A](as: Option[A])
    override def foldRight[B](acc: B)(f: (A, B) => B) = as match
```

```
      case None => acc
      case Some(a) => f(a, acc)
    override def foldLeft[B](acc: B)(f: (B, A) => B) = as match
      case None => acc
      case Some(a) => f(acc, a)
    override def foldMap[B](f: A => B)(using mb: Monoid[B]): B =
      as match
        case None => mb.empty
        case Some(a) => f(a)
```

■ ANSWER 10.15

```
trait Foldable[F[_]]:
  extension [A](as: F[A])
    def toList: List[A] =
      as.foldRight(List.empty[A])(_ :: _)
```

Note that we can also override this `toList` implementation in the `Foldable[List]` instance:

```
given Foldable[List] with
  extension [A](as: List[A])
    override def foldRight[B](acc: B)(f: (A, B) => B) =
      as.foldRight(acc)(f)
    override def foldLeft[B](acc: B)(f: (B, A) => B) =
      as.foldLeft(acc)(f)
    override def toList: List[A] = as
```

■ ANSWER 10.16

To implement `combine`, we combine the first element of the input pairs with `ma` and the second element with `mb`, returning the result as a pair. For `empty` we pair the empty elements of `ma` and `mb`:

```
given productMonoid[A, B](
  using ma: Monoid[A], mb: Monoid[B]
): Monoid[(A, B)] with
  def combine(x: (A, B), y: (A, B)) =
    (ma.combine(x(0), y(0)), mb.combine(x(1), y(1)))
  val empty = (ma.empty, mb.empty)
```

■ ANSWER 10.17

Looking at the types tells us that `combine` merges two functions, f and g, of type A => B into a single function, A => B. To implement this we return an anonymous function that upon receiving an A value, invokes both f and g and combines their results using the supplied Monoid[B]. To implement empty, we return an anonymous function that ignores the input and always returns the empty element of Monoid[B]:

```
given functionMonoid[A, B](using mb: Monoid[B]): Monoid[A => B] with
  def combine(f: A => B, g: A => B): A => B = a => mb.combine(f(a), g(a))
  val empty: A => B = a => mb.empty
```

■ ANSWER 10.18

We can foldMap the input sequence, converting each element to a singleton Map with a key equal to the element and a value equal to one. The singleton maps will be merged using the mapMergeMonoid given, instantiated with the intAddition given to combine values, returning a map containing a count of each unique element.

We'll need to import the syntax for Foldable (i.e., Scala needs to know where to look for the foldMap extension method). Assuming we've defined the various Foldable given instances in the Foldable companion object, we can import the foldMap syntax via import Foldable.given:

```
def bag[A](as: IndexedSeq[A]): Map[A, Int] =
  import Foldable.given
  as.foldMap(a => Map(a -> 1))
```

Alternatively, we could manually create the mapMergeMonoid and pass that to the foldMapV function we wrote earlier in this chapter:

```
def bagManualComposition[A](as: IndexedSeq[A]): Map[A, Int] =
  val bagMonoid = mapMergeMonoid[A, Int](using intAddition)
  foldMapV(as, bagMonoid)(a => Map(a -> 1))
```

11

Monads

This chapter covers

- Discussing type constructors
- Introducing functors
- Defining monads

In the previous chapter, we introduced a simple algebraic structure: the monoid. This was our first instance of a completely abstract, purely algebraic interface, and it led us to think about interfaces in a new way. A useful interface may be defined only by a collection of operations related by laws.

In this chapter, we'll continue this mode of thinking and apply it to the problem of factoring out code duplication across some of the libraries we wrote in parts 1 and 2. We'll discover two new abstract interfaces—Functor and Monad—and get more general experience with spotting these sorts of abstract structures in our code.[1]

---

[1] The names *functor* and *monad* come from the branch of mathematics called *category theory*, but it isn't necessary to have any category theory background to follow the content in this chapter or to be a proficient functional programmer. You may be interested in following some of the references in the chapter notes (https://github.com/fpinscala/fpinscala/wiki) for more information.

11.1 *Functors: Generalizing the map function*

In parts 1 and 2, we implemented several different combinator libraries. In each case, we proceeded by writing a small set of primitives and then a number of combinators defined purely in terms of those primitives, and we noted some similarities between derived combinators across the libraries we wrote. For instance, we implemented a map function for each data type to lift a function taking one argument into the context of some data type. For Gen, Parser, and Option, the type signatures were as follows:

```
extension [A](ga: Gen[A])
  def map[B](f: A => B): Gen[B]

extension [A](pa: Parser[A])
  def map[B](f: A => B): Parser[B]

extension [A](oa: Option[A])
  def map[B](f: A => B): Option[B]
```

These type signatures differ only in the concrete data type (Gen, Parser, or Option). We can capture the idea of a data type that implements map in a Scala trait:

```
trait Functor[F[_]]:
  extension [A](fa: F[A])
    def map[B](f: A => B): F[B]
```

Here we've parameterized the trait on the type constructor, F[_], much like we did with Foldable in the previous chapter.[2] Instead of picking a particular F[_], like Gen or Parser, the Functor trait is parametric in the choice of F. Here's an instance for List:

```
given listFunctor: Functor[List] with
  extension [A](as: List[A])
    def map[B](f: A => B): List[B] =
      as.map(f)
```

We say that a type constructor like List (or Option or F) is a functor, and the Functor[F] instance constitutes proof that F is in fact a functor.[3]

What can we do with this abstraction? As we did in several places throughout this book, we can discover useful functions just by playing with the operations of the interface in a purely algebraic way. You may want to pause here to see what (if any) useful operations you can define only in terms of map.

Let's look at one example. If we have F[(A, B)], where F is a functor, we can distribute the F over the pair to get (F[A], F[B]):

---

[2] Recall that a type constructor is applied to a type to produce a type. For example, List is a type constructor, not a type. There are no values of the List type, but we can apply it to the type Int to produce the type List[Int]. Likewise, Parser can be applied to String to yield Parser[String].

[3] Note that writing an instance that compiles does not imply the instance is a functor. We need to ensure the instance adheres to various algebraic laws.

```
trait Functor[F[_]]:
  ...
  extension [A, B](fab: F[(A, B)])
    def distribute: (F[A], F[B]) =
      (fab.map(_(0)), fab.map(_(1)))
```

Defined as an extension method instead of a regular method, so users don't need to manually get a functor instance to use this operation

We wrote this by just following the types, but let's think about what it means for concrete data types, like `List`, `Gen`, `Option`, and so on. For example, if we `distribute` a `List[(A, B)]`, then we get two lists of the same length—one with all the `A`s and the other with all the `B`s. That operation is sometimes called *unzip*. So we just wrote a generic unzip function that works not only for lists but for any functor! When we have an operation on a product like this, we should see if we can construct the opposite operation over a sum or coproduct:

```
trait Functor[F[_]]:
  ...
  extension [A, B](e: Either[F[A], F[B]])
    def codistribute: F[Either[A, B]] =
      e match
        case Left(fa) => fa.map(Left(_))
        case Right(fb) => fb.map(Right(_))
```

What does `codistribute` mean for `Gen`? If we have either a generator for `A` or a generator for `B`, then we can construct a generator that produces either `A` or `B`, depending on which generator we actually have.

We just came up with two very general and potentially useful combinators based purely on the abstract interface of `Functor`, and we can reuse them for any type that allows an implementation of `map`.

11.1.1 Functor laws

Whenever we create an abstraction like `Functor`, we should consider not only what abstract methods it should have but which laws we expect to hold for the implementations. The laws you stipulate for an abstraction are entirely up to you,[4] and of course Scala won't enforce any of these laws. But laws are important for two reasons:

- Laws help an interface form a new semantic level whose algebra may be reasoned about independently of the instances. For example, when we take the product of a `Monoid[A]` and a `Monoid[B]` to form a `Monoid[(A, B)]`, the monoid laws let us conclude that the fused monoid operation is also associative. We don't need to know anything about `A` and `B` to conclude this.
- More concretely, we often rely on laws when writing various combinators derived from the functions of some abstract interface like `Functor`. We'll see examples of this later.

---

[4] Though if you're going to borrow the name of some existing mathematical abstraction like functor or monoid, we recommend using the laws already specified by mathematics.

For `Functor`, we'll stipulate the familiar law we first introduced in chapter 7 for our
`Par` data type:[5]

```
x.map(a => a) == x
```

In other words, mapping over a structure x with the identity function should itself be
an identity. This law is quite natural, and we saw later in part 2 that this law was satisfied by the map functions of other types besides `Par`. This law (and its corollaries given
by parametricity) capture the requirement that x.map preserves the structure of x.
Implementations satisfying this law are restricted from doing strange things like
throwing exceptions, removing the first element of a `List`, converting a `Some` to `None`,
and so on. Only the elements of the structure are modified by map; the shape or structure itself is left intact. Note that this law holds for `List`, `Option`, `Par`, `Gen`, and most
other data types that define map!

To give a concrete example of this preservation of structure, we can consider
`distribute` and `codistribute`, defined earlier. Here are their signatures again:

```
extension [A, B](fab: F[(A, B)])
  def distribute: (F[A], F[B])

extension [A, B](e: Either[F[A], F[B]])
  def codistribute: F[Either[A, B]]
```

Since we know nothing about F other than that it's a functor, the law assures us that
the returned values will have the same shape as the arguments. If the input to
`distribute` is a list of pairs, then the returned pair of lists will be of the same length as
the input, and corresponding elements will appear in the same order. This kind of
algebraic reasoning can potentially save us a lot of work since we don't have to write
separate tests for these properties.

We'll define one other law for `Functor`, which ensures function composition is
preserved:

```
x.map(f).map(g) == x.map(f andThen g)
```

This law says that first mapping a function f over a structure x and mapping another
function g over the result must be equivalent to mapping the single, composed function f andThen g. Like the identity law, this law also holds for `List`, `Option`, `Par`, `Gen`,
and most other data types that define map.[6]

---

[5] This law also comes from the mathematical definition of functor.
[6] If we allow impure functions, then Scala's built-in immutable `Set` is an example of a data type that defines a
map operation that doesn't adhere to this law. See https://mng.bz/yaQe for more details.

11.2 Monads: Generalizing the flatMap and unit functions

Functor is just one of many abstractions we can factor out of our libraries. But Functor isn't too compelling, as there aren't many useful operations that can be defined purely in terms of map. Next we'll look at a more interesting interface: Monad. Using this interface, we can implement a number of useful operations once and for all, factoring out what would otherwise be duplicated code. And it comes with laws with which we can reason that our libraries work the way we expect.

Recall that for several of the data types in this book so far, we've implemented map2 to lift a function taking two arguments. For Gen, Parser, and Option the map2 function could be implemented as follows.

Listing 11.1 Implementing map2 for Gen, Parser, and Option

```
extension [A](fa: Gen[A])
  def map2[B, C](fb: Gen[B])(f: (A, B) => C): Gen[C] =      ⟵  This makes a generator
    fa.flatMap(a => fb.map(b => f(a, b)))                        of a random C that runs
                                                                 random generators fa and
                                                                 fb, combining their results
                                                                 with the function f.

extension [A](fa: Parser[A])
  def map2[B, C](
    fb: Parser[B])(f: (A, B) => C
  ): Parser[C] =                        ⟵  This makes a parser that produces C
    fa.flatMap(a => fb.map(b => f(a, b)))   by combining the results of parsers fa
                                            and fb with the function f.

extension [A](fa: Option[A])
  def map2[B, C](
    fb: Option[B])(f: (A, B) => C
  ): Option[C] =                        ⟵  This combines two Options with the
    fa.flatMap(a => fb.map(b => f(a, b)))   function f when both have a value;
                                            otherwise, it returns None.
```

These functions have more in common than just the name. In spite of operating on data types that seemingly have nothing to do with one another, the implementations are identical! The only thing that differs is the particular data type being operated on. This confirms what we've suspected all along—that these are individual instances of a more general pattern. We should be able to exploit that fact to avoid repeating ourselves. For example, we should be able to write map2 once and for all in such a way that it can be reused for all of these data types.

We've made the code duplication particularly obvious here by choosing uniform names for our functions, taking the arguments in the same order, and so on. It may be more difficult to spot in your everyday work, but the more libraries you write, the better you'll get at identifying patterns you can factor out into common abstractions.

11.2.1 The Monad trait

What unites Parser, Gen, Par, Option, and many of the other data types we've looked at is that they're monads. Much like we did with Functor and Foldable, we can come up with a Scala trait for Monad that defines map2 and numerous other functions once and for all, rather than having to duplicate their definitions for every concrete data type.

In part 2 of this book, we concerned ourselves with individual data types, finding a minimal set of primitive operations from which we could derive a large number of useful combinators. We'll do the same kind of thing here to refine an *abstract* interface to a small set of primitives.

Let's start by introducing a new trait, called Mon for now. Since we know we want to eventually define map2, let's add that.

Listing 11.2 Creating a Mon trait for map2

```
trait Mon[F[_]]:
  extension [A](fa: F[A])
    def map2[B, C](fb: F[B])(f: (A, B) => C): F[C] =          ┐ This won't compile since map
      fa.flatMap(a => fb.map(b => f(a, b)))           ◄─────┤ and flatMap are undefined in
                                                             ┘ this context.
```

Here we've just taken the implementation of map2 and changed Parser, Gen, and Option to the polymorphic F of the Mon[F] interface in the signature.[7] But in this polymorphic context, this won't compile! We don't know anything about F here, so we certainly don't know how to flatMap or map over an F[A]. Here we can simply add map and flatMap to the Mon interface and keep them abstract.

Listing 11.3 Adding map and flatMap to our trait

```
trait Mon[F[_]]:
  extension [A](fa: F[A])
    def map[B](f: A => B): F[B]
    def flatMap[B](f: A => F[B]): F[B]

    def map2[B, C](fb: F[B])(f: (A, B) => C): F[C] =        ┐ We're calling the (abstract)
      fa.flatMap(a => fb.map(b => f(a, b)))          ◄─────┤ functions map and flatMap in
                                                            ┘ the Mon interface.
```

This translation was rather mechanical. We just inspected the implementation of map2 and added all the functions it called, map and flatMap, as suitably abstract methods on our interface. This trait will now compile, but before we declare victory and move on to defining instances of Mon[List], Mon[Parser], Mon[Option], and so on, let's see if we can refine our set of primitives. Our current set of primitives is map and flatMap, from which we can derive map2. Are flatMap and map a minimal set of primitives? Well, the data types that implemented map2 all had a unit, and we know map can be implemented in terms of flatMap and unit. For example, on Gen

```
def map[B](f: A => B): Gen[B] =
  flatMap(a => unit(f(a)))
```

---

[7] Our decision to call the type constructor argument F here was arbitrary. We could have called this argument Foo, w00t, or Blah2, though by convention, we usually give type constructor arguments one-letter uppercase names, such as F, G, and H or sometimes M and N or P and Q.

So let's pick unit and flatMap as our minimal set. We'll unify all data types that have these functions defined under a single concept. The trait is called Monad, flatMap and unit are abstract, and it provides default implementations for map and map2.

Listing 11.4   Creating our Monad trait

```
trait Monad[F[_]] extends Functor[F]:
  def unit[A](a: => A): F[A]

  extension [A](fa: F[A])
    def flatMap[B](f: A => F[B]): F[B]

    def map[B](f: A => B): F[B] =
      flatMap(a => unit(f(a)))

    def map2[B, C](fb: F[B])(f: (A, B) => C): F[C] =
      fa.flatMap(a => fb.map(b => f(a, b)))
```

> Since Monad provides a default implementation of map, it can extend Functor. All monads are functors, but not all functors are monads.

> ### The name monad
>
> We could have called Monad anything at all, like FlatMappable, Unicorn, or Bicycle, but monad is already a perfectly good name in common use. The name comes from category theory, a branch of mathematics that has inspired a lot of functional programming concepts. The name monad is intentionally similar to monoid, and the two concepts are related in a deep way. See the chapter notes (https://github.com/fpinscala/fpinscala/wiki) for more information.

To tie this back to a concrete data type, we can implement the Monad instance for Gen.

Listing 11.5   Implementing Monad for Gen

```
object Monad:
  given genMonad: Monad[Gen] with
    def unit[A](a: => A): Gen[A] = Gen.unit(a)
    extension [A](fa: Gen[A])
      def flatMap[B](f: A => Gen[B]): Gen[B] =
        Gen.flatMap(fa)(f)
```

We only need to implement unit and flatMap, and we get map and map2 at no additional cost. We've implemented them once and for all for any data type for which it's possible to supply an instance of Monad! But we're just getting started. There are many more functions we can implement once and for all in this manner.

EXERCISE 11.1

Write monad instances for Option, List, LazyList, Par, and Parser.

■ ── **EXERCISE 11.2** ──

Hard: State looks like it would be a monad too, but it takes two type arguments, and you need a type constructor of one argument to implement Monad. Try to implement a State monad, see what problems you run into, and think about possible solutions. We'll discuss the solution later in this chapter.

11.3 *Monadic combinators*

Now that we have our primitives for monads, we can look back at previous chapters and see if there were some other functions we implemented for each of our monadic data types. Many of them can be implemented once for all monads, so let's do that now.

■ ── **EXERCISE 11.3** ──

The sequence and traverse combinators should be familiar to you by now, and your implementations of them from various prior chapters are probably all very similar. Implement them once and for all on Monad[F]:

```
def sequence[A](fas: List[F[A]]): F[List[A]]
def traverse[A,B](as: List[A])(f: A => F[B]): F[List[B]]
```

One combinator we saw for Gen and Parser was listOfN, which allowed us to replicate a parser or generator n times to get a parser or generator of lists of that length. We can implement this combinator for all monads F by adding it to our Monad trait. We should also give it a more generic name, such as replicateM (meaning *replicate in a monad*).

■ ── **EXERCISE 11.4** ──

Implement replicateM:

```
def replicateM[A](n: Int, fa: F[A]): F[List[A]]
```

EXERCISE 11.5

Think about how `replicateM` will behave for various choices of F. For example, how does it behave in the `List` monad? What about `Option`? Describe in your own words the general meaning of `replicateM`.

There was also a combinator for our `Gen` data type, `product`, to take two generators and turn them into a generator of pairs, and we did the same thing for `Par` computations. In both cases, we implemented `product` in terms of `map2`, so we can definitely write it generically for any monad F:

```
extension [A](fa: F[A]) def product[B](fb: F[B]): F[(A, B)] =
  fa.map2(mb)((_, _))
```

We don't have to restrict ourselves to combinators we've already seen. It's important to play around and see what we find.

EXERCISE 11.6

Hard: Here's an example of a function we haven't seen before. Implement the function `filterM`—it's a bit like `filter`, except instead of a function from A => Boolean, we have an A => F[Boolean]. (Replacing various ordinary functions like this with the monadic equivalent often yields interesting results.) Implement this function, and then think about what it means for various data types:

```
def filterM[A](as: List[A])(f: A => F[Boolean]): F[List[A]]
```

The combinators we've seen here are only a small sample of the full library that `Monad` lets us implement once and for all. We'll see some more examples in chapter 13.

11.4   Monad laws

In this section, we'll introduce laws to govern our `Monad` interface.[8] Certainly, we'd expect the functor laws to also hold for `Monad`, since a `Monad[F]` *is* a `Functor[F]`, but what else do we expect? What laws should constrain `flatMap` and `unit`?

---

[8] These laws, once again, come from the concept of monads from category theory, but a background in category theory isn't necessary to understand this section.

11.4.1 *The associative law*

For example, if we wanted to combine three monadic values into one, which two should we combine first? Should it matter? To answer this question, let's take a step down from the abstract level for a moment and look at a simple concrete example using the Gen monad.

Say we're testing a product order system and we need to mock up some orders. We might have an Order case class and a generator for that class.

Listing 11.6 Defining our Order class

```
case class Order(item: Item, quantity: Int)
case class Item(name: String, price: Double)

val genOrder: Gen[Order] = for
  name <- Gen.stringN(3)
  price <- Gen.uniform.map(_ * 10)
  quantity <- Gen.choose(1, 100)
yield Order(Item(name, price), quantity)
```

A random string of length 3

A uniform random Double between 0 and 10

A random Int between 0 and 100

Here we're generating the Item inline (from name and price), but there might be places where we want to generate an Item separately. So we could pull that into its own generator:

```
val genItem: Gen[Item] = for
  name <- Gen.stringN(3)
  price <- Gen.uniform.map(_ * 10)
yield Item(name, price)
```

Then we can use that in genOrder:

```
val genOrder: Gen[Order] = for
  item <- genItem
  quantity <- Gen.choose(1, 100)
yield Order(item, quantity)
```

And that should do exactly the same thing, right? It seems safe to assume that—but not so fast. How can we be sure? It's not exactly the same code.

Let's expand both implementations of genOrder into calls to map and flatMap to better see what's going on. In the former case, the translation is straightforward:

```
Gen.nextString.flatMap(name =>
  Gen.nextDouble.flatMap(price =>
    Gen.nextInt.map(quantity =>
      Order(Item(name, price), quantity))))
```

But the second case looks like this (inlining the call to genItem):

```
Gen.nextString.flatMap(name =>
  Gen.nextInt.map(price =>
    Item(name, price))
).flatMap(item =>
  Gen.nextInt.map(quantity =>
    Order(item, quantity)))
```

Once we expand them, it's clear those two implementations aren't identical. And yet when we look at the for-comprehension it seems perfectly reasonable to assume the two implementations do exactly the same thing. In fact, it would be surprising and weird if they didn't. This is because we're assuming flatMap obeys an associative law:

```
x.flatMap(f).flatMap(g) == x.flatMap(a => f(a).flatMap(g))
```

And this law should hold for all values x, f, and g of the appropriate types—not just for Gen, but for Parser, Option, and any other monad.

11.4.2 *Proving the associative law for a specific monad*

Let's prove this law holds for Option. All we have to do is substitute None or Some(v) for x in the preceding equation and expand both sides of it.

   We start with the case in which x is None, and then both sides of the equal sign are None:

```
None.flatMap(f).flatMap(g) == None.flatMap(a => f(a).flatMap(g))
```

Since None.flatMap(f) is None for all f, this simplifies to

```
None == None
```

Thus the law holds if x is None. What about if x is Some(v) for an arbitrary choice of v? In that case, we have

```
x.flatMap(f).flatMap(g) ==
  x.flatMap(a => f(a).flatMap(g))    ◁——— Original law

Some(v).flatMap(f).flatMap(g) ==            │ Substitute Some(v)
  Some(v).flatMap(a => f(a).flatMap(g))  ◁——┘ for x on both sides.

f(v).flatMap(g) ==                  │ Apply the definition of
  (a => f(a).flatMap(g))(v)    ◁────┘ Some(v).flatMap(...).

f(v).flatMap(g)  . == f(v).flatMap(g)   ◁────┐ Simplify the function
                                             │ application (a => ..)(v).
```

Thus the law also holds when x is Some(v) for any v. We're now done, as we've shown that the law holds when x is None or Some, and these are the only two possibilities for Option.

KLEISLI COMPOSITION: A CLEARER VIEW OF THE ASSOCIATIVE LAW

It's not so easy to see that the law we just discussed is an associative law. Remember the associative law for monoids? That was clear:

```
combine(combine(x, y), z) == combine(x, combine(y, z))
```

But our associative law for monads doesn't look anything like that! Fortunately, there's a way we can make the law clearer if we consider not the monadic values of types like `F[A]` but monadic functions of types like `A => F[B]`. Functions like that are called *Kleisli arrows*,[9] and they can be composed with one another:

```
def compose[A, B, C](f: A => F[B], g: B => F[C]): A => F[C]
```

EXERCISE 11.7

Implement the Kleisli composition function `compose`.

We can now state the associative law for monads in a much more symmetric way:

```
compose(compose(f, g), h) == compose(f, compose(g, h))
```

EXERCISE 11.8

Hard: Implement `flatMap` in terms of `compose`. It seems we've found another minimal set of monad combinators: `compose` and `unit`.

EXERCISE 11.9

Show that the two formulations of the associative law, the one in terms of `flatMap` and the one in terms of `compose`, are equivalent.

11.4.3 The identity laws

The other monad law is now pretty easy to see. Just like `empty` was an *identity element* for `combine` in a monoid, there's an identity element for `compose` in a monad. Indeed, that's exactly what `unit` is, and that's why we chose this name for this operation:[10]

```
def unit[A](a: => A): F[A]
```

---

[9] *Kleisli arrow* comes from category theory and is named after the Swiss mathematician Heinrich Kleisli.

[10]The name *unit* is often used in mathematics to mean an identity for some operation.

This function has the right type to be passed as an argument to compose.[11] The effect should be that anything composed with unit is that same thing. This usually takes the form of two laws, *right identity* and *left identity*:

```
compose(f, unit) == f          ←──────────  Right identity law
compose(unit, f) == f          ◁──── Left identity law
```

We can also state these laws in terms of flatMap, but they're less clear that way:

```
x.flatMap(unit) == x           ◁──── Right identity law
unit(y).flatMap(f) == f(y)     ◁────
                                      Left identity law
```

■ **EXERCISE 11.10** ──

Prove that these two statements of the identity laws are equivalent.

■ **EXERCISE 11.11** ──

Prove that the identity laws hold for a monad of your choice.

■ **EXERCISE 11.12** ──

There's a third minimal set of monadic combinators: map, unit, and join. Implement join in terms of flatMap:

```
def join[A](ffa: F[F[A]]): F[A]
```

■ **EXERCISE 11.13** ──

Implement either flatMap or compose in terms of join and map.

□ **EXERCISE 11.14** ──

Restate the monad laws to mention only join, map, and unit.

────────────────────────────

[11]This is not quite true, since it takes a nonstrict A to F[A] (it's an (=> A) => F[A]), and in Scala this type is different from an ordinary A => F[A]. We'll ignore this distinction for now, though.

EXERCISE 11.15

Write down an explanation in your own words of what the associative law means for
Par and Parser.

EXERCISE 11.16

Explain in your own words what the identity laws are stating in concrete terms for Gen
and List.

11.5 *Just what is a monad?*

Let's now take a wider perspective. There's something unusual about the Monad interface: the data types for which we've given monad instances don't seem to have much
to do with each other. Yes, Monad factors out code duplication among them, but what
is a monad exactly? What does monad mean?

You may be used to thinking of interfaces as providing a relatively complete API
for an abstract data type, merely abstracting over the specific representation. After all,
a singly linked list and an array-based list may be implemented differently behind the
scenes, but they'll share a common interface in terms that lots of useful and concrete
application code can be written. Monad, like Monoid, is a more abstract, purely algebraic interface. The Monad combinators are often just a small fragment of the full API
for a given data type that happens to be a monad. So Monad doesn't generalize one
type or another; rather, many vastly different data types can satisfy the Monad interface
and laws.

We've seen three minimal sets of primitive Monad combinators, and instances of
Monad will have to provide implementations of one of these sets:

- unit and flatMap
- unit and compose
- unit, map, and join

And we know there are two monad laws to be satisfied, associativity and identity, that
can be formulated in various ways. So we can state plainly what a monad is:

*A monad is an implementation of one of the minimal sets of monadic combinators,
satisfying the laws of associativity and identity.*

That's a perfectly respectable, precise, and terse definition. And if we're being precise,
this is the only correct definition. A monad is precisely defined by its operations and
laws—no more, no less. But it's a little unsatisfying. It doesn't say much about what it
implies—what a monad means. The problem is that it's a self-contained definition. Even

if you're a beginning programmer, you have by now obtained a vast amount of knowledge related to programming, and this definition integrates with none of that.

To really understand what's going on with monads, try thinking about monads in terms of things you already know, and then connect them to a wider context. To develop some intuition for what monads mean, let's look at another couple of monads and compare their behavior.

11.5.1 *The identity monad*

To distill monads to their essentials, let's look at the simplest interesting specimen, the identity monad, given by the following type:

```
case class Id[A](value: A)
```

 EXERCISE 11.17

Implement `map` and `flatMap` as methods on this class, and give an implementation for `Monad[Id]`.

`Id` is just a simple wrapper; it doesn't really add anything. Applying `Id` to `A` is an identity, since the wrapped type and the unwrapped type are totally isomorphic (we can go from one to the other and back again without any loss of information). But what is the meaning of the identity monad? Let's try using it in the REPL:

```
scala> Id("Hello, ").flatMap(a =>
     |     Id("monad!").flatMap(b =>
     |       Id(a + b)))
res0: Id[String] = Id(Hello, monad!)
```

When we write the exact same thing with a for-comprehension, it might be clearer:

```
scala> for
     |    a <- Id("Hello, ")
     |    b <- Id("monad!")
     | yield a + b
res1: Id[String] = Id(Hello, monad!)
```

So what is the action of `flatMap` for the identity monad? It's simply variable substitution. The variables a and b get bound to `"Hello, "` and `"monad!"`, respectively, and then substituted into the expression a + b. We could have written the same thing without the `Id` wrapper using just Scala's own variables:

```
scala> val a = "Hello, "
a: String = "Hello, "

scala> val b = "monad!"
```

```
b: String = monad!

scala> a + b
res2: String = Hello, monad!
```

Besides the `Id` wrapper, there's no difference. So now we have at least a partial answer to the question of what monads mean. We could say monads provide a context for introducing and binding variables and performing variable substitution. Let's see if we can get the rest of the answer.

11.5.2 *The State monad and partial type application*

Look back at the discussion of the `State` data type in chapter 6. Recall that we implemented some combinators for `State`, including `map` and `flatMap`.

Listing 11.7 Revisiting our `State` data type

```
opaque type State[S, +A] = S => (A, S)

object State:
  extension [S, A](underlying: State[S, A])
    def map[B](f: A => B): State[S, B] =
      flatMap(a => unit(f(a)))

    def flatMap[B](f: A => State[S, B]): State[S, B] =
      s =>
        val (a, s1) = underlying(s)
        f(a)(s1)
```

It looks like `State` definitely fits the profile for being a monad. However, its type constructor takes two type arguments, and `Monad` requires a type constructor of one argument, so we can't just say `Monad[State]`. But if we choose some particular `S`, then we have something like `State[S, *]`, which is the kind of thing expected by `Monad`. So `State` doesn't just have one monad instance but a whole family of them—one for each choice of `S`. We'd like to be able to partially apply `State` to where the `S` type argument is fixed to be some concrete type.

This is much like how we might partially apply a function, except at the type level. For example, we can create an `IntState` type constructor, which is an alias for `State` with its first type argument fixed to be `Int`:

```
type IntState[A] = State[Int, A]
```

And `IntState` is exactly the kind of thing we can build a `Monad` for:

```
given intStateMonad: Monad[IntState] with
  def unit[A](a: => A): IntState[A] = State(s => (a, s))
  def flatMap[A,B](st: IntState[A])(f: A => IntState[B]): IntState[B] =
    State.flatMap(st)(f)
```

Of course, it would be really repetitive if we had to manually write a separate `Monad` instance for each state type. Fortunately, Scala allows us to create anonymous type constructors. For example, we could have declared `IntState` directly inline like this:

```
given intStateMonad: Monad[[x] =>> State[Int, x]] with ...
```

This defines a monad for the anonymous type constructor `[x] =>> State[Int, x]`—a type constructor that takes a single argument of type x and returns the type `State[Int, x]`. You can think of this as the type-level equivalent of anonymous functions. And just like anonymous functions have an abbreviated form (e.g., `_ + 1` instead of `x => x + 1`), anonymous type constructors do too. With the `-Ykind-projector:underscores` compiler option enabled, we can rewrite `[x] =>> State[Int, x]` as `State[Int, _]`.[12]

An anonymous type constructor declared inline like this is called a *type lambda* in Scala. We can use this feature to partially apply the `State` type constructor and declare a monad instance for any state type `S`:

```
given stateMonad[S]: Monad[[x] =>> State[S, x]] with      ⟵ Alternatively,
  def unit[A](a: => A): State[S,A] = State(s => (a, s))        given stateMonad[S]:
  extension [A](st: State[S, A])                                Monad[State[S, _]] with ...
    def flatMap[B](f: A => State[S, B]): State[S, B] =
      State.flatMap(st)(f)
```

Again, just by giving implementations of `unit` and `flatMap`, we get implementations of all the other monadic combinators for free.

■ EXERCISE 11.18

Now that we have a `State` monad, we should try it out to see how it behaves. What is the meaning of `replicateM` in the `State` monad? How does `map2` behave? What about `sequence`?

Let's now look at the difference between the `Id` monad and the `State` monad. Remember that the primitive operations on `State` (besides the monadic operations `unit` and `flatMap`) are that we can read the current state with `get`, and we can set a new state with `set`:

```
def get[S]: State[S, S]
def set[S](s: => S): State[S, Unit]
```

Remember that we also discovered that these combinators constitute a minimal set of primitive operations for `State`. So together with the monadic primitives (`unit` and

---

[12]Anonymous type constructors are a Scala 3 feature inspired by so-called *type lambdas* from Scala 2. Type lambdas weren't an intentional language feature but rather a pattern that was discovered and then codified in the popular kind-projector compiler plugin.

flatMap), they completely specify everything we can do with the State data type. This is true in general for monads—they all have unit and flatMap, and each monad brings its own set of additional primitive operations that are specific to it.

What laws do you expect to mutually hold for get, set, unit, and flatMap?

What does this tell us about the meaning of the State monad? Let's study a simple example. The details of this code aren't too important, but notice the use of get and set in the for block.

Listing 11.8 Getting and setting state with a for-comprehension

```
val F = stateMonad[Int]

def zipWithIndex[A](as: List[A]): List[(Int, A)] =
  as.foldLeft(F.unit(List[(Int, A)]()))((acc, a) =>
    for
      xs <- acc
      n  <- State.get
      _  <- State.set(n + 1)
    yield (n, a) :: xs
  ).run(0)._1.reverse
```

This function numbers all the elements in a list using a State action. It keeps a state that's an Int, which is incremented at each step. We run the whole composite state action starting from 0, and then we reverse the result, since we constructed it in reverse order.[13]

Note what's going on with get and set in the for-comprehension. We're obviously getting variable binding just like in the Id monad—we're binding the value of each successive state action (get, acc, and then set) to variables. But there's more going on, literally, between the lines. At each line in the for-comprehension, the implementation of flatMap is making sure that the current state is available to get and the new state gets propagated to all actions that follow a set.

What does the difference between the action of Id and the action of State tell us about monads in general? We can see that a chain of flatMap calls (or an equivalent for-comprehension) is like an imperative program with statements that assign to variables, and the monad specifies what occurs at statement boundaries. For example, with Id, nothing at all occurs except unwrapping and rewrapping in the Id constructor. With State, the most current state gets passed from one statement to the next.

---

[13]This is asymptotically faster than appending to the list in the loop.

With the `Option` monad, a statement may return `None` and terminate the program. With the `List` monad, a statement may return many results, which causes statements that follow it to potentially run multiple times—once for each result.

The `Monad` contract doesn't specify what is happening between the lines, only that whatever *is* happening satisfies the laws of associativity and identity.

■ EXERCISE 11.20

Hard: To cement your understanding of monads, give a monad instance for the following type, and explain what it means. What are its primitive operations? What is the action of `flatMap`? What meaning does it give to monadic functions like `sequence`, `join`, and `replicateM`? What meaning does it give to the monad laws?[14]

```
opaque type Reader[-R, +A] = R => A

object Reader:
  given readerMonad[R]: Monad[Reader[R, _]] with
    def unit[A](a: => A): Reader[R, A] =
      ???
    extension [A](fa: Reader[R, A])
      override def flatMap[B](f: A => Reader[R, B]) =
        ???
```

11.6 Conclusion

In this chapter, we took a pattern we've seen repeated throughout the book and unified it under a single concept: the monad. This allowed us to write a number of combinators once and for all for many different data types that, at first glance, don't seem to have anything in common. We discussed laws they all satisfy, the monad laws, from various perspectives, and we developed some insight into what it all means.

An abstract topic like this can't be fully understood all at once. It requires an iterative approach through which we keep revisiting the topic from different perspectives. When we discover new monads, discover new applications of them, or see them appear in a new context, we'll inevitably gain new insight. And each time it happens, you might think to yourself, OK, I thought I understood monads before, but now I *really* get it.

Summary

- A functor is an implementation of `map` that preserves the structure of the data type.
- The functor laws are
  - Identity: `x.map(a => a) == x`
  - Composition: `x.map(f).map(g) == x.map(f andThen g)`

---

[14]See the chapter notes (https://github.com/fpinscala/fpinscala/wiki) for further discussion of this data type.

- A monad is an implementation of one of the minimal sets of monadic combinators, satisfying the laws of associativity and identity.
- The minimal sets of monadic combinators are
  - unit and flatMap
  - unit and compose
  - unit, map, and join
- The monad laws are
  - *Associativity*—x.flatMap(f).flatMap(g) == x.flatMap(a => f(a).flatMap(g))
  - *Right identity*—x.flatMap(unit) == x
  - *Left identity*—unit(y).flatMap(f) == f(y)
- All monads are functors, but not all functors are monads.
- There are monads for many of the data types encountered in this book, including Option, List, LazyList, Par, and State[S, _].
- The Monad contract doesn't specify what is happening between the lines, only that whatever is happening satisfies the laws of associativity and identity.
- Providing a Monad instance for a type constructor has practical usefulness. Doing so gives access to all of the derived operations (or combinators) in exchange for implementing one of the minimal sets of monadic combinators.

11.7 *Exercise answers*

■ **ANSWER 11.1**

The Option, List, and LazyList instances directly delegate to the flatMap method on each type:

```
given optionMonad: Monad[Option] with
  def unit[A](a: => A) = Some(a)
  extension [A](fa: Option[A])
    override def flatMap[B](f: A => Option[B]) =
      fa.flatMap(f)

given listMonad: Monad[List] with
  def unit[A](a: => A) = List(a)
  extension [A](fa: List[A])
    override def flatMap[B](f: A => List[B]) =
      fa.flatMap(f)

given lazyListMonad: Monad[LazyList] with
  def unit[A](a: => A) = LazyList(a)
  extension [A](fa: LazyList[A])
    override def flatMap[B](f: A => LazyList[B]) =
      fa.flatMap(f)
```

Recall that Par is an opaque type alias that has a flatMap method defined via an extension method. We have to be careful to tell Scala that we want the flatMap extension method defined in the `Par` companion and not the one we're defining on `Monad` (or else we'd have an infinite loop, where `flatMap` just calls itself until we exhaust the stack):

```
given parMonad: Monad[Par] with
  def unit[A](a: => A) = Par.unit(a)
  extension [A](fa: Par[A])
    override def flatMap[B](f: A => Par[B]): Par[B] =
      Par.flatMap(fa)(f)
```

Defining a `Monad` instance for a parser is a bit syntactically trickier due to the `Parsers` trait. One solution is defining a function that provides a `Monad[P]` instance, given a value of type `Parsers[P]`:

```
def parserMonad[P[+_]](p: Parsers[P]): Monad[P] = new:
  def unit[A](a: => A) = p.succeed(a)
  extension [A](fa: P[A])
    override def flatMap[B](f: A => P[B]): P[B] =
      p.flatMap(fa)(f)
```

■ ANSWER 11.2

The `State` type constructor takes two type parameters, but `Monad` requires a type constructor of a single type parameter. We can create a type alias that takes a single type parameter and pick an arbitrary type for `S`:

```
type IntState[A] = State[Int, A]
```

Here we chose `Int` for the `S` type parameter, but we could have chosen anything. With this type alias, we can define a `Monad[IntState]` instance:

```
given stateIntMonad: Monad[StateInt] with
  def unit[A](a: => A) = State(s => (a, s))
  extension [A](fa: StateInt[A])
    override def flatMap[B](f: A => StateInt[B]) =
      State.flatMap(fa)(f)
```

Our implementation didn't take advantage of the fact that we instantiated `State` with `S = Int`. This is a good clue that we can define a monad for any choice of `S`. Later in this chapter, we'll see how to accomplish that.

■ ANSWER 11.3

We can implement `sequence` in terms of `traverse` by passing the identity function:

```
def sequence[A](fas: List[F[A]]): F[List[A]] =
  traverse(fas)(identity)
```

To implement `traverse`, let's first look at the implementation we wrote for `Option` in chapter 4:

```
def traverse[A, B](as: List[A])(f: A => Option[B]): Option[List[B]] =
  as.foldRight(Some(Nil): Option[List[B]])((a, acc) =>
    map2(f(a), acc)(_ :: _))
```

We should also look at the implementation we wrote for `State` in chapter 6:

```
def traverse[S, A, B](as: List[A])(f: A => State[S, B]): State[S, List[B]] =
  as.foldRight(unit[S, List[B]](Nil))((a, acc) => f(a).map2(acc)(_ :: _))
```

Both implementations involve a right fold over the elements in the list, applying each element to the supplied function and consing the result onto an accumulated list with the help of `map2`. We can implement `traverse` for any monad by using the `unit` and `map2` operations:

```
def traverse[A, B](as: List[A])(f: A => F[B]): F[List[B]] =
  as.foldRight(unit(List.empty[B]))((a, acc) => f(a).map2(acc)(_ :: _))
```

■ **ANSWER 11.4** ───

We can implement this in various ways. First let's try a recursive solution:

```
def replicateM[A](n: Int, fa: F[A]): F[List[A]] =
  if n <= 0 then unit(Nil)
  else fa.map2(replicateM(n - 1, fa))(_ :: _)
```

This works but has a subtle flaw. The recursive call is not in tail position, resulting in stack overflows for large values of n. Forgetting stack safety, this implementation also seems to duplicate logic we already wrote—we have a base case using `unit` and an recursive case using `map2` and `::`. It seems like we've reimplemented parts of `traverse` here. Let's avoid that duplication:

```
def replicateM[A](n: Int, fa: F[A]): F[List[A]] =
  sequence(List.fill(n)(fa))
```

Here we've created a list of n copies of `fa`, which has type `List[F[A]]`. We then `sequence` that into an `F[List[A]]`, swapping the positions of the `List` and `F` type constructors.

ANSWER 11.5

Let's first try a few examples. Starting with List, let's try replicating a single element list:

```scala
scala> summon[Monad[List]].replicateM(1, List(1))
val res0: List[List[Int]] = List(List(1))

scala> summon[Monad[List]].replicateM(2, List(1))
val res1: List[List[Int]] = List(List(1, 1))

scala> summon[Monad[List]].replicateM(3, List(1))
val res2: List[List[Int]] = List(List(1, 1, 1))
```

We're getting a single element result, which contains a list whose size is equal to the n parameter passed to replicateM. Let's try with a two-element list:

```scala
scala> summon[Monad[List]].replicateM(1, List(1, 2))
val res3: List[List[Int]] = List(List(1), List(2))

scala> summon[Monad[List]].replicateM(2, List(1, 2))
val res4: List[List[Int]] = List(List(1, 1), List(1, 2),
⮕ List(2, 1), List(2, 2))

scala> summon[Monad[List]].replicateM(3, List(1, 2))
val res5: List[List[Int]] = List(List(1, 1, 1), List(1, 1, 2),
⮕ List(1, 2, 1), List(1, 2, 2), List(2, 1, 1), List(2, 1, 2),
⮕ List(2, 2, 1), List(2, 2, 2))
```

We're getting lots of output lists now—again, each inner list has a size equal to n. The inner lists represent all the ways three ordered elements can be chosen from two values. That is, replicateM(n, xs) appears to return a list with a size equal to xs.size raised to the power n. In this case, $2^3 = 8$.

Let's test this hypothesis with a few more examples:

```scala
scala> summon[Monad[List]].replicateM(4, List(1, 2, 3)).size
val res6: Int = 81

scala> summon[Monad[List]].replicateM(5, List(1, 2, 3, 4)).size
val res7: Int = 1024
```

$4^3 = 81$ and $5^4 = 1024$, so our hypothesis is looking good.

Let's look at Option now:

```scala
scala> summon[Monad[Option]].replicateM(0, Some(0))
val res0: Option[List[Int]] = Some(List())

scala> summon[Monad[Option]].replicateM(0, None)
val res1: Option[List[Nothing]] = Some(List())
```

```
scala> summon[Monad[Option]].replicateM(1, Some(1))
val res2: Option[List[Int]] = Some(List(1))

scala> summon[Monad[Option]].replicateM(1, Some(0))
val res3: Option[List[Int]] = Some(List(0))

scala> summon[Monad[Option]].replicateM(1, None)
val res4: Option[List[Nothing]] = None

scala> summon[Monad[Option]].replicateM(2, Some(0))
val res5: Option[List[Int]] = Some(List(0, 0))

scala> summon[Monad[Option]].replicateM(3, Some(0))
val res6: Option[List[Int]] = Some(List(0, 0, 0))
```

Replicating a Some(x) n times results in a list of size n, where every element is equal to x, all wrapped in some. Replicating a None one or more times results in a None, and replicating a None zero times results in an empty list wrapped in some.

Given that List and Option seem to have wildly different behaviors, how can we generically describe the behavior of replicateM? We can say replicateM repeats the supplied monadic value n times, combining the results into a single value, where the monadic type defines how that combination is performed.

■ ANSWER 11.6

We can implement this a bit like traverse, where we right fold the input list and use map2 to combine an accumulated output list with the current element. Unlike traverse, we only cons the current element onto the output when the predicate function returns true. To access the Boolean result of the predicate function, we need to flatMap the resulting monadic value:

```
def filterM[A](as: List[A])(f: A => F[Boolean]): F[List[A]] =
  as.foldRight(unit(List[A]()))((a, acc) =>
    f(a).flatMap(b => if b then unit(a).map2(acc)(_ :: _) else acc))
```

■ ANSWER 11.7

Let's return an anonymous function that invokes f and then flatMap's result with g:

```
def compose[A, B, C](f: A => F[B], g: B => F[C]): A => F[C] =
  a => f(a).flatMap(g)
```

■ **ANSWER 11.8**

To implement `flatMap`, we need to create an `F[B]`, given an `fa: F[A]`, an `f: A => F[B]`, and the compose function. Compose takes two functions: `A => F[B]` and `B => F[C]`. If we could somehow create a function that returns `fa`, then we could compose that function with `f`. We can create such a function, which given any value, returns `fa`. After composing that function with `f`, we can apply a value to it to compute the desired `F[B]`:

```
extension [A](fa: F[A])
  def flatMap[B](f: A => F[B]): F[B] =
    compose(_ => fa, f)(())
```

■ **ANSWER 11.9**

We start with the associative law in terms of `compose` and perform successive substitutions until we arrive at the associative law in terms of `flatMap`:

```
compose(f, compose(g, h)) ==
  compose(compose(f, g), h)
```

```
a => f(a).flatMap(compose(g, h)) ==
  a => compose(f, g)(a).flatMap(h)
```
Substitute the outer compose with the definition.

```
a => f(a).flatMap(b => g(b).flatMap(h)) ==
  a => (b => f(b).flatMap(g))(a).flatMap(h)
```
Substitute the inner compose with the definition.

```
a => f(a).flatMap(b => g(b).flatMap(h)) ==
  a => f(a).flatMap(g).flatMap(h)
```
On the right-hand side, simplify (b => f(b).flatMap(g))(a) to f(a).flatMap(g).

```
x.flatMap(b => g(b).flatMap(h)) ==
  x.flatMap(g).flatMap(h)
```
Replace a => f(a) on both sides with an arbitrary x.

■ **ANSWER 11.10**

First let's prove that `compose(f, unit) == f` is equivalent to `x.flatMap(unit) == x`:

Substitute compose with the definition.

```
compose(f, unit)            == f
a => f(a).flatMap(unit) == f
a => f(a).flatMap(unit) == a => f(a)
x.flatMap(unit)             == x
```
Introduce an anonymous function on the right-hand side.

Replace a => f(a) on both sides with an arbitrary x.

Now let's prove compose(unit, f) == f is equivalent to unit(y).flatMap(f) == f(y):

```
                                          Substitute compose
                                          with the definition.

compose(unit, f)              == f        Apply y to both sides.
a => unit(a).flatMap(f)       == f
(a => unit(a).flatMap(f))(y)  == f(y)     Simplify the left-hand side
unit(y).flatMap(f)            == f(y)     by substituting a with y.
```

ANSWER 11.11

Let's prove that the identity laws hold for Option. As a reminder, the definition of flatMap on Option is

```
enum Option[+A]:
  case Some(get: A)
  case None

  def flatMap[B](f: A => Option[B]): Option[B] =
    this match
      case None => None
      case Some(a) => f(a)
```

Let's first prove compose(f, unit) == f; recall that this law is equivalent to x.flatMap (unit) == x. When x is None, the left-hand side reduces to None by the definition of flatMap. When x is Some(a), it reduces to unit(a), and unit(a) reduces to Some(a).

Now let's prove that compose(unit, f) == f; this is equivalent to unit(y).flat-Map(f) == f(y). Using the definition of unit, the left-hand side simplifies to Some(y).flatMap(f). Using the definition of flatMap, that simplifies to f(y).

ANSWER 11.12

We can flatMap with an identity function to flatten the nested type constructors into a single type constructor. This operation is typically called flatten in Scala:

```
extension [A](ffa: F[F[A]]) def join: F[A] =
  ffa.flatMap(identity)
```

ANSWER 11.13

```
extension [A](fa: F[A])
  def flatMapViaJoinAndMap[B](f: A => F[B]): F[B] =
    fa.map(f).join
```

```
def composeViaJoinAndMap[A, B, C](f: A => F[B], g: B => F[C]): A => F[C] =
  a => f(a).map(g).join
```

ANSWER 11.14

We have three laws to restate: the associative law and the two identity laws. First let's rewrite the associative law:

```
x.flatMap(f).flatMap(g) ==
  x.flatMap(a => f(a).flatMap(g))
```

```
x.map(f).join.map(g).join ==
  x.map(a => f(a).map(g).join).join  ◁
```
Substitute all uses of flatMap(h) with map(h).join.

```
x.join.map(g).join == x.map(a => a.map(g).join).join  ◁
```
Choose f = identity, and simplify using the functor law that x.map(identity) = x.

```
x.join.join == x.map(a => a.join).join  ◁──── Choose g = identity, and simplify.
```

```
x.join.join == x.map(_.join).join  ◁──── Use lambda on the right-hand side.
```

Next let's rewrite the right identity law (using the version expressed in terms of flatMap):

```
x.flatMap(unit)    == x
x.map(unit).join == x  ◁──── Substitute the definition of flatMap.
```

Finally, let's rewrite the left identity law:

```
unit(y).flatMap(f)    == f(y)
unit(y).map(f).join == f(y)  ◁──── Substitute the definition of flatMap.
unit(y).join          == y  ◁──── Choose f = identity, and simplify.
```

ANSWER 11.15

Let's use the `join` version of the associative law: `x.join.join == x.map(_.join).join`. Note that x has the `F[F[F[A]]]` type here.

For `Par`, the associative law says that if you have a three-level deep parallel computation, you can await the results of the computations inside out or outside in, and the result is equivalent. For `Parser`, the associative law says that in a series of dependent parsers, only the order of the parsers matters, not the way in which they are nested.

⬛ ▬▬ **ANSWER 11.16** ▬▬▬▬▬▬▬▬▬▬▬▬▬▬▬▬▬▬▬▬▬▬▬▬▬▬▬▬▬▬▬▬▬▬▬▬▬▬

Let's use the `flatMap` versions of the identity laws:

- *Right identity law*—x.`flatMap` (`unit`) == x
- *Left identity law*—`uint(y).flatMap(f)` == `f(y)`

For `Gen`, the right identity law means that flat mapping the unit generator over a generator doesn't change it in any way. The left identity law means that the generator you get from lifting an arbitrary value via the unit generator and then flat mapping that over an arbitrary function is equivalent to simply applying that value directly to the function. Travelling through the unit generator and `flatMap` has no effect on the generated values.

For `List`, the right identity law means that flat mapping a singleton list constructor over each element results in the original list—that `flatMap` can't drop, filter, or otherwise change the elements. The left identity law means that `flatMap` can't increase or decrease the number of elements (e.g., by applying the supplied function multiple times to each element before joining the results).

⬛ ▬▬ **ANSWER 11.17** ▬▬▬▬▬▬▬▬▬▬▬▬▬▬▬▬▬▬▬▬▬▬▬▬▬▬▬▬▬▬▬▬▬▬▬▬▬▬

```scala
case class Id[+A](value: A):
  def map[B](f: A => B): Id[B] =
    Id(f(value))
  def flatMap[B](f: A => Id[B]): Id[B] =
    f(value)

object Id:
  given idMonad: Monad[Id] with
    def unit[A](a: => A) = Id(a)
    extension [A](fa: Id[A])
      override def flatMap[B](f: A => Id[B]) =
        fa.flatMap(f)
```

⬛ ▬▬ **ANSWER 11.18** ▬▬▬▬▬▬▬▬▬▬▬▬▬▬▬▬▬▬▬▬▬▬▬▬▬▬▬▬▬▬▬▬▬▬▬▬▬▬

Let's create a state action to experiment with:

```scala
val getAndIncrement: State[Int, Int] =
  for
    i <- State.get
    _ <- State.set(i + 1)
  yield i
```

Here we have a state type of `Int` and a state action that increments the state and returns the old value.

```
scala> getAndIncrement.run(0)
res0: (Int, Int) = (0, 1)
```

Let's try replicating `getAndIncrement`:

```
scala> val replicated = summon[Monad[State[Int, *]]].
                        replicateM(10, getAndIncrement)
val replicated: State[Int, List[Int]] = ...

scala> replicated.run(0)
val res1: (List[Int], Int) = (List(0, 1, 2, 3, 4, 5, 6, 7, 8, 9),10)
```

`replicateM` wires up all the state actions one after another, so the output state of the first action is the input state to the second action and so on and collects the output value from each action into a list.

Now let's look at `map2` and `sequence`:

```
scala> getAndIncrement.map2(getAndIncrement)((_, _)).run(0)
val res2: ((Int, Int), Int) = ((0,1),2)

scala> val actions = List(getAndIncrement, getAndIncrement, getAndIncrement)
scala> summon[Monad[State[Int, *]]].sequence(actions).run(0)
val res3: (List[Int], Int) = (List(0, 1, 2),3)
```

These operations also evaluate state actions sequentially, passing the output state of an action as the input state to the next action in the sequence. `map2` allows the result values of the two state actions to be combined into a new value via an arbitrary function, while `sequence` collects the various output values into a list.

■ **ANSWER 11.19**

One law is that `get` followed by `set` must be equivalent to `unit`:

```
State.get.flatMap(s => State.set(s)) == State.unit(())
```

We get another law by reversing the order of `get` and `set`—setting the state to some value and then getting it must be equivalent to a unit of that value:

```
s => (State.set(s).flatMap(_ => State.get)) == s => State.unit(s)
```

```
opaque type Reader[-R, +A] = R => A

object Reader:
  def ask[R]: Reader[R, R] = r => r
  def apply[R, A](f: R => A): Reader[R, A] = f

  extension [R, A](ra: Reader[R, A])
    def run(r: R): A = ra(r)

  extension [R, A](ra: Reader[R, A])
    def run(r: R): A = ra(r)

  given readerMonad[R]: Monad[Reader[R, _]] with
    def unit[A](a: => A): Reader[R, A] = _ => a
    extension [A](fa: Reader[R, A])
      override def flatMap[B](f: A => Reader[R, B]) =
        r => f(fa(r))(r)
```

The Reader type is an opaque type alias for a function R => A. Rather than thinking of Reader as a function, it's useful to think of it as a computation that produces a value of type A, which has access to a value of type R, often called the environment, when running. That is, think of it as a computation that may read the environment R in the computation of A. This is essentially dependency injection. It's similar to the State type we've been working with, except the environment (i.e., state) cannot be changed, only read.

Its primitive operations are

- Lifting a function R => A into a Reader[R, A] via Reader.apply
- Running the function given an environment of type R via reader.run(r)

Using Reader.apply, we can build the ask operation by simply passing the identity function. This gives us a Reader[R, R]—a reader that returns the environment.

The unit(a) operation returns a function that ignores the environment and instead returns a. The flatMap(f) operation creates a reader that propagates the environment to both the original reader and the reader computed by f. The sequence operation converts a list of readers into a single reader that propagates the environment to each constituent and collects all their results into a single list. The join operation is interesting if we recall that Reader[R, A] is an alias for R => A. Hence, Reader[R, Reader[R, A]] is an alias for R => R => A, which can be written as (R, R) => A. So join lets us propagate an environment to a binary function. The replicateM(n) operation creates a reader that computes a result from the environment and copies it n times. The monad laws provide us a guarantee that we can refactor reader-based computations without changing the overall computed result.

Applicative and traversable functors

In the previous chapter on monads, we saw how many of the functions we've been writing for different combinator libraries can be expressed in terms of a single interface: Monad. Monads provide a powerful interface, as evidenced by the fact that we can use flatMap to essentially write imperative programs in a purely functional way.

In this chapter, we'll learn about a type of related abstractions, *applicative functors*, which are less powerful than monads but more general (and hence more common). The process of arriving at applicative functors will also provide some insight into how to discover such abstractions, and we'll use some of these ideas to uncover another useful abstraction: *traversable functors*. It may take some time for the full significance and usefulness of these abstractions to sink in, but you'll see them popping up again and again in your daily work with FP if you pay attention.

313

12.1   *Generalizing monads*

By now we've seen various operations, like `sequence` and `traverse`, implemented many times for different monads, and in the last chapter, we generalized the implementations to work for any monad `F`:

```
def sequence[A](fas: List[F[A]]): F[List[A]]
  traverse(fas)(fa => fa)

def traverse[A, B](as: List[A])(f: A => F[B]): F[List[B]]
  as.foldRight(unit(List[B]()))((a, acc) => f(a).map2(acc)(_ :: _))
```

Here the implementation of `traverse` is using `map2` and `unit`, and we've seen that `map2` can be implemented in terms of `flatMap`:

```
extension [A](fa: F[A])
  def map2[B, C](fb: F[B])(f: (A, B) => C): F[C] =
    fa.flatMap(a => fb.map(b => f(a, b)))
```

You may not have noticed that a large number of the useful combinators on `Monad` can be defined using only `unit` and `map2`. The `traverse` combinator is one example—it doesn't call `flatMap` directly and is therefore agnostic to whether `map2` is primitive or derived. Furthermore, for many data types, `map2` can be implemented directly, without using `flatMap`.

All this suggests a variation on `Monad`—the `Monad` interface has `flatMap` and `unit` as primitives and derives `map2`, but we can obtain a different abstraction by letting `unit` and `map2` be the primitives. We'll see that this new abstraction, called an *applicative functor*, is less powerful than a monad, but we'll also see that limitations come with benefits.

12.2   *The Applicative trait*

Applicative functors can be captured by a new interface, `Applicative`, in which `unit` and `map2` are primitives.

Listing 12.1   Creating the `Applicative` interface

```
trait Applicative[F[_]] extends Functor[F]:
  // primitive combinators
  def unit[A](a: => A): F[A]
  extension [A](fa: F[A])
    def map2[B, C](fb: F[B])(f: (A, B) => C): F[C]

  // derived combinators
  extension [A](fa: F[A])                            We can implement map in
    def map[B](f: A => B): F[B] =                    terms of unit and map2.
      fa.map2(unit(()))((a, _) => f(a))
                                                     Recall () is the sole value of type
  def traverse[A, B](                                Unit, so unit(()) is calling unit
    as: List[A])(f: A => F[B]): F[List[B]] =         with the dummy value ().
      as.foldRight(unit(List[B]()))((a, acc) => f(a).map2(acc)(_ :: _))
```

The definition of traverse is identical.

This establishes that all applicatives are functors. We implement map in terms of map2 and unit, as we've done before for particular data types. The implementation is suggestive of laws for Applicative that we'll examine later, since we expect this implementation of map to preserve structure, as dictated by the Functor laws.

Note that the implementation of traverse is unchanged. We can similarly move other combinators into Applicative that don't depend directly on flatMap or join.

EXERCISE 12.1

Move the implementations of sequence, traverse, replicateM, and product from Monad to Applicative, using only map2 and unit or methods implemented in terms of them:

```
def sequence[A](fas: List[F[A]]): F[List[A]]
def traverse[A,B](as: List[A])(f: A => F[B]): F[List[B]]
def replicateM[A](n: Int, fa: F[A]): F[List[A]]
extension [A](fa: F[A]) def product[B](fb: F[B]): F[(A, B)]
```

EXERCISE 12.2

Hard: The name *applicative* comes from the fact that we can formulate the Applicative interface using an alternate set of primitives, unit and the function apply, rather than unit and map2. Show that this formulation is equivalent in expressiveness by defining map2 and map in terms of unit and apply. Also establish that apply can be implemented in terms of map2 and unit:

```
trait Applicative[F[_]] extends Functor[F]:                    Define in terms
    def apply[A, B](fab: F[A => B], fa: F[A]): F[B]  ◁──┘       of map2.
    def unit[A](a: => A): F[A]
                                         Define in terms of
    extension [A](fa: F[A])              apply and unit.
        def map[B](f: A => B): F[B]  ◁──┘                      Define in terms of
        def map2[B, C](fb: F[B])(f: (A, B) => C): F[C]  ◁──┘   apply and map.
```

EXERCISE 12.3

The apply method is useful for implementing map3, map4, and so on, and the pattern is straightforward. Implement map3 and map4 using only unit, apply, and the curried method available on functions:[1]

---

[1] Recall that given f: (A, B) => C, f.curried has type A => B => C. A curried method exists for functions of any arity in Scala.

```
extension [A](fa: F[A])
  def map3[B, C, D](
    fb: F[B],
    fc: F[C])(f: (A, B, C) => D): F[D]

  def map4[B, C, D, E](
    fb: F[B],
    fc: F[C],
    fd: F[D])(f: (A, B, C, D) => E): F[E]
```

We could define `map3` and `map4` as regular methods instead of extension methods (e.g., `def map3[A, B, C, D](fa: F[A], fb: F[B], fc: F[C])(f: (A, B, C) => D): F[D]`). One disadvantage of doing so is that call sites become more verbose. For example, with `map3` defined as a regular method on the `Applicative` trait, summing three `Option[Int]` values is `summon[Applicative[Option]].map3(oa, ob, oc)(_ + _ + _)` instead of `oa.map3(ob, oc)(_ + _ + _)`, with `map3` as an extension method. In the extension method case, Scala searches for a `map3` extension method for an `Option[Int]` and finds one on the `Applicative[Option]` given. There's no need to even mention `Applicative`.

Furthermore, we can now make `Monad[F]` a subtype of `Applicative[F]` by providing the default implementation of `map2` in terms of `flatMap`. This tells us that all monads are applicative functors, and we don't need to provide separate `Applicative` instances for all our data types that are already monads.

Listing 12.2 Making `Monad` a subtype of `Applicative`

```
trait Monad[F[_]] extends Applicative[F]:
  extesnion [A](fa: F[A])
    def flatMap[B](f: A => F[B]): F[B] = fa.map(f).join   ◁┐  A minimal implementation
                                                          │  of Monad must implement
  extension [A](ffa: F[F[A]])                             │  unit and override either
    def join: F[A] = ffa.flatMap(identity)                ┘  flatMap or join and map.

  def compose[A, B, C](f: A => F[B], g: B => F[C]): A => F[C] =
    a => f(a).flatMap(g)

  extension [A](fa: F[A])
    def map[B](f: A => B): F[B] =
      fa.flatMap(a => unit(f(a)))

    def map2[B,C](fb: F[B])(f: (A, B) => C): F[C] =
      fa.flatMap(a => fb.map(b => f(a, b)))
```

So far we've just rearranged the functions of our API and followed the type signatures. Let's take a step back to understand the difference in expressiveness between `Monad` and `Applicative` and what it all means.

12.3   The difference between monads and applicative functors

In the last chapter, we noted there were several minimal sets of operations that defined a `Monad`:

- unit and `flatMap`
- unit and `compose`
- unit, map, and `join`

Are the `Applicative` operations unit and `map2` yet another minimal set of operations for monads? No. There are monadic combinators, such as `join` and `flatMap`, that can't be implemented with just `map2` and unit. To see convincing proof of this, take a look at `join`:

```
extension [A](ffa: F[F[A]])
  def join: F[A]
```

Just reasoning algebraically, we can see that unit and `map2` have no hope of implementing this function. The `join` function removes a layer of `F`. But the unit function only lets us add an `F` layer, and `map2` lets us apply a function within `F` but does no flattening of layers. By the same argument, we can see that `Applicative` has no means of implementing `flatMap` either.

So `Monad` is clearly adding some extra capabilities beyond `Applicative`. But what exactly? Let's look at some concrete examples.

12.3.1   The Option applicative versus the Option monad

Suppose we're using `Option` to work with the results of lookups in two `Map` objects. If we simply need to combine the results from two (independent) lookups, then `map2` is fine.

Listing 12.3   Combining results with the Option applicative

```
val depts: Map[String, String] = ...     ◁—— Department indexed by employee name
val salaries: Map[String, Double] = ...  ◁—┐
val o: Option[String] =                      │ Salaries indexed by employee name
  depts.get("Alice").map2(salaries.get("Alice"))(
    (dept, salary) =>                        ┌ String interpolation substitutes
      s"Alice in $dept makes $salary per year"  ◁—┘ values for dept and salary.
  )
```

Here we're doing two lookups, but they're independent, and we merely want to combine their results within the `Option` context. If we want the result of one lookup to affect what lookup we do next, then we need `flatMap` or `join`, as the following listing shows.

Listing 12.4   Combining results with the `Option` **monad**

Employee ID indexed by employee name

Department indexed by employee ID

```
val idsByName: Map[String, Int] = ...  ◁
val depts: Map[Int,String] = ...  ◁
val salaries: Map[Int,Double] = ...  ◁─── Salaries indexed by employee ID
val o: Option[String] =
  idsByName.get("Bob").flatMap(id =>  ◁───
    depts.get(id).map2(salaries.get(id))(
      (dept, salary) => s"Bob in $dept makes $salary per year"
    )
  )
```

Look up Bob's ID; then use the
result to do further lookups.

Here `depts` is a `Map[Int, String]` indexed by employee ID, which is an `Int`. If we want to print out Bob's department and salary, we need to first resolve Bob's name to his ID and then use this ID to do lookups in `depts` and `salaries`. We might say that with `Applicative`, the structure of our computation is fixed; with `Monad`, the results of previous computations may influence what computations to run next.

Effects in FP

Functional programmers often informally call type constructors like `Par`, `Option`, `List`, `Parser`, `Gen`, and so on *effects*. This usage is distinct from the term *side effect*, which implies some violation of referential transparency. These types are called *effects* because they augment ordinary values with extra capabilities. (`Par` adds the ability to define parallel computation, `Option` adds the possibility of failure, and so on.) We sometimes use the terms *monadic effects* or *applicative effects* to mean types with an associated `Monad` or `Applicative` instance.

12.3.2 *The Parser applicative versus the Parser monad*

Let's look at one more example. Suppose we're parsing a file of comma-separated values with two columns: *date* and *temperature*. Here's an example file:

```
1/1/2010, 25
2/1/2010, 28
3/1/2010, 42
4/1/2010, 53
...
```

If we know ahead of time that the file will have the *date* and *temperature* columns in that order, we can just encode this order in the `Parser` we construct:

```
case class Row(date: Date, temperature: Double)

val d: Parser[Date] = ...
```

```
val temp: Parser[Double] = ...

val row: Parser[Row] = d.map2(temp)(Row(_, _))
val rows: Parser[List[Row]] = row.sep("\n")
```

If we don't know the order of the columns and need to extract this information from the header, then we need `flatMap`. Here's an example file where the columns happen to be in the opposite order:

```
# Temperature, Date
25, 1/1/2010
28, 2/1/2010
42, 3/1/2010
53, 4/1/2010
...
```

To parse this format, where we must dynamically choose our `Row` parser based on first parsing the header (the first line starting with #), we need `flatMap`:

```
case class Row(date: Date, temperature: Double)

val d: Parser[Date] = ...
val temp: Parser[Double] = ...

val header: Parser[Parser[Row]] = ...
val rows: Parser[List[Row]] =
  header.flatMap(row => row.sep("\n"))
```

Here we're parsing the header, which gives us a `Parser[Row]` as its result. We then use this parser to parse the subsequent rows. Since we don't know the order of the columns up front, we're selecting our `Row` parser dynamically, based on the result of parsing the header.

There are many ways to state the distinction between `Applicative` and `Monad`. Of course, the type signatures tell us all we really need to know, and we can understand the difference between the interfaces algebraically, but here are a few other common ways of stating the difference:

- Applicative computations have a fixed structure and simply sequence effects, whereas monadic computations may choose a structure dynamically, based on the result of previous effects.
- Applicative constructs *context-free* computations, while `Monad` allows for *context sensitivity*.[2]
- `Monad` makes effects first class; they may be generated at interpretation time, rather than chosen ahead of time by the program. We saw this in our `Parser` example, where we generated our `Parser[Row]` as part of the act of parsing and used this `Parser[Row]` for subsequent parsing.

---

[2] For example, a monadic parser allows for context-sensitive grammars, while an applicative parser can only handle context-free grammars.

12.4   *The advantages of applicative functors*

The `Applicative` interface is important for a few reasons:

- In general, it's preferable to implement combinators like `traverse` using as few assumptions as possible. It's better to assume a data type can provide `map2` than `flatMap`. Otherwise, we'd have to write a new `traverse` every time we encountered a type that's `Applicative` but not a `Monad`! We'll look at examples of such types next.

- Because `Applicative` is weaker than `Monad`, the interpreter of applicative effects has more flexibility. To take just one example, consider parsing. If we describe a parser without resorting to `flatMap`, this implies that the structure of our grammar is determined before we begin parsing. Therefore, our interpreter or runner of parsers has more information about what it'll be doing up front and is free to make additional assumptions and possibly use a more efficient implementation strategy for running the parser, based on this known structure. Adding `flatMap` is powerful, but it means we're generating our parsers dynamically, so the interpreter may be more limited in what it can do—power comes at a cost. See the chapter notes (https://github.com/fpinscala/fpinscala/wiki) for more discussion of this problem.

- Applicative functors compose, whereas monads (in general) don't. We'll see how this works later.

12.4.1   *Not all applicative functors are monads*

Let's look at two examples of data types that are applicative functors but not monads. These are certainly not the only examples. If you do more functional programming, you'll undoubtedly discover or create lots of data types that are applicative but not monadic.[3]

AN APPLICATIVE FOR LAZY LISTS

The first example we'll look at is an alternative applicative for lazy lists. In the last chapter, we defined a `Monad[LazyList]` that behaved much like the `Monad[List]` we defined—unit lifted a value to a `LazyList` of one element, and `flatMap` concatenated the inner lists. For example:

```scala
scala> LazyList(1, 2, 3).flatMap(i => LazyList.fill(i)(i)).toList
val res0: List[Int] = List(1, 2, 2, 3, 3, 3)
```

The concatenation monad results in `map2` generating the cross product of the inputs:

```scala
scala> LazyList(1, 2, 3).map2(LazyList('a', 'b'))((_, _)).toList
val res1: List[(Int, Char)] = List((1,a), (1,b), (2,a), (2,b), (3,a), (3,b))
```

There's an alternative way of implementing `unit` and `map2`, though, yielding a different applicative instance. The idea is zipping the input lists, combining corresponding

---

[3] *Monadic* is the adjective form of *monad.*

elements from each input with the function passed to map2. Resultingly, the shorter input determines the length of the output. To maintain the structure-preserving property of map2, we need an implementation of unit that has at least as many elements as any other lazy list. We achieve that by returning an infinite lazy list:

```
val zipLazyListApplicative: Applicative[LazyList] = new:
  def unit[A](a: => A): LazyList[A] =
    LazyList.continually(a)          ◁────── The infinite, constant

  extension [A](fa: LazyList[A])
    def map2[B, C](fb: LazyList[B])(        ◁────── Combine elements pairwise.
             f: (A, B) => C): LazyList[C] =
      fa.zip(fb).map(f.tupled)
```

It's impossible to define flatMap or join for this instance in a way that's compatible with map2—that is, in a way in which fa.map2(fb)(f) returns the same result as fa.flatMap(a => fb.map(b => f(a, b))).

  We defined this Applicative[LazyList] instance as a regular value instead of a given instance since we can only have a single given instance per type (or otherwise introduce ambiguity errors). This works, but it's a bit cumbersome to use, as we have to explicitly pass it to any operations that take an applicative as a context parameter. Instead, we can introduce a new type and associate it with the zipping applicative using a given instance:

```
opaque type ZipList[+A] = LazyList[A]
object ZipList:
  def fromLazyList[A](la: LazyList[A]): ZipList[A] = la
  extension [A](za: ZipList[A]) def toLazyList: LazyList[A] = za

  given zipListApplicative: Applicative[ZipList] with
    def unit[A](a: => A): ZipList[A] =
      LazyList.continually(a)
    extension [A](fa: ZipList[A])
      override def map2[B, C](fb: ZipList[B])(f: (A, B) => C) =
        fa.zip(fb).map(f.tupled)
```

At the cost of some boilerplate conversions between LazyList and ZipList, we ensure we're always using the zip-based applicative.

■ ─ EXERCISE 12.4 ──

Hard: What is the meaning of sequence for a ZipList? Specializing the signature of sequence to ZipList, we have this:

```
def sequence[A](as: List[ZipList[A]]): ZipList[List[A]]
```

VALIDATED: AN EITHER VARIANT THAT ACCUMULATES ERRORS

In chapter 4, we looked at the Either data type and considered the question of how such a data type would have to be modified to allow us to report multiple errors. As a concrete example, think of validating a web form submission. Only reporting the first error means the user would have to repeatedly submit the form and fix one error at a time.

This is the situation with Either if we use it monadically. First, let's actually write the monad for the partially applied Either type.

■　EXERCISE 12.5
───

Write a monad instance for Either:

```
given eitherMonad[E]: Monad[Either[E, _]] with
  def unit[A](a: => A): Either[E, A] = ???
  extension [A](fa: Either[E, A])
    def flatMap[B](f: A => Either[E, B]): Either[E, B] = ???
```

───

Now consider what happens in a sequence of flatMap calls like the following, where the functions validName, validBirthdate, and validPhone each has the Either [String, T] type for a given type T:

```
validName(field1).flatMap(f1 =>
  validBirthdate(field2).flatMap(f2 =>
    validPhone(field3).map(f3 => WebForm(f1, f2, f3))))
```

If validName fails with an error, then validBirthdate and validPhone won't even run. The computation with flatMap inherently establishes a linear chain of dependencies. The variable f1 will never be bound to anything, unless validName succeeds.

Now think of doing the same thing with map3:

```
validName(field1).map3(
  validBirthdate(field2),
  validPhone(field3)
)(WebForm(_, _, _))
```

Here no dependency is implied between the three expressions passed to map3, and in principle, we can imagine collecting any errors from each Either into a List. But if we use the Either monad, then its implementation of map3 in terms of flatMap will halt after the first error.

In chapter 4, we created a data type called Validated that provided support for error accumulation (note we're using the final formulation of Validated, where we store the error as a single value of type E). Let's define that again here:

```
enum Validated[+E, +A]:
  case Valid(get: A)
  case Invalid(error: E)
```

■   EXERCISE 12.6

Write an `Applicative` instance for `Validated` that accumulates errors in `Invalid`. In chapter 4, we modified the signature of map2 to take an extra `combineErrors: (E, E) => E` function. In this exercise, use the monoid for the error type to combine errors. Remember that the summon method can be used to get an explicit reference to a context parameter:

```
given validatedApplicative[E: Monoid]: Applicative[Validated[E, _]] with
  def unit[A](a: => A) = ???
  extension [A](fa: Validated[E, A])
    override def map2[B, C](fb: Validated[E, B])(f: (A, B) => C) =
      ???
```

To continue the example, consider a web form that requires a name, birth date, and phone number:

```
case class WebForm(name: String, birthdate: LocalDate, phoneNumber: String)
```

This data will likely be collected from the user as strings, and we must make sure that the data meets a certain specification. If it doesn't, we must give a list of errors to the user indicating how to fix the problem. The specification might say that name can't be empty, birthdate must be in the "yyyy-MM-dd" format, and phoneNumber must contain exactly 10 digits.

Listing 12.5   Validating user input in a web form

```
def validName(name: String): Validated[List[String], String] =
  if name != "" then Validated.Valid(name)
  else Validated.Invalid(List("Name cannot be empty"))

def validBirthdate(birthdate: String): Validated[List[String], LocalDate] =
  try Validated.Valid(LocalDate.parse(birthdate))
  catch case _: java.time.format.DateTimeParseException =>
    Validated.Invalid(List("Birthdate must be in the form yyyy-MM-dd"))

def validPhone(phoneNumber: String): Validated[List[String], String] =
  if phoneNumber.matches("[0-9]{10}") then Validated.Valid(phoneNumber)
  else Validated.Invalid(List("Phone number must be 10 digits"))
```

To validate an entire web form, we can simply lift the WebForm constructor with map3:

```
def validateWebForm(name: String,
                    birthdate: String,
                    phone: String): Validated[List[String], WebForm] =
  validName(name).map3(
```

```
    validBirthdate(birthdate),
    validPhone(phone)
  )(WebForm(_, _, _))
```

If any or all of the functions produce `Invalid`, then the whole `validateWebForm` method will return all of those failures combined.

Note that we used `List[String]` as our error type, allowing us to return multiple errors (this requires a `Monoid[List[A]]` instance, which is provided in the GitHub repository). One downside to this choice of error type is that we have to handle the case where we get an `Invalid(Nil)`. What does it mean for our validation to fail with no errors? Let's prohibit this from occurring by using a different type for error accumulation. Instead of a `List[String]`, let's create a list that must have at least one element:

```
case class NonEmptyList[+A](head: A, tail: List[A]):
  def toList: List[A] = head :: tail

object NonEmptyList:
  def apply[A](head: A, tail: A*): NonEmptyList[A] =
    NonEmptyList(head, tail.toList)
```

Problem solved? Not quite. Recall that our applicative instance for `Validated` required a monoid instance for the error type. Let's try to write a `Monoid[NonEmptyList[A]]` instance:

```
given nelMonoid: Monoid[NonEmptyList[A]] with
  def combine(x: NonEmptyList[A], y: NonEmptyList[A]) =
    NonEmptyList(x.head, x.tail ++ y.toList)
  val empty: NonEmptyList[A] = ???
```

The `combine` operation is straightforward, but we've hit a problem with `empty`. We cannot construct an empty nonempty list, and we have no way of constructing a single element list because we have no way of conjuring a value of type `A` (and even if we could create a singleton list, our instance wouldn't pass the monoid identity laws). Let's look more closely at our definition of `Applicative[Validated[E, _]]`, though—our implementation used `combine` but not `empty`. Let's extract a trait from `Monoid` that only contains `combine`. We'll call this `Semigroup`,[4] but we could call it anything:

```
trait Semigroup[A]:
  def combine(a1: A, a2: A): A

trait Monoid[A] extends Semigroup[A]:
  def empty: A
```

---

[4] The name `Semigroup` comes from abstract algebra, which studies *groups*—monoids with an inverse for each element. As the name implies, *semigroups* are weaker than groups and monoids, only requiring the combine operation to be associative and closed on the set. Group theory defines many similar algebraic structures, but semigroups and monoids are the ones seen most in functional programming.

With this new abstraction, we can modify our `Applicative[Validated[E, _]]` instance to only require a `Semigroup[E]`:

```
given nelSemigroup[A]: Semigroup[NonEmptyList[A]] with
  def combine(x: NonEmptyList[A], y: NonEmptyList[A]) =
    NonEmptyList(x.head, x.tail ++ (y.head :: y.tail))

given validatedApplicative[E: Semigroup]: Applicative[Validated[E, _]] with
  def unit[A](a: => A) = Valid(a)
  extension [A](fa: Validated[E, A])
    override def map2[B, C](fb: Validated[E, B])(f: (A, B) => C) =
      (fa, fb) match
        case (Valid(a), Valid(b)) => Valid(f(a, b))
        case (Invalid(e1), Invalid(e2)) =>
          Invalid(summon[Semigroup[E]].combine(e1, e2))
        case (e @ Invalid(_), _) => e
        case (_, e @ Invalid(_)) => e
```

Can we do this? Yes! When creating a new abstraction like this, by extraction from an existing abstraction, we should extract the relevant algebraic laws as well. Otherwise, we risk creating abstractions that provide no meaning beyond the existence of an operation (i.e., no ability to build derived operations that are guaranteed to work for any instance). Let's do this for `Semigroup`. We defined three laws for monoids: associativity, left identity, and right identity. The associativity law can be extracted to the definition of `Semigroup`, which leaves us with the following definitions:

- A semigroup for a type `A` has an associative `combine` operation that returns an `A` given two input `A` values.
- A monoid is a semigroup with an `empty` element such that `combine(empty, a)` == `combine(a, empty)` == a for all a: A.

Why build weaker abstractions out of stronger ones? As we saw with `NonEmptyList`, weaker abstractions often have more instances—instances that cannot be promoted to a stronger abstraction due to the additional constraints demanded by the stronger abstraction. Like the relationship between `Semigroup` and `Monoid`, the `Applicative` abstraction is weaker than `Monad`, providing more instances and hence more ubiquity. `Validated` having an applicative but not a monad is similar to `NonEmptyList` having a semigroup but not a monoid.

12.5 The applicative laws

This section walks through the laws for applicative functors.[5] You may want to verify that each of these laws is satisfied by some of the data types we've been working with so far (an easy one to verify is `Option`).

---

[5] There are various other ways of presenting the laws for `Applicative`. See the chapter notes (https://github.com/fpinscala/fpinscala/wiki) for more information.

12.5.1 Left and right identity

What types of laws should we expect applicative functors to obey? Well, we should definitely expect them to obey the functor laws:

```
x.map(a => a) == x
x.map(f).map(g) == x.map(f andThen g)
```

This implies some other laws for applicative functors because of how we've implemented map in terms of map2 and unit. Recall the definition of map:

```
extension [A](fa: F[A])
  def map[B](f: A => B): F[B] =
    fa.map2(unit(()))((a, _) => f(a))
```

Of course, there's something rather arbitrary about this definition—we could have just as easily put the unit on the left side of the call to map2:

```
extension [A](fa: F[A])
  def map[B](f: A => B): F[B] =
    unit(()).map2(fa)((_, a) => f(a))
```

The first two laws for Applicative might be summarized by saying that both these implementations of map respect the functor laws. In other words, map2 of some fa: F[A] with unit preserves the structure of fa. We'll call these the left and right identity laws (shown here in the first and second lines of code, respectively):

```
unit(()).map2(fa)((_, a) => a) == fa
fa.map2(unit(()))((a, _) => a) == fa
```

12.5.2 Associativity

To see the next law, associativity, let's look at the signature of map3:

```
extension [A](fa: F[A])
  def map3[B,C,D](
    fb: F[B],
    fc: F[C]
  )(f: (A, B, C) => D): F[D]
```

We can implement map3 using apply and unit, but let's think about how we might define it in terms of map2. We have to combine our effects two at a time, and we seem to have two choices: we could combine fa and fb and then combine the result with fc, or we could associate the operation the other way, grouping fb and fc together and combining the result with fa. The associativity law for applicative functors tells us we should get the same result either way. This should remind you of the associativity laws for monoids (and semigroups) and monads:

```
combine(a, combine(b, c)) == combine(combine(a, b), c)
compose(f, compose(g, h)) == compose(compose(f, g), h)
```

The associativity law for applicative functors is the same general idea. If we didn't have this law, then we'd need two versions of map3—perhaps map3L and map3R—depending on the grouping, and we'd get an explosion of other combinators based on having to distinguish between different groupings.

We can state the associativity law in terms of product.[6] Recall that product just combines two effects into a pair using map2:

```
extension [A](fa: F[A])
  def product[B](fb: F[B]): F[(A, B)] =
    fa.map2(fb)((_, _))
```

If we have pairs nested on the right, we can always turn those into pairs nested on the left:

```
def assoc[A, B, C](p: (A, (B, C))): ((A, B), C) =
  p match
    case (a, (b, c)) => ((a, b), c)
```

Using these combinators, product and assoc, the law of associativity for applicative functors is as follows:

```
fa.product(fb).product(fc) == fa.product(fb.product(fc)).map(assoc)
```

Note that the calls to product are associated to the left on one side and to the right on the other side of the == sign. On the right side, we're then mapping the assoc function to make the resulting tuples line up.

12.5.3 *Naturality of product*

Our final law for applicative functors is *naturality*. To illustrate, let's look at a simple example using Option.

Listing 12.6   Retrieving employee names and annual pay

```
case class Employee(name: String, id: Int)
case class Pay(rate: Double, hoursPerYear: Double)

def format(employee: Option[Employee], pay: Option[Pay]): Option[String] =
  employee.map2(pay)((e, p) =>
    s"${e.name} makes ${p.rate * p.hoursPerYear}")

val employee: Option[Employee] = ...
val pay: Option[Pay] = ...
format(employee, pay)
```

---

[6] product, map, and unit are an alternate formulation of Applicative. Can you see how map2 can be implemented using product and map?

Here we're applying a transformation to the result of map2—from Employee we extract the name, and from Pay we extract the yearly wage. But we could just as easily apply these transformations separately before calling format, giving format an Option[String] and Option[Double] rather than an Option[Employee] and Option[Pay]. This might be a reasonable refactoring, so format doesn't need to know the details of how the Employee and Pay data types are represented.

Listing 12.7 Refactoring `format`

```
def format(name: Option[String], pay: Option[Double]): Option[String] =   ◀──┐
  name.map2(pay)((e, p) => s"$e makes $p")              format now takes the employee name as
                                                         an Option[String] rather than extracting
val employee: Option[Employee] = ...                     the name from an Option[Employee], and
val pay: Option[Pay] = ...                                             it's similar for pay.

format(
  employee.map(_.name),
  pay.map(p => p.rate * p.hoursPerYear))
```

We're applying the transformation to extract the name and pay fields before calling map2. We expect this program to have the same meaning as before; this sort of pattern comes up frequently. When working with Applicative effects, we generally have the option of applying transformations before or after combining values with map2. The naturality law states that it doesn't matter; we get the same result either way. Stated more formally

```
fa.map2(fb)((a, b) => (f(a), g(b))) == fa.map(f).product(fb.map(g))
```

The applicative laws are not surprising or profound. Just like the monad laws, these are simple checks that the applicative functor works in the way we'd expect—they ensure unit, map, and map2 behave in a consistent and reasonable manner.

EXERCISE 12.7

Hard: Prove all monads are applicative functors by showing that if the monad laws hold, then the Monad implementations of map2 and map satisfy the applicative laws.

EXERCISE 12.8

Just like we can take the product of two monoids A and B to get the monoid (A, B), we can take the product of two applicative functors. Implement this function on the Applicative trait:

```
trait Applicative[F[_]] extends Functor[F]:
  def product[G[_]](G: Applicative[G]): Applicative[[x] =>> (F[x], G[x])] =
    ???
```

Hard: Applicative functors also compose another way! If F[_] and G[_] are applicative functors, then so is F[G[_]]. Implement this function on the Applicative trait:

```
trait Applicative[F[_]] extends Functor[F]:
  def compose[G[_]](G: Applicative[G]): Applicative[[x] =>> F[G[x]]] =
    ???
```

Very hard: Prove that this composite applicative functor meets the applicative laws. This is an extremely challenging exercise and is best accomplished via automated proof assistant software.

Try to write compose on the Monad trait. It's not possible, but it is instructive to attempt it and understand why this is the case:

```
trait Monad[F[_]] extends Applicative[F]:
  def compose[G[_]](G: Monad[G]): Monad[[x] =>> F[G[x]]] =
    ???
```

12.6 Traversable functors

At the start of this chapter, we discovered applicative functors by noticing that our traverse and sequence functions (and several other operations) didn't depend directly on flatMap. We can spot another abstraction by generalizing traverse and sequence once again. Look again at the signatures of traverse and sequence:

```
def traverse[F[_], A, B](as: List[A])(f: A => F[B]): F[List[B]]
def sequence[F[_], A](fas: List[F[A]]): F[List[A]]
```

Any time you see a concrete type constructor, like List showing up in an abstract interface, like Applicative, you may want to ask the question, *What happens if I abstract over this type constructor?* Recall from chapter 10 that a number of data types other than

List are Foldable. Are there data types other than List that are traversable? Of course!

■ **EXERCISE 12.12**

On the Applicative trait, implement sequence over a Map rather than a List:

```
def sequenceMap[K, V](ofv: Map[K, F[V]]): F[Map[K, V]]
```

But traversable data types are too numerous for us to write specialized sequence and traverse methods for each of them. We need a new abstraction—we'll call it Traverse:[7]

```
trait Traverse[F[_]]:
  extension [A](fa: F[A])
    def traverse[G[_]: Applicative, B](f: A => G[B]): G[F[B]] =
      fa.map(fp).sequence

  extension [G[_]: Applicative, A](fga: F[G[A]])
    def sequence: G[F[A]] =
      fga.traverse(ga => ga)
```

The interesting operation here is sequence. Look at its signature closely. It takes F[G[A]] and swaps the order of F and G, so long as G is an applicative functor. This is a rather abstract, algebraic notion; we'll get to what it all means in a minute, but first, let's look at a few instances of Traverse.

■ **EXERCISE 12.13**

Write Traverse instances for List, Option, Tree, and [x] =>> Map[K, x]:

```
case class Tree[+A](head: A, tail: List[Tree[A]])
```

We now have instances for List, Option, Map, and Tree. What does this generalized traverse/sequence mean? Let's try plugging in some concrete type signatures for calls to sequence. We can speculate about what these functions do based on their signatures:

- List[Option[A]] => Option[List[A]] (a call to Traverse[List].sequence, with Option as the Applicative) returns None if any of the input List is None; otherwise, it returns a Some containing a List of all the values in the input List.

---

[7] The name Traversable is already taken by an unrelated trait in the Scala standard library.

- Tree[Option[A]] => Option[Tree[A]] (a call to Traverse[Tree].sequence, with Option as the Applicative) returns None if any of the input Tree is None; otherwise, it returns a Some containing a Tree of all the values in the input Tree.
- Map[K, Par[A]] => Par[Map[K, A]] (a call to Traverse[Map[K, _]].sequence with Par as the Applicative) produces a parallel computation that evaluates all values of the map in parallel.

It turns out that there is a startling number of operations that can be defined in the most general possible way in terms of sequence and traverse. We'll explore these in the next section.

A traversal is similar to a fold in that both take some data structure and apply a function to the data within to produce a result. The difference is that traverse preserves the original structure, whereas foldMap discards the structure and replaces it with the operations of a monoid. Look at the signature Tree[Option[A]] => Option[Tree[A]], for instance. We're preserving the Tree structure, not merely collapsing the values using some monoid.

12.7 Uses of Traverse

Let's now explore the large set of operations that can be implemented quite generally using Traverse. We'll only scratch the surface here; if you're interested, follow some of the references in the chapter notes (https://github.com/fpinscala/fpinscala/wiki) to learn more, and do some exploring on your own.

EXERCISE 12.14

Hard: Implement map in terms of traverse as a method on Traverse[F]. This establishes that Traverse is an extension of Functor and the traverse function is a generalization of map (for this reason, we sometimes call these *traversable functors*). Note that when implementing map, you can call traverse with your choice of Applicative[G]:

```
trait Traverse[F[_]] extends Functor[F]:

  extension [A](fa: F[A])
    def traverse[G[_]: Applicative, B](f: A => G[B]): G[F[B]] =
      fa.map(f).sequence

    def map[B](f: A => B): F[B] = ???

  extension [G[_]: Applicative, A](fga: F[G[A]])
    def sequence: G[F[A]] =
      fga.traverse(ga => ga)
```

But what is the relationship between Traverse and Foldable? The answer involves a connection between Applicative and Monoid.

12.7.1 *From monoids to applicative functors*

We've just learned that traverse is more general than map. Next we'll learn that traverse can also express foldMap and, by extension, foldLeft and foldRight! Take another look at the signature of traverse:

```
extension [A](fa: F[A])
  def traverse[G[_]: Applicative, B](f: A => G[B]): G[F[B]]
```

Suppose that our G is a type constructor ConstInt that takes any type to Int, so ConstInt[A] throws away its type argument A and just gives us Int:

```
type ConstInt[A] = Int
```

Then, in the type signature for traverse, if we instantiate G to be ConstInt, it becomes

```
extension [A](fa: F[A])
  def traverse(f: A => Int): Int
```

This looks a lot like foldMap from Foldable. Indeed, if F is something like List, then to implement this signature, we need a way of combining the Int values returned by f for each element of the list and a starting value for handling the empty list. In other words, we only need a Monoid[Int], and that's easy to come by. In fact, given a constant functor like we have here, we can turn any Monoid into an Applicative.

Listing 12.8   Turning a Monoid into an Applicative

```
type Const[A, B] = A          ◁──────  This is ConstInt
                                        generalized to any
given monoidApplicative[M](              A, not just Int.
  using m: Monoid[M]
): Applicative[Const[M, _]] with          This signature looks different from
  def unit[A](a: => A): M = m.empty       apply on Applicative, but due to
  override def apply[A, B](m1: M)(m2: M): M =   Const[M, _], the normal signature,
    m.combine(m1, m2)         ◁──────     def apply[A, B](fab: F[A => B])(fa:
                                          F[A]): F[B], simplifies to what's here.
```

This means Traverse can extend Foldable, and we can give a default implementation of foldMap in terms of traverse:

```
trait Traverse[F[_]] extends Functor[F], Foldable[F]:   ◁──  A trait may list multiple
  ...                                                        super traits, separated
    extension [A](fa: F[A])                                  by commas.
      override def foldMap[B: Monoid](f: A => B): B =         Scala can't infer the partially
        fa.traverse[Const[B, _], Nothing](f)   ◁──────       applied Const type alias here, so
                                                             we have to provide an annotation.
```

Traverse now extends both Foldable and Functor! Importantly, Foldable itself can't extend Functor. Even though it's possible to write map in terms of a fold for most foldable data structures, like List, it's not possible in general.

Answer, to your own satisfaction, the question of why it's not possible for `Foldable` to extend `Functor`. Can you think of a `Foldable` that isn't a functor?

So what is `Traverse` really for? We've already seen practical applications of particular instances, such as turning a list of parsers into a parser that produces a list, but in what kinds of cases do we want the generalization? What sort of generalized library does `Traverse` allow us to write?

12.7.2 Traversals with State

The `State` applicative functor is a particularly powerful one. Using a `State` action to traverse a collection, we can implement complex traversals that keep some kind of internal state.

To demonstrate, here's a `State` traversal that labels every element with its position. We keep an integer state, starting with 0, and add 1 at each step. Note that this implementation depends on a given instance of `Applicative[State[S, _]]` being available.

Listing 12.9   Numbering the elements in a traversable

```
extension [A](fa: F[A])
  def zipWithIndex: F[(A, Int)] =
    fa.traverse(a =>
      for
        i <- State.get[Int]
        _ <- State.set(i + 1)
      yield (a, i)
    ).run(0)(0)
```

This definition works for `List`, `Tree`, or any other traversable.

Continuing along these lines, we can keep a state of type `List[A]` to turn any traversable functor into a `List`.

Listing 12.10   Turning traversable functors into lists

```
extension [A](fa: F[A])
  def toList: List[A] =
    fa.traverse(a =>
      for
        as <- State.get[List[A]]      ◁─┐   Get the current state—
        _ <- State.set(a :: as)       ◁─┘   the accumulated list.
      yield ()
    ).run(Nil)(1).reverse                   Add the current element, and
                                            set the new list as the new state.
```

We begin with the empty list Nil as the initial state, and at every element in the traversal, we add it to the front of the accumulated list. This will construct the list in the reverse order of the traversal, so we end by reversing the list we get from running the completed state action. Note that we yield () because in this instance, we don't want to return any value other than the state.

Notice that the code for toList and zipWithIndex is nearly identical. And in fact, most traversals with State will follow this exact pattern: we get the current state, compute the next state, set it, and yield some value. We should capture that in a function.

Listing 12.11   Factoring out our mapAccum function

```
extension [A](fa: F[A])
  def mapAccum[S, B](s: S)(f: (A, S) => (B, S)): (F[B], S) =
    fa.traverse(a =>
      for
        s1 <- State.get[S]
        (b, s2) = f(a, s1)
        _ <- State.set(s2)
      yield b
    ).run(s)

  override def toList: List[A] =
    fa.mapAccum(List[A]())((a, s) => ((), a :: s))(1).reverse

  def zipWithIndex: F[(A, Int)] =
    fa.mapAccum(0)((a, s) => ((a, s), s + 1))(0)
```

EXERCISE 12.16

There's an interesting consequence of being able to turn any traversable functor into a reversed list: we can write, once and for all, a function to reverse any traversable functor! Write this function, and think about what it means for List, Tree, and other traversable functors:

```
extension [A](fa: F[A])
  def reverse: F[A]
```

It should obey the following law for all x and y of the appropriate types:

```
x.reverse.toList ++ y.reverse.toList == (y.toList ++ x.toList).reverse
```

EXERCISE 12.17

Use mapAccum to give a default implementation of foldLeft for the Traverse trait.

12.7.3 *Combining traversable structures*

The nature of a traversal necessitates preserving the shape of its argument, which is both its strength and weakness. This is well demonstrated when we try to combine two structures into one.

Given Traverse[F], can we combine a value of some type F[A] and another of some type F[B] into an F[C]? We could try using mapAccum to write a generic version of zip.

Listing 12.12 Combining two different structure types

```
extension [A](fa: F[A])
  def zip[B](fb: F[B]): F[(A, B)] =
    fa.mapAccum(fb.toList):
      case (a, Nil) => sys.error("zip: Incompatible shapes.")
      case (a, b :: bs) => ((a, b), bs)
    .apply(0)
```

This version of zip is unable to handle arguments of different shapes. For example, if F is List, then it can't handle lists of different lengths. In this implementation, the list fb must be at least as long as fa. If F is Tree, then fb must have at least the same number of branches as fa at every level. We can change the generic zip slightly and provide two versions, so the shape of one side or the other is dominant.

Listing 12.13 A more flexible implementation of `zip`

```
extension [A](fa: F[A])
  def zipL[B](fb: F[B]): F[(A, Option[B])] =
    fa.mapAccum(fb.toList):
      case (a, Nil) => ((a, None), Nil)
      case (a, b :: bs) => ((a, Some(b): Option[B]), bs)
    .apply(0)

  def zipR[B](fb: F[B]): F[(Option[A], B)] =
    fb.mapAccum(fa.toList):
      case (b, Nil) => ((None, b), Nil)
      case (b, a :: as) => ((Some(a): Option[A], b), as)
    .apply(0)
```

These implementations work out nicely for List and other sequence types. In the case of List, for example, the result of zipR will have the shape of the fb argument, and it will be padded with None on the left if fb is longer than fa.

For types with more interesting structures, like Tree, these implementations may not be what we want. Note that in zipL, we're simply flattening the right argument to a List[B] and discarding its structure. For Tree, this will amount to a preorder traversal of the labels at each node. We're then zipping this sequence of labels with the values of our left Tree, fa; we aren't skipping over nonmatching subtrees. For trees, zipL and zipR are most useful if we happen to know that both trees share the same shape.

12.7.4 *Traversal fusion*

In chapter 5, we talked about how multiple passes over a structure can be fused into one. In chapter 10, we looked at how we can use monoid products to carry out multiple computations over a foldable structure in a single pass. Using products of applicative functors, we can likewise fuse multiple traversals of a traversable structure.

EXERCISE 12.18

Use applicative functor products to write the fusion of two traversals. This function will, given two functions f and g, traverse `fa` a single time, collecting the results of both functions at once. Define this as an extension method on the `Traverse` trait:

```
extension [A](fa: F[A])
  def fuse[M[_]: Applicative, N[_]: Applicative, B](
    f: A => M[B], g: A => N[B]
  ): (M[F[B]], N[F[B]])
```

12.7.5 *Nested traversals*

Not only can we use composed applicative functors to fuse traversals, traversable functors themselves compose. If we have a nested structure, like `Map[K, Option[List[V]]]`, then we can traverse the map, the option, and the list at the same time and easily get to the `V` value inside because `Map`, `Option`, and `List` are all traversable.

EXERCISE 12.19

Implement the composition of two `Traverse` instances. Define this as a method on the `Traverse` trait:

```
def compose[G[_]: Traverse]: Traverse[[x] =>> F[G[x]]] = ???
```

12.7.6 *Monad composition*

Let's now return to the problem of composing monads. As we saw earlier in this chapter, `Applicative` instances always compose, but `Monad` instances do not. If you tried to implement general monad composition earlier, then you would have found that to implement `join` for nested monads F and G, you'd have to write something of a type like `F[G[F[G[A]]]] => F[G[A]]`—and that can't be written generally. But if G also happens to have a `Traverse` instance, then we can `sequence` to turn `G[F[_]]` into `F[G[_]]`, leading to `F[F[G[G[A]]]]`. Then we can join the adjacent F as well as G layers, using their respective `Monad` instances.

EXERCISE 12.20

Hard: Implement the composition of two monads, where one of them is traversable. Define this on the Monad companion object:

```
def composeM[G[_]: Monad, H[_]: Monad: Traverse]: Monad[[x] =>> G[H[x]]] =
  ???
```

Expressivity and power sometimes come at the price of compositionality and modularity. The problem of composing monads is often addressed with a custom-written version of each monad that's specifically constructed for composition. This kind of thing is called a *monad transformer.* For example, the OptionT monad transformer composes Option with any other monad:

```
opaque type OptionT[F[_], A] = F[Option[A]]
```
Option is added to the inside of the monad F.

```
object OptionT:
  def apply[F[_], A](fa: F[Option[A]]): OptionT[F, A] = fa
  extension [F[_], A](o: OptionT[F, A])
    def value: F[Option[A]] = o

  given optionTMonad[F[_]](using F: Monad[F]): Monad[OptionT[F, _]] with
    def unit[A](a: => A): OptionT[F, A] = F.unit(Some(a))
    extension [A](fa: OptionT[F, A])
      override def flatMap[B](f: A => OptionT[F, B]): OptionT[F, B] =
        F.flatMap(fa):
          case None => F.unit(None)
          case Some(a) => f(a).value
```

The flatMap definition here maps over both F and Option and flattens structures like F[Option[F[Option[A]]]] to just F[Option[A]]. But this implementation is specific to Option, and the general strategy of taking advantage of Traverse works only with traversable functors. To compose with State (which can't be traversed), for example, a specialized StateT monad transformer has to be written. There's no generic composition strategy that works for every monad. See the chapter notes (https://github.com/fpinscala/fpinscala/wiki) for more information about monad transformers.

12.8 Conclusion

In this chapter, we discovered two new useful abstractions, Applicative and Traverse, simply by playing with the signatures of our existing Monad interface. Applicative functors are a less expressive but more compositional generalization of monads. The functions unit and map allow us to lift values and functions, whereas map2 and apply give us the power to lift functions of higher arities. Traversable functors are the result of generalizing the sequence and traverse functions we've seen many times. Together,

Applicative and Traverse let us construct complex nested and parallel traversals out of simple elements that only need to be written once. As you write more functional code, you'll learn how to spot instances of these abstractions and make better use of them in your programs.

This is the final chapter in part 3, but there are many abstractions beyond Monad, Applicative, and Traverse, and you can apply the techniques we've developed here to discover new structures yourself. Functional programmers have, of course, been discovering and cataloguing for a while, and there is by now a whole zoo of such abstractions that captures various common patterns (*arrows*, *categories*, and *comonads*, just to name a few). Our hope is that these chapters have given you enough of an introduction to start exploring this wide world on your own; the material linked in the chapter notes (https://github.com/fpinscala/fpinscala/wiki) is a good place to start.

In part 4, we'll complete the functional programming story. So far, we've been writing libraries that might constitute the core of a practical application, but such applications will ultimately need to interface with the outside world. In part 4, we'll see that referential transparency can be made to apply even to programs that perform I/O operations or make use of mutable state. Even there, the principles and patterns we've learned so far allow us to write such programs in a compositional and reusable way.

Summary

- Functional programmers often informally call type constructors, like Par, Option, Gen, and so on *effects* because they augment ordinary values with extra capabilities.
- Applicative functors provide us the ability to combine effectful values and lift values and functions into an effect.
- An Applicative instance is defined by providing implementations of unit and map2.
- Applicative functors have a number of derived operations, including map3, map4, ..., and product.
- All applicative functors are functors, but not all functors are applicative functors.
- All monads are applicative functors, but not all applicative functors are monads.
- Applicative functors are less powerful than monads but, in exchange, are more composable and have more instances.
- Applicative functors are limited to context-free computations, while monads allow for context-sensitive computations.
- The applicative laws are
  - *Left identity*—unit(()).map2(fa)((_, a) => a) == fa
  - *Right identity*—fa.map2(unit(()))((a, _) => a) == fa
  - *Associativity*—fa.product(fb).product(fc) == fa.product(fb.product (fc)).map(assoc)
  - *Naturality*—fa.map2(fb)((a, b) => (f(a), g(b))) == fa.map(f).product (fb.map(g))

- The `Validated` type provides an alternative to `Either` that has accumulating error behavior. `Validated` has an applicative instance but no monad instance.
- A `Semigroup` is a generalization of a `Monoid` that removes the requirement for an identity element.
- All monoids are semigroups, but not all semigroups are monoids.
- The `NonEmptyList` data type has a `Semigroup` instance but not a `Monoid` instance.
- Traversable functors let us compose applicative effects with various iteration patterns, avoiding the need to write specialized logic for each effect.
- A `Traverse` instance is defined by providing implementations of either `traverse` or both `map` and `sequence`.
- The `sequence` operation converts an `F[G[A]]` into a `G[F[A]]`, swapping the order of `F` and `G`, as long as there's a `Traverse[F]` instance and an `Applicative[G]` instance.
- The `traverse` operation takes an `F[A]` and `A => G[B]` and returns a `G[F[B]]`, as long as there's a `Traverse[F]` instance and an `Applicative[G]` instance.
- Any `fa.map(f).sequence` can be written as `fa.traverse(f)`, and vice versa.
- All traversable functors are both functors and foldable instances. Not all functors are traversable functors, and not all foldables are traversable functors.
- Traversing with the `State` type lets us express a variety of stateful computations, like `zipWithIndex` and `mapAccum`.
- Applicative functors compose, whereas monads do not (generically) compose. That is, any two applicative functors can be composed to a new applicative functor, without relying on any concrete properties of the type constructors.
- Some monads can be composed with other arbitrary monads. This composition often comes in the form of a specific monad transformer, which allows a concrete monadic data type to be composed with another arbitrary monad, yielding a composed monad.
- The `OptionT` monad transformer is an example, yielding a specialized monad for the type `F[Option[A]]` for any monadic type constructor `F[_]`. The `OptionT` monad transformer lets us zoom in on the inner `A` value, moving both the effect of `Option` and the effect of `F` to the background.

12.9   Exercise answers

ANSWER 12.1

```
def sequence[A](fas: List[F[A]]): F[List[A]] =
  traverse(fas)(fa => fa)

def traverse[A,B](as: List[A])(f: A => F[B]): F[List[B]] =
  as.foldRight(unit(List[B]()))((a, acc) => f(a).map2(acc)(_ :: _))
```

```
def replicateM[A](n: Int, fa: F[A]): F[List[A]] =
  sequence(List.fill(n)(fa))

extension [A](fa: F[A])
  def product[B](fb: F[B]): F[(A, B)] =
    fa.map2(fb)((_, _))
```

■   **ANSWER 12.2**

To implement `apply`, notice that `fab` has a function A => B and `fa` has an A, each in the effect F. By passing `fab` and `fa` to `map2`, we get those inner values and apply the A to the function A => B:

```
def apply[A, B](fab: F[A => B])(fa: F[A]): F[B] =
  fab.map2(fa)((f, a) => f(a))
```

To implement `map`, we lift the `f`: A => B into F via `unit`, giving us an F[A => B]. We then pass that value along with F[A] to `apply` to get the final F[B]:

```
extension [A](fa: F[A])
  def map[B](f: A => B): F[B] =
    apply(unit(f))(fa)
```

`map2` is the most challenging. First let's curry the function f, giving us a function A => B => C. Then let's lift that function into our effect type F via `unit`, giving us an F[A => B => C]. We can use `apply` with that value and `fa` to reduce to a F[B => C]. Finally, we can pass that F[B => C] and F[B] to `apply` to get the desired F[C]:

```
def map2[B, C](fb: F[B])(f: (A, B) => C): F[C] =
  apply(apply(unit(f.curried))(fa))(fb)
```

Note that the inner usage of `apply(unit(f.curried))(fa)` could be replaced with `fa.map(f.curried)`, since that's exactly the definition of `map`.

■   **ANSWER 12.3**

A pattern is starting in the definitions of `map` and `map2` from the previous exercise; we can extend that pattern to implement `map3`, `map4`, and so on. For each additional parameter, we add another outer layer of `apply`:

```
extension [A](fa: F[A])
  def map3[B, C, D](
    fb: F[B],
    fc: F[C]
```

```
)(f: (A, B, C) => D): F[D] =
  apply(apply(apply(unit(f.curried))(fa))(fb))(fc)

def map4[B, C, D, E](
  fb: F[B],
  fc: F[C],
  fd: F[D]
)(f: (A, B, C, D) => E): F[E] =
  apply(apply(apply(apply(unit(f.curried))(fa))(fb))(fc))(fd)
```

We can make it a bit clearer that mapN can be implemented in terms of apply and
map(N - 1), though we can no longer use f.curried for arity 3 or greater, which
makes the syntax a bit noisy:

```
extension [A](fa: F[A])
  def map[B](f: A => B): F[B] =
    apply(unit(f))(fa)

  def map2[B, C](fb: F[B])(f: (A, B) => B): F[C] =
    apply(fa.map(f.curried))(fb)

  def map3[B, C, D](
    fb: F[B],
    fc: F[C]
  )(f: (A, B, C) => D): F[D] =
    apply(fa.map2(fb)((a, b) => f(a, b, _)))(fc)

  def map4[B, C, D, E](
    fb: F[B],
    fc: F[C],
    fd: F[D]
  )(f: (A, B, C, D) => E): F[E] =
    apply(fa.map3(fb, fc)((a, b, c) => f(a, b, c, _)))(fd)
```

■ ANSWER 12.4

sequence turns a finite list of potentially infinite lists into a potentially infinite list of
finite lists. The resulting zip list first emits a list of all the first elements from the
inputs, then a list of all second elements, and so on, until we reach the end of one of
the input lists.

■ ANSWER 12.5

```
given eitherMonad[E]: Monad[Either[E, _]] with
  def unit[A](a: => A): Either[E, A] = Right(a)
  extension [A](fa: Either[E, A])
    def flatMap[B](f: A => Either[E, B]): Either[E, B] =
```

```
fa match
  case Right(a) => f(a)
  case Left(e) => Left(e)
```

> Alternatively, we could delegate directly to
> the flatMap method defined on Either.

To implement `map2`, we pattern match on the two validated values. When both are
valid, we invoke the supplied function and wrap the result in `Valid`. When both are
invalid, we combine the errors via the given `Monoid[E]`; otherwise, we return the
invalid value:

```
enum Validated[+E, +A]:
  case Valid(get: A) extends Validated[Nothing, A]
  case Invalid(error: E) extends Validated[E, Nothing]

object Validated:
  given validatedApplicative[E: Monoid]: Applicative[Validated[E, _]] with
    def unit[A](a: => A) = Valid(a)
    extension [A](fa: Validated[E, A])
      override def map2[B, C](fb: Validated[E, B])(f: (A, B) => C) =
        (fa, fb) match
          case (Valid(a), Valid(b)) => Valid(f(a, b))
          case (Invalid(e1), Invalid(e2)) =>
            Invalid(summon[Monoid[E]].combine(e1, e2))
          case (e @ Invalid(_), _) => e
          case (_, e @ Invalid(_)) => e
```

We need to show that each of the applicative laws hold when we implement `map2` in
terms of `flatMap`: left identity, right identity, associativity, and naturality. We'll use this
definition of `map2`:

```
extension [A](fa: F[A])
  def map2[B, C](fb: F[B])(f: (A, B) => C): F[C] =
    fa.flatMap(a => fb.map(b => f(a, b)))
```

The following is a proof of the left identity:

```
unit(()).map2(fa)((_, a) => a)             == fa
unit(()).flatMap(_ => fa.map(a => a))      == fa
unit(()).flatMap(_ => fa)                  == fa
compose(unit, _ => fa)(())                 == fa
(_ => fa)(())                              == fa
fa                                         == fa
```

The left identity law

Substitute definition of map2

**By the functor identity law,
substitute fa for fa.map(a => a).**

**Rewrite flatMap in terms of compose,
substituting compose(unit, _ => fa)(())
for unit(()).flatMap(_ => a).**

**By the monad left identity, substitute _
=> fa for compose(unit, _ => fa).**

Apply () to _ => fa.

The following is a proof of the right identity:

		The right identity law
		Substitute definition of map2

```
fa.map2(unit(()))((a, _) => a)          == fa  ◄──┘
fa.flatMap(a => unit(()).map(_ => a))   == fa  ◄────────   Rewrite flatMap in terms
fa.flatMap(a => unit(a))                == fa             of compose, substituting
compose(_ => fa, unit)(())              == fa  ◄────      compose(_ => fa, unit)(())
(_ => fa)(())                           == fa  ◄────      for fa.flatMap(unit).
fa                                      == fa  ◄─┐
```

By the functor identity law, substitute
unit(a) for unit(()).map(_ => a).

Apply () to
_ => fa.

By the monad right identity, substitute _
=> fa for compose(_ => fa, unit).

The following is a proof of associativity. Let's start with the definition of the associativity law:

```
fa.product(fb).product(fc) == fa.product(fb.product(fc)).map(assoc)
```

Now let's simplify the left-hand side:

	Left-hand side of the associativity law

```
fa.product(fb).product(fc)  ◄──────┘
```

	Substitute definition of
	product in terms of map2

```
fa.map2(fb)((_, _)).map2(fc)((_, _))  ◄──┘
```

```
fa.flatMap(a => fb.map(b => (a, b)))          Substitute definition of map2
  .flatMap(ab => fc.map(c => (ab, c)))  ◄──┘  in terms of flatMap and map
```

```
fa.flatMap(a => fb.map(b => (a, b))            By the monad associativity
  .flatMap(ab => fc.map(c => (ab, c))))  ◄──┘  law, reassociate flatMaps.
```

```
fa.flatMap(a =>
  fb.flatMap(b => unit((a, b)))               Substitute definition of map
    .flatMap(ab => fc.map(c => (ab, c))))  ◄──┘  in terms of flatMap and unit
```

```
fa.flatMap(a =>                                         By the monad
  fb.flatMap(b =>                                       associativity law,
    unit((a, b)).flatMap(ab => fc.map(c => (ab, c)))))  ◄──┘  reassociate flatMaps.
```

```
fa.flatMap(a =>
  fb.flatMap(b =>                         By the monad left identity law,
    fc.map(c => ((a, b), c))))  ◄──┘      simplify unit((a, b)).flatMap(f).
```

```
fa.flatMap(a =>
  fb.flatMap(b =>                              Substitute definition of map
    fc.flatMap(c => unit(((a, b), c)))))  ◄──┘ in terms of flatMap and unit
```

Let's do the same for the right-hand side:

	Right-hand side of the associativity law

```
fa.product(fb.product(fc)).map(assoc)  ◄──┘
```

	Substitute definition of
	product in terms of map2

```
fa.map2(fb.map2(fc)((_, _)))((_, _)).map(assoc)  ◄──┘
```

```
fa.flatMap(a =>   ◄──┤ Substitute definition of map2
  fb.flatMap(b =>     in terms of flatMap and map
    fc.map(c => (b, c)))
```

```
            .map(bc => (a, bc))).map(assoc)
fa.flatMap(a =>      ◁─┤ Substitute definition of map
  fb.flatMap(b =>        in terms of flatMap and unit
    fc.flatMap(c => unit((b, c))))
    .map(bc => (a, bc))).map(assoc)
```

```
fa.flatMap(a =>      ◁─┤ Substitute definition of map
  fb.flatMap(b =>        in terms of flatMap and unit
    fc.flatMap(c => unit((b, c))))
    .flatMap(bc => unit((a, bc)))).map(assoc)
```

```
fa.flatMap(a =>      ◁─┤ By the monad associativity
  fb.flatMap(b =>        law, reassociate flatMaps.
    fc.flatMap(c => unit((b, c)))
     .flatMap(bc => unit((a, bc))))).map(assoc)
```

```
fa.flatMap(a =>      ◁─┤ By the monad associativity
  fb.flatMap(b =>        law, reassociate flatMaps.
    fc.flatMap(c => unit((b, c))
     .flatMap(bc => unit((a, bc)))))).map(assoc)
```

```
fa.flatMap(a =>      ◁─┤ By the monad left identity law,
  fb.flatMap(b =>        simplify unit((b, c)).flatMap(f).
    fc.flatMap(c => unit((a, (b, c)))))).map(assoc)
```

```
fa.flatMap(a =>      ◁─┤ Substitute definition of map
  fb.flatMap(b =>        in terms of flatMap and unit
    fc.flatMap(c => unit((a, (b, c))))))
.flatMap(abc => unit(assoc(abc)))
```

```
fa.flatMap(a =>      ◁─┤ By the monad associativity law, reassociate flatMaps,
  fb.flatMap(b =>        moving the outermost to innermost position.
    fc.flatMap(c =>
      unit((a, (b, c))).flatMap(abc => unit(assoc(abc)))))))
fa.flatMap(a =>                                               ◁──┤ By the monad
  fb.flatMap(b => fc.flatMap(c => unit(((a, b), c))))))           left identity law,
                                                                   simplify unit((a,
                                                                   (b, c))).flatMap(f).
```

The following is the proof of naturality; let's start with the definition of the naturality law:

```
fa.map2(fb)((a, b) => (f(a), g(b))) == fa.map(f).product(fb.map(g))
```

Now let's simplify the left-hand side: The left-hand
                                                          side of the   Substitute definition
```                                                       naturality law      of map2 in terms of
fa.map2(fb)((a, b) => (f(a), g(b)))  ◁──┘                                     flatMap and map
fa.flatMap(a => fb.map(b => (f(a), g(b))))  ◁────────┘
```

Then let's simplify the right-hand side: The right-hand side of
                                             the naturality law
```
fa.map(f).product(fb.map(g))  ◁──┘
                                             Substitute definition of
fa.map(f).map2(fb.map(g))((_, _))  ◁──┘      product in terms of map2
```

```
fa.map(f).flatMap(x => fb.map(g).map(y => (x, y)))
```
⟵ Substitute definition of map2 in terms of flatMap and map

```
fa.map(f).flatMap(x => fb.map(b => (x, g(b))))
```
⟵ By functor identity law, simplify consecutive map calls to a single call.

```
fa.flatMap(a => unit(f(a)))
  .flatMap(x => fb.map(b => (x, g(b))))
```
⟵ Substitute definition of map in terms of flatMap and unit

```
fa.flatMap(a =>
  unit(f(a)).flatMap(x => fb.map(b => (x, g(b)))))
```
⟵ By the monad associativity law, reassociate flatMaps.

```
fa.flatMap(a => fb.map(b => (f(a), g(b))))
```
⟵ By the monad left identity law, simplify unit(f(a)).flatMap(...).

■ **ANSWER 12.8**

The unit operation lifts the supplied a into both F and G and returns the result as a pair. The apply operation receives a pair of functions—one in F and one in G and a pair of F[A] and G[A]. It applies the F[A => B] with F[A] and the G[A => B] with G[A], returning the result as a pair:

```
trait Applicative[F[_]] extends Functor[F]:
  self =>                    ⟵
  def product[G[_]](
    G: Applicative[G]
  ): Applicative[[x] =>> (F[x], G[x])] = new:
    def unit[A](a: => A) = (self.unit(a), G.unit(a))
    override def apply[A, B](fs: (F[A => B], G[A => B]))(p: (F[A], G[A])) =
      (self.apply(fs(0))(p(0)), G.apply(fs(1))(p(1)))
```
We alias this to self so we can reference self.unit and self.apply in the anonymous instance.

■ **ANSWER 12.9**

The unit operation first lifts the supplied a into G via G.unit and then lifts the result into F, resulting in a value of the F[G[A]] type.

Unlike exercise 12.8, where we chose to implement apply, we'll choose map2 as a primitive this time. We implement map2 by nested invocations of map2 on the F and G applicatives:

```
trait Applicative[F[_]] extends Functor[F]:
  self =>
  def compose[G[_]](G: Applicative[G]): Applicative[[x] =>> F[G[x]]] = new:
    def unit[A](a: => A) = self.unit(G.unit(a))
    extension [A](fga: F[G[A]])
      override def map2[B, C](fgb: F[G[B]])(f: (A, B) => C) =
        self.map2(fga)(fgb)(G.map2(_)(_)(f))
```

ANSWER 12.10

This proof is best accomplished via an automated proof assistant, like Coq or Agda. A Coq-based proof is available here: https://mng.bz/M2DQ.

ANSWER 12.11

Implementing unit is straightforward; we first lift the A into a G[A] with the supplied Monad[G] and then lift the result to F[G[A]] with the Monad[F]. Unfortunately, it isn't possible to implement flatMap. We need to eventually get at the A value to apply it to our function f. No matter which way we get at it, we end up with types that don't quite fit together. In the following example, we flatMap the outer F[G[A]] and then map the inner G[A], but we're left with a type that doesn't work with our existing combinators—a G[F[G[B]]]:

> It doesn't compile because G.map(ga)(a => f(a)) returns G[F[G[B]]], but self.flatMap needs F on the outside.

```
trait Monad[F[_]] extends Applicative[F]:
  self =>
  def compose[G[_]](G: Monad[G]): Monad[[x] =>> F[G[x]]] = new:
    def unit[A](a: => A): F[G[A]] = self.unit(G.unit(a))
    extension [A](fga: F[G[A]])
      override def flatMap[B](f: A => F[G[B]]): F[G[B]] =
        self.flatMap(fga)(ga => G.map(ga)(a => f(a)))   <----
```

We could flatMap the inner G instead—self.flatMap(fga)(ga => G.flatMap(ga)(a => f(a)))—but again we end up with F and G in the wrong position with no way to swap. f(a) returns a F[G[B]], but G.flatMap demands G on the outside. If we could somehow swap the positions of F and G, we'd have a solution—more on that later.

ANSWER 12.12

Let's fold over the entries of the Map, starting with an empty map lifted to our type constructor via unit. On each iteration, we use map2 to combine the entry value of type F[V] with the accumulator of type Map[K, V], yielding a new map with one new entry:

```
def sequenceMap[K, V](ofv: Map[K, F[V]]): F[Map[K, V]] =
  ofv.foldLeft(unit(Map.empty[K, V])):
    case (acc, (k, fv)) =>
      acc.map2(fv)((m, v) => m + (k -> v))
```

■ **ANSWER 12.13**

We need to implement both `traverse` and `map` for each data type. For `map`, we can reuse the `map` operation on these data types.

To implement the `List` instance, let's use a right fold that uses `map2` to cons each element onto the accumulated output list. The initial accumulator is an empty list lifted into G via the `unit` of the `Applicative[G]` instance:

```
given listTraverse: Traverse[List] with
  extension [A](as: List[A])
    override def traverse[G[_]: Applicative, B](f: A => G[B]): G[List[B]] =
      val g = summon[Applicative[G]]
      as.foldRight(g.unit(List[B]()))((a, acc) => f(a).map2(acc)(_ :: _))
    def map[B](f: A => B): List[B] =
      as.map(f)
```

The `Option` instance is implemented by pattern matching on the original optional. If it's a `Some(a)`, we invoke `f(a)` and map the `Some` constructor over the result, converting `G[B]` to `G[Option[B]]`. If instead the original option is a `None`, then we lift `None` into G via the `unit` operation of the `Applicative[G]`:

```
given optionTraverse: Traverse[Option] with
  extension [A](oa: Option[A])
    override def traverse[G[_]: Applicative, B](
      f: A => G[B]
    ): G[Option[B]] =
      oa match
        case Some(a) => f(a).map(Some(_))
        case None    => summon[Applicative[G]].unit(None)
    def map[B](f: A => B): Option[B] =
      oa.map(f)
```

The `Tree` instance is a little bit different due to branching recursion. We immediately invoke `f` with the head value, which gives us a `G[B]`. We then traverse the tail list of subtree and recursively traverse each of them, which gives us a `G[List[B]]`. We use `map2` to combine the head `G[B]` and subtree `G[List[B]]` into a single `G[Tree[B]]`:

```
given treeTraverse: Traverse[Tree] = new:
  extension [A](ta: Tree[A])
    override def traverse[G[_]: Applicative, B](f: A => G[B]): G[Tree[B]] =
      f(ta.head).map2(ta.tail.traverse(a => a.traverse(f)))(Tree(_, _))
    def map[B](f: A => B): Tree[B] =
      Tree(f(ta.head), ta.tail.map(_.map(f)))
```

Finally, the instance for a `Map[K, _]` is implemented with a left fold, starting with an empty `Map[K, B]` lifted into G via the `unit` of `Applicative[G]`. For each entry in the original map of type `(K, A)`, we call the supplied function with the entry value. This leaves us with an accumulator of the G[Map[K, B]] type, a transformed value of the G[B] type, and a key of the K type. We use map2 on the accumulator and transformed value and add a new entry to the inner map, associating the transformed B with the key K:

```
given mapTraverse[K]: Traverse[Map[K, _]] with
  extension [A](m: Map[K, A])
    override def traverse[G[_]: Applicative, B](
      f: A => G[B]
    ): G[Map[K, B]] =
      m.foldLeft(summon[Applicative[G]].unit(Map.empty[K, B])):
        case (acc, (k, a)) =>
          acc.map2(f(a))((m, b) => m + (k -> b))
    def map[B](f: A => B): Map[K, B] =
      m.map((k, a) => (k, f(a)))
```

ANSWER 12.14

Let's compare the signature of map to traverse:

```
def map[B](f: A => B): F[B]
def traverse[G[_]: Applicative, B](f: A => G[B]): G[F[B]]
```

Note that traverse is similar to map but introduces an extra type constructor G. Can we select a type for G that causes the type constructor to evaporate? Consider a slightly different version of the Id type we saw in the previous chapter, this time defined as a type alias instead of a case class:

```
type Id[A] = A
given idMonad: Monad[Id] with
  def unit[A](a: => A) = a
  extension [A](a: A)
    override def flatMap[B](f: A => B): B = f(a)
```

Now let's substitute Id for G in the signature of traverse:

```
def traverse[G[_]: Applicative, B](
  f: A => G[B]): G[F[B]]              ←—— The signature of traverse

def traverseId[B](f: A => Id[B]): Id[F[B]]   ←—— Substituting Id for G

def traverseId[B](f: A => B): F[B]    ←—— Simplifying Id[X] to X
```

So traversing with the identity type constructor results in a definition of map! The full implementation is the following:

```
trait Traverse[F[_]] extends Functor[F]:

  extension [A](fa: F[A])
    def traverse[G[_]: Applicative, B](f: A => G[B]): G[F[B]] =
```

```
          fa.map(f).sequence

      def map[B](f: A => B): F[B] =
          fa.traverse[Id, B](f)(using idMonad)
```

The simplest approach is finding a counterexample—a data type that has a `Foldable` instance but cannot have a `Functor` instance. Consider the following:

```
case class Iteration[A](a: A, f: A => A, n: Int)
```

This type has a lawful `Foldable` instance:

```
given iterationFoldable: Foldable[Iteration] with
  extension [A](i: Iteration[A])
    override def foldMap[B](g: A => B)(using m: Monoid[B]): B =
      def iterate(n: Int, b: B, c: A): B =
        if n <= 0 then b else iterate(n - 1, g(c), i.f(i.a))
      iterate(i.n, m.empty, i.a)
```

When we try to implement `Functor[Iteration]`, we run into a problem:

```
given iterationFunctor: Functor[Iteration] with
  extension [A](i: Iteration[A])
    def map[B](g: A => B): Iteration[B] =
      Iteration(g(i.a), b => ???, i.n)
```

The types guide us into needing to implement a function `B => B`, but we only have functions `i.f: A => A` and `g: A => B`. There's no way of putting these functions together to implement `B => B`.

One way of thinking about this is that `Foldable` lets us visit each element, whereas `Functor` lets us change elements while preserving the overall structure. However, `Foldable` doesn't let us construct new values of the foldable type.

One way of thinking about `mapAccum` is that each element in `F[A]` is replaced with a transformed element of `B` (resulting in an `F[B]`), but unlike `map`, the computation depends on an accumulated state. With this model, `reverse` becomes a matter of replacing the element with its corresponding element in its reversal at the same position. We implement this by converting the input `F[A]` to a list, reversing that list, and doing a `mapAccum` traversal. On each element, we discard the input `A` and replace it with the head of the remaining reversed list, returning the tail of the remaining reversed list for the next element. When the traversal completes, the state is an empty list, which we discard:

```
extension [A](fa: F[A])
  def reverse: F[A] =
    fa.mapAccum(fa.toList.reverse)((_, as) => (as.head, as.tail))(0)
```

ANSWER 12.17

mapAccum accumulates state, like `foldLeft`, and also outputs each transformed element, unlike `foldLeft`. To implement `foldLeft` in terms of `mapAccum`, we use the state accumulation feature and discard the accumulated transformed elements. Because we're only using the final accumulated state, we return () for each transformed element, though we could have returned anything, really—a, 0, true, and so on. We're immediately discarding the resulting F[Unit]:

```
extension [A](fa: F[A])
  override def foldLeft[B](acc: B)(f: (B, A) => B): B =
    fa.mapAccum(acc)((a, b) => ((), f(b, a)))(1)    ◀
```

mapAccum returns (F[Unit], B) here, so we discard the F[Unit] and return just the accumulated B.

ANSWER 12.18

To implement `fuse`, we first take the product of the `Applicative[M]` and `Applicative[N]` instances, and then we traverse the original input, applying each element to both f and g and pairing the result. We have to be explicit about the type of applicative used in the traversal; otherwise, Scala infers a different type constructor:

```
extension [A](fa: F[A])
  def fuse[M[_], N[_], B](
    f: A => M[B], g: A => N[B])(using m: Applicative[M], n: Applicative[N]
  ): (M[F[B]], N[F[B]]) =
    fa.traverse[[x] =>> (M[x], N[x]), B](a =>
      (f(a), g(a)))(using m.product(n))
```

ANSWER 12.19

We first traverse the F[G[A]] with an anonymous function that receives a G[A]. In that anonymous function, we then traverse the G[A] with the supplied function f, resulting in an H[G[B]]. Consequently, the outer traversal has the type H[F[G[B]]]:

```
def compose[G[_]: Traverse]: Traverse[[x] =>> F[G[x]]] = new:
  extension [A](fga: F[G[A]])
```

```
override def traverse[H[_]: Applicative, B](f: A => H[B]): H[F[G[B]]] =
  self.traverse(fga)(ga => ga.traverse(f))
```

━━ ◻ ━**ANSWER 12.20**━━━

The `unit` operation is straightforward: lift the value into `H` and then into `G`, resulting in a `G[H[A]]`.

The `flatMap` operation is more challenging. We first `flatMap` the gha: `G[H[A]]`, which means we have to implement an anonymous function that receives an `H[A]`. We traverse that `H[A]` with the supplied function `f`, resulting in a value of `G[H[H[B]]]`. We then map over that and `join` the inner `H` layers into a single `H` layer:

```
def composeM[G[_], H[_]](
  using G: Monad[G], H: Monad[H], T: Traverse[H]
): Monad[[x] =>> G[H[x]]] = new:
  def unit[A](a: => A): G[H[A]] = G.unit(H.unit(a))
  extension [A](gha: G[H[A]])
    override def flatMap[B](f: A => G[H[B]]): G[H[B]] =
      G.flatMap(gha)(ha => G.map(T.traverse(ha)(f))(H.join))   ◄────────
```

> **We must explicitly call G.flatMap and G.map, or else we inadvertently get the extension methods from this composed instance.**

Part 4

Effects and I/O

Functional programming is a complete programming paradigm. All programs we can imagine can be expressed functionally, including those that mutate data in place and interact with the external world by writing to files or reading from databases. In this part, we'll apply what we covered in parts 1–3 of this book to show how FP can express these effectful programs.

We'll begin in the next chapter by examining the most straightforward handling of external effects: using an I/O monad. This is a simple embedding of an imperative programming language into a functional language. The same general approach can be used for handling local effects and mutation, which we'll introduce in chapter 14. Both of these chapters will motivate the development of more composable ways of dealing with effects. In chapter 15, our final chapter, we'll develop a library for streaming I/O and discuss how to write compositional and modular programs that incrementally process I/O streams.

Our goal in this part of the book is not covering absolutely every technique relevant to handling I/O and mutation but introducing the essential ideas and equipping you with a conceptual framework for future learning. You'll undoubtedly encounter problems that don't look exactly like those discussed here, but after finishing this part, along with parts 1–3, you'll be in good position to apply FP to whatever programming tasks you may face.

13

External effects and I/O

This chapter covers

- Contrasting effects and side effects
- Introducing trampolining
- Discussing free monads
- Defining capability traits

In this chapter, we'll take what we've learned so far about monads and algebraic data types and extend it to handling *external effects*, like reading from databases and writing to files. We'll develop a monad for I/O, aptly called IO, that will allow us to handle such external effects in a purely functional way.

We'll make an important distinction in this chapter between effects and side effects. The IO monad provides a straightforward way of embedding imperative programming with I/O effects in a pure program, while preserving referential transparency. It clearly separates *effectful* code—code that needs to have some effect on the outside world—from the rest of our program.

This will also illustrate a key technique for dealing with external effects: using pure functions to compute a description of an effectful computation, which is then executed by a separate interpreter that actually performs those effects. Essentially, we're crafting an embedded domain-specific language (EDSL) for imperative programming. This is a powerful technique we'll use throughout the rest of part 4. Our goal is equipping you with the skills needed to craft your own EDSLs for describing effectful programs.

13.1   *Factoring effects*

We'll work our way up to the IO monad by first considering a simple example of a program with side effects.

Listing 13.1   Program with side effects

```
case class Player(name: String, score: Int)

def contest(p1: Player, p2: Player): Unit =
  if p1.score > p2.score then
    println(s"${p1.name} is the winner!")
  else if p2.score > p1.score then
    println(s"${p2.name} is the winner!")
  else
    println("It's a draw.")
```

The contest function couples the I/O code for displaying the result to the pure logic for computing the winner. We can factor the logic into its own pure function—winner:

```
def winner(p1: Player, p2: Player): Option[Player] =      ◁──┐  Contains the logic for
  if p1.score > p2.score then Some(p1)                        computing the winner
  else if p1.score < p2.score then Some(p2)                   or a draw
  else None

                                              Has the responsibility of declaring
def contest(p1: Player, p2: Player): Unit =   the winner on the console
  winner(p1, p2) match      ◁──
    case Some(Player(name, _)) => println(s"$name is the winner!")
    case None => println("It's a draw.")
```

It is always possible to factor an impure procedure into a pure core function and two procedures with side effects: one that supplies the pure function's input and one that does something with the pure function's output. In listing 13.1, we factored the pure function winner out of contest. Conceptually, contest had two responsibilities: computing the result of the contest and displaying the computed result. With the refactored code, winner has a single responsibility: computing the winner. The contest method retains the responsibility of printing the result of winner to the console.

We can refactor this even further. The contest function still has two responsibilities: computing which message to display and then printing that message to the console. We could factor out a pure function here as well, which might be beneficial if we later decide to display the result in some sort of UI or write it to a file instead. Let's perform this refactoring now:

```
def winnerMsg(p: Option[Player]): String = p
  .map:
    case Player(name, _) => s"$name is the winner!"
  .getOrElse("It's a draw.")
```
⟵ **Has the responsibility of determining which message is appropriate**

```
def contest(p1: Player, p2: Player): Unit =
  println(winnerMsg(winner(p1, p2)))
```
⟵ **Has the responsibility of printing the message to the console**

Note how the side effect, `println`, is now only in the outermost layer of the program, and what's inside the call to `println` is a pure expression.

This might seem like an overly simple example, but the same principle applies in larger, more complex programs, and we hope you can see how this sort of refactoring is quite natural. We aren't changing what our program does, just the internal details of how it's factored into smaller functions. The insight here is that inside every function with side effects is a pure function waiting to get out.

We can formalize this insight a bit. Given an impure function `f` of type `A => B`, we can split `f` into two functions:

- A pure function of type `A => D`, where `D` is some description of the result of `f`.
- An impure function of type `D => B`, which can be thought of as an interpreter of these descriptions.

We'll extend this to handle input effects shortly. For now, let's consider applying this strategy repeatedly to a program. Each time we apply it, we make more functions pure and push side effects to the outer layers. We could call these impure functions the *imperative shell* around the pure core of the program. Eventually, we reach functions that seem to necessitate side effects like the built-in `println`, which has type `String => Unit`. What do we do then?

13.2 A simple IO type

It turns out that even procedures like `println` are doing more than one thing. They can even be factored in much the same way by introducing a new data type we'll call `IO`:

```
trait IO:
  def unsafeRun: Unit

def PrintLine(msg: String): IO = new:
  def unsafeRun = println(msg)

def contest(p1: Player, p2: Player): IO =
  PrintLine(winnerMsg(winner(p1, p2)))
```

Our `contest` function is now pure; it returns an `IO` value, which simply describes an action that needs to take place but doesn't actually execute it. We say `contest` has (or produces) an effect or is effectful, but it's only the interpreter of `IO`, its `unsafeRun` method, that actually has a side effect.[1] Now `contest` only has one responsibility, which

---

[1] The `unsafe` prefix is used to differentiate the interpreter from other methods that have no side effects.

is composing the parts of the program together: winner to compute who the winner is, winnerMsg to compute what the resulting message should be, and PrintLine to indicate that the message should be printed to the console. But the responsibility of interpreting the effect and manipulating the console is held by the run method on IO.

Other than technically satisfying the requirements of referential transparency, has the IO type actually bought us anything? That's a personal value judgment. As with any other data type, we can assess the merits of IO by considering what sort of algebra it provides—is it something interesting, from which we can define a large number of useful operations and programs, with nice laws that give us the ability to reason about what these larger programs will do? Not really. Let's look at the operations we can define:

```
trait IO:                    The self argument lets us refer to
  self =>            ◀────── this object as self instead of this.
  def unsafeRun: Unit
  def ++(io: IO): IO = new:
    def unsafeRun =
      self.unsafeRun     ◀────── self refers to the outer IO.
      io.unsafeRun

object IO:
  def empty: IO = new:
    def unsafeRun = ()
```

The only thing we can perhaps say about IO as it stands is that it forms a Monoid (empty is the identity, and ++ is the associative operation). So if we have, for example, a List[IO], we can reduce that to a single IO, and the associativity of ++ means we can do this either by folding left or right. On its own, this isn't very interesting. All it seems to have given us is the ability to delay when a side effect occurs.

Now we'll let you in on a secret: you, as the programmer, get to invent whatever API you wish to represent your computations, including those that interact with the universe external to your program. This process of crafting pleasing, useful, and composable descriptions of what you want your programs to do is, at its core, *language design*. You're crafting a little language and an associated interpreter that will allow you to express various programs. If you don't like something about the language you've created, change it! You should approach this like any other design task.

13.2.1 *Handling input effects*

As you've seen before, sometimes when building up a little language, you'll encounter a program that it can't express. So far, our IO type can represent only output effects. There's no way of expressing IO computations that must, at various points, wait for input from some external source. Suppose we want to write a program that prompts the user for a temperature in degrees Fahrenheit and then converts this value to Celsius and echoes it to the user. A typical imperative program might look something like the following listing.[2]

---

[2] We're not doing any sort of error handling here. This is just meant to be an illustrative example.

```
def fahrenheitToCelsius(f: Double): Double =
  (f - 32) * 5.0/9.0

def converter: Unit =
  println("Enter a temperature in degrees Fahrenheit: ")
  val d = readLine.toDouble
  println(fahrenheitToCelsius(d))
```

Unfortunately, we run into problems if we want to make converter into a pure function that returns an IO:

```
def fahrenheitToCelsius(f: Double): Double =
  (f - 32) * 5.0/9.0

def converter: IO =
  val prompt: IO =
    PrintLine("Enter a temperature in degrees Fahrenheit: ")
  // now what ???
```

In Scala, readLine is a def with the side effect of capturing a line of input from the console; it returns a String. We could wrap a call to readLine in IO, but we have nowhere to put the result! We don't yet have a way of representing this sort of effect. The problem is that our current I/O type can't express computations that yield a value of some meaningful type—our interpreter of IO just produces Unit as its output. Should we give up on our IO type and resort to using side effects? Of course not! We extend our IO type to allow input by adding a type parameter:

```
trait IO[A]:
  self =>
  def unsafeRun: A
  def map[B](f: A => B): IO[B] = new:
    def unsafeRun = f(self.unsafeRun)
  def flatMap[B](f: A => IO[B]): IO[B] = new:
    def unsafeRun = f(self.unsafeRun).unsafeRun
```

An IO computation can now return a meaningful value by returning an A from unsafeRun. We've added map and flatMap functions here, so IO can be used in for-comprehensions, and IO now forms a Monad:[3]

```
object IO:
  def apply[A](a: => A): IO[A] = new:     ◁——— This method lets us use the function
    def unsafeRun = a                            application syntax to construct IO
                                                 blocks, as in IO(...).
  given monad: Monad[IO] with
```

[3] We're using the Monad type from chapter 11 here, but in the companion GitHub repository, we define the Monad trait anew in the package corresponding to this chapter, as we'll add a number of combinators throughout this chapter.

```
def unit[A](a: => A): IO[A] = IO(a)
extension [A](fa: IO[A])
  override def flatMap[B](f: A => IO[B]) =
    fa.flatMap(f)
```

We can now write our converter example:

```
def ReadLine: IO[String] = IO(readLine())
def PrintLine(msg: String): IO[Unit] = IO(println(msg))

def converter: IO[Unit] = for
  _ <- PrintLine("Enter a temperature in degrees Fahrenheit: ")
  d <- ReadLine.map(_.toDouble)
  _ <- PrintLine(fahrenheitToCelsius(d).toString)
yield ()
```

Our converter definition no longer has side effects; it's a referentially transparent description of a computation with effects, and converter.unsafeRun is the interpreter that will actually execute those effects. And because IO forms a Monad, we can use all the monadic combinators we wrote previously. Here are some other example usages of IO:

- val echo = ReadLine.flatMap(PrintLine)—An IO[Unit] that reads a line from the console and echoes it back
- val readInt = ReadLine.map(_.toInt)—An IO[Int] that parses an Int by reading a line from the console
- val readInts = readInt ** readInt—An IO[(Int, Int)] that parses an (Int, Int) by reading two lines from the console[4]
- ReadLine.replicateM(10)—An IO[List[String]] that will read 10 lines from the console and return the list of results[5]

Let's look at a larger example—an interactive program that prompts the user for input in a loop and then computes the factorial of the input. Here's an example run:

```
The Amazing Factorial REPL, v2.0
q - quit
<number> - compute the factorial of the given number
<anything else> - crash spectacularly
3
factorial: 6
7
factorial: 5040
q
```

The code for this is shown in listing 13.3. It uses a few Monad functions we haven't seen yet: when, foreachM, and sequence_. For the full listing, see the associated chapter

---

[4] Recall that a ** b is the same as a.map2(b)((_, _))—it combines two effects into a pair of their results.
[5] Recall that fa.replicateM(3) is the same as List(fa, fa, fa).sequence.

code. The details of this code aren't too important; the point here is just demonstrating how we can embed an imperative programming language into the purely functional subset of Scala. All the usual imperative programming tools are here; we can write loops, perform I/O, and so on.

Listing 13.3 An imperative program with a `doWhile` loop

```
def factorial(n: Int): IO[Int] =      ⟵──── Imperative factorial using a mutable IO reference
  for
    acc <- IO.ref(1)       ⟵──── Allocation of a mutable reference
    _ <- foreachM((1 to n)                                    Modifying a
         .to(LazyList))(i => acc.modify(_ * i).void) ⟵─┘     reference in a loop
    result <- acc.get              ⟵──────────┐
  yield result                                 Dereference to obtain the
                                               value inside a reference
val factorialREPL: IO[Unit] = sequence_(
  PrintLine(helpstring),
  ReadLine.doWhile: line =>
    val ok = line != "q"
    when(ok):
      for
        n <- factorial(line.toInt)
        _ <- PrintLine("factorial: " + n)
      yield ()
)
```

Additional monad combinators

Listing 13.3 makes use of some monad combinators that we haven't seen before, although they can be defined for any `Monad`. You may want to think about what these combinators mean for types other than `IO`. Note that not all of them make sense for every monadic type (e.g., what does `forever` mean for `Option` or `LazyList`?):

```
extension [A](fa: F[A])
  def void: F[Unit] = fa.map(_ => ())  ⟵─┤  Replaces the
                                            value with a unit

  def doWhile(cond: A => F[Boolean]): F[Unit] =  ⟵─┐
    for                                               Repeats the effect of the
      a <- fa                                         first argument as long as
      ok <- cond(a)                                   the cond function yields
      _ <- if ok then doWhile(cond) else unit(())     true
    yield ()

  def forever[B]: F[B] =     ⟵──── Repeats the effect of its argument infinitely
    lazy val t: F[B] = fa.forever
    fa.flatMap(_ => t)                              Folds the stream
                                                    with the function f,
def foldM[A, B](                                    combining the
  l: LazyList[A])(z: B)(f: (B, A) => F[B]): F[B] =  ⟵─┤ effects and return-
  l match                                              ing the result
```

```
(continued)
    case h #:: t => f(z, h).flatMap(z2 => foldM(t)(z2)(f))
    case _ => unit(z)

def foldM_[A,B](
    l: LazyList[A])(z: B)(f: (B,A) => F[B]): F[Unit] =    ◁────
    foldM(l)(z)(f).void

def foreachM[A](
    l: LazyList[A])(f: A => F[Unit]): F[Unit] =    ◁────
    foldM_(l)(())((u,a) => f(a).void)
```

The same as the previous foldM function, except it ignores the result

Calls the function f for each element of the stream and combines the effects

We don't necessarily endorse writing code this way in Scala.[6] But it does demonstrate that FP is not in any way limited in its expressiveness—every program can be expressed in a purely functional way, even if that functional program is a straightforward embedding of an imperative program into the IO monad.

13.2.2 Benefits and drawbacks of the simple IO type

An IO monad like what we have so far is a kind of least-common denominator for expressing programs with external effects. Its usage is important mainly because it clearly separates pure code from impure code, forcing us to be honest about where interactions with the outside world are occurring. It also encourages the beneficial factoring of effects we discussed earlier. But when programming within the IO monad, we have many of the same difficulties as we would in ordinary imperative programming, which has motivated functional programmers to look for more composable ways of describing effectful programs.[7] Nonetheless, our IO monad does provide some real benefits:

- IO computations are ordinary values. We can store them in lists, pass them to functions, create them dynamically, and so on. Any common pattern can be wrapped up in a function and reused.
- Reifying IO computations as values means we can craft a more interesting interpreter than the simple run method baked into the IO type itself. Later in this chapter, we'll build a more refined IO type and sketch out an interpreter that uses nonblocking I/O in its implementation. What's more, as we vary the interpreter, client code like the converter example remains identical; we don't expose the representation of IO to the programmer at all! It's entirely an implementation detail of our IO interpreter.

---

[6] If you have a monolithic block of impure code like this, you can always just write a definition that performs actual side effects and then wrap it in IO—this will be more efficient, and the syntax is nicer than what's provided using a combination of for-comprehension syntax and the various Monad combinators.

[7] We'll see an example of this in chapter 15 when we develop a data type for composable streaming I/O.

Our naive `IO` monad also has a few problems:

- *Many* `IO` *programs will overflow the runtime call stack and throw a* `StackOverflow Error`. If you haven't encountered this problem yet in your own experimenting, you will certainly run into it if you write larger programs using our current `IO` type. For example, if you keep typing numbers into the `factorialREPL` program from earlier, it eventually overflows the stack.
- *A value of type* `IO[A]` *is completely opaque.* It's really just a lazy identity—a function that takes no arguments. When we call `unsafeRun`, we hope it will eventually produce a value of type `A`, but there's no way for us to inspect such a program and see what it might do. It might hang forever and do nothing, or it might eventually do something productive—there's no way to tell. We could say it's too general, and as a result, there's little reasoning we can do with `IO` values. We can compose them with the monadic combinators, or we can run them, but that's all we can do.
- *Our simple* `IO` *type has nothing at all to say about concurrency or asynchronous operations.* The primitives we have so far only allow us to sequence opaque blocking `IO` actions one after another. Many I/O libraries, such as the java.nio package that comes with the standard libraries, allow nonblocking and asynchronous I/O. Our `IO` type is incapable of making use of such operations. We'll rectify that by the end of this chapter when we develop a more practical `IO` monad. Let's start by solving the first problem (overflowing the call stack), since it will inform our solution for the other two.

13.3 Avoiding the StackOverflowError

To better understand the `StackOverflowError`, consider this very simple program that demonstrates the problem:

```
val p = PrintLine("Still going...").forever
```

If we evaluate `p.unsafeRun`, it will crash with a `StackOverflowError` after printing a few thousand lines. If you look at the stack trace, you'll see that `unsafeRun` is calling itself over and over. The problem is in the definition of `flatMap`:

```
def flatMap[B](f: A => IO[B]): IO[B] = new:
  def unsafeRun = f(self.unsafeRun).unsafeRun
```

This method creates a new `IO` object whose `unsafeRun` definition calls `unsafeRun` again before calling `f`. This will keep building up nested `unsafeRun` calls on the stack and eventually overflow it. What can we do about this?

13.3.1 Reifying control flow as data constructors

The answer is surprisingly simple. Instead of letting program control just flow through with function calls, we explicitly bake the control flow we want to support into our data type. For example, instead of making flatMap a method that constructs a new IO in terms of unsafeRun, we can just make it a data constructor of the IO data type, and then the interpreter can be a tail-recursive loop. Whenever it encounters a constructor like FlatMap(x, k), it will interpret x, and then it will call k on the result. Here's a new IO type that implements that idea.

Listing 13.4   Creating a new IO type

```
enum IO[A]:
  case Return(a: A)
  case Suspend(resume: () => A)
  case FlatMap[A, B](
      sub: IO[A], k: A => IO[B]) extends IO[B]

  def flatMap[B](f: A => IO[B]): IO[B] =
    FlatMap(this, f)
  def map[B](f: A => B): IO[B] =
    flatMap(a => Return(f(a)))
```

> **This is a pure computation that immediately returns an A without any further steps. When unsafeRun sees this constructor, it knows the computation has finished.**

> **This is a suspension of the computation, where resume is a function that takes no arguments but has some effect and yields a result.**

This is a composition of two steps. It reifies flatMap as a data constructor rather than a function. When run sees this, it should first process the subcomputation sub and then continue with k once sub produces a result.

This new IO type has three data constructors, representing the three different kinds of control flow we want the interpreter of this data type to support. Return represents an IO action that has finished, meaning we want to return the value a, without any further steps. Suspend means we want to execute some effect to produce a result, and the FlatMap data constructor lets us extend or continue an existing computation by using the result of the first computation to produce a second computation. The flatMap method's implementation can now simply call the FlatMap data constructor and return immediately. When the interpreter encounters FlatMap(sub, k), it can interpret the subcomputation sub and then remember to call the continuation k on the result. Then k will continue executing the program. Let's add some convenience constructors as well:

```
object IO:
  def apply[A](a: => A): IO[A] =
    suspend(Return(a))

  def suspend[A](ioa: => IO[A]): IO[A] =
    Suspend(() => ioa).flatMap(identity)
```

> **Delays the computation of a until the returned program is interpreted**

> **Delays the computation of the ioa program until the returned program is interpreted**

Note that the definitions of apply and suspend do not evaluate their by-name arguments—rather, evaluation is delayed until later, when the thunk passed to the internal Suspend value is forced.

We'll get to the interpreter shortly, but first let's rewrite our printLine example to use this new IO type:

```
def printLine(s: String): IO[Unit] =
  IO(println(s))

val p = printLine("Still going...").forever
```

What this actually creates is an infinite nested structure, much like a `LazyList`. The *head* of the stream is a `Function0`, and the rest of the computation is like the *tail*:

```
FlatMap(
  FlatMap(
    Suspend(() => Return(println(s))),
    identity
  ),
  _ => FlatMap(
    FlatMap(
      Suspend(() => Return(println(s))),
      identity
    ),
    _ => FlatMap(...)))
```

The following is the tail-recursive interpreter, defined as a method on `IO`, that traverses the structure and performs the effects:

```
@annotation.tailrec final def unsafeRun(): A = this match
  case Return(a) => a
  case Suspend(r) => r()
  case FlatMap(x, f) => x match       <───
    case Return(a) => f(a).unsafeRun()
    case Suspend(r) => f(r()).unsafeRun()   <───
    case FlatMap(y, g) =>
      y.flatMap(a => g(a).flatMap(f)).unsafeRun()
```

> We could just say f(x.unsafeRun()).unsafeRun() here, but then the inner call to unsafeRun wouldn't be in tail position. Instead, we match on x to see what it is.

> Here x is a Suspend(r), so we force the r thunk and call f on the result.

> In this case, io is an expression like FlatMap(FlatMap(y, g), f). We reassociate this to the right to be able to call unsafeRun in tail position, and the next iteration will match on y.

Instead of saying `f(x.unsafeRun()).unsafeRun()` in the `FlatMap(x, f)` case (thereby losing tail recursion), we pattern match on x, since it can only be one of three things. If it's a `Return`, we can just call f on the pure value inside. If it's a `Suspend`, then we can just execute its resumption, pass the result to the f from the outer `FlatMap`, and recurse. But if x is itself a `FlatMap` constructor, then we know io consists of two `FlatMap` constructors nested on the left, like this: `FlatMap(FlatMap(y, g), f)`.

To continue running the program in that case, we next want to look at y to see if it is another `FlatMap` constructor, but the expression may be arbitrarily deep, and we want to remain tail recursive. We reassociate this to the right, effectively turning `y.flatMap(g).flatMap(f)` into `y.flatMap(a => g(a).flatMap(f))`. We're taking advantage of the monad associativity law! Then we call `unsafeRun` on the rewritten expression, letting us remain tail recursive. Thus, when we actually interpret our program, it will be incrementally rewritten to be a right-associated sequence of `FlatMap` constructors:

```
FlatMap(a1, a1 =>
  FlatMap(a2, a2 =>
    FlatMap(a3, a3 =>
      ...
        FlatMap(aN, aN => Return(aN)))))
```

If we now call `unsafeRun` on our example program `p`, it'll continue running indefinitely without a stack overflow, which is what we want. Our `unsafeRun` function won't overflow the stack, even for infinitely recursive IO programs.

What have we done here? When a program running on the JVM makes a function call, it'll push a frame onto the call stack to remember where to return after the call has finished, so the execution can continue. We've made this program control explicit in our IO data type. When `unsafeRun` interprets an IO program, it'll determine whether the program is requesting to execute some effect with a `Suspend(s)` or it wants to call a subroutine with `FlatMap(x, f)`. Instead of the program making use of the call stack, `unsafeRun` will call `x()` and then continue by calling `f` on the result of that, and `f` will immediately return either a `Suspend`, `FlatMap`, or `Return`, transferring control to `unsafeRun` again. Our IO program is therefore a kind of *coroutine* that executes cooperatively with `unsafeRun`. It continually makes either `Suspend` or `FlatMap` requests, and every time it does so, it suspends its own execution and returns control to `unsafeRun`. And it's actually `unsafeRun` that drives the execution of the program forward, one such suspension at a time. A function like `unsafeRun` is sometimes called a *trampoline*, and the overall technique of returning control to a single loop to eliminate the stack is called *trampolining*.

13.3.2 *Trampolining: A general solution to stack overflow*

There is no requirement for the `resume` functions in our IO monad to perform side effects. The IO type we have so far is, in fact, a general data structure for trampolining computations—even pure computations that don't do any I/O at all!

The `StackOverflowError` problem manifests itself in Scala wherever we have a composite function that consists of more function calls than there's space for on the call stack. This problem is easy to demonstrate:

> **We construct a composite function g that consists of 100,000 functions, where each one calls the next.**

```
scala> val f = (x: Int) => x
val f: Int => Int = <function1>

scala> val g = List.fill(100000)(f).foldLeft(f)(_ compose _)    <─────
val g: Int => Int = <function1>

scala> g(42)
java.lang.StackOverflowError
```

It will likely fail for much smaller compositions. Fortunately, we can solve this with our IO monad:

```
scala> val f = (x: Int) => IO.Return(x)
val f: Int => IO[Int] = <function1>
```

```
scala> val g = List.fill(10000)(f).foldLeft(f)((a, b) =>
     |     x => IO.suspend(a(x).flatMap(b)))    ◁─┐
val g: Int => IO[Int] = <function1>              │   Create a large, left-nested
                                                 │   chain of flatMap calls.
scala> val x1 = g(0).unsafeRun()
val x1: Int = 0

scala> val x2 = g(42).unsafeRun()
val x2: Int = 42
```

But there's no I/O going on here at all. So IO is a bit of a misnomer. It really gets that name from the fact that Suspend can contain a side-effecting function. But what we have is not really a monad for I/O—it's actually a monad for tail-call elimination! Let's change its name to reflect that:

```
enum TailRec[A]:
  case Return(a: A)
  case Suspend(resume: () => A)
  case FlatMap[A,B](sub: TailRec[A],
                    k: A => TailRec[B]) extends TailRec[B]

  def flatMap[B](f: A => TailRec[B]): TailRec[B] =
    FlatMap(this, f)

  def map[B](f: A => B): TailRec[B] =                We renamed this function
    flatMap(a => Return(f(a)))                       as run since it's no longer
                                                     being used to capture side
  @annotation.tailrec final def run: A = this match  ◁─  effects.
    case Return(a) => a
    case Suspend(r) => r()
    case FlatMap(x, f) => x match
      case Return(a) => f(a).run
      case Suspend(r) => f(r()).run
      case FlatMap(y, g) => y.flatMap(a => g(a).flatMap(f)).run
```

We can use the TailRec data type to add trampolining to any function type A => B by modifying the return type B to TailRec[B] instead. We just saw an example where we changed a program that used Int => Int to use Int => TailRec[Int]. The program just had to be modified to use flatMap in function composition[8] and Suspend before every function call.

Using TailRec can be slower than direct function calls, but its advantage is that we gain predictable stack usage.[9]

---

[8] This is the Kleisli composition from chapter 11. In other words, the trampolined function uses the Kleisli composition in the TailRec monad instead of ordinary function composition.

[9] When we use TailRec to implement tail calls that wouldn't be otherwise optimized, it's faster than using direct calls (not to mention stack safe). It seems the overhead of building and tearing down stack frames is greater than the overhead of having all calls wrapped in a Suspend. There are variations on TailRec that we haven't investigated in detail—it isn't necessary to transfer control to the central loop after every function call, only periodically for avoiding stack overflows. We can, for example, implement the same basic idea using exceptions. See Throw.scala in the chapter code.

`TailRec` in the standard library

The `TailRec` type we defined here is built into the Scala standard library in the `scala.util.control.TailCalls` object. The object defines the `TailRec[A]` type as well as `done` and `tailcall` constructors, which correspond to `Return` and the `suspend` convenience constructor. The `TailRec` type has a method `result`, which interprets a `TailRec[A]` value to an `A` value. Besides naming, `scala.util.control .TailCalls` is implemented exactly like the `TailRec` we defined here (see the implementation at https://mng.bz/do81). Here's the same example using `TailCalls` instead of our `TailRec`:

```
scala> import scala.util.control.TailCalls.*

scala> val f = (x: Int) => done(x)
val f: Int => scala.util.control.TailCalls.TailRec[Int] = ...

scala> val g = List.fill(10000)(f).foldLeft(f)((a, b) =>
     |   x => tailcall(a(x).flatMap(b)))
val g: Int => scala.util.control.TailCalls.TailRec[Int] = ...

scala> val x1 = g(0).result
x1: Int = 0

scala> val x2 = g(42).result
x2: Int = 42
```

13.4   A more nuanced I/O type

If we use `TailRec` as our `IO` type, we avoid the stack overflow problem, but the other two problems with the monad still remain: it's inexplicit about what kinds of effects may occur, and it has no concurrency mechanism or means of performing I/O without blocking the current thread of execution.

During execution, the `run` interpreter will look at a `TailRec` program such as `FlatMap(Suspend(s), k)`, in which case the next thing to do is to call `s()`. The program is returning control to `run`, requesting it executes some effect `s`, waiting for the result, and responding by passing the resulting value to `k` (which may subsequently return a further request). At the moment, the interpreter can't know anything about what kind of effects the program will have. It's completely opaque, so the only thing it can do is call `s()`. Not only can that have an arbitrary and unknowable side effect, but there's no way the interpreter could allow asynchronous calls if it wanted to. Since the suspension is a `Function0`, all we can do is call it and wait for it to complete.

What if we used `Par` from chapter 7 for the suspension instead of `Function0`? Let's call this type `Async` since the interpreter can now support asynchronous execution.

Listing 13.5   Defining our `Async` type

```
enum Async[A]:
  case Return(a: A)
```

```
  case Suspend(resume: Par[A])
  case FlatMap[A, B](sub: Async[A],
                     k: A => Async[B]) extends Async[B]

  def flatMap[B](f: A => Async[B]): Async[B] =
    FlatMap(this, f)

  def map[B](f: A => B): Async[B] =
    flatMap(a => Return(f(a)))
```

Note that the resume argument to `Suspend` is a `Par[A]` rather than a `() => A` (or a `Function0[A]`). The implementation of run changes accordingly; it now returns a `Par[A]` rather than an `A`, and we rely on a separate tail-recursive `step` function to reassociate the `FlatMap` constructors:

```
@annotation.tailrec final def step: Async[A] = this match
  case FlatMap(FlatMap(x, f), g) => x.flatMap(a => f(a).flatMap(g)).step
  case FlatMap(Return(x), f) => f(x).step
  case _ => this

def run: Par[A] = step match
  case Return(a) => Par.unit(a)
  case Suspend(r) => r
  case FlatMap(x, f) => x match
    case Suspend(r) => r.flatMap(a => f(a).run)
    case _ => sys.error("Impossible, since `step` eliminates these cases")
```

Our `Async` data type now supports asynchronous computations; we can embed them using the `Suspend` constructor, which takes an arbitrary `Par`. This works, but we take this idea one step further and abstract over the choice of type constructor used in `Suspend`. To do that, we'll generalize `Async` and parameterize it on some type constructor `F`, rather than use `Function0` or `Par` specifically. We'll name this more abstract data type `Free`:

```
enum Free[F[_], A]:          ◁──
  case Return(a: A)
  case Suspend(s: F[A]) ◁──
  case FlatMap[F[_], A, B](
    s: Free[F, A],
    f: A => Free[F, B]) extends Free[F, B]
```

> The difference between Free and TailRec is that Free is parameterized with a type constructor, F. TailRec is a special case of Free where F is fixed to be Function0

> The suspension is now of some arbitrary type F, rather than Function0.

Then `TailRec` and `Async` are simply type aliases:

```
type TailRec[A] = Free[Function0, A]
type Async[A] = Free[Par, A]
```

13.4.1 *Free monads*

The `Return` and `FlatMap` constructors witness that this data type is a monad for any choice of F, and since they're exactly the operations required to generate a monad, we say it's a *free* monad.[10]

■ EXERCISE 13.1

Free is a monad for any choice of F. Implement `map` and `flatMap` methods on the Free enum, and give the `Monad` instance for `Free[F,_]`:

```
given freeMonad[F[_]]: Monad[[x] =>> Free[F, x]] with
  def unit[A](a: => A): Free[F, A] = ???
  extension [A](fa: Free[F, A])
    def flatMap[B](f: A => Free[F, B]): Free[F, B] = ???
```

■ EXERCISE 13.2

Implement a specialized tail-recursive interpreter, `runTrampoline`, for running a `Free[Function0, A]`:

```
extension [A](fa: Free[Function0, A])
  @annotation.tailrec
  def runTrampoline: A = ???
```

■ EXERCISE 13.3

Hard: Implement a generic interpreter for `Free[F, A]`, given a `Monad[F]`. Define this interpreter as a method on the Free type. You can pattern your implementation after the Async interpreter given previously, including using a tail-recursive `step` function:

```
enum Free[F[_], A]:
  ...

  def run(using F: Monad[F]): F[A] = ???

  @annotation.tailrec
  final def step: Free[F, A] = ???
```

---

[10] In this context *free* means *generated freely* in the sense that F doesn't need to have any monadic structure of its own. See the chapter notes (https://github.com/fpinscala/fpinscala/wiki) for a more formal statement of the definition of free.

What is the meaning of Free[F, A]? Essentially, it's a recursive structure that contains a value of type A wrapped in zero or more layers of F.[11] It's a monad because flatMap lets us take the A and from it generate more layers of F. Before getting the result, an interpreter of the structure must be able to process all of those F layers. We can view the structure and its interpreter as interacting coroutines, and the type F defines the protocol of this interaction. By choosing our F carefully, we can precisely control what kinds of interactions are allowed.

13.4.2 A monad that supports only console I/O

Function0 is not just the simplest possible choice for the type parameter F but also one of the least restrictive in terms of what's allowed. This lack of restriction gives us no ability to reason about what a value of type Function0[A] might do. A more restrictive choice for F in Free[F, A] might be an algebraic data type that only models interaction with the console.

Listing 13.6 Creating our Console type

```
enum Console[A]:
  case ReadLine extends Console[Option[String]]
  case PrintLine(line: String) extends Console[Unit]

  def toPar: Par[A] = this match                              ← Interpret this Console[A] as a Par[A].
    case ReadLine => Par.lazyUnit(Try(readLine()).toOption)
    case PrintLine(line) => Par.lazyUnit(println(line))
                                                              ← Interpret this Console[A] as a Function0[A].
  def toThunk: () => A = this match
    case ReadLine => () => Try(readLine()).toOption
    case PrintLine(line) => () => println(line)
```

A Console[A] represents a computation that yields an A, but it's restricted to one of two possible forms: ReadLine (with type Console[Option[String]]) or PrintLine. We bake two interpreters into Console, one that converts to a Par, and another that converts to a Function0. The implementations of these interpreters are straightforward.

We can now embed this data type into Free to obtain a restricted IO type allowing for only console I/O. We just use the Suspend constructor of Free:

```
object Console:
  def readLn: Free[Console, Option[String]] =
    Suspend(ReadLine)

  def printLn(line: String): Free[Console, Unit] =
    Suspend(PrintLine(line))
```

---

[11]Put another way, it's a tree with data of type A at the leaves, where the branching is described by F. Put yet another way, it's an abstract syntax tree for a program in a language whose instructions are given by F, with free variables in A.

Using the `Free[Console, A]` type, we can write programs that interact with the console, and we reasonably expect they won't perform other kinds of I/O:[12]

```
val f1: Free[Console, Option[String]] =
  for
    _  <- printLn(
      "I can only interact with the console.")   <─┐
    ln <- readLn
  yield ln
```

These aren't Scala's standard readLine and println but the monadic methods we defined earlier.

This sounds good, but how do we actually run a `Free[Console, A]`? Recall our signature for run:

```
def run(using F: Monad[F]): F[A]
```

To run a `Free[Console, A]`, we seem to need a `Monad[Console]`, which we don't have. It isn't possible to implement `flatMap` for `Console`:

```
enum Console[A]:
  def flatMap[B](f: A => Console[B]): Console[B] = this match
    case ReadLine => ???
    case PrintLine(s) => ???
```

In the `case ReadLine`, we need a value of type `Option[String]` to pass to f, but we don't have one. The result of reading a line doesn't occur until `ReadLine` is interpreted. It seems like we need some way of defering the `flatMap` to the interpreter.

We must translate our `Console` type, which doesn't form a monad, to some other type (e.g., `Function0` or `Par`) that does. We can generalize our definition of run to capture this transformation to a target monad:

```
enum Free[F[_], A]:
  ...
  def runFree[G[_]](t: [x] => F[x] => G[x])(using G: Monad[G]): G[A] =   <─┐
    step match
      case Return(a) => G.unit(a)
      case Suspend(r) => t(r)
      case FlatMap(Suspend(r), f) => t(r).flatMap(a => f(a).runFree(t))
      case FlatMap(_, _) =>
        sys.error("Impossible, `step` eliminates these cases")
```

runFree interprets a Free[F, A] into a monad, G.

runFree uses the provided translation t to convert each `F[x]` to a `G[x]` as it interprets the `Free[F, A]` program. The parameter t is using syntax we haven't seen before; this parameter is a *polymorphic function type*—a function that accepts type parameters. t is a function from `F[x]` to `G[x]` for every x. Hence, t can convert an `F[Unit]` to a `G[Unit]` or an `F[Int]` to a `G[Int]` but not an `F[Int]` to a `G[Boolean]`. The type of t, `[x] => F[x] => G[x]`, requires the type applied to G to be equal to the type applied to F.

---

[12]Of course, a Scala program could always technically have side effects, but we're assuming the programmer has adopted the discipline of programming without side effects, since Scala can't guarantee this for us.

Why do we need a polymorphic function here? Why not take a `F[A] => G[A]` instead? Or perhaps we could modify the signature of `runFree` to `def runFree[G[_], B](t: F[B] => G[B])(using G: Monad[G]): G[A]`. As we interpret a `Free[F, A]`, we may encounter various free programs of differing types. Consider the free program that reads an integer from the console:

```
def readInt: Free[Console, Option[Int]] =
  for
    ln <- readLn
  yield ln.toIntOption
```

The `readInt` program has the structure `FlatMap(Suspend(ReadLine), ln => Return(ln.toIntOption))`. When interpreting this program, we encounter a `Free[Console, String]`, despite the overall program having the `Free[Console, Option[Int]]` type. The function passed to `FlatMap` converts `String` to `Option[Int]`, but the interpreter needs a way of converting an `F[x]` to a `G[x]` for any x it encounters. Hence, any normal function, like `F[A] => G[A]`, is insufficient.

> ## Polymorphic function types
>
> Throughout this book, we've been rather informal with the terms *function* and *method*, using them interchangeably. Let's be more precise by saying `def` defines a method, whereas a function is a value—something we assign to a `val` or take as a parameter to another method, class, or trait.
>
> In the following example, `magnitude` is a method, whereas `f` is a function. Scala lets us treat any method as a function through a process called eta expansion. (See the documentation here: https://mng.bz/5mw8.) In this example, Scala performs eta expansion of `magnitude` into a function of type `Option[Int] => Int`:
>
> ```
> scala> def magnitude(o: Option[Int]): Int = o.getOrElse(0)
> def magnitude(o: Option[Int]): Int
>
> scala> val f = magnitude
> val f: Option[Int] => Int = Lambda$8358/0x0000000801654410@70e77cb6
> ```
>
> Methods that take type parameters are called polymorphic methods; we've written many polymorphic methods throughout this book. Consider the polymorphic method `headOption` and what happens when we eta expand it:
>
> ```
> scala> def headOption[A](as: List[A]): Option[A] =
>      |   if as.isEmpty then None else Some(as.head)
> def headOption[A](as: List[A]): Option[A]
>
> scala> val f = headOption
> val f: List[Any] => Option[Any] = Lambda$8352/0x0000000801855c10@66925d67
> ```
>
> Scala inferred a function type of `List[Any] => Option[Any]`. It made each type parameter concrete—in this case, selecting A = Any.

> *(continued)*
> Polymorphic function types allow us to refer to polymorphic methods while retaining
> the type parameters—that is, without selecting a concrete type for each type param-
> eter. We have to be explicit about our intent to retain the type parameters, though,
> since Scala won't infer a polymorphic function type when eta-expanding a polymor-
> phic method:
>
> ```
> scala> val f = [x] => (as: List[x]) => headOption(as)
> val f: [x] => (List[x]) => Option[x] = <function1>
> ```
>
> Polymorphic function types were added in Scala 3 (see the official documentation here:
> https://mng.bz/7WaV). In Scala 2, polymorphic functions are simulated using a trait.
> The equivalent of our `[x] => F[x] => G[x]` type is represented as the following:
>
> ```
> trait FunctionK[F[_], G[_]]:        ◁──┐ A universally quantified function from
>   def apply[x](fx: F[x]): G[x]          └ one type constructor to another
>
> type ~>[F[_], G[_]] = FunctionK[F, G]  ◁──┐ Allows us to write the type F ~>
>                                            └ G instead of FunctionK[F, G]
> def runFree[G[_]](t: F ~> G)(using G: Monad[G]): G[A] = ...
>
> runFree(new (Console ~> Par):        ◁────┐ Constructs an anonymous instance
>   def apply[x](c: Console[x]) = c.toPar    └ of the trait at the use site
> )
> ```
>
> This encoding is used in libraries like Cats, which cross compile for both Scala 2 and
> Scala 3.

Using `runFree` we can implement the convenience functions `toThunk` and `toPar` to
convert a `Free[Console, A]` to either `+() => A` or `Par[A]`:

```
extension [A](fa: Free[Console, A])
  def toThunk: () => A =
    fa.runFree([x] => (c: Console[x]) => c.toThunk)

  def toPar: Par[A] =
    fa.runFree([x] => (c: Console[x]) => c.toPar)
```

This relies on having `Monad[Function0]` and `Monad[Par]` instances:

```
given function0Monad: Monad[Function0] with
  def unit[A](a: => A) = () => a
  extension [A](fa: Function0[A])
    def flatMap[B](f: A => Function0[B]) =
      () => f(fa())()

given parMonad: Monad[Par] with
  def unit[A](a: => A) = Par.unit(a)
```

```
extension [A](fa: Par[A])
  def flatMap[B](f: A => Par[B]) =
    Par.flatMap(fa)(f)
```

EXERCISE 13.4

Hard: It turns out our toThunk convenience function isn't stack safe, since flatMap isn't stack safe for Function0 (it has the same problem as our original, naive IO type in which unsafeRun called itself in the implementation of flatMap). Implement translate using runFree, and then use translate to implement unsafeRunConsole in a stack-safe manner:

```
enum Free[F[_], A]:
  ...
  def translate[G[_]](fToG: [x] => F[x] => G[x]): Free[G, A] = ???

extension [A](fa: Free[Console, A])
  def unsafeRunConsole: A = ???
```

A value of the Free[F, A] type is like a program written in an instruction set provided by F. In the case of Console, the two instructions are PrintLine and ReadLine. The recursive scaffolding (Suspend) and monadic variable substitution (FlatMap and Return) are provided by Free itself. We can introduce other choices of F for different instruction sets—for example, different I/O capabilities, such as a file system, F, granting read/write access (or even just read access) to the file system. Or we could have a network F granting the ability to open network connections and read from them, and so on.

13.4.3 Pure interpreters

Note that nothing about the Free[Console, A] type implies that any effects must actually occur! That decision is the responsibility of the interpreter. We could choose to translate our Console actions into pure values that perform no I/O at all! For example, an interpreter for testing purposes could ignore PrintLine requests and always return a constant string in response to ReadLine requests. We would do this by translating our Console requests to a String => A, which forms a monad in A, as we saw in exercise 11.20 (readerMonad).

Listing 13.7 Creating our ConsoleReader class

```
case class ConsoleReader[A](run: String => A):        ◁─┐  A specialized reader monad,
  def map[B](f: A => B): ConsoleReader[B] =                │  implemented as a case class, instead
    ConsoleReader(r => f(run(r)))                          │  of an opaque type, for brevity
  def flatMap[B](f: A => ConsoleReader[B]): ConsoleReader[B] =
    ConsoleReader(r => f(run(r)).run(r))
```

```
object ConsoleReader:
  given monad: Monad[ConsoleReader] with
    def unit[A](a: => A) = ConsoleReader(_ => a)
    extension [A](fa: ConsoleReader[A])
      def flatMap[B](f: A => ConsoleReader[B]) = fa.flatMap(f)
```

We introduce another function on Console, toReader, and then use that to implement toReader for a Free[Console, A]:

```
enum Console[A]:
  ...
  def toReader: ConsoleReader[A]

extension [A](fa: Free[Console, A])
  def toReader: ConsoleReader[A] =
    fa.runFree([x] => (c: Console[x]) => c.toReader)
```

Or for a more complete simulation of console I/O, we could write an interpreter that uses two lists—one to represent the input buffer and another to represent the output buffer. When the interpreter encounters a ReadLine, it can pop an element off the input buffer, and when it encounters a PrintLine(s), it can push s onto the output buffer:

```
enum Console[A]:
  ...
  def toState: ConsoleState[A]

case class Buffers(in: List[String], out: List[String])    ◁

case class ConsoleState[A](
  run: Buffers => (A, Buffers))    ◁────── A specialized state action

object ConsoleState:
  given monad: Monad[ConsoleState] = ...

extension [A](fa: Free[Console, A])
  def toState: ConsoleState[A] =                    Converts to a pure state action
    fa.runFree([x] => (c: Console[x]) => c.toState)    ◁──┘
```

This represents a pair of buffers. The in buffer will be fed to ReadLine requests, and the out buffer will receive strings contained in PrintLine requests.

This will allow us to have multiple interpreters for our little languages! We could, for example, use toState for testing console applications with our property-based testing library from chapter 8 and then use unsafeRunConsole to actually run our program.[13]

The fact that we can write a generic runFree that turns Free programs into State or Reader values demonstrates something amazing: there's nothing about our Free type that requires side effects of any kind. For example, from the perspective of our

---

[13] Note that toReader and toState aren't stack safe as implemented for the same reason toThunk wasn't stack safe. We can fix this by changing the representations to String => TailRec[A] for ConsoleReader and Buffers => TailRec[(A, Buffers)] for ConsoleState.

`Free[Console, A]` programs, we can't know (and don't care) whether they're going to be run with an interpreter that uses real side effects, like `unsafeRunConsole`, or one, like `toState`, that doesn't. As far as we're concerned, a program is just a referentially transparent expression—a pure computation that may occasionally make requests of some interpreter. The interpreter is free to use side effects or not. That's now an entirely separate concern.

13.5   Non-blocking and asynchronous I/O

Let's turn our attention now to the last remaining problem with our original IO monad: performing non-blocking or asynchronous I/O. When performing I/O, we frequently need to invoke operations that take a long time to complete and don't occupy the CPU. These include accepting a network connection from a server socket, reading a chunk of bytes from an input stream, writing a large number of bytes to a file, and so on. Let's think about what this means in terms of the implementation of our `Free` interpreter.

When `unsafeRunConsole`, for example, encounters a `Suspend(s)`, s will be of `Console` type, and we'll have a translation f from `Console` to the target monad. To allow for non-blocking asynchronous I/O, we simply change the target monad from `Function0` to `Par` or another concurrency monad, such as `scala.concurrent.Future`. So just as we were able to write both pure and effectful interpreters for `Console`, we can write both blocking and non-blocking interpreters as well, just by varying the target monad.[14]

Let's look at an example. Here `toPar` will turn the `Console` requests into `Par` actions and then combine them all into one `Par[A]`. We can think of it as a kind of compilation—we're replacing the abstract `Console` requests with more concrete `Par` requests that will actually read from and write to the standard input and output streams when the resulting `Par` value is run:

```scala
scala> def p: Free[Console, Unit] =
     |   for
     |     _ <- printLn("What's your name?")
     |     n <- readLn
     |     _ <- n match
     |       case Some(n) => printLn(s"Hello, $n!")
     |       case None => printLn(s"Fine, be that way.")
     |   yield ()
val p: Free[Console, Unit] =
FlatMap(Suspend(PrintLine(What's your name?)),<function1>)

scala> val q = p.toPar
val q: Par[Unit] = <function1>
```

---

[14] Our `Par` monad from chapter 7 doesn't handle any exceptions. See the Task.scala file in the answer source code accompanying this chapter for an example of an asynchronous I/O monad with proper exception handling.

Although this simple example runs in Par, which, in principle, permits asynchronous actions, it doesn't make use of any asynchronous actions—readLine and println are both blocking I/O operations. But there are I/O libraries that support non-blocking I/O directly, and Par will let us bind to such libraries. The details of these libraries vary, but to give the general idea, a non-blocking source of bytes might have an interface like this:

```
trait Source:
  def readBytes(
    numBytes: Int,
    callback: Either[Throwable, Array[Byte]] => Unit): Unit
```

Here it's assumed that readBytes returns immediately. We give readBytes a callback function indicating what to do when the result becomes available or the I/O subsystem encounters an error.

Using this sort of library directly is painful.[15] We want to program against a compositional monadic interface and abstract over the details of the underlying non-blocking I/O library. Luckily, the Par type lets us wrap these callbacks:

```
opaque type Future[+A] = (A => Unit) => Unit
opaque type Par[+A] = ExecutorService => Future[A]
```

The representation of Future is remarkably similar to that of Source. It's a function that returns immediately but takes a callback or continuation it will invoke once the value of type A becomes available. It's straightforward to adapt Source.readBytes to a Future, but we'll need to add a primitive to our Par algebra:[16]

```
def async[A](f: (A => Unit) => Unit): Par[A] =
  es => cb => f(cb)
```

With this in place, we can now wrap the asynchronous readBytes function in the nice monadic interface of Par:

```
def nonblockingRead(source: Source, numBytes: Int):
    Par[Either[Throwable, Array[Byte]]] =
  async: (cb: Either[Throwable, Array[Byte]] => Unit) =>
    source.readBytes(numBytes, cb)

def readPar(source: Source, numBytes: Int):
    Free[Par, Either[Throwable, Array[Byte]]] =
  Suspend(nonblockingRead(source, numBytes))
```

We can now use regular for-comprehensions to construct chains of non-blocking computations:

---

[15] Even this API is nicer than what's offered directly by the nio package in Java (see the API at http://mng.bz/uojM), which supports non-blocking I/O.

[16] This may, in fact, be the most primitive Par operation. The other primitives we developed for Par in chapter 7 could be implemented in terms of this one.

```
val src: Source = ...
val prog: Free[Par, Unit] =
  for
    chunk1 <- readPar(src, 1024)
    chunk2 <- readPar(src, 1024)
    ...
  yield ...
```

EXERCISE 13.5

Hard: We won't be working through a full-fledged implementation of a non-blocking I/O library here, but you may be interested in exploring this on your own by building off the java.nio library (see the API at http://mng.bz/uojM). As a start, try implementing an asynchronous read from an AsynchronousFileChannel (see the API at http://mng.bz/X30L):

```
def read(file: AsynchronousFileChannel,
         fromPosition: Long,
         numBytes: Int): Free[Par, Either[Throwable, Array[Byte]]]
```

13.5.1 Composing free algebras

Instead of performing file I/O directly in terms of Free[Par, A], we can introduce a new algebraic data type representing the set of supported file I/O operations, just like we did with Console:

```
enum Files[A]:
  case ReadLines(file: String) extends Files[List[String]]
  case WriteLines(file: String, lines: List[String]) extends Files[Unit]

  def toPar: Par[A] = ???
  def toThunk: () => A = ???

object Files:
  def readLines(file: String): Free[Files, List[String]] =
    Free.Suspend(Files.ReadLines(file))

  def writeLines(file: String, lines: List[String]): Free[Files, Unit] =
    Free.Suspend(Files.WriteLines(file, lines))
```

The toPar method converts each of our primitives to a Par value, using the non-blocking implementations we wrote earlier. The toThunk method perhaps uses blocking implementations of file system access.

Files gives us the same benefits we saw with Console. We could provide various pure interpreters, like toState, which perform no file system operations whatsoever. More importantly, when we see a value of type Free[Files, A], we know that program only interacts with the file system—it doesn't perform network calls, interact with the console, or perform any other effects. Its expressive power is limited to sequencing the operations defined in `Files`.

Using this approach, we can systematically turn any set of I/O operations into an algebraic data type and then use `Free` to represent programs consisting of sequences of those primitive operations. Let's try writing a `cat` utility, which reads the lines from a file and prints them to the console:

```scala
def cat(file: String) =
  Files.readLines(file).flatMap: lines =>
    Console.printLn(lines.mkString("\n"))
```

Unfortunately, this doesn't compile! Scala reports an error like the following:

```
-- [E007] Type Mismatch Error: ---------------------------------------
 |     Console.printLn(lines.mkString("\n"))
 |     ^^^^^^^^^^^^^^^^^^^^^^^^^^^^^^^^^^^^^^^
 |     Found:    Free[Console, Unit]
 |     Required: Free[Files, B]
 |
 |     where:    B is a type variable with constraint
```

What's going on here? `Files.readLines(file)` returns a `Free[Files, List[String]]`. We `flatMap` that value and try to return a `Free[Console, Unit]`. Scala complains because a `Free[Console, Unit]` can't be unified with a `Free[Files, B]` for some arbitrary type B. In essence, `Files` and `Console` are different algebras, and we can't just mix and match them.

Let's think about the type we want Scala to infer for `cat`. We want a program that can use operations from either `Console` or `Files`. We can use Scala 3's union types to represent this notion.[17] Let's create a type constructor that represents the union of the operations from `Console` and `Files`—that is, `[x] =>> Console[x] | Files[x]`. The return type of `cat` then becomes `Free[[x] => Console[x] | Files[x], Unit]`.

Now that we know the desired type, how can we implement it? Let's add a method to Free that lets us convert a `Free[F, A]` to a `Free[[x] =>> F[x] | G[x], A]` for an arbitrary type `G[_]`:

```scala
enum Free[F[_], A]:
  ...
  def union[G[_]]: Free[[x] =>> F[x] | G[x], A] = this match
    case Return(a) => Return(a)
    case Suspend(s) => Suspend(s: F[A] | G[A])
    case FlatMap(s, f) => FlatMap(s.union, a => f(a).union)
```

> s has the type F[A], so we can ascribe the type F[A] | G[A].

> This propagates the union through both arguments of a FlatMap.

---

[17] Unfortunately, Scala 2 does not support union types, which makes composing algebras much clunkier. A popular technique is representing the composed algebra as a *coproduct* of the individual algebras. This typically requires a lot of boilerplate to manage conversions between individual algebras and coproduct algebras.

The magic happens in the case of `Suspend`, where we lift `s: F[A]` to a value of `F[A] |` `G[A]`. Given a union type `X | Y`, values of `X` and `Y` are inhabitants of that type. Here we're taking `X = F[A]` and `Y = G[A]`.

The union method gives us the ability to express `cat`:

```
def cat(file: String) =
  Files.readLines(file).union[Console].flatMap: lines =>
    Console.printLn(lines.mkString("\n")).union[Files]
```

This is a lot of syntax. Every free expression needs to be manually converted to the proper type via union; we can do better. Notice how we were able to implement union for every `Free[F, A]`, without any constraints on F or G. This tells us that a `Free[F, A]` can be used anywhere we expect a `Free[[x] =>> F[x] | G[x], A]`—that a value of the former is always convertible to a value of the latter. We can use covariance to declare this equivalence to Scala, removing the need to manually insert calls to union:

```
enum Free[+F[_], A]:                          ⟵──── +F[_] defines F as covariant.
  case Return(a: A) extends Free[Nothing, A]  ⟵┐
  case Suspend(s: F[A])                         │  Return doesn't use F, so we declare
  case FlatMap[F[_], A, B](                     │  that by extending Free[Nothing, A],
    s: Free[F, A],                              │  instead of the default Free[F, A].
    f: A => Free[F, B]) extends Free[F, B]

  def flatMap[F2[x] >: F[x], B](               Scala forces us to alter the definition of
    f: A => Free[F2, B]): Free[F2, B] =   ⟵─┘  flatMap to account for the covariance of F.
    FlatMap(this, f)
```

By declaring `Free` to be covariant in its type parameter `F`, `Free[G, A]` is a subtype of `Free[H, A]` if `G` is a subtype of `H`. This, in turn, means a `Free[Console, A]` is a subtype of `Free[[x] =>> Console[x] | Files[x]]` as a result of `Console` being a subtype of `[x] =>> Console[x] | Files[x]`.

What happened to the signature of `flatMap`? If we make no changes, Scala complains with an error:

```
|     def flatMap[B](f: A => Free[F, B]): Free[F, B] =
|                       ^^^^^^^^^^^^^^^^^^^^
|covariant type F occurs in contravariant position
|in type A => Free[F, B] of parameter f
```

We're trying to use F unsoundly here—roughly, as a result of the variance of `Free` and `Function1`, a caller of `flatMap` may return a `Free[G, B]`, where G is a supertype of F. Yet our type signature claims it returns a `Free[F, B]` in that case. Scala forces us to be more explicit about this possibility. The new signature says the function may return a `Free[F2, B]`, where F2 is a supertype of F. The overall result ends up being a `Free` `[F2, B]` instead of `Free[F, B]`.

If this seems confusing, that's because it is! Understanding variance and subtyping takes significant effort and practice. The good news is that we can often mechanically transform definitions to account for variance. When making a type parameter covariant, we replace each contravariant usage (as reported by the compiler) with a new type parameter that's a supertype of the covariant type parameter. In the case of flatMap, Scala reported that F was used in a contravariant position, so we introduced a type param, F2[x] >: F[x], and replaced the contravariant use of F with F2.

With this new formulation of Free, union becomes much simpler:

```
enum Free[+F[_], A]:
  ...
  def union[G[_]]: Free[[x] =>> F[x] | G[x], A] = this
```

We can even generalize union to a new operation, which lets us specify an explicit type for F, without having to repeat the full type of the expression:

```
enum Free[+F[_], A]:
  ...
  def covary[F2[x] >: F[x]]: Free[F2, A] = this
```

The covary operation doesn't provide any new functionality—it's simply syntactic sugar. For any value fa: Free[F, A] and type F2[x] >: F[x], fa.covary[F2] can always be written as fa: Free[F2, A] instead. Both covary and union end up providing subtle hints about Scala's type inference, rather than introducing new functionality.

Let's now return to cat—this new definition of Free lets us compose free programs in the Files and Console algebras with little boilerplate:

```
def cat(file: String): Free[[x] =>> Files[x] | Console[x], Unit] =
  Files.readLines(file).flatMap: lines =>
    Console.printLn(lines.mkString("\n"))
```

We must explicitly provide a type for the cat definition, as Scala won't infer the union type automatically. This isn't a bad trade-off though, as explicitly defining return types of methods is a common practice.

EXERCISE 13.6

Hard: Define run, step, runFree, and translate on Free[+F[_], A]. Start with the definitions from the invariant encoding, and alter type signatures and implementations to account for the covariance of F.

Now that we have a Free[[x] =>> Files[x] | Console[x], Unit], how do we run it? We use runFree just like before, but we pattern match on the effect and dispatch to an effect-specific conversion to our target monad:

```
extension [A](fa: Free[[x] =>> Files[x] | Console[x], A])
  def toThunk: () => A =
    fa.runFree([x] => (fx: Files[x] | Console[x]) => fx match
      case c: Console[x] => c.toThunk
      case f: Files[x] => f.toThunk
    )
```

13.6 Capabilities

Let's recap our approach to I/O so far: We define algebras for I/O operations, which enumerate primitive actions. Each algebra defines a set of related actions, covering operations that are likely to be performed together and reasoned about as a collective unit (e.g., Console, Files, or Database). We sequence these primitive operations into programs using Free, gradually building up expressiveness by taking the union of the various effect algebras. Finally, we interpret free programs to a target monad (e.g., Par or Thunk) using an interpreter per algebra and then eventually run that monad to execute our program.

The primary advantage of this approach is constraining our effectful programs to a small set of operations, improving reasoning and reuse. A program of the Free [Console, Unit] type can only interact with the console—not read the file system. A program of the Free[[x] =>> Files[x] | Console[x]] type can interact with the file system and console but not the database or network. This is an application of the principle of least power[18]—constraining our programs to the minimal set of functionality needed to accomplish their job—promoting local reasoning.

The encoding and composition of these least-powerful programs introduce their own complexities, though. There's boilerplate via suspension constructors for each operation, complex types (e.g., union algebras), and the indirection of first building a free program and then interpreting it to a target monad. Can we do better without giving up the principle of least power?

Instead of modeling a primitive set of I/O actions as an algebra, we'll model it as a *capability trait*. We define a trait parameterized by a target monad[19] and then define each primitive operation as a method on the trait returning a value of the target monad:

```
trait Console[F[_]]:
  def readLn: F[Option[String]]
  def printLn(line: String): F[Unit]
```

The operations of the Console trait provide constructors of the primitive console operations in the target monad. For example, given a Console[F], we can construct an F[Option[String]] program that reads a line from the console—without knowing anything about the target monad F.

---

[18]For more on the principle of least power, see https://mng.bz/aDpX.

[19]More precisely, a target type constructor. In practice, these type constructors are always monads, so you can sequence multiple operations.

We then provide given instances of this trait for each target monad we want to support:

```
given parConsole: Console[Par] with
  def readLn =
    Par.lazyUnit(Try(readLine()).toOption)
  def printLn(line: String) =
    Par.lazyUnit(println(line))

given thunkConsole: Console[Function0] with
  def readLn =
    () => Try(readLine()).toOption
  def printLn(line: String) =
    () => println(line)
```

These instances are analagous to the interpreters we wrote for Free algebras, but note that we're not first constructing a Free program and then later interpreting it. Instead, we're directly creating instances of our target monad using given instances.

When building Free programs, the Free data type provided the ability to sequence multiple operations. What's providing the sequencing functionality with this capability trait approach? The target monad provides it directly! This becomes evident when we use a capability trait. Let's define the same greeting program we defined earlier—this time with the Console[F] capability trait:

```
def greet[F[_]](using c: Console[F], m: Monad[F]): F[Unit] =
  for
    _ <- c.printLn("What's your name?")
    n <- c.readLn
    _ <- n match
      case Some(n) => c.printLn(s"Hello, $n!")
      case None => c.printLn(s"Fine, be that way.")
  yield ()
```

The greet function is now defined for an abstract target monad F, which has both a Console and Monad instance. In the body of the function, we construct console operations by calling c.printLn and c.readLn, and we sequence those actions using the given Monad[F] instance. Without the Monad[F] context parameter, we'd be unable to call flatMap on the result of printLn and readLn, since we wouldn't know any details about the type F.

We say Console imbues the type constructor F with the ability to perform console operations, while Monad imbues F with sequencing (i.e., flatMap). Instead of passing free algebras around, we pass abstract effectful programs. When we eventually want to execute our program, we instantiate it for a concrete effect (e.g., greet[Function0]) and execute the resulting concrete monad.

How about composition? Let's revisit the definition of cat—this time defined with capability traits:

```
trait Files[F[_]]:
  def readLines(file: String): F[List[String]]
  def writeLines(file: String, lines: List[String]): F[Unit]

def cat[F[_]](file: String)(
  using c: Console[F], f: Files[F], m: Monad[F]
): F[Unit] =
  f.readLines(file).flatMap: lines =>
    c.printLn(lines.mkString("\n"))
```

The `cat` operation directly combines the results of `Console` and `Files` capabilities. It's able to do this without ceremony since both capabilities offer constructors in the same target monad. There's no need for unions or any explicit composition because the capability traits return programs in the target monad. Composition of capability trait programs is much simpler than composition of free algebra programs.

How about stack safety? We previously used `Free` to provide stack-safe sequencing of our primitive operations. Our capability trait encoding relies on the target monad to provide that stack-safe sequencing; if the target monad defines a stack safe `flatMap`, then the resulting program is stack safe. Hence, instead of choosing `Function0` as our target monad, we may want to choose `TailRec` or `[x] =>> Free[Par, x]`. Doing so affects only the outermost part of our program, where we select a concrete target monad!

Any set of I/O operations that can be represented as a free algebra can alternatively be represented as a capability trait.[20] The capability trait encoding is much simpler to work with, while retaining the primary advantages of the free encoding.

13.7 A general-purpose I/O type

We can now formulate a general methodology of writing programs that perform I/O. For any given set of I/O operations we want to support, we can write a capability trait whose methods represent the individual operations. We could have a `Files` capability for file I/O, a `Database` capability for database access, and something like `Console` for interacting with standard input and output. For any such capability trait, we can provide instances for various concrete monads. In particular, each capability trait can provide an instance for a lower-level I/O type with unconstrained power—what we earlier called `Async`:

```
opaque type IO[A] = Free[Par, A]
```

This `IO` type supports both trampolined sequential execution (because of `Free`) and asynchronous execution (because of `Par`). In our main program, we instantiate our various capabilities for this unconstrained, general `IO` type. All we need is an instance of `IO` for each capability.

---

[20]Capability traits are also known as *tagless final* interpreters, while free encodings are also known as *initial encodings*. For full details on this correspondence, see *Typed Tagless Final Interpreters* by Oleg Kiselyov, available at https://mng.bz/g4KG.

13.7.1 *The main program at the end of the universe*

When the JVM calls into our main program, it expects a main method with a specific signature. The return type of this method is Unit, meaning it's expected to have some side effects. But we can delegate to a pureMain program that's entirely pure! The only thing the main method does in that case is interpret our pure program, actually performing the effects.

```
trait IOApp:
  import java.util.concurrent.{Executors, ExecutorService}

  extension [A](ioa: IO[A])
    def unsafeRunSync(pool: ExecutorService): A =
      ioa.run.run(pool)

  def main(args: Array[String]): Unit =
    val pool = Executors.newFixedThreadPool(8)
    pureMain(args.toList).unsafeRunSync(pool)

  def pureMain(args: List[String]): IO[Unit]
```

This interprets the IO action and performs the effect by turning IO[A] into Par[A] and then A. The name of this method reflects that it's unsafe to call (because it has side effects).

Our actual program goes here as an implementation of pureMain in a subclass of IOApp. It also takes the arguments as an immutable List rather than a mutable Array.

The only thing the main method does is interpret our pureMain.

We want to make a distinction here between effects and side effects. The pureMain program itself isn't going to have any side effects; it should be a referentially transparent expression of the IO[Unit] type. Performing effects is entirely contained within main, which is outside the universe of our actual program, pureMain. Since our program can't observe these effects occurring, but they nevertheless occur, we say our program has effects but not side effects.

13.8 *Why the IO type is insufficient for streaming I/O*

Despite the flexibility of the IO monad and the advantage of having I/O actions as first-class values, the IO type fundamentally provides us with the same level of abstraction as ordinary imperative programming. This means that writing efficient, streaming I/O will generally involve monolithic loops.

Let's look at an example. Suppose we wanted to write a program to convert a file, fahrenheit.txt, containing a sequence of temperatures in degrees Fahrenheit, separated by line breaks, to a new file, celsius.txt, containing the same temperatures in degrees Celsius:[21]

```
trait Files[F[_]]:
  def readLines(file: String): F[List[String]]
  def writeLines(file: String, lines: List[String]): F[Unit]
```

---

[21] We're ignoring exception handling in this example.

With the `Files` capability, we might try writing the program we want in the following way:

```
def convert[F[_]](using f: Files[F]): F[Unit] =
  for
    lines <- f.readLines("fahrenheit.txt")
    cs = lines.map(s => fahrenheitToCelsius(s.toDouble).toString)
    _ <- f.writeLines("celsius.txt", cs)
  yield ()
```

This works, although it requires loading the contents of fahrenheit.txt entirely into memory to work on it, which could be problematic if the file is very large. We'd prefer performing this task using roughly constant memory—reading a line or a fixed-size buffer full of lines from farenheit.txt, converting to Celsius, dumping to `celsius.txt`, and repeating. To achieve this efficiency, we could expose a lower-level file API that provides access to I/O handles:

```
trait Files[F[_]]:
  def openRead(file: String): F[HandleR]
  def openWrite(file: String): F[HandleW]
  def readLine(h: HandleR): F[Option[String]]
  def writeLine(h: HandleW, line: String): F[Unit]

trait HandleR
trait HandleW
```

The only problem is that we now need to write a monolithic loop:

```
def loop[F[_]](
  hr: HandleR, hw: HandleW)(using f: Files[F]): F[Unit] =
  f.readLine(hr).flatMap:
    case None => IO.unit(())
    case Some(s) =>
      f.writeLine(hw, fahrenheitToCelsius(s.toDouble))
        .flatMap(_ => loop(f, c))

def convertFiles[F[_]](using f: Files[F]): F[Unit] =
  for
    hr <- f.openRead("fahrenheit.txt")
    hw <- f.openWrite("celsius.txt")
    _ <- loop(hr, hw)
  yield ()
```

> Explicit flatMap is used instead of a for-comprehension to ensure monadic recursion is in tail position.

There's nothing inherently wrong with writing a monolithic loop like this, but it's not composable. Suppose we decide later that we'd like to compute a five-element moving average of the temperatures. Modifying our `loop` function to do this would be somewhat painful. Compare that to the equivalent change we might make to `List`-based code, where we could define a `movingAvg` function and just stick it before or after our conversion to Celsius:

```
def movingAvg(n: Int)(l: List[Double]): List[Double] = ???
val cs = movingAvg(5)(
  lines.map(s =>fahrenheitToCelsius(s.toDouble))).map(_.toString)
```

Even `movingAvg` could be composed from smaller pieces; we could build it using a generic combinator—windowed:

```
def windowed[A](n: Int, l: List[A])(f: A => B)(using m: Monoid[B]): List[B]
```

The point is that programming with a composable abstraction, like `List`, is much nicer than programming directly with the primitive I/O operations. Lists aren't really special in this regard; they're just one instance of a composable API that's pleasant to use, and we shouldn't have to give up all the nice compositionality we've come to expect from FP just to write programs that make use of efficient, streaming I/O.[22] Luckily, we don't have to. As we'll see in chapter 15, we get to build whatever abstractions we want for creating computations that perform I/O. If we like the metaphor of lists, we can design a list-like API for expressing I/O computations. If we discover some other composable abstraction, we can find a way of using that instead. Functional programming gives us that flexibility.

13.9 *Conclusion*

This chapter introduced a simple model for handling external effects and I/O in a purely functional way. We began with a discussion of factoring effects and demonstrated how they can be moved to the outer layers of a program. We generalized this to an `IO` data type that lets us describe interactions with the outside world, without resorting to side effects.

We discovered that monads in Scala suffer from a stack overflow problem, and we solved it in a general way, using the technique of trampolining. This led us to the even more general idea of free monads, which we employed to write a very capable `IO` monad with an interpreter that used non-blocking asynchronous I/O internally.

The `IO` monad is not the final word in writing effectful programs. It's important because it represents a kind of lowest common denominator when interacting with the external world, but in practice, we want to use `IO` directly as rarely as possible because `IO` programs tend to be monolithic and have limited reuse. In chapter 15, we'll discuss how to build nicer, more composable, more reusable abstractions, using essentially the same technique we used here.

Before getting to that, we'll apply what we've learned so far to fill in the other missing piece of the puzzle: local effects. In various parts of this book, we've made use of local mutation rather casually, with the assumption that these effects weren't observable. In the next chapter, we'll explore what this means in more detail, see more examples of using local effects, and show how effect scoping can be enforced by the type system.

---

[22] One might ask whether we could just have various `Files` operations return the `LazyList` type we defined in chapter 5. This is called *lazy I/O,* and it's problematic for several reasons that we'll discuss in chapter 15.

Finally, note that real-world IO monads, like the IO type provided by the Cats Effect library (https://mng.bz/p2vw), typically have much more functionality than we built here, including better support for concurrency, cancellation, and resource management.

Summary

- It is always possible to factor an impure procedure into a pure core function and two procedures with side effects: one that supplies the pure function's input and one that does something with the pure function's output. In other words, inside every function with side effects is a pure function waiting to get out.
- The first IO[A] type developed in this chapter has a number of benefits, despite its simple implementation. It allows computations to be expressed as ordinary values, which allows them to be stored in lists, passed to functions, created dynamically, and so on. The interpreter of our computations is defined separately from the computations themselves, allowing the interpreter to be changed without affecting client code.
- The first IO[A] type developed in this chapter also has a number of problems: it's not stack safe; it's completely opaque, disallowing all inspection; and it doesn't support concurrency.
- Trampolining can be used to make monads stack safe.
- The TailRec[A] type uses trampolining to provide stack-safe function composition.
- The Async[A] type is similar to TailRec[A] but allows composition of Par[A] values instead of functions.
- The Free[F[_], A] type generalizes TailRec[A] and Async[A], providing a way of sequencing primitive operations of the supplied F[_] algebra.
- Free monads allow us to sequence primitive operations defined by an algebra into a value representing a program and later interpret that value into a target monad.
- Free monads limit the expressive power of a computation to sequencings of the primitive operations of the algebra.
- Polymorphic function types are function types parameterized by one or more type parameters.
- Free monads of different algebras can be composed into free monads of unioned algebras. For example, Free[[x] =>> Files[x] | Console[x]] describes a computation that may use operations from either the Files algebra or the Console algebra.
- Capability traits, also known as tagless final interpreters, allow us to compose programs consisting of various primitive I/O algebras, while retaining the local reasoning and constrained power benefits of free monads.
- The general-purpose IO data type allows us to maintain referential transparency while writing programs that perform input and output—programs that, at first glance, appear to be inextricably linked to side effects and incompatible with pure functional programming.

13.10 Exercise answers

We implement `map` in terms of `flatMap` and `Return`. The implementation of `flatMap` creates a `Free.FlatMap` value that references `this` and the function `f`:

```
enum Free[F[_], A]:
  case Return(a: A)
  case Suspend(s: F[A])
  case FlatMap[F[_], A, B](
    s: Free[F, A],
    f: A => Free[F, B]) extends Free[F, B]

  def flatMap[B](f: A => Free[F, B]): Free[F, B] =
    FlatMap(this, f)

  def map[B](f: A => B): Free[F, B] =
    flatMap(a => Return(f(a)))

object Free:
  given freeMonad[F[_]]: Monad[[x] =>> Free[F, x]] with
    def unit[A](a: => A) = Return(a)
    extension [A](fa: Free[F, A])
      def flatMap[B](f: A => Free[F, B]) = fa.flatMap(f)
```

We pattern match on the initial `Free[Function0, A]`. If we encounter a `FlatMap`, we pattern match on the inner `Free[Function0, X]`. If that inner free is a `Return`, then we can call the original continuation `f` with that returned value and run the result. If the inner free is a `Suspend`, then we can force the thunk and similarly call the original continuation `f` with the result of the thunk. If the inner free is another `FlatMap`, then we reassociate the `flatMap` calls to the right—that is, we turn `FlatMap(FlatMap(fy, g), f)` into `FlatMap(fy, y => FlatMap(g(y), f))`—and then run the result:

```
extension [A](fa: Free[Function0, A])
  @annotation.tailrec
  def runTrampoline: A = fa match
    case Return(a) => a
    case Suspend(ta) => ta()
    case FlatMap(fx, f) => fx match
      case Return(x) => f(x).runTrampoline
      case Suspend(tx) => f(tx()).runTrampoline
      case FlatMap(fy, g) => fy.flatMap(y => g(y).flatMap(f)).runTrampoline
```

Let's first implement step:

```
@annotation.tailrec
final def step: Free[F, A] = this match
  case FlatMap(FlatMap(fx, f), g) => fx.flatMap(x => f(x).flatMap(g)).step
  case FlatMap(Return(x), f) => f(x).step
  case _ => this
```

The main goal of step is converting the input into one of three cases:

- Return
- Suspend
- Right-associated FlatMap(Suspend(fx), f)

To implement this, we pattern match on the input. If we encounter left-associated FlatMaps, then we reassociate them to the right and step the result. If we encounter a FlatMap(Return(x), f), then we simplify and return the result. Otherwise, we can return the input directly, as it is one of Return, Suspend, or FlatMap (Suspend(fx), f).

This implementation of step makes the implementation of run straightforward. We first step the input and then pattern match on the result, handling each of the three possible cases that step returns. Scala doesn't know step has eliminated the possibility of various shapes, like FlatMap(Return(a), f) and FlatMap(FlatMap(fy, g), f), so we add a wildcard case that fails with a runtime error to satisfy Scala's exhaustiveness checker:

```
def run(using F: Monad[F]): F[A] = step match
  case Return(a) => F.unit(a)
  case Suspend(fa) => fa
  case FlatMap(Suspend(fa), f) => fa.flatMap(a => f(a).run)
  case FlatMap(_, _) =>
    sys.error("Impossible, `step` eliminates these cases")
```

runFree lets us convert a Free[F, A] to a G[A] for some type constructor G, whereas translate converts a Free[F, A] to a Free[G, A] for some type constructor G. Let's restate runFree after renaming G to H—runFree lets us convert a Free[F, A] to an H[A] for some type constructor H. We can implement translate in terms of runFree by taking H[x] = Free[G, x]. We then need a polymorphic function that converts an F[x] into a Free[G, x]. We can get that by suspending the result of translating F[x] to G[x]:

```
def translate[G[_]](fToG: [x] => F[x] => G[x]): Free[G, A] =
  runFree([x] => (fx: F[x]) => Suspend(fToG(fx)))
```

We can then implement unsafeRunConsole by translating each Console[x] to a thunk of type x, yielding a Free[Function0, A], and running that Free[Function0, A] using runTrampoline:

```
extension [A](fa: Free[Console, A])
  def unsafeRunConsole: A =
    fa.translate([x] => (c: Console[x]) => c.toThunk).runTrampoline
```

ANSWER 13.5

The non-blocking asynchronous NIO APIs work via callbacks. When calling an asynchronous NIO API, we pass a callback when requesting an I/O operation. NIO will invoke the callback once the requested I/O operation has finished.

The Par.async constructor lets us adapt callback-based APIs into Par values. To implement read, we call Par.async and pass a function that receives a callback. Our function performs the I/O request to the AsynchronousFileChannel and, as part of that request, passes a completion handler that invokes the callback given to use by Par.async. By wiring up the completion handler to the callback, the Par value created by Par.async completes when the completion handler is invoked:

```
def read(file: AsynchronousFileChannel,
         fromPosition: Long,
         numBytes: Int): Free[Par, Either[Throwable, Array[Byte]]] =
  Suspend(Par.async: (cb: Either[Throwable, Array[Byte]] => Unit) =>
    val buf = ByteBuffer.allocate(numBytes)
    file.read(buf, fromPosition, (), new CompletionHandler[Integer, Unit]:
      def completed(bytesRead: Integer, ignore: Unit) =
        val arr = new Array[Byte](bytesRead)
        buf.slice.get(arr, 0, bytesRead)
        cb(Right(arr))
      def failed(err: Throwable, ignore: Unit) =
        cb(Left(err))
    )
  )
```

ANSWER 13.6

Like flatMap, the run method uses F in a contravariant position. Hence, we need to perform the mechanical transformation of introducing a type parameter that's a super type of F:

```
def run[F2[x] >: F[x]](using F: Monad[F2]): F2[A] = step match
  case Return(a) => F.unit(a)
  case Suspend(fa) => fa
```

```
case FlatMap(Suspend(fa), f) => fa.flatMap(a => f(a).run)
case FlatMap(_, _) =>
  sys.error("Impossible, since `step` eliminates these cases")
```

Note that we need to take a `Monad[F2]` now, instead of a `Monad[F]`.

The other operations—`step`, `runFree`, and `translate`—can be reused with no changes in signature. There are a few places in their definitions in which Scala needs some help with type inference: via type ascription, explicitly passing type parameters, or using `covary`. See the answer key in the GitHub repository for details.

14

Local effects
and mutable state

This chapter covers

- Introducing mutable state
- Discussing the ST monad
- Providing a better definition of referential transparency

In the first chapter of this book, we introduced the concept of referential transparency, setting the premise for purely functional programming. We declared that pure functions can't mutate data in place or interact with the external world. In chapter 13, we learned this isn't exactly true; we can write purely functional and compositional programs that describe interactions with the outside world. These programs are unaware that they can be interpreted with an evaluator that has an effect on the world.

In this chapter, we'll develop a more mature concept of referential transparency. We'll consider the idea that effects can occur locally inside an expression and that we can guarantee no other part of the larger program can observe these effects occurring. We'll also introduce the idea that expressions can be referentially transparent with regard to some programs and not others.

14.1 Purely functional mutable state

Up until this point, you may have had the impression that in purely functional programming you're not allowed to use mutable state. But if we look carefully, there's nothing about the definitions of referential transparency and purity that disallows mutation of local state. Let's refer to our definitions from chapter 1.

> **Definitions of referential transparency and purity**
>
> *Referential transparency*—An expression e is referentially transparent if for all programs p, all occurrences of e in p can be replaced by the result of evaluating e without affecting the meaning of p.
>
> *Purity*—A function f is pure if the expression f(x) is referentially transparent for all referentially transparent x.

By these definitions, the following function is pure, even though it uses a while loop, an updatable var, and a mutable array.

Listing 14.1 In-place quicksort with a mutable array

```scala
def quicksort(xs: List[Int]): List[Int] =
  if xs.isEmpty then xs
  else
    val arr = xs.toArray
    def swap(x: Int, y: Int) =            <── Swaps two elements in an array
      val tmp = arr(x)
      arr(x) = arr(y)
      arr(y) = tmp
    def partition(n: Int, r: Int, pivot: Int) =   <── Partitions a portion of the array into elements less than and greater than pivot, respectively
      val pivotVal = arr(pivot)
      swap(pivot, r)
      var j = n
      for i <- n until r if arr(i) < pivotVal do
        swap(i, j)
        j += 1
      swap(j, r)
      j
    def qs(n: Int, r: Int): Unit =        <── Sorts a portion of the array in place
      if n < r then
        val pi = partition(n, r, n + (n - r) / 2)
        qs(n, pi - 1)
        qs(pi + 1, r)
    qs(0, arr.length - 1)
    arr.toList
```

The quicksort function sorts a list by turning it into a mutable array, sorting the array in place using the well-known quicksort algorithm and then turning the array back into a list. It's not possible for any caller to know that the individual subexpressions inside the body of quicksort aren't referentially transparent or that the local methods swap, partition, and qs aren't pure because at no point does any code outside the quicksort function hold a reference to the mutable array. Since all of the mutation is locally scoped, the overall function is pure. That is, for any referentially transparent expression xs of type List[Int], the expression quicksort(xs) is also referentially transparent.

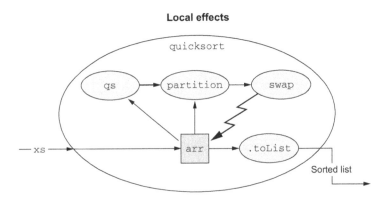

A mutation that happens inside a function
is not a side effect if nothing outside the
function refers to the mutated object.

Figure 14.1
Local effects

Some algorithms, like quicksort, need to mutate data in place to work correctly or efficiently. Fortunately for us, we can always safely mutate data that's created locally. Any function can use side-effecting components internally and still present a pure external interface to its callers, and we should feel no shame taking advantage of this in our own programs. We may prefer purely functional components in our implementations for other reasons—they're easier to get right, they can be assembled more easily from other pure functions, and so on—but in principle, there's nothing wrong with building a pure function using local side effects in the implementation.

14.2   *A data type to enforce the scoping of side effects*

The preceding section makes it clear that pure functions may have side effects with respect to data that's locally scoped. The quicksort function may mutate the array because it allocated that array, it's locally scoped, and it's not possible for any outside code to observe the mutation. If, on the other hand, quicksort somehow mutated its input list directly (as is common in mutable collection APIs), that side effect would be observable to all callers of quicksort.

There's nothing wrong with doing this sort of loose reasoning to determine the scoping of side effects, but it's sometimes desirable to enforce effect scoping using Scala's type system. The constituent parts of `quicksort` would have direct side effects if used on their own, and with the types we're using, we get no help controlling the scope of these side effects from the compiler. Additionally, we aren't alerted if we accidentally leak side effects or mutable state to a broader scope than intended. In this section, we'll develop a data type that uses Scala's type system to enforce the scoping of mutations.[1]

Note that we could just work in `IO`, but that's really not appropriate for local mutable state. If `quicksort` returned `IO[List[Int]]`, then it would be an `IO` action that's perfectly safe to run and would have no side effects, which isn't the case for arbitrary `IO` actions in general. We want to be able to distinguish between effects that are safe to run (like locally mutable state) and external effects like I/O, so a new data type is in order.

14.2.1 A little language for scoped mutation

The most natural approach is making a little language for talking about mutable state. Writing and reading a state is something we can already do with the `State[S, A]` monad, which you'll recall is just a function of type `S => (A, S)` that takes an input state and produces a result and an output state. However, when we're talking about mutating the state in place, we're not really passing it from one action to the next. Instead, we'll pass a kind of token marked with the type `S`. A function called with the token then has the authority to mutate data that's tagged with the same type `S`.

This new data type will employ Scala's type system to gain two static guarantees. We want our code to not compile if it violates these invariants:

- If we hold a reference to a mutable object, then nothing can observe us mutating it.
- A mutable object can never be observed outside of the scope in which it was created.

We relied on the first invariant for our implementation of `quicksort`—we mutated an array, but since no one else had a reference to that array, the mutation wasn't observable outside our function definition. The second invariant is more subtle; it's saying we won't leak references to any mutable state as long as that mutable state remains in scope. This invariant is important for some use cases (see the sidebar).

> ### Another use case for typed scoping of mutation
> Imagine writing a file I/O library. At the lowest level, the underlying OS file read operation might fill up a mutable buffer of type `Array[Byte]`, reusing the same array on every read instead of allocating a new buffer each time. In the interest of efficiency, it might be nice if the I/O library could simply return a read-only view of type `Seq[Byte]` that's backed by this array, rather than defensively copying the bytes to a fresh data structure.

---

[1] There's an efficiency cost and notational convenience, so think of this as another technique you have at your disposal, not something that must be employed every time you make use of local mutation.

> *(continued)*
> But this isn't quite safe—the caller may keep around this (supposedly) immutable
> sequence, and when we overwrite the underlying array on the next read, that caller
> will observe the data changing out from under it! To make the recycling buffers safe,
> we need to restrict the scope of the `Seq[Byte]` view we give to callers and make sure
> callers can't retain references (directly or indirectly) to these mutable buffers when
> we begin the next read operation that clobbers the underlying `Array[Byte]`. See the
> chapter notes for chapter 15 (https://github.com/fpinscala/fpinscala/wiki) for more
> discussion of this sort of use case.

We'll call this new local-effects monad `ST`, which could stand for *state thread, state transition, state token*, or *state tag*. It's different from the `State` monad in that there's no way of directly calling the underlying function, but otherwise, its structure is exactly the same.

Listing 14.2 Our new `ST` data type

```
opaque type ST[S, A] = S => (A, S)
object ST:
  extension [S, A](self: ST[S, A])
    def map[B](f: A => B): ST[S, B] =
      s =>
        val (a, s1) = self(s)
        (f(a), s1)

    def flatMap[B](f: A => ST[S, B]): ST[S, B] =
      s =>
        val (a, s1) = self(s)
        f(a)(s1)

  def apply[S, A](a: => A): ST[S, A] =          Cache the value in case the returned
    lazy val memo = a              ⟵─────────   ST is run more than once.
    s => (memo, s)

  def lift[S, A](f: S => (A, S)): ST[S, A] = f
```

There's no mechanism provided for directly invoking the underlying function because an `S` represents the ability to mutate state, and we don't want the mutation to escape. So how do we run an `ST` action, giving it an initial state? This question is actually two separate questions. We'll start by answering the question of how we specify the initial state.

As we explore the `ST` type, keep in mind that it's not necessary to understand every detail of the implementation. What matters is the idea that we can use the type system to constrain the scope of mutable state.

14.2.2 *An algebra of mutable references*

Our first example of an application for the `ST` monad is a little language for talking about mutable references. This language takes the form of a combinator library with some primitives. The language for talking about mutable memory cells should have these primitive commands:

- Allocate a new mutable cell
- Write to a mutable cell
- Read from a mutable cell

The data structure we'll use for mutable references is just a wrapper around a private var:

```
final class STRef[S, A] private (private var cell: A):
  def read: ST[S,A] = ST(cell)
  def write(a: => A): ST[S, Unit] = ST.lift[S, Unit]:
    s =>
      cell = a
      ((), s)

object STRef:
  def apply[S, A](a: A): ST[S, STRef[S, A]] =
    ST(new STRef[S, A](a))
```

The methods on STRef to read and write the cell are pure since they just return ST actions. Note that the type S is not the type of the cell being mutated, and we never actually use the value of type S. Nevertheless, to call apply and actually run one of these ST actions, we do need to have a value of type S. That value therefore serves as a kind of token—an authorization to mutate or access the cell—but it serves no other purpose.

The only way to construct an instance of STRef is by calling the apply method on the STRef companion object. The STRef is constructed with an initial value for the cell of type A. However, a naked STRef isn't returned, but rather an ST[S, STRef[S, A]] action that constructs the STRef when run and given the token of type S. It's important to note that the ST action and the STRef it creates are tagged with the same S type.

At this point, let's try writing a trivial ST program. It's awkward right now because we have to choose a type S arbitrarily. Here we arbitrarily choose Nothing:

```
for
  r1 <- STRef[Nothing, Int](1)
  r2 <- STRef[Nothing, Int](1)
  x  <- r1.read
  y  <- r2.read
  _  <- r1.write(y + 1)
  _  <- r2.write(x + 1)
  a  <- r1.read
  b  <- r2.read
yield (a, b)
```

This little program allocates two mutable Int cells, swaps their contents, adds one to both, and then reads their new values. But we can't yet run this program because the underlying function is still encapsulated by the opaqueness of ST (and we could never actually pass it a value of the Nothing type anyway). Let's work on that.

14.2.3   *Running mutable state actions*

By now you may have figured out what's going on with the ST monad. The plan is to use ST to build up a computation that, when run, allocates some local mutable state, proceeds to mutate it to accomplish some task, and then discards the mutable state. The whole computation is referentially transparent because all the mutable state is private and locally scoped, but we want to be able to guarantee that. For example, an STRef contains a mutable var, and we want Scala's type system to guarantee we can never extract an STRef out of an ST action. That would violate the invariant that the mutable reference is local to the ST action, breaking referential transparency in the process.

So how do we safely run ST actions? First we must differentiate between actions that are safe to run and those that aren't. Spot the difference between these types:

- ST[S, STRef[S, Int]] (not safe to run)
- ST[S, Int] (completely safe to run)

The former is an ST action that returns a mutable reference, but the latter is different. A value of type ST[S, Int] is literally just an Int, even though computing the Int may involve some local mutable state. There's an exploitable difference between these two types: the STRef involves the type S, but Int doesn't.

We want to disallow running an action of type ST[S, STRef[S, A]] because that would expose the STRef, and in general, we want to disallow running any ST[S, T], where T involves the type S. On the other hand, it's easy to see that it should always be safe to run an ST action that doesn't expose a mutable object. If we have a pure action like this of a type like ST[S, Int], it should be safe to pass it an S to get the Int out of it. Furthermore, we don't care what S actually is in that case because we're going to throw it away. The action might as well be polymorphic in S.

To represent this, we'll use a polymorphic function that represents ST actions that are safe to run—in other words, actions that are polymorphic in S:

```
[s] => () => ST[s, A]
```

This is similar to the idea behind the polymorphic function used with translate from chapter 13. A value of type [s] => () => ST[s, A] is a function that takes a type s and produces a value of type ST[s, A].[2]

In the previous section, we arbitrarily chose Nothing as our S type. Let's instead wrap it in a polymorphic function, making it polymorphic in S—then we don't have to choose the type S at all. It will be supplied by whatever invokes the function:

```
val p = [s] => () =>
  for
    r1 <- STRef[s, Int](1)
    r2 <- STRef[s, Int](2)
```

---

[2] We're using a polymorphic thunk here because Scala does not directly support polymorphic values (e.g., [s] => ST[s, A]).

```
      x   <- r1.read
      y   <- r2.read
      _   <- r1.write(y + 1)
      _   <- r2.write(x + 1)
      a   <- r1.read
      b   <- r2.read
  yield (a, b)
```

We're now ready to write the run function that will call a polymorphic function by
arbitrarily choosing a type for S. Since the action is polymorphic in S, it's guaranteed
to not make use of the value that gets passed in. This means it's actually completely
safe to pass (), the value of type Unit!

We'll define the run function on the ST companion object where it's known that an
ST[S, A] is equivalent to a S => (A, S) function:

```
object ST:
  def run[A](st: [s] => () => ST[s, A]): A =
    val su: ST[Unit, A] = st[Unit]()
    su(())(0)
```

We can now run our trivial program p from earlier:

```
scala> val p = [s] => () =>
     |     for
     |       r1 <- STRef[s, Int](1)
     |       r2 <- STRef[s, Int](2)
     |       x   <- r1.read
     |       y   <- r2.read
     |       _   <- r1.write(y + 1)
     |       _   <- r2.write(x + 1)
     |       a   <- r1.read
     |       b   <- r2.read
     |     yield (a, b)
val p: [s] => () => ST[s, (Int, Int)] = <function0>
scala> val r = ST.run(p)
val r: (Int, Int) = (3,2)
```

The expression run(p) uses mutable state internally, but it doesn't have any side
effects. As far as any other expression is concerned it's just a pair of integers like any
other. It will always return the same pair of integers, and it'll do nothing else.

But this isn't the most important part. Most importantly, we cannot run a program
that tries to return a mutable reference. It isn't possible to create a polymorphic function that returns a naked STRef:

```
scala> val p: [s] => () => ST[s, STRef[Nothing, Int]] =
     |     [s] => () => STRef(1)
-- [E007] Type Mismatch Error: ---------------------------------------------
2 |    [s] => () => STRef(1)
  |                     ^
  |                          Found:     [s] => () =>
```

```
|                        ST[Nothing,
|                          STRef[Nothing, Int]
|                        ]
|              Required: [s] => () =>
|                        ST[s,
|                          STRef[Nothing, Int]
|                        ]
```

In this example, we arbitrarily chose Nothing to illustrate the point. The important part is that the type s is bound at the time the polymorphic function is called and may even be called multiple times with different types. We can't know that type until the function has been invoked.

Because an STRef is always tagged with the type S of the ST action it lives in, it can never escape. And this is guaranteed by Scala's type system! As a corollary, the fact that you can't get an STRef out of an ST action guarantees that if you have an STRef, then you are inside of the ST action that created it, so it's always safe to mutate the reference.

A note on the wildcard type

It's possible to bypass the type system in run by using the *wildcard type*. Passing it a [s] => () => ST[s, STRef[?, Int]] will allow an STRef to escape:

```
scala> val ref = ST.run[STRef[?, Int]](
         [s] => () => STRef[s, Int](1).map(ref => ref: STRef[?, Int]))
val ref: STRef[?, Int] = STRef@5decdb3
```

The wildcard type is an artifact of Scala's interoperability with Java's type system. Fortunately, when you have an STRef[?, Int], using it will cause a type error:

```
scala> val p: [r] => () => ST[r, Int] = [r] => () => ref.read
-- [E007] Type Mismatch Error: ---------------------------------------------
1 |val p: [r] => () => ST[r, Int] = [r] => () => ref.read
  |                                                       ^
  |         Found:    [r] => () => ST[ref.S, Int]
  |         Required: [r] => () => ST[r, Int]
```

This type error is caused by the fact that the wildcard type in ref represents some concrete type that only ref knows about. In this case, it's the s type that was bound in the polymorphic method where it was created. Scala is unable to prove that this is the same type as r. Therefore, even though it's possible to misuse the wildcard type to get the naked STRef out, it's still safe, since we can't use it to mutate or access the state.

14.2.4 *Mutable arrays*

Mutable references on their own aren't all that useful. Mutable arrays are a much more compelling use case for the ST monad. In this section, we'll define an algebra for manipulating mutable arrays in the ST monad and then write an in-place quicksort algorithm compositionally. We'll need primitive combinators to allocate, read, and write mutable arrays.

Listing 14.3   An array class for our ST monad

```
final class STArray[S, A] private (private var value: Array[A]):

  def size: ST[S, Int] = ST(value.size)

  def write(i: Int, a: A): ST[S, Unit] =        Write a value at the given
    ST.lift[S, Unit]:                           index of the array.
      s =>
        value(i) = a
        ((), s)
                                                Read the value at the
  def read(i: Int): ST[S, A] = ST(value(i))     given index of the array.

  def freeze: ST[S, List[A]] = ST(value.toList)
                                                Turn the array into
object STArray:                                 an immutable list.
  def apply[S, A: ClassTag](
    sz: Int, v: A                               Construct an array of the given
  ): ST[S, STArray[S, A]] =                     size filled with the value v.
    ST(new STArray[S, A](Array.fill(sz)(v)))
```

Note that Scala can't create arrays for every type A. It requires a given ClassTag[A] instance existing in scope, which we provide here via the A: ClassTag context bound. Scala's standard library provides class tags for various concrete types.

As with STRef, we always return an STArray packaged in an ST action with a corresponding S type, and any manipulation of the array (even reading it) is an ST action tagged with the same type S. It's therefore impossible to observe a naked STArray outside of the ST monad (except by code in the Scala source file in which the STArray data type itself is declared). Using these primitives, we can write more complex functions on arrays.

■ EXERCISE 14.1

Add a combinator on STArray to fill the array from a Map, where each key in the map represents an index into the array, and the value under that key is written to the array at that index. For example, xs.fill(Map(0->"a", 2->"b")) should write the value "a" at index 0 in the array xs and "b" at index 2. Use the existing combinators to write your implementation:

```
def fill(xs: Map[Int, A]): ST[S, Unit]
```

Not everything can be done efficiently using these existing combinators. For example, the Scala library already has an efficient way of turning a list into an array. Let's make that a primitive as well:

```
def fromList[S, A: ClassTag](xs: List[A]): ST[S, STArray[S, A]] =
  ST(new STArray[S, A](xs.toArray))
```

14.2.5 A purely functional in-place quicksort

The components for `quicksort` are now easy to write in `ST`. For example, the `swap` function that swaps two elements of the array can be defined as a method on `STArray`:

```
def swap(i: Int, j: Int): ST[S, Unit] =
  for
    x <- read(i)
    y <- read(j)
    _ <- write(i, y)
    _ <- write(j, x)
  yield ()
```

■ **EXERCISE 14.2**

Write the purely functional versions of `partition` and `qs`:

```
def partition[S](a: STArray[S, Int], l: Int, r: Int, pivot: Int): ST[S, Int]
def qs[S](a: STArray[S, Int], l: Int, r: Int): ST[S, Unit]
```

With those components written, `quicksort` can now be assembled out of them in the `ST` monad:

```
def quicksort(xs: List[Int]): List[Int] =
  if xs.isEmpty then xs else ST.run([s] => () =>
    for
      arr    <- STArray.fromList[s, Int](xs)
      size   <- arr.size
      _      <- qs(arr, 0, size - 1)
      sorted <- arr.freeze
    yield sorted
  )
```

As you can see, the `ST` monad allows us to write pure functions that nevertheless mutate the data they receive. Scala's type system ensures we don't combine things in an unsafe way.

■ **EXERCISE 14.3**

Give the same treatment to `scala.collection.mutable.HashMap` as we've given here to references and arrays. Come up with a minimal set of primitive combinators for creating and manipulating hash maps.

14.3   Purity is contextual

In the preceding section, we talked about effects that aren't observable because they're entirely local to some scope. A program can't observe mutation of data unless it holds a reference to that data.

But there are other effects that may be unobservable, depending on who's looking. As a simple example, let's take a kind of side effect that occurs all the time in ordinary Scala programs, even ones we'd usually consider purely functional:

```scala
scala> case class Foo(s: String)

scala> val b = Foo("hello") == Foo("hello")
val b: Boolean = true

scala> val c = Foo("hello") eq Foo("hello")
val c: Boolean = false
```

Here `Foo("hello")` looks pretty innocent; we could be forgiven if we assumed it was a completely referentially transparent expression. But each time it appears, it produces a different `Foo`, in a certain sense. If we test two appearances of `Foo("hello")` for equality using the `==` function, we get `true`, as we'd expect. But when testing for *reference equality* (a notion inherited from the Java language) with `eq`, we get `false`. The two appearances of `Foo("hello")` aren't references to the same object if we look under the hood.

Note that if we evaluate `Foo("hello")` and store the result as x and then substitute x to get the expression x eq x, it has a different result:

```scala
scala> val x = Foo("hello")
val x: Foo = Foo(hello)

scala> val d = x eq x
val d: Boolean = true
```

Therefore, by our original definition of referential transparency, every data constructor in Scala has a side effect. The effect is that a new and unique object is created in memory, and the data constructor returns a reference to that new object.

For most programs, this makes no difference because most programs don't check for reference equality. It's only the `eq` method that allows our programs to observe this side effect occurring. We could therefore say that it's not a side effect at all for the vast majority of programs.

Our definition of referential transparency doesn't take this into account. Referential transparency is with regard to some context, and our definition doesn't establish this context.

A more general definition of referential transparency

An expression e is referentially transparent with regard to a program p if every occurrence of e in p can be replaced by the result of evaluating e without affecting the meaning of p.

This definition is only slightly modified to reflect the fact that not all programs observe the same effects. We say that an effect of e is *unobservable* by p if it doesn't affect the referential transparency of e with regard to p. For instance, most programs can't observe the side effect of calling a constructor because they don't make use of eq.

This definition is still somewhat vague. For example, what is meant by *evaluating*? And what's the standard by which we determine whether the meaning of two programs is the same?

In Scala, there's a kind of standard answer to this first question. We'll take evaluation to mean reduction to some normal form. Since Scala is a strictly evaluated language, we can force the evaluation of an expression e into normal form in Scala by assigning it to a val:

```
val v = e
```

Referential transparency of e with regard to a program p means we can rewrite p, replacing every appearance of e with v without changing the meaning of our program. But what do we mean by *changing the meaning of our program*? Just what is the meaning of a program?

This is a somewhat philosophical question, and there are various ways of answering it that we won't explore in detail here.[3] But the general point is that when we talk about referential transparency, it's always with regard to some context. The context determines what sort of programs we're interested in as well as how we assign meaning to our programs. Establishing this context is a choice; we need to decide which aspects of a program participate in that program's meaning. Let's explore this subtlety a bit further.

14.3.1 *What counts as a side effect?*

Earlier we talked about how the eq method is able to observe the side effect of object creation. Let's look more closely at this idea of observable behavior and program meaning. It requires that we delimit what we consider observable and what we don't. Take, for example, this method that has a definite side effect:

```
def timesTwo(x: Int): Int =
  if x < 0 then println("Got a negative number")
  x * 2
```

If we replace timesTwo(1) with 2 in our program, then we don't have the same program in every respect. It may compute the same result, but we can say that the meaning of the program has changed. But this isn't true for all programs that call timesTwo, nor for all notions of program equivalence.

We need to decide up front whether changes in standard output are factors we care to observe—whether they are changes in behavior that matter in our context. In this case, it's exceedingly unlikely that any other part of the program will be able to observe the println side effect occurring inside timesTwo.

---

[3] See the chapter notes (https://github.com/fpinscala/fpinscala/wiki) for links to further reading.

Of course, timesTwo has a hidden dependency on the I/O subsystem. It requires access to the standard output stream, but as we've seen, most programs that we'd consider purely functional also require access to some of the underlying machinery of Scala's environment, like being able to construct objects in memory and discard them. Ultimately, we need to decide for ourselves which effects are important enough to track. We could use the IO monad to track println calls, but maybe we wouldn't feel that was necessary. If we were just using the console to do some temporary debug logging, it would seem like a waste of time to track that. But in a situation where the program's correct behavior depends in some way on what it prints to the console (like if it's a command-line utility), then we definitely want to track it.

This brings us to an essential point: tracking effects is a choice we make as programmers. It's a value judgement, and there are trade-offs associated with what we choose. We can take it as far as we want, but as with the context of referential transparency, in Scala there's a kind of standard choice. For example, it would be completely valid and possible to track memory allocations in the type system if that really mattered to us, but in Scala we have the benefit of automatic memory management, so the cost of explicit tracking is usually higher than the benefit.

The policy we should adopt is tracking those effects that program correctness depends on. If a program is fundamentally about reading and writing files, then file I/O should be tracked in the type system to the extent feasible. If a program relies on object reference equality, it would be nice to know that statically as well. Static type information lets us know what kinds of effects are involved and thereby lets us make educated decisions about whether they matter to us in a given context.

The ST type in this chapter and the IO monad in the previous chapter should have given you a taste of what tracking effects in the type system is like. But this isn't the end of the road. You're limited only by your imagination and the expressiveness of Scala's types.

14.4   Conclusion

In this chapter, we discussed two different implications of referential transparency. We saw that we can get away with mutating data that never escapes a local scope. At first blush, it may seem that mutating state can't be compatible with pure functions, but we've learned that we can write components that have a pure interface and mutate local state behind the scenes, as well as use Scala's type system to guarantee purity.

We also discussed that what counts as a side effect is actually a choice made by the programmer or language designer. When we talk about functions being pure, we should already have a context we've chosen that establishes what it means for two things to be equal, what it means to execute a program, and which effects we care to take into account when assigning meaning to our program.

Summary

- Unobservable mutation is a completely valid implementation technique in functional programming.
- Scala's type system is expressive enough to track many types of effects.
- The ST data type allows us to track the effect of the mutation of some shared state within some locally defined scope.
- The STRef data type provides the ability to allocate, read, and write a mutable cell.
- The STArray data type provides the ability to allocate, read, and write a mutable array.
- Both STRef and STArray return ST actions for every access and mutation, ensuring access is limited to the same ST action.
- Choosing which effects to track is a judgment call based on the needs of the program; track those effects that program correctness depends on.

14.5 Exercise answers

ANSWER 14.1

Let's fold over the elements of the map, using the `write` operation on STArray to set the value at each index. To start the fold, we lift a unit value into ST:

```
def fill(xs: Map[Int, A]): ST[S, Unit] =
  xs.foldRight(ST[S, Unit](())):
    case ((k, v), st) => st.flatMap(_ => write(k, v))
```

ANSWER 14.2

We can port the original definition of `partition`, replacing each array access and update with the equivalent operation on STArray. The original definition used a var j, which we can replace with an STRef:

```
def partition[S](
  a: STArray[S, Int], l: Int, r: Int, pivot: Int
): ST[S, Int] =
  for
    vp <- a.read(pivot)
    _ <- a.swap(pivot, r)
    j <- STRef(l)
    _ <- (l until r).foldLeft(ST[S, Unit](()))((s, i) =>
      for
        _ <- s
        vi <- a.read(i)
        _ <- if vi < vp then
```

```
    for
      vj <- j.read
      _ <- a.swap(i, vj)
      _ <- j.write(vj + 1)
    yield ()
  else ST[S, Unit]((()))
  yield (())
x <- j.read
_ <- a.swap(x, r)
yield x
```

Porting the original definition of qs is simpler; the logic doesn't need to change. The only change needed is returning the ST[S, Unit] value we create instead of a Unit:

```
def qs[S](a: STArray[S,Int], l: Int, r: Int): ST[S, Unit] =
  if l < r then for
    pi <- partition(a, l, r, l + (r - 1) / 2)
    _ <- qs(a, l, pi - 1)
    _ <- qs(a, pi + 1, r)
  yield () else ST[S, Unit]((()))
```

■ **ANSWER 14.3**

Let's wrap a HashMap[K, B] with a class just like we did with STArray, providing constructors as methods on the companion object that provide the initial value of the HashMap. Then we can add methods to the class for each operation that accesses or mutates the map, wrapping the delegated call in ST:

```
final class STMap[S, K, V] private (private val table: HashMap[K, V]):
  def size: ST[S, Int] = ST(table.size)

  def apply(k: K): ST[S, V] = ST(table(k))

  def get(k: K): ST[S, Option[V]] = ST(table.get(k))

  def +=(kv: (K, V)): ST[S, Unit] = ST(table += kv)

  def -=(k: K): ST[S, Unit] = ST(table -= k)

object STMap:
  def empty[S, K, V]: ST[S, STMap[S, K, V]] =
    ST(new STMap(HashMap.empty))

  def fromMap[S, K, V](m: Map[K, V]): ST[S, STMap[S, K, V]] =
    ST(new STMap((HashMap.newBuilder ++= m).result()))
```

Stream processing and incremental I/O

We mentioned in the introduction to part 4 that functional programming is a complete paradigm. Every imaginable program can be expressed functionally, including programs that interact with the external world—but it would be disappointing if the IO type were the only way of constructing such programs. IO and ST work by simply embedding an imperative programming language into the purely functional subset of Scala. While programming within the IO monad, we have to reason about our programs, much like we would in ordinary imperative programming.

We can do better. In this chapter, we'll show how to recover the high-level compositional style developed in parts 1–3 of this book, even for programs that interact with the outside world. The design space in this area is enormous, and our goal here is not to explore it completely but to convey ideas and give you a sense of what's possible. We'll build up a compositional streaming API that's similar to the Functional Streams for Scala (FS2) library (https://fs2.io).

15.1   Problems with imperative I/O: An example

We'll start by considering a simple concrete usage scenario, which we'll use to highlight some of the problems with imperative I/O embedded in the IO monad. Our first challenge in this chapter is writing a program that checks whether the number of lines in a file is greater than 40,000.

This is a deliberately simple task that illustrates the essence of the problem our library is intended to solve. We could certainly accomplish this task with ordinary imperative code inside the IO monad. Let's look at that first.

Listing 15.1   Counting line numbers in imperative style

```
def linesGt40k(filename: String): IO[Boolean] = IO:
  val src = io.Source.fromFile(filename)        ←———————  scala.io.Source has convenience
  try                                                     functions for reading from
    var count = 0                                         external sources, like files.
    val lines: Iterator[String] = src.getLines()  ←———
    while count <= 40000 && lines.hasNext do              Obtain a stateful Iterator
      lines.next                    ←———————              from the Source.
      count += 1
    count > 40000           Has the side effect of
  finally src.close      advancing to the next element
```

We can then run this IO action with `linesGt40k("lines.txt").unsafeRunSync()`, where `unsafeRunSync` is a side-effecting method that takes `IO[A]`, returning `A` and actually performing the desired effects (see section 13.7.1).

Although this code uses low-level primitives, like a `while` loop, mutable `Iterator`, and `var`, there are some good things about it. First, it's incremental—the entire file isn't loaded into memory up front. Instead, lines are fetched from the file only when needed. If we didn't buffer the input, we could keep as little as a single line of the file in memory at a time. It also terminates early—as soon as the answer is known.

There are some bad things about this code, too. For one, we have to remember to close the file when we're done. This might seem obvious, but if we forget to do this, or (more commonly) if we close the file outside of a `finally` block and an exception occurs first, the file will remain open.[1] This is called a *resource leak*. A file handle is an example of a scarce resource, since the operating system can only have a limited number of files open at any given time. If this task were part of a larger program—say we were scanning an entire directory recursively, building up a list of all files with more than 40,000 lines—our larger program could easily fail because too many files were left open.

---

[1] The JVM will actually close an `InputStream` (which is what backs a `scala.io.Source`) when it's garbage collected, but there's no way of guaranteeing this will occur in a timely manner, or at all! This is especially true in generational garbage collectors that perform full collections infrequently.

We want to write programs that are *resource-safe*. They should close file handles as soon as they're no longer needed (whether because of normal termination or an exception); they shouldn't attempt to read from a closed file; and they should do the same for other resources, like network sockets, database connections, and so on. Using IO directly can be problematic because it means our programs are entirely responsible for ensuring their own resource safety, and we get no help from the compiler in making sure they do this. It would be nice if our library would ensure programs are resource-safe by construction.

But even aside from the problems with resource safety, there's something unsatisfying about this code. It entangles the high-level algorithm with low-level concerns about iteration and file access. Of course, we have to obtain the elements from some resource, handle any errors that occur, and close the resource when we're done, but our program isn't about any of those things. Instead, it's about counting elements and returning a value as soon as we hit 40,000, which happens between all of those I/O actions. Intertwining the algorithm and the I/O concerns is not just ugly—it's a barrier to composition, and our code will be difficult to extend later. To see this, consider a few variations of the original scenario:

- Check whether the number of nonempty lines in the file exceeds 40,000.
- Find a line index before 40,000 where the first letters of consecutive lines spell out "abracadabra".

For the first case, we could imagine passing a String => Boolean into our linesGt40k function. But for the second case, we'd need to modify our loop to keep track of some further state. Besides being uglier, the resulting code will likely be tricky to get right. In general, writing efficient code in the IO monad means writing monolithic loops, and monolithic loops are not composable.

Let's compare this to the case in which we have a LazyList[String] for the lines being analyzed:

```
lines.zipWithIndex.exists(_(1) + 1 >= 40000)
```

Much nicer! With a LazyList, we get to assemble our program from preexisting combinators, zipWithIndex and exists. If we want to consider only nonempty lines, then we can easily use filter:

```
lines.filter(!_.trim.isEmpty).zipWithIndex.exists(_(1) + 1 >= 40000)
```

And for the second scenario, we can use the indexOfSlice function defined on LazyList[2] in conjunction with take (to terminate the search after 40,000 lines) and map (to pull out the first character of each line):

---

[2] If the argument to indexOfSlice doesn't exist as a subsequence of the input, it returns -1. See the API docs for details, or experiment with this function in the REPL.

```
lines
  .filter(!_.trim.isEmpty)
  .take(40000)
  .map(_.head)
  .indexOfSlice("abracadabra".toList)
```

We want to write something like the preceding when reading from an actual file. The problem is that we don't have a `LazyList[String]`; we have a file from which we can read. We could cheat by writing a function named `lines` that returns an `IO[LazyList[String]]`:

```
def lines(filename: String): IO[LazyList[String]] = IO:
  val src = io.Source.fromFile(filename)
  src.getLines().to(LazyList).append {
    src.close
    LazyList.empty
  }
```

This is called *lazy I/O*. We're cheating because the `LazyList[String]` inside the IO monad isn't actually a pure value. As elements of the stream are forced, it'll execute side effects of reading from the file, and only if we examine the entire stream and reach its end will we close the file. Although lazy I/O is appealing in that it lets us recover the compositional style to some extent, it's problematic for several reasons:

- *It isn't resource-safe.* The resource (in this case, a file) will be released only if we traverse to the end of the stream. But we'll frequently want to terminate traversal early (here, `exists` will stop traversing the `LazyList` as soon as it finds a match), and we certainly don't want to leak resources every time we do this.

- *Nothing stops us from traversing that same* `LazyList` *again after the file has been closed.* This will result in one of two things, depending on whether the `LazyList` *memoizes* (caches) its elements once they're forced. If they're memoized, we'll see excessive memory usage, since all of the elements will be retained in memory. If they're not memoized, traversing the stream again will cause a read from a closed file handle.

- *Since forcing elements of the stream has I/O side effects, two threads traversing a* `LazyList` *at the same time can result in unpredictable behavior.*

- *In more realistic scenarios, we won't necessarily have full knowledge of what's happening with the* `LazyList[String]`. It could be passed to some function we don't control, which might store it in a data structure for a long period of time before ever examining it. Proper usage now requires some out-of-band knowledge: we can't just manipulate this `LazyList[String]` like a typical pure value—we have to know something about its origin. This is bad for composition, where we shouldn't have to know anything about a value other than its type.

15.2 *Simple stream transformations*

Our first step toward recovering the high-level style we're accustomed to from Lazy-
List and List while doing I/O is introducing the notion of *stream processors*. A stream
processor specifies a transformation from one stream to another. We're using the
term *stream* quite generally here to refer to a sequence, possibly lazily generated or
supplied by an external source. This could be a stream of lines from a file, HTTP
requests, mouse click positions, or anything else. Let's consider a simple data type,
Pull, that lets us express stream transformations.[3]

Listing 15.2   The `Pull` data type

```
enum Pull[+O, +R]:
  case Result[+R](result: R) extends Pull[Nothing, R]
  case Output[+O](value: O) extends Pull[O, Unit]
  case FlatMap[X, +O, +R](
    source: Pull[O, X],
    f: X => Pull[O, R]) extends Pull[O, R]       Interprets the pull
                                                  while rewriting left
  def step: Either[R, (O, Pull[O, R])] = this match  ◁── nested flatMap calls
    case Result(r) => Left(r)
    case Output(o) => Right(o, Pull.done)
    case FlatMap(source, f) =>
      source match
        case FlatMap(s2, g) =>
          s2.flatMap(x => g(x).flatMap(y => f(y))).step
        case other => other.step match
          case Left(r) => f(r).step             Steps the pull
          case Right((hd, tl)) => Right((hd, tl.flatMap(f)))  until a final result
                                                  is produced,
                                                  accumulating an
  @annotation.tailrec                             output value
  final def fold[A](init: A)(f: (A, O) => A): (R, A) =  ◁──
    step match
      case Left(r) => (r, init)
      case Right((hd, tl)) => tl.fold(f(init, hd))(f)

  def toList: List[O] =                           ◁──
    fold(List.newBuilder[O])((bldr, o) => bldr += o)(1).result    Folds the pull,
                                                  collecting all
  def flatMap[O2 >: O, R2](                       output elements
    f: R => Pull[O2, R2]      Operates on the final result value  into a single list,
  ): Pull[O2, R2] =          of a pull, not each output value     and discards the
    Pull.FlatMap(this, f)                         R value

  def >>[O2 >: O, R2](next: => Pull[O2, R2]): Pull[O2, R2] =
    flatMap(_ => next)

  def map[R2](f: R => R2): Pull[O, R2] =
    flatMap(r => Result(f(r)))
```

---

[3] We've chosen to omit some trampolining in this chapter for simplicity.

A Pull[O, R] outputs any number of values of type O and then terminates with a single value of type R. A pull can be incrementally evaluated via step, either outputting a final value of R or outputting a value O and a new pull representing the remainder of the input stream. With this model, we can construct arbitrarily complex pulls from a variety of sources of data by sequencing Pull.Output calls using flatMap. When we want to run the final stream transformation, we can use fold, which repeatedly steps the pull until termination.

Of particular note is the flatMap operation. Rather than converting each output value to a new pull and concatenating all of the results, flatMap operates on the final result value of type R. This means we can concatenate the values of two pulls using the derived >> method. We'll look at this in a moment.

The Pull type is covariant in both the output type and the result type. This covariance lets us define Result[+R] as a Pull[Nothing, R] and Output[+O] as a Pull[O, Unit]. These subtyping relationships are similar to how None is an Option[Nothing] and Nil is a List[Nothing]. Thus, we get an API that works better with type inference. We'll take a deeper look at type inference later.

15.2.1 *Creating pulls*

One of the simplest pulls we can create is one that outputs no values and terminates with a unit:

```
val done: Pull[Nothing, Unit] = Result(())
```

We can construct pulls that output single values and concatenate them:

```
scala> val p = Pull.Output(1) >> Pull.Output(2)
val p: Pull[Int, Unit] = FlatMap(Output(1),...)

scala> val q = p.toList
val q: List[Int] = List(1, 2)
```

The p1 >> p2 operation is shorthand for writing p1.flatMap(_ => p2).

We can use recursion with done and >> to construct pulls from lists and lazy lists:

```
def fromList[O](os: List[O]): Pull[O, Unit] =
  os match
    case Nil => done
    case hd :: tl => Output(hd) >> fromList(tl)

def fromLazyList[O](os: LazyList[O]): Pull[O, Unit] =
  os match
    case LazyList() => done
    case hd #:: tl => Output(hd) >> fromLazyList(tl)
```

In both fromList and fromLazyList, we construct a pull using recursion. We convert each input element into an Output pull and then use >> to lazily recurse. This is stack safe due to >> taking its only argument lazily. This is similar to how we used lazy evaluation to construct lazy lists in chapter 5, but here we're relying on the laziness of `flatMap` to defer the evaluation of the tail. Let's generalize this recursion pattern into a higher-level pull constructor:

```
def unfold[O, R](init: R)(f: R => Either[R, (O, R)]): Pull[O, R] =
  f(init) match
    case Left(r) => Result(r)
    case Right((o, r2)) => Output(o) >> unfold(r2)(f)
```

`unfold` starts with an initial seed value of type `R` and an iteration function, which is repeatedly invoked, producing either a final result of `R` or an output of `O` and a new seed of `R`. This is essentially the same operation as we defined in exercise 5.11 for `LazyList`.

Implement `fromListViaUnfold` and `fromLazyListViaUnfold` as methods on the `Pull` companion object, using `unfold`:

```
def fromListViaUnfold[O](os: List[O]): Pull[O, Unit]
def fromLazyListViaUnfold[O](os: LazyList[O]): Pull[O, Unit]
```

Like we did for `LazyList`, we can create a `continually` constructor:

```
def continually[A](a: A): Pull[A, Nothing] =
  Output(a) >> continually(a)
```

The return type of `continually` is interesting—the result type is `Nothing`, since the pull is infinite and hence never terminates in a value. We can again extract the recursion out into a more general combinator:

```
enum Pull[+O, +R]:
  def repeat: Pull[O, R] =
    this >> repeat

object Pull:
  def continually[A](a: A): Pull[O, Nothing] =
    Output(a).repeat
```

Define `iterate` as a method on the `Pull` companion object. It should return an infinite stream which first outputs the supplied initial value, then outputs the result of applying that value to the supplied function, and so on:

```
def iterate[O](initial: O)(f: O => O): Pull[O, Nothing]
```

So far, we don't have a way to partially evaluate a pull. Partial evaluation is particularly helpful with infinite pulls, like those returned from `continually`, `repeat`, and `iterate`. Let's define `take(n)` on `Pull`, which evaluates the pull until the specified number of output values has been generated:

```
def take(n: Int): Pull[O, Option[R]] =
  if n <= 0 then Result(None)
  else step match
    case Left(r) => Result(Some(r))
    case Right((hd, tl)) => Output(hd) >> tl.take(n - 1)
```

When n is less than or equal to zero, `take` returns a `Result(None)`. Otherwise, we step the pull; if we've reached the end of the input, then we return the final result of the source wrapped in a `Some`. Otherwise, we get an output value, which we output, and a remainder pull, which we recursively call `take` on, decrementing the number of elements.

This implementation has one subtlety, though: when n is positive, we eagerly step the source pull. This eager evaluation can be surprising, since evaluation currently only occurs when folding a pull (or using an operation, like `toList`, which is built on `fold`), so let's delay this evaluation via a new combinator on `Pull`:

```
def uncons: Pull[Nothing, Either[R, (O, Pull[O, R])]] =
  Pull.done >> Result(step)

def take(n: Int): Pull[O, Option[R]] =
  if n <= 0 then Result(None)
  else uncons.flatMap:
    case Left(r) => Result(Some(r))
    case Right((hd, tl)) => Output(hd) >> tl.take(n - 1)
```

The uncons operation wraps `step` in a `Result` constructor and delays its creation via `flatMap`. In the implementation of `take`, instead of matching on the result of `step`, we now `flatMap` on the result of `uncons`. With this definition, we can make partially evaluated infinite streams:

```
scala> val ints = Pull.iterate(0)(_ + 1)
val ints: Pull[Int, Nothing] = FlatMap(Output(0),...)

scala> val firstFive = ints.take(5).toList
val firstFive: List[Int] = List(0, 1, 2, 3, 4)
```

■ **EXERCISE 15.3** ───

Implement `drop`, `takeWhile`, and `dropWhile` on `Pull`:

```
def drop(n: Int): Pull[O, R]
def takeWhile(p: O => Boolean): Pull[O, Pull[O, R]]
def dropWhile(p: O => Boolean): Pull[Nothing, Pull[O, R]]
```

We can build lots of interesting pull transformations by combining recursive functions with uncons. Here's how we can transform the output elements of a pull:

```
def mapOutput[O2](f: O => O2): Pull[O2, R] =
  uncons.flatMap:
    case Left(r) => Result(r)
    case Right((hd, tl)) => Output(f(hd)) >> tl.mapOutput(f)
```

We can use the same approach for adding or removing the elements of a pull. Here's a combinator that filters the output elements based on a predicate:

```
def filter(p: O => Boolean): Pull[O, R] =
  uncons.flatMap:
    case Left(r) => Result(r)
    case Right((hd, tl)) =>
      (if p(hd) then Output(hd) else Pull.done) >> tl.filter(p)
```

We can even maintain state in our pull transformations by passing the state as an argument to our recursive function:

```
def count: Pull[Int, R] =
  def go(total: Int, p: Pull[O, R]): Pull[Int, R] =
    p.uncons.flatMap:
      case Left(r) => Result(r)
      case Right((_, tl)) =>
        val newTotal = total + 1
        Output(newTotal) >> go(newTotal, tl)
  Output(0) >> go(0, this)
```

■ **EXERCISE 15.4**

Implement a method on `Pull` that outputs a running tally of all inputs, using a monoid to combine elements. For each input element, combine it with the accumulated tally, outputting the result:

```
def tally[O2 >: O](using m: Monoid[O2]): Pull[O2, R]

scala> val t = ints.tally.take(10).toList
val t: List[Int] = List(0, 0, 1, 3, 6, 10, 15, 21, 28, 36)
```

■ **EXERCISE 15.5**

Implement an extension method on `Pull[Int, R]`, which outputs the mean of the last n values as a `Pull[Double, R]`:

```
extension [R](self: Pull[Int, R])
  def slidingMean(n: Int): Pull[Double, R]
```

Just as we've seen many times throughout this book, when we notice common patterns when defining a series of functions, we can factor these patterns out into generic combinators. The functions count, tally, and slidingMean all share a common pattern: each has a single piece of state, has a state transition function that updates this state in response to input, and produces a single output. We can generalize this to a combinator, which we'll call mapAccumulate:

```
def mapAccumulate[S, O2](init: S)(f: (S, O) => (S, O2)): Pull[O2, (S, R)] =
  uncons.flatMap:
    case Left(r) => Result((init, r))
    case Right((hd, tl)) =>
      val (s, out) = f(init, hd)
      Output(out) >> tl.mapAccumulate(s)(f)
```

■ **EXERCISE 15.6**

Reimplement count, tally, and slidingMean, using mapAccumulate instead of explicit recursion.

THE PULL MONAD

The flatMap operation along with the Result constructor form a monad instance for [x] =>> Pull[O, x]:

```
given [O]: Monad[[x] =>> Pull[O, x]] with
  def unit[A](a: => A): Pull[O, A] = Result(a)
  extension [A](pa: Pull[O, A])
    def flatMap[B](f: A => Pull[O, B]): Pull[O, B] =
      pa.flatMap(f)
```

We can create an alternative monad instance by taking Output as the implementation of unit and coming up with a different implementation of flatMap. Output(a) gives us a Pull[A, Unit]—the result type is Unit—so let's define a Monad[[x] =>> Pull[x, Unit]]. By plugging in this type to the definition of Monad and following the types, we find we need to define a version of flatMap with the following signature:

```
extension [O](self: Pull[O, Unit])
  def flatMap[O2](f: O => Pull[O2, Unit]): Pull[O2, Unit]
```

Notice that the function passed to flatMap takes an output from the original Pull. This suggests that our flatMap implementation will be similar to the monads for List and LazyList, where the supplied function is invoked on each output element and the results are all concatenated. Since we already have a flatMap method on Pull, let's rename this extension to flatMapOutput and implement this map-then-concat behavior:

```
extension [O](self: Pull[O, Unit])
  def flatMapOutput[O2](f: O => Pull[O2, Unit]): Pull[O2, Unit] =
    self.uncons.flatMap:
      case Left(()) => Result(())
      case Right((hd, tl)) =>
        f(hd) >> tl.flatMapOutput(f)
```

We uncons the original pull, and if we receive an output element and remainder, then we apply the output element to the supplied function to create a `Pull[O2, Unit]`. We return that pull followed by calling `flatMapOutput` on the remainder. This implementation has the desired map-then-concat behavior:

```
scala> val out = ints.flatMapOutput(i =>
                        Pull.fromList(List(i, i))).take(10).toList
val out: List[Int] = List(0, 0, 1, 1, 2, 2, 3, 3, 4, 4)
```

Given this implementation, we can provide the alternative monad instance:

```
val outputMonad: Monad[[x] =>> Pull[x, Unit]] = new:
  def unit[A](a: => A): Pull[A, Unit] = Output(a)
  extension [A](pa: Pull[A, Unit])
    def flatMap[B](f: A => Pull[B, Unit]): Pull[B, Unit] =
      pa.flatMapOutput(f)
```

This is a legitimate monad instance, but it can be awkward to work with. The `Monad[[x] =>> Pull[O, x]]` is a given instance, so to use the `Monad[[x] =>> Pull[x, Unit]]` instance instead, we need to either explicitly reference the instance or otherwise bring it into scope with higher precedence than the regular instance:

```
scala> val p = Pull.Result(true).void   ◁─────┐   void is an extension
val p: Pull[Nothing, Unit] = ...               │   method from Monad.

scala> val q = Pull.Output(1).void   ◁──────┐
val q: Pull[Int, Unit] = ...              │   Uses Monad[[x] =>> Pull[O, x]]

scala> val r = Pull.outputMonad.void(Pull.Output(1))   ◁───│  Uses Monad[[x]
val r: Pull[Unit, Unit] = ...                              │  =>> Pull[x, Unit]]
```

Instead, we can define an opaque type alias for `Pull[O, Unit]` and associate the map-then-concat behavior with that new type. Let's call this new type `Stream`, since it fixes the result of the pull to be `Unit` and hence shifts the focus to the output values:

```
opaque type Stream[+O] = Pull[O, Unit]

object Stream:
  def apply[O](os: O*): Stream[O] =
    Pull.fromList(os.toList).toStream

  extension [O](self: Stream[O])                 Converts a Stream[O]
    def toPull: Pull[O, Unit] = self    ◁──────│  to a Pull[O, Unit]
```

```
    def fold[A](init: A)(f: (A, O) => A): A =
      self.fold(init)(f)(1)

    def toList: List[O] =
      self.toList

    def take(n: Int): Stream[O] =
      self.take(n).void

    def ++(that: => Stream[O]): Stream[O] =
      self >> that

  given Monad[Stream] with
    def unit[A](a: => A): Stream[A] = Pull.Output(a)
    extension [A](sa: Stream[A])
      def flatMap[B](f: A => Stream[B]): Stream[B] =
        sa.flatMapOutput(f)

object Pull:
  extension [O](self: Pull[O, Unit])              Converts a Pull[O,
    def toStream: Stream[O] = self   ◁─────┘      Unit] to a Stream[O]
```

Besides the opaque type definition and the monad instance, we've provided some additional APIs. The `toPull` and `toStream` methods allow us to convert back and forth between `Stream` and `Pull`. We've also provided some APIs for working directly with streams, delegating to the corresponding operations on `Pull` but adjusting the return type when necessary. For example, the `take` operation on `Stream` returns a `Stream[O]`, discarding the `Option[R]` result provided by `take` on `Pull`. Another interesting example is the `++` operation, which concatenates two streams using monadic sequencing of the underlying pulls.

Do we need both `Pull` and `Stream`? `Pull` is more powerful than `Stream` (implied by the fact that `Stream` fixes the result type to `Unit`), so why not just stick with `Pull` and simply not provide the problematic monad instance? `Stream` is often the more convenient type to work with, modeling streaming computations as a collection like `LazyList`, whereas `Pull` excels at defining custom streaming computations in terms of uncons and `flatMap`. We can appeal to these strengths when designing the APIs of `Pull` and `Stream`—adding high-level, collection-like combinators directly to `Stream`, while adding operations that simplify building new streaming computations to `Pull`.

15.2.2 Composing stream transformations

The `Pull` type lets us describe arbitrarily complex data sources in terms of monadic recursion, and the `Stream` type provides us a collection like API that operates on the individual elements being output by a pull. The various stream transformations we've defined so far have all been methods on `Pull` or `Stream`. We'd like to be able to define stream transformations independent from the stream itself and compose multiple stream transformations into a single value. We can accomplish this with function composition!

```
type Pipe[-I, +O] = Stream[I] => Stream[O]
```

A `Pipe[I, O]` is a type alias for a function from a stream of input values of type `I` to a stream of output values of type `O`. Note that `Pipe` doesn't add any expressiveness—it's simply a type alias for a function. Why give it a name? Doing so encourages the users of our stream library to think in terms of independent stream transformations. Let's take a look at a few examples:

```
val nonEmpty: Pipe[String, String] =
  _.filter(_.nonEmpty)

val lowerCase: Pipe[String, String] =
  _.map(_.toLowerCase)
```

The `nonEmpty` pipe converts a `Stream[String]` to a `Stream[String]` with all the empty strings removed, and the `lowerCase` pipe converts each input string to lowercase. In both cases, the bulk of the transformation work is done by a high-level stream combinator (`filter` and `map`, respectively). Extracting these operations out into values lets us describe them independently. Furthermore, we're able to compose these values using function composition:

```
val normalize: Pipe[String, String] =
  nonEmpty andThen lowerCase
```

Here we're using the built-in `andThen` operation on Scala's function type to compose the two transformations into a higher-level pipe.

Since `Pipe` is a type alias for a function, we can apply pipes to streams by directly calling those functions. Alternatively, we can use the `scala.util.chaining.pipe` utility method, which allows us to write `f(a)` as `a.pipe(f)`. The following are all equivalent:

```
val lines: Stream[String] = Stream("Hello", "", "World!")

val normalized: Stream[String] = normalize(lines)

import scala.util.chaining.scalaUtilChainingOps       ⟵—— Provides the pipe extension method
val normalized2: Stream[String] = lines.pipe(normalize)
val normalized3: Stream[String] = lines.pipe(nonEmpty).pipe(lowerCase)
```

■ EXERCISE 15.7

Implement exists. There are multiple ways to implement it, given that `exists(_ % 2 == 0)(Stream(1, 3, 5, 6, 7))` could produce `Stream(true)` (halting and only yielding the final result), `Stream(false, false, false, true)` (halting and yielding all intermediate results), or `Stream(false, false, false, true, true)` (not halting and yielding all the intermediate results):

```
def exists[I](f: I => Boolean): Pipe[I, Boolean]
```

We can now express the core transformation for our line-counting problem as count andThen exists(_ > 40000), and it's easy to attach filters and other transformations to our pipeline.

15.2.3 Processing files

Our original problem of answering whether a file has more than 40,000 elements is now easy to solve—but so far we've just been transforming pure streams. Luckily, we can just as easily use a file as the source of elements in a Stream, and instead of generating a Stream as the result, we can combine all the outputs of the stream into a single final value.

Listing 15.3   Using Stream with files instead of LazyList

```
def fromIterator[O](itr: Iterator[O]): Stream[O] =
  Pull.unfold(itr)(itr =>
    if itr.hasNext then Right((itr.next(), itr))
    else Left(itr)
  ).void.toStream

def processFile[A](
  file: java.io.File,
  p: Pipe[String, A],
)(using m: Monoid[A]): IO[A] = IO:
  val source = scala.io.Source.fromFile(file)
  try fromIterator(source.getLines).pipe(p).fold(m.empty)(m.combine)
  finally source.close()
```

The processFile function opens the file and uses fromIterator to create a Stream[String] representing the lines of the file. It then applies the supplied pipe to that stream to get a Stream[A] and subsequently reduces that Stream[A] to a single A by folding over the outputs using a Monoid[A]. This entire computation is wrapped in an IO to ensure processFile remains referentially transparent. We can now solve the original problem with the following:

```
def checkFileForGt40K(file: java.io.File): IO[Boolean] =
  processFile(file, count andThen exists(_ > 40000))(using Monoid.booleanOr)
```

EXERCISE 15.8

Write a program that reads degrees Fahrenheit as Double values from a file one value per line, sends each value through a pipe to convert it to degrees Fahrenheit, and writes the result to another file. Your program should ignore blank lines in the input file as well as lines that start with the # character. You can use the function toCelsius:

```
def toCelsius(fahrenheit: Double): Double =
  (5.0 / 9.0) * (fahrenheit - 32.0)

def convert(inputFile: String, outputFile: String): IO[Unit]
```

15.3   *Extensible pulls and streams*

Our `Pull` and `Stream` types provide an alternative way of describing lazy computations, but they are not more expressive than `LazyList`. In fact, we could have written our file conversion program in a similar way had we defined `Pipe[I, O]` as an alias for `LazyList[I] => LazyList[O]`. Rather than relying on a monolithic `IO` wrapper that hides the effectful source of a stream, we can augment the definition of `Pull` and `Stream` to support evaluation of arbitrary effects. Let's parameterize both `Pull` and `Stream` with the ability to evaluate an effect to generate either a result value or an output value. To do this, we'll add an additional data constructor to `Pull`:

```
enum Pull[+F[_], +O, +R]:
  case Result[+R](result: R) extends Pull[Nothing, Nothing, R]
  case Output[+O](value: O) extends Pull[Nothing, O, Unit]
  case Eval[+F[_], R](action: F[R]) extends Pull[F, Nothing, R]
  case FlatMap[+F[_], X, +O, +R](
    source: Pull[F, O, X], f: X => Pull[F, O, R]) extends Pull[F, O, R]
```

We've added a new `Eval` data constructor, which wraps an action of type `F[R]`. `Eval[F, R]` extends `Pull[F, Nothing, R]`, indicating that it does not output any values (and hence is usable anywhere we need a `Pull[F, O, R]`). We've also added the type parameter `+F[_]` to `Pull`. The parameter is covariant, which allows `Result` and `Output` to fix the effect type to `Nothing`, indicating they do not evaluate any effects.[4]

> **Variance annotations on `Pull`**
>
> We've chosen to define all of the type parameters of `Pull` as covariant, which provides us with better type inference and more precise types. We could instead define each parameter as invariant like this:
>
> ```
> enum Pull[F[_], O, R]:
>   case Result(result: R)
>   case Output(value: O)
>   case Eval(action: F[R])
>   case FlatMap[F[_], X, O, R](
>     source: Pull[F, O, X], f: X => Pull[F, O, R]) extends Pull[F, O, R]
> ```
>
> This version certainly looks much simpler! Unfortunately, it's not as nice to use. Consider the following examples:
>
> ```
> scala> Pull.Output(1)
> val res0: Pull[Nothing, Int, Nothing] = Output(1)
>
> scala> Pull.Result(true)
> val res1: Pull[Nothing, Nothing, Boolean] = Result(true)
> ```

---

[4] We could have instead defined F to be `+F[+_]`, since we'll always use effect types that are functors (and functors are covariant by nature). Doing so would simplify the definition of various methods but would require the effect types we use to be covariant in their own type parameter. In practice, it's rare for effect types like `IO` to define their type parameter covariantly, so here we've chosen `+F[_]`.

So far, these types look the same as in the covariant definition. The problem occurs when we try combining these values. For example, we should be able to write `res0 >> res1`, but doing so results in the following error:

```scala
scala> res0 >> res1
-- [E007] Type Mismatch Error: ------------------------------------------
1 |res0 >> res1
  |        ^^^^
  |        Found:    (res1 : Pull[Nothing, Nothing, Boolean])
  |        Required: Pull[Nothing, Int, Nothing]
```

In this example, `res0` has fixed F = Nothing, O = Int, R = Nothing and can't be unified with a pull that has fixed F = Nothing, O = Nothing, R = Boolean. However, we can avoid this by deferring the application of concrete types:

```scala
scala> Pull.Output(1) >> Pull.Result(true)
val res2: Pull[Nothing, Int, Boolean] = Result(true)
```

In this case, Scala is able to infer O = Int and R = Boolean while typing the combined expression.

The version of `Pull` with variance annotations does not suffer from this problem. Overall, the variance annotations add a lot of noise to the definition of `Pull` and, as we'll soon see, the methods on `Pull`. But the resulting API is much nicer to use.

Let's see how the addition of an effect parameter affects the definitions of various operations on `Pull`. First, let's look at `step`: The previous definition returned an `Either[R, (O, Pull[O, R])]`. We need to modify the return type to account for the case where `step` encounters an `Eval` node. We can map over the wrapped `F[R]` to convert it to an `Either`, putting the result of type R on the left. This suggests that `step` now needs to return a `F[Either[R, (O, Pull[O, R])]]`. As a consequence of that change, when we recursively call `step`, we need to sequence our computation with `flatMap`. How can we `map` and `flatMap` on an abstract type constructor F, though? We can ask for `Monad[F]`:

```scala
def step[F2[x] >: F[x], O2 >: O, R2 >: R](        │ Monad instance for
  using F: Monad[F2]                              │ the effect type
): F2[Either[R2, (O2, Pull[F2, O2, R2])]] =
  this match
    case Result(r) => F.unit(Left(r))            │ Lift the pure result into
    case Output(o) => F.unit(Right(o, Pull.done)) │ the effect type via unit.
    case Eval(action) => action.map(Left(_))
    case FlatMap(source, f) =>                     │ Wrap the result of
      source match                                 │ the action in a Left.
        case FlatMap(s2, g) =>
          s2.flatMap(x => g(x).flatMap(y => f(y))).step  │ Recursively step, using
        case other => other.step.flatMap:          │ flatMap to access the
          case Left(r) => f(r).step                 │ result of the first step.
          case Right((hd, tl)) => F.unit(Right((hd, tl.flatMap(f))))
```

The simple change of adding an `Eval` constructor has had profound consequences for `step`! We've picked up a `Monad` constraint for our effect type, and we've used monadic recursion instead of regular recursion to sequence computation. As a result, `step` is only stack safe when the effect type has a stack-safe `flatMap` (due to the `other.step.flatMap(…)` call).

The signature of `step` has also gotten much more complex. We've picked up three type parameters with bounds that indicate they are supertypes of F, O, and R. Without these type parameters, Scala complains that we're trying to use covariant parameters in invariant positions. Like we've done in previous chapters, we can mechanically convert such errors into working definitions through the introduction of type parameters with supertype constraints, though doing so gets very complex. Alternatively, we could define `step` as an extension method, avoiding the need for new type parameters:

```
def step(using F: Monad[F]): F[Either[R, (O, Pull[F, O, R])]] =
  self match
    case Result(r) => F.unit(Left(r))
    case Output(o) => F.unit(Right(o, Pull.done))
    case Eval(action) => action.map(Left(_))
    case FlatMap(source, f) =>
      source match
        case FlatMap(s2, g) =>
          s2.flatMap(x => g(x).flatMap(y => f(y))).step
        case other => other.step.flatMap:
          case Left(r) => f(r).step
          case Right((hd, tl)) => F.unit(Right((hd, tl.flatMap(f))))
```

We'll use methods throughout this chapter, but if the type constraints become overwhelming, feel free to define operations with extension methods instead. Doing so is often simpler in exchange for the loss of some type inference.

The `fold` and `toList` methods need similar treatments, since `fold` calls `step` recursively and `toList` calls `fold`:

```
def fold[F2[x] >: F[x], R2 >: R, A](init: A)(f: (A, O) => A)(
  using F: Monad[F2]
): F2[(R2, A)] =
  step.flatMap:
    case Left(r) => F.unit((r, init))
    case Right((hd, tl)) => tl.fold(f(init, hd))(f)

def toList[F2[x] >: F[x]: Monad, O2 >: O]: F2[List[O2]] =
  fold(List.newBuilder[O])((bldr, o) => bldr += o).map(_(1).result)
```

`fold` can no longer be annotated with the `tailrec` annotation, since it's now using monadic recursion instead of regular recursion. Again, we rely on `flatMap` of the effect monad to be stack safe.

The uncons operation is more interesting. Recall the previous definition:

```
def uncons: Pull[Nothing, Either[R, (O, Pull[O, R])]] =
  Pull.done >> Result(step)
```

We can adapt this to the effectful version of pull by creating an `Eval` node that wraps the call to `step`:

```
def uncons[F2[x] >: F[x], O2 >: O, R2 >: R](
  using Monad[F2]
): Pull[F2, Nothing, Either[R2, (O2, Pull[F2, O2, R2])]] =
  Eval(step)
```

Since we're calling `step`, we're forced to add a monad constraint on the effect type, and doing so means we can no longer call `uncons` on a non-effectful pull—that is, a pull with `F = Nothing`—because there's no `Monad[Nothing]` instance. Likewise, every operation that uses `uncons`, like `take`, would need to carry a `Monad[F]` constraint as well.

To fix this, we can defer the invocation of `step` until the resultant pull is being evaluated. Let's create a new `Uncons` data constructor that stores a reference to the source pull. Then let's augment the definition of `step` to handle this constructor:

```
case Uncons(source: Pull[F, O, R])
  extends Pull[F, Nothing, Either[R, (O, Pull[F, O, R])]]

def step[F2[x] >: F[x], O2 >: O, R2 >: R](
  using F: Monad[F2]
): F2[Either[R2, (O2, Pull[F2, O2, R2])]]] =
  this match
    case Result(r) => F.unit(Left(r))
    case Output(o) => F.unit(Right(o, Pull.done))
    case Eval(action) => action.map(Left(_))
    case Uncons(source) =>
      source.step.map(s => Left(s.asInstanceOf[R2]))
    case FlatMap(source, f) =>
      source match
        case FlatMap(s2, g) =>
          s2.flatMap(x => g(x).flatMap(y => f(y))).step
        case other => other.step.flatMap:
          case Left(r) => f(r).step
          case Right((hd, tl)) => F.unit(Right((hd, tl.flatMap(f))))
```

The definition of `Uncons` is interesting—it extends `Pull[F, Nothing, Either[R, (O, Pull[F, O, R])]]` and references an underlying `Pull[F, O, R]`. The type says that unconsing a `Pull[F, O, R]` results in a pull that may evaluate effects in `F`, outputs no elements, and results in either the final value `R` of the source pull or an output value `O` and a remainder `Pull[F, O, R]`.

When we encounter an `Uncons` node in the implementation of `step`, we step the source pull and wrap its result in a `Left`. We need a `Monad[F2]` instance to do so, and `step` already has that instance in scope.

The remaining operations on `Pull` port to the effectful version with little change—often just needing an adjustment to pass a type parameter for the effect. See the chapter code for more examples.[5] How about `Stream` and `Pipe`?

```
opaque type Stream[+F[_], +O] = Pull[F, O, Unit]
```

Like `Pull`, `Stream` picks up a new covariant type parameter for the effect type. The various constructors and methods defined for `Stream` all need to be modified to account for this additional type parameter, but since all the heavy lifting is performed by `Pull`, this is an entirely mechanical transformation:

```
object Stream:
  def empty: Stream[Nothing, Nothing] = Pull.done    ◁——

  def apply[O](os: O*): Stream[Nothing, O] =    ◁———
    fromList(os.toList)

  def fromList[O](os: List[O]): Stream[Nothing, O] =
    os match
      case Nil => Pull.done
      case hd :: tl => Pull.Output(hd) >> fromList(tl)

  extension [F[_], O](self: Stream[F, O])
    def toPull: Pull[F, O, Unit] = self

    def fold[A](
      init: A)(f: (A, O) => A)(using Monad[F]): F[A] =    ◁——
      self.fold(init)(f).map(_(1))

    def toList(using Monad[F]): F[List[O]] =    ◁———
      self.toList
```

Returns a Stream[Nothing, Nothing] indicating there's neither effect evaluation nor output

Returns a Stream[Nothing, O] indicating there's no effect evaluation

The return type is now F[A].

The return type is now F[List[O]].

Like `fold` and `toList` on `Pull`, the equivalent operations on `Stream` now return an effectful action. We say that `fold` and `toList` are *eliminators* of the `Stream` type—interpreting or compiling the algebra of streams into a target monad.

Can we still use these eliminators with non-effectful streams? Yes, but it's a bit awkward. We need to pass an appropriate monad instance explicitly:

```
scala> val x = Stream(1, 2, 3).
        repeat.    ◁———
        take(5).
        toList(using Monad.tailrecMonad).
        result
val x: List[Int] = List(1, 2, 3, 1, 2)
```

repeat and take delegate to their Pull counterparts. See the chapter code for full definitions.

---

[5] The chapter code generally defines operations on `Stream` instead of `Pull`, unless the operation is useful when building recursive pulls.

In this example, we used the `TailRec` monad, so the overall stream computation is stack safe. We need to pass the monad instance explicitly (or otherwise ascribe the type of our stream as `Stream[TailRec, Int]`), and we need to run the trampoline by calling `result` on the result of `toList`. We can provide non-effectful versions of each eliminator to avoid this boilerplate:

```
extension [O](self: Stream[Nothing, O])
  def fold[A](init: A)(f: (A, O) => A): A =
    self.fold(init)(f)(using Monad.tailrecMonad).result(1)

  def toList: List[O] =
    self.toList(using Monad.tailrecMonad).result

scala> val s = Stream(1, 2, 3).repeat.take(5)
val s: Stream[Nothing, Int] = ...
                                         │ Calling toList when F =
                                         │ Nothing results in a List[O].
scala> val x = s.toList          ⟵──────┘
val x: List[Int] = List(1, 2, 3, 1, 2)
                                           │ Calling toList when F = IO
                                           │ results in an IO[O].
scala> val y = (s: Stream[IO, Int]).toList ⟵──┘
val y: IO[List[Int]] = ...
```

Let's add some new constructors and combinators to `Stream` that work with effects.

EXERCISE 15.9

Implement the `eval` constructor on the `Stream` companion object:

```
object Stream:
  def eval[F[_], O](fo: F[O]): Stream[F, O]
```

EXERCISE 15.10

Implement the `mapEval` extension method on the `Stream` type:

```
extension [F[_], O](self: Stream[F, O])
  def mapEval[O2](f: O => F[O2]): Stream[F, O2]
```

EXERCISE 15.11

Implement `unfoldEval` on both the `Stream` and `Pull` companion objects:

```
object Stream:
  def unfoldEval[F[_], O, R](
    init: R)(f: R => F[Option[(O, R)]]): Stream[F, O]
```

```
object Pull:
  def unfoldEval[F[_], O, R](
    init: R)(f: R => F[Either[R, (O, R)]]): Pull[F, O, R]
```

Finally, let's update `Pipe` to account for effects:

```
type Pipe[F[_], -I, +O] = Stream[F, I] => Stream[F, O]
```

We now have a design choice for the `Pipe` type. We've chosen to add a single type parameter `F[_]` to the definition of `Pipe`, which specifies the effect type of both the input stream and the output stream. By using this type parameter in both input and output, we are forced to define the parameter invariantly (try to define it covariantly, and see what the compiler complains about). Yet in doing so, we give up a bit of generality. Instead, we could define `Pipe` like this:

```
type Pipe[-F[_], -I, +G[_], +O] = Stream[F, I] => Stream[G, O]
```

While this definition is more expressive, it's also more complicated. And since `Pipe` is only a type alias, we can always use an explicit function type in the cases where we need the additional expressiveness. Therefore, we'll stick with the simpler definition.

15.3.1 *Effectful streaming computations*

Now that `Pull`, `Stream`, and `Pipe` support evaluation of arbitrary effects, we can build computations that incrementally acquire data from a source, transform it, and send the results to a sink. If sources are represented by streams and transformations are represented by pipes, how do we represent sinks?

It turns out that we don't need any special support for sinks! In fact, the `mapEval` method from exercise 15.10 provides the basis for effectful sinks. We adopt the convention that a sink is a pipe that changes the output to either `Unit` or `Nothing`—in essence, consuming each output value from the source stream. Consider these example sinks:

```
def log[O]: Pipe[IO, O, Unit] = _.mapEval(o => IO(println(o)))

def drain[F[_], O]: Pipe[F, O, Nothing] = _.flatMap(_ => Stream.empty)
```

The `log` sink uses `mapEval` to print each output value of the source to the console. The `drain` sink discards all of the output elements of the source. Putting all the pieces together, we can describe an effectful streaming computation:

```
case class Message(id: UUID, timestamp: Instant, ...)

def format(m: Message): String = s"id: $id, timestamp: $timestamp, ..."
```

```
val dequeue: IO[Message] = ...

val logAll: Stream[IO, Unit] =
  Stream.eval(dequeue).repeat.map(format).pipe(log)
```

In this example, the `dequeue` operation blocks until a message is available (perhaps from a distributed message queue). The `logAll` operation repeatedly evaluates `dequeue` and, for each received message, formats messages to a string and logs the result to the console. The overall stream computation has the `Stream[IO, Unit]` type. How do we run this stream? Our only eliminators are `fold` and `toList`. Calling `toList` would be a problem, as each log action would output a unit value, which would accumulate in a list builder, eventually using all of our heap. Instead, let's fold and discard each output value. This comes up often when working with effectful streams, so we can create a new eliminator:

```
extension [F[_], O](self: Stream[F, O])
  def run(using Monad[F]): F[Unit] =
    fold(())((_, _) => ()).map(_(1))

val program: IO[Unit] = logAll.run
```

15.3.2 *Handling errors*

Some effect types provide the ability to handle errors that occur during evaluation. The chapter code for chapter 13 defines the `Task[A]` type as an opaque type around an `IO[Try[A]]`. Task lets us ignore the presence of potential errors until we want to handle them:

```
val a: Task[Int] = Task("asdf".toInt)
val b: Task[Int] = a.map(_ + 1)
val c: Task[Try[Int]] = b.attempt
val d: Try[Int] = c.unsafeRunSync(pool)
```

When the task assigned to a is evaluated, the conversion from a string to an integer fails with a `NumberFormatException`. Task handles that exception and stores it internally wrapped in a `Failure` (recall that `Failure` is a data constructor of `Try`). In the definition of b, the map invocation ends up being a no-op. In the definition of c, the call to `attempt` exposes the underlying `Try[Int]`.

Task adds an *error channel* to `IO`—a conduit for passing errors that have occurred through computation, in much the same way as `Try` and `Either` provide for non-effectful computations. We can define a `Monad[Task]` instance that works just like the monad instances for `Try` and `Either`, short circuiting upon encountering a `Failure`. Task also provides the `handleErrorWith` combinator, derived from `attempt` and `flatMap`:

```
def handleErrorWith(h: Throwable => Task[A]): Task[A] =
  attempt.flatMap:
    case Failure(t) => h(t)
    case Success(a) => Task(a)
```

```
val a: Task[Int] = Task("asdf".toInt)
val b: Task[Int] = a.map(_ + 1)
val c: Task[Int] = b.handleErrorWith(_ => Task(0))
```

handleErrorWith is somewhat similar to flatMap in that it provides sequencing—but of the error channel instead of the result channel. What happens when we use Task with Stream? We can use eval just like we did with IO:

```
val s: Stream[Task, Int] = Stream.eval(Task("asdf".toInt))
```

When we convert this stream to a task via one of the stream eliminators (e.g., toList or run), we'll end up with a failure that wraps a NumberFormatException. It's useful to be able to handle such errors as part of the Stream and Pull APIs, so let's add handleErrorWith to each:

```
enum Pull[+F[_], +O, +R]:
  case Handle(
    source: Pull[F, O, R],
    handler: Throwable => Pull[F, O, R]
  ) extends Pull[F, O, R]

  def handleErrorWith[F2[x] >: F[x], O2 >: O, R2 >: R](
    handler: Throwable => Pull[F2, O2, R2]): Pull[F2, O2, R2] =
    Pull.Handle(this, handler)

extension [F[_], O](self: Stream[F, O])
  def handleErrorWith(handler: Throwable => Stream[F, O]): Stream[F, O] =
    Pull.Handle(self, handler)
```

We've added a new constructor to Pull that captures the original pull and the error handler. We then need to augment the definition of step to interpret this Handle constructor. When stepping and encountering a Handle, we need to step the inner pull and handle any errors that occurred while doing so. But step is defined to work for an arbitrary effect F[_] that has a monad instance, and monad doesn't provide the ability to handle errors. To address this, let's introduce a new type class that adds error-handling abilities to Monad:

```
trait MonadThrow[F[_]] extends Monad[F]:
  extension [A](fa: F[A])
    def attempt: F[Try[A]]
    def handleErrorWith(h: Throwable => F[A]): F[A] =
      attempt.flatMap:
        case Failure(t) => h(t)
        case Success(a) => unit(a)

  def raiseError[A](t: Throwable): F[A]
```

MonadThrow extends Monad and adds the ability to raise errors and later handle them.

■ EXERCISE 15.12

Define laws for `MonadThrow`. Consider how `attempt` should interact with `raiseError` and `unit`.

We can now update the definition of `step` to take a `MonadThrow` instance:

```
def step[F2[x] >: F[x], O2 >: O, R2 >: R](
  using F: MonadThrow[F2]
): F2[Either[R2, (O2, Pull[F2, O2, R2])]] =
  this match
    ...
    case Handle(source, f) =>
      source match
        case Handle(s2, g) =>
          s2.handleErrorWith(x =>
            g(x).handleErrorWith(y => f(y))).step
        case other =>
          other.step
            .map:
              case Right((hd, tl)) => Right((hd, Handle(tl, f)))
              case Left(r) => Left(r)
            .handleErrorWith(t => f(t).step)
```

Rewrite left-nested handlers as right-nested handlers. (annotation pointing to `case Handle(s2, g)` block)

Handle errors that occurred when stepping source pull. (annotation pointing to `.map:` / `.handleErrorWith` block)

This implementation first checks for left-nested error handlers and rewrites such nesting to be right nested, just like we do for left-nested calls to `flatMap`. Otherwise, it steps the original pull and handles any errors that occurred[6] by delegating to the `handleErrorWith` method for the target effect `F`. If no errors occur, then we propagate the error handler to the remainder pull.

As a result of `step` taking a `MonadThrow`, the various eliminators all must take a `MonadThrow` as well: `fold`, `toList`, and `run`. We can similarly add support for explicitly raising errors in a pull and stream by introducing a `raiseError` constructor for each. See the chapter code for full details.

Now that we have `handleErrorWith` and `raiseError` for stream, we can define `onComplete`:

```
extension [F[_], O](self: Stream[F, O])
  def onComplete(that: => Stream[F, O]): Stream[F, O] =
    self.handleErrorWith(t => that ++ raiseError(t)) ++ that
```

The `onComplete` method allows us to evaluate a stream after the completion of a source stream, regardless of whether the source stream completed successfully or failed with an

---

[6] This implementation is not catching exceptions thrown from the handler itself (i.e., when `f(t)` throws).

error. This is particularly powerful when the stream passed to onComplete evaluates an effect.

Does onComplete let us to safely acquire and release resources, such as file handles? Let's take a look:

```
def acquire(path: String): Task[Source] =
  Task(Source.fromFile(path))

def use(source: Source): Stream[Task, Unit] =
  Stream.eval(Task(source.getLines))
    .flatMap(itr => Stream.fromIterator(itr))
    .mapEval(line => Task(println(line)))

def release(source: Source): Task[Unit] =
  Task(source.close())

val printLines: Stream[Task, Unit] =
  Stream.eval(acquire("path/to/file")).flatMap(resource =>
    use(resource).onComplete(Stream.eval(release(resource))))
```

We first evaluate the acquire task to open a file, and then we flatMap the result, building a stream that uses the opened file and releases it via onComplete. We then print each line of the file to the console. If we run this, perhaps with some added logging on resource acquisition and finalization, we'll see that it does exactly what we want.

Unfortunately, this approach has a major limitation; it is not composable. Consider what happens if we refactor things a bit, extracting the printing of each line until after the call to onComplete:

```
val printLines: Stream[Task, Unit] =
  Stream.eval(acquire("path/to/file"))
    .flatMap: resource =>
      Stream.eval(source => Task(source.getLines))
        .flatMap(itr => Stream.fromIterator(itr))
        .onComplete(Stream.eval(release(resource)))
      .mapEval(line => Task(println(line)))
```

This program should behave the same as the original, and in fact, it does when there are no errors. However, if the final mapEval fails with an exception, then the error handler registered by onComplete isn't called, the overall computation fails, and the resource is never finalized.

Another problematic case is early termination as a result of only taking some of the elements of the source stream. Imagine if we changed use to take the first 10 lines of the file. If we put the take(10) in the body of use, then the overall stream behaves correctly. However, if we move take(10) until after the call to onComplete, then the first 10 lines are returned and the resource is never finalized.

In both of these cases, we expect a resource to be finalized regardless of what else happens in the stream. Relying solely on flatMap and onComplete doesn't give us enough power to provide this guarantee—we'll return to this guarantee shortly.

Adding support for error handling to `Stream` results in a stronger constraint on its elimination forms. Consequently, it's no longer possible to convert a `Stream[IO, X]` into an `IO[List[X]]` or any other `IO` value, since `IO` doesn't have a `MonadThrow` instance. Is this the right trade-off? In practice, most monadic effect types have support for error handling, so this constraint is not as limiting as it first seems, but it's worth experimenting with other API choices.

What about non-effectful streams? We previously evaluated them in the `TailRec` monad, which also doesn't have a `MonadThrow` instance. This is more easily addressed—we can add error handling to `TailRec` in much the same way as we added it to `IO`, by embedding a `Try` inside it:

```
opaque type SyncTask[A] = TailRec[Try[A]]
```

We can define a `MoandThrow[SyncTask]` instance and modify the non-effectful eliminators to evaluate streams using `SyncTask` instead of `TailRec`. In general, each time we add additional functionality to streams and pulls, we have to be careful about how that functionality changes the requirements on the eliminators.

15.3.3 *Ensuring resource safety*

`Stream` can be used for talking to arbitrary resources—not just files but database connections, network sockets, and so on. In the last section, we attempted to open a file and ensure it was closed no matter how our stream computation terminated, and we found that doing so was more difficult than adding support for error handling. Let's revisit the various types of termination we need to support.

Suppose we have `lines: Stream[Task, String]` representing the lines of a large file. This is a *source* or *producer*, and it references a resource (a file handle) we want to ensure is closed, regardless of how this producer is consumed.

When should we close this file handle—at the very end of our program? No. Ideally, we'd close the file once we know we're done reading from `lines`. We're certainly done if we reach the last line of the file; at that point, there are no more values to produce, and it's safe to close the file. So this gives us our first rule to follow: a producer should free any underlying resources as soon as it knows it has no further values to produce, whether due to normal exhaustion or an exception.

This isn't sufficient, though, because the consumer of a stream may itself decide to terminate consumption early. Consider `lines.take(5).toList`. The call to `take(5)` will halt after only five lines have been received, possibly before the file has been exhausted. In this case, we want to make sure that any necessary resource cleanup is run before the overall stream completes. Note that `toList` can't be responsible for this, since `toList` has no idea that the `Stream` it's interpreting is internally composed of other streams, one of which requiring finalization. Thus we have our second rule to follow: any stream s that consumes values from another stream t must ensure cleanup actions of t are run before s halts.

To summarize, a stream s may terminate due to

- Producer exhaustion when the source has no further values to output
- Early termination when the remainder of a source is discarded
- Abnormal termination when an exception is thrown

No matter the cause, we want to close the underlying resource(s) in each case.

Now that we have our guidelines, how do we actually implement this? To handle early termination, we need a way of running cleanup actions of a source stream even when it is discarded. This suggests a design where the cleanup actions of acquired resources are tracked by the interpreter instead of being primitive actions in the stream composed with flatMap and handleErrorWith. Let's introduce a new stream constructor that captures this pattern:

```
def resource[F[_], R](acquire: F[R])(release: R => F[Unit]): Stream[F, R]
```

The resource operation creates a single element stream from acquire and guarantees that the release action is evaluated according to the guidelines we've established. How can we implement resource? In the rest of this section, we'll walk through one approach, but don't worry about all the details of the implementation. The important concept here is how resource behaves, not how it's implemented.

To start, we'll introduce the notion of a *scope* in which stream interpretation occurs. A scope is either *open* or *closed*. An *open scope* has an associated cleanup action, which we'll refer to as a *finalizer*. An open scope may also have any number of subscopes. We can register a new finalizer on a scope by opening a subscope that references that finalizer. An open scope can be closed, which has the effect of first closing all subscopes and then running the finalizer.

Since we're representing finalizers as values of type F[Unit], the Scope type must be parameterized by our effect type. To implement the various state transitions, like opening a subscope and closing a scope tree, we need the ability to manipulate state in the effect F. We can do this using a new type—Ref:

```
final class Ref[F[_], A] private (
  underlying: AtomicReference[A],
  delay: [A] => (() => A) => F[A]       ◄——┐ Lifts an arbitrary thunk
):                                          │ to an effectful action

  def get: F[A] = delay(() => underlying.get)

  def set(a: A): F[Unit] = delay(() => underlying.set(a))

  def modify[B](f: A => (A, B)): F[B] = delay: () =>
    @annotation.tailrec
    def loop(): B =
      val oldA = underlying.get
      val (newA, result) = f(oldA)
      if underlying.compareAndSet(oldA, newA) then result else loop()
    loop()
```

```
object Ref:
  def apply[F[_], A](initial: A)(using F: Monad[F]): Ref[F, A] =
    new Ref(new AtomicReference[A](initial),
      [A] => (th: () => A) => F.unit(()).map(_ => th()))
```

A `Ref[F, A]` is a purely functional equivalent of a variable of type `A` where all access and mutation is performed in the effect `F`. This implementation uses a `java.util .concurrent.AtomicReference` as the underlying storage while exposing effectful accessors and mutators.

The `modify` operation is particularly useful. It atomically computes a new value from the current value and allows an arbitrary additional value to be returned. Using `Ref` and `modify`, we can implement `Scope` as a state machine with `Open` and `Closed` states:

```
class Scope[F[_]](
  parent: Option[Scope[F]],
  val id: Id,
  state: Ref[F, Scope.State[F]]
)(using F: MonadThrow[F]):
  import Scope.State

  def open(finalizer: F[Unit]): F[Scope[F]] = ???
  def close: F[Unit] = ???

object Scope:
  enum State[F[_]]:
    case Open(
      finalizer: F[Unit], subscopes: Vector[Scope[F]]) extends State[F]
    case Closed() extends State[F]

  def root[F[_]](using F: MonadThrow[F]): Scope[F[_]] =
    new Scope(None, new Id, Ref(State.Open(F.unit(()), Vector.empty)))
```

A `Scope` stores its mutable state in a `Ref[F, State[F]]`. The `State[F]` type is an enum consisting of `Open` and `Closed` cases. `Open` stores a reference to the finalizer for this scope and the subscopes.

A subscope can be opened by computing a new `Open` state with a new subscope registered:

```
def open(finalizer: F[Unit]): F[Scope[F]] =
  state
    .modify:
      case State.Open(myFinalizer, subscopes) =>
        val sub = new Scope(Some(this), new Id,
                            Ref(State.Open(finalizer, Vector.empty)))
        State.Open(myFinalizer, subscopes :+ sub) -> F.unit(sub)
      case State.Closed() =>
        val next = parent match
          case None =>
            F.raiseError(new RuntimeException("root scope already closed"))
```

```
        case Some(p) => p.open(finalizer)
      State.Closed() -> next
   .flatten
```

We have two cases to handle: when open is called on an Open scope and when it is
called on a Closed scope. If the scope is open, then we first construct a new scope for
the new finalizer, and we then compute a new Open state that references the new scope
in its subscopes. Recall that the signature of modify allows us to return an arbitrary
value along with the updated state; here we return an F[Scope[F]] as that arbitrary
value. Ignoring the Closed case for a moment, we have a state.modify(…) that
returns an F[F[Scope[F]]], which we flatten into an F[Scope[F]].

This pattern is extensible to any state machine we can imagine. We store the current state in a Ref and perform transitions in terms of ref.modify(f).flatten,
where f computes the next state from the current state and returns an action to evaluate after successful modification of the Ref's state.

Returning to the Closed case, we could choose to make opening a subscope on a
closed scope an error. Instead, we'll propagate the open request to the parent scope.
That scope may be closed as well, which will result in recursive propagation up the
tree until we either encounter an open scope or we reach the root. We only signal an
error if we reach the root without encountering an open scope. The close operation
is implemented in a similar fashion:

```
def close: F[Unit] =
  state
    .modify:
      case State.Open(finalizer, subscopes) =>
        val finalizers = (subscopes.reverseIterator.map(_.close) ++
          Iterator(finalizer)).toList
        def go(rem: List[F[Unit]], error: Option[Throwable]): F[Unit] =
          rem match
            case Nil => error match
              case None => F.unit(())
              case Some(t) => F.raiseError(t)
            case hd :: tl =>
              hd.attempt.flatMap(res =>
                go(tl, error orElse res.toEither.swap.toOption))
        State.Closed() -> go(finalizers, None)
      case State.Closed() => State.Closed() -> F.unit(())
    .flatten
```

Calling close on an open scope transitions the scope's state to Closed. We compute an
action that closes all subscopes and then runs the finalizer of the original scope. We
have to be careful to reverse the order of the subscopes to ensure finalizers are run in
a stack-like fashion (i.e., finalizers must be run in *last in, first out* order). We also have
to be careful to run all finalizers, even if errors occur. We can't just traverse the list of
actions; otherwise, we'd short-circuit on the first error.

Now let's integrate `Scope` into `Stream` and `Pull`. We'll start by creating two new cases in the `Pull` enum:

```
case OpenScope[+F[_], +O, +R](
  source: Pull[F, O, R], finalizer: Option[F[Unit]]
) extends Pull[F, O, R]

case WithScope[+F[_], +O, +R](
  source: Pull[F, O, R], scopeId: Id, returnScope: Id
) extends Pull[F, O, R]
```

`OpenScope` references a source pull and finalizer. Upon encountering `OpenScope`, the interpreter calls `open` on the active scope, passing the finalizer. It then interprets the source pull using the newly opened scope as the new active scope. `WithScope` references a source pull, the ID of a scope to use during the interpretation of that source pull, and the ID of a scope to return to when the source pull has terminated.

Implied by these new cases, the interpreter (i.e., `fold` and `step`) needs to track the active scope and allow a step to change the current scope. To allow active scope changes, we need to change the result of `step` to include the new active scope. We could change the result type from `Either[R, (O, Pull[F, O, R])]` to `(Scope[F], Either[R, (O, Pull[F, O, R])])`, but that's a bit overwhelming. Instead, let's introduce a new type representing the result of a step:

```
enum StepResult[F[_], +O, +R]:
  case Done(scope: Scope[F], result: R)
  case Out(scope: Scope[F], head: O, tail: Pull[F, O, R])
```

Let's modify `fold` to manage the active scope. We need to construct a root scope and close it after the fold completes, and we need to change the active scope on each `StepResult.Out`:

```
def fold[F2[x] >: F[x], R2 >: R, A](init: A)(f: (A, O) => A)(
  using F: MonadThrow[F2]
): F2[(R2, A)] =
  val scope = Scope.root[F2]
  def go(scope: Scope[F2], p: Pull[F2, O, R2], acc: A): F2[(R2, A)] =
    p.step(scope).flatMap:
      case StepResult.Done(_, r) => F.unit((r, init))
      case StepResult.Out(newScope, hd, tl) =>
        go(newScope, tl, f(init, hd))
  go(scope, this, init).attempt.flatMap(res =>
    scope.close.flatMap(_ => res.fold(F.raiseError, F.unit))
  )
```

The `step` operation takes the active scope as an argument now, and the result of `step` indicates the next scope to use. Modifying `step` to handle `OpenScope` is fairly straightforward: we delegate to `open` on the active scope, and then we use `WithScope` to evaluate the original source stream using the newly opened subscope. Upon termination, we restore the original scope:

```
case OpenScope(source, finalizer) =>
  scope.open(finalizer.getOrElse(F.unit(()))).flatMap(subscope =>
    WithScope(source, subscope.id, scope.id).step(subscope))
```

Modifying `step` for `WithScope` is a bit more involved. We first search the scope tree for the target scope, and then we use that scope to step the source stream. If doing so results in a `Done`, then we close the target scope and look up the scope to return to. Otherwise, we propagate `WithScope` through the remaining stream returned in `Out`:

```
case WithScope(source, scopeId, returnScopeId) =>
  scope.findScope(scopeId)
    .map(_.map(_ -> true).getOrElse(scope -> false))
    .flatMap:
      case (newScope, closeAfterUse) =>                    │ The source outputs an element,
        source.step(newScope).attempt.flatMap:            │ so we must propagate WithScope
          case Success(Out(scope, hd, tl)) =>    ◄────────┘ through the tail.
            F.unit(Out(scope, hd,
                        WithScope(tl, scopeId, returnScopeId)))
          case Success(Done(outScope, r)) =>      ◄────────
            scope.findScope(returnScopeId)                 │ The source terminated, so we close
              .map(_.getOrElse(outScope))                  │ the target scope and reset the next
              .flatMap: nextScope =>                       │ scope to the return scope.
                scope.close.as(Done(nextScope, r))
          └─► case Failure(t) =>
                scope.close.flatMap(_ => F.raiseError(t))
```

An error occurred while stepping, so close the target scope, and reraise the error.

With these changes, we can implement `resource` in terms of `Eval` and `OpenScope`:

```
def resource[F[_], R](acquire: F[R])(release: R => F[Unit]): Stream[F, R] =
  Pull.Eval(acquire).flatMap(r =>
    Pull.OpenScope(Pull.Output(r), Some(release(r))))
```

This implementation handles both producer exhaustion and abnormal termination. We still need to do one more thing to handle early termination, though: any time we could potentially discard the remainder of a stream, we must do so in a fresh scope. Doing so ensures that all resources get allocated to subscopes and the entire scope subtree is closed at the earliest appropriate time.

Let's add a `scope` method to `Stream` that opens a new scope, and then let's introduce such scopes on any operations that may partially evaluate streams—operations like `take`, `takeWhile`, and so on:

```
def scope: Stream[F, O] =
  Pull.OpenScope(self, None)

def take(n: Int): Stream[F, O] =
  self.take(n).void.scope
```

With this change, `take` introduces a new scope. If `take` partially evaluates its source, then the Done case of the source is never reached. But the scope introduced by `take` reaches its end, and the entire subtree is closed, including any resources allocated during the partially evaluated source stream.

Putting all of these pieces together, we can return to exercise 15.8, this time using our effectful version of `Stream`:

```
def file(path: String): Stream[Task, Source] =
  Stream.resource(Task(Source.fromFile(path)))(s => Task(s.close()))

def lines(path: String): Stream[Task, String] =
  file(path).flatMap(source =>
    Stream.eval(Task(source.getLines)).flatMap(Stream.fromIterator)
  )

def fileWriter(path: String): Stream[Task, BufferedWriter] =
  Stream.resource(
    Task(Files.newBufferedWriter(Paths.get(path))))(w => Task(w.close()))

def writeLines(path: String): Pipe[Task, String, Unit] =
  lines => fileWriter(path).flatMap(writer =>
    lines.mapEval(line => Task:
      writer.write(line)
      writer.newLine
    ))

val conversion: Pipe[Task, String, String] =
  trimmed andThen
  nonEmpty andThen
  nonComment andThen
  asDouble andThen
  convertToCelsius andThen
  toString

def convert(inputFile: String, outputFile: String): Task[Unit] =
  lines(inputFile).pipe(conversion).pipe(writeLines(outputFile)).run
```

15.3.4 Dynamic resource allocation

Realistic programs may need to allocate resources dynamically, while transforming some input stream. For example, we may encounter scenarios like the following:

- *Dynamic resource allocation*—Read a file, fahrenheits.txt, containing a list of filenames. Concatenate these files into a single logical stream, convert this stream to Celsius, and output the joined stream to celsius.txt.
- *Multi-sink output*—This is similar to dynamic resource allocation, but rather than producing a single output file, produce an output file for each input file in fahrenheits.txt. Name the output file by appending .celsius onto the input filename.

Can these capabilities be incorporated into our definition of `Stream` in a way that preserves resource safety? Yes, they can! We actually already have the power to do these things, using the `flatMap` combinator we've already defined for an arbitrary `Stream` type.

For instance, `flatMap` plus our existing combinators let us write this first scenario as follows:

```
def convertAll(inputFile: String, outputFile: String): Task[Unit] =
  lines(inputFile)
    .flatMap(lines).pipe(conversion).pipe(writeLines(outputFile)).run
```

This code is completely resource safe, meaning all file handles will be closed automatically by the runner as soon as they're finished, even in the presence of exceptions.

We can write to multiple files just by switching the order of the calls to `flatMap`:

```
def convertMultisink(inputFile: String): Task[Unit] =
  lines(inputFile).flatMap(file =>
    lines(file).pipe(conversion).pipe(writeLines(file + ".celsius"))).run
```

15.4 Applications

The ideas presented in this chapter are widely applicable. A surprising number of programs can be cast in terms of stream processing—once you're aware of the abstraction, you begin to see it everywhere. Let's look at some domains where it's applicable:

- *File I/O*—We've already demonstrated how to use stream processing for file I/O. Although we've focused on line-by-line reading and writing for the examples here, we can also use the library for processing binary files.

- *Message processing, state machines, and actors*—Large systems are often organized as a system of loosely coupled components that communicate via message passing. These systems are often expressed in terms of *actors*, which communicate via explicit message sends and receives. We can express components in these architectures as stream computations, which lets us describe extremely complex state machines and behaviors using a high-level, compositional API.

- *Servers and web applications*—A web application can be thought of as converting a stream of HTTP requests to a stream of HTTP responses.

- *UI programming*—We can view individual UI events such as mouse clicks as streams, and the UI as one large network of stream computations determining how the UI responds to user interaction.

- *Big data and distributed systems*—Stream-processing libraries can be distributed and parallelized for processing large amounts of data. The key insight here is that the nodes of a stream-processing network need not all live on the same machine.

If you're curious about learning more about these applications (and others), see the chapter notes (https://github.com/fpinscala/fpinscala/wiki) for additional discussion and links to further reading.

The FS2 library (https://fs2.io/) builds upon the ideas in this chapter to provide an industrial-grade streaming library. FS2 provides `Stream`, `Pull`, and `Pipe` and supports a wide variety of features not discussed here, including concurrency, fan-in–fan-out, interruption–resumption, and support for modern effect types, which themselves are much more powerful than the `IO` and `Task` types developed in this book. It also has a rich set of APIs for interacting with files, network sockets, and various other sources and sinks. Various higher-level libraries are built on FS2, including the popular web framework http4s (https://http4s.org) and database libraries like Skunk (https://tpolecat.github.io/skunk/) and doobie (https://tpolecat.github.io/doobie/).

15.5 Conclusion

We began this book with a simple premise: we assemble our programs using only pure functions. From this sole premise and its consequences, we were led to explore a completely new approach to programming that's both coherent and principled. In this final chapter, we constructed a library for stream processing and incremental I/O, demonstrating that we can retain the compositional style developed throughout this book even for programs that interact with the outside world. Our story, of how to use FP to architect programs both large and small, is now complete.

FP is a deep subject, and we've only scratched the surface. By now, you should have everything you need to continue the journey on your own, making functional programming a part of your own work. Though good design is always difficult, expressing your code functionally will become effortless over time. As you apply FP to more problems, you'll discover new patterns and more powerful abstractions. Enjoy the journey, keep learning, and good luck!

Summary

- Imperative I/O is monolithic, mixing high-level algorithms with low-level details related to iteration and resource safety.
- Streaming computations have a number of important properties: they are incremental, resource safe, and compositional. They also may support early termination (i.e., partial evaluation), error handling, and evaluating effects.
- `Stream` and `Pull` allow for composable, resource-safe, streaming computations that build on top of the effect types built in previous chapters.
- `take(5)` and `takeWhile(_ > 10)` are examples of operations that may terminate a streaming computation early.
- The `Pull` type provides expressive constructors and combinators for constructing streaming computations, making heavy use of monadic recursion.

- `Pull[F, O, R]` describes a streaming computation that may evaluate effects of type `F[_]`, output zero or more values of type `O`, and complete with a final result of type `R`.
- The `Stream` type provides a different API on `Pull` that shifts the focus from the constituent subcomputations to the output elements of a computation. `Stream` complements `Pull` rather than supplanting it.
- `Stream[F, O]` describes a streaming computation that may evaluate effects of type `F[_]` and output zero or more values of type `O`.
- A `Stream[F, O]` can be converted to a `Pull[F, O, Unit]`, and vice versa.
- Both `Stream` and `Pull` have monad instances that differ in behavior. The `Stream` instance provides list-like map-then-concat behavior, while the `Pull` instance provides sequencing of streaming computations.
- `Pipe[F, I, O]` is an alias for `Stream[F, I] => Stream[F, O]`.
- Pipe composition is simply function composition (e.g., `p1 andThen p2`).
- Sinks are pipes that output a stream of either `Unit` or `Nothing` values.
- To ensure that resource safety resources must be finalized when the producer is exhausted, stream evaluation terminates early, or stream evaluation terminates due to an unhandled error.
- The `resource` operation on `Stream` constructs a `Stream[F, R]` from an acquisition effect `F[R]` and a finalizer `R => F[Unit]`.
- The `Ref[F, A]` type models a mutable cell that stores a value of `A` and provides accessors or mutators via the effect `F`.
- Streaming computations have wide applicability within a variety of domains, including file and network I/O, message passing systems, HTTP servers, user interfaces, and distributed data processing.

15.6   *Exercise answers*

■ ANSWER 15.1

For both `fromListViaUnfold` and `fromLazyListViaUnfold`, we start the unfold with the initial input, and on each iteration, we pattern match on the current state, returning a left if the input is empty or a right wrapping a head and tail if it isn't. We must map over the result to discard the final unfold state:

```
def fromListViaUnfold[O](os: List[O]): Pull[O, Unit] =
  unfold(os):
    case Nil => Left(Nil)
    case hd :: tl => Right((hd, tl))
  .map(_ => ())

def fromLazyListViaUnfold[O](os: LazyList[O]): Pull[O, Unit] =
  unfold(os):
```

```
    case LazyList() => Left(LazyList())
    case hd #:: tl => Right((hd, tl))
  .map(_ => ())
```

■ **ANSWER 15.2**

We output the initial value and then call `iterate` recursively, with the result of `f(initial)` as the new initial value:

```
def iterate[O](initial: O)(f: O => O): Pull[O, Nothing] =
  Output(initial) >> iterate(f(initial))(f)
```

■ **ANSWER 15.3**

We implement `drop` with a recursive function that unconses a single element and recurses until the remaining number to drop reaches zero:

```
def drop(n: Int): Pull[O, R] =
  if n <= 0 then this
  else uncons.flatMap:
    case Left(r) => Result(r)
    case Right((_, tl)) => tl.drop(n - 1)
```

`takeWhile` is similar in that we first uncons an element and then decide whether to recurse. If the unconsed element passes the predicate, then we output it and then call `takeWhile` on the tail. If the unconsed element fails the predicate, then we return that element prepended to the tail as the result of the pull. If instead we exhaust the source, then we return the result:

```
def takeWhile(f: O => Boolean): Pull[O, Pull[O, R]] =
  uncons.flatMap:
    case Left(r) => Result(Result(r))
    case Right((hd, tl)) =>
      if f(hd) then Output(hd) >> tl.takeWhile(f)
      else Result(Output(hd) >> tl)
```

`dropWhile` is very similar to `takeWhile`, except we don't output the elements that pass the predicate:

```
def dropWhile(f: O => Boolean): Pull[Nothing, Pull[O, R]] =
  uncons.flatMap:
    case Left(r) => Result(Result(r))
    case Right((hd, tl)) =>
      if f(hd) then tl.dropWhile(f)
      else Result(Output(hd) >> tl)
```

We use a recursive function that takes the accumulated total as an argument, along with the next pull. We uncons the next element from the pull and combine it with the total so far. We output the new total and recurse, passing the new total and the tail of the uncons. If instead we exhaust the source pull, then we return the result of the source pull:

```
def tally[O2 >: O](using m: Monoid[O2]): Pull[O2, R] =
  def go(total: O2, p: Pull[O, R]): Pull[O2, R] =
    p.uncons.flatMap:
      case Left(r) => Result(r)
      case Right((hd, tl)) =>
        val newTotal = m.combine(total, hd)
        Output(newTotal) >> go(newTotal, tl)
  Output(m.empty) >> go(m.empty, this)
```

As with `tally` from the previous exercise, we use a recursive function that takes the current state and the next pull as arguments, representing the state as an immutable queue of integers. The function uncons an element and adds it to the queue, ensuring the queue doesn't grow beyond the specified size. We then output the mean of the queue and recurse on the tail:

```
extension [R](self: Pull[Int, R])
  def slidingMean(n: Int): Pull[Double, R] =
    def go(
      window: collection.immutable.Queue[Int],
      p: Pull[Int, R]
    ): Pull[Double, R] =
      p.uncons.flatMap:
        case Left(r) => Result(r)
        case Right((hd, tl)) =>
          val newWindow = if window.size < n then window :+ hd
                          else window.tail :+ hd
          val meanOfNewWindow = newWindow.sum / newWindow.size.toDouble
          Output(meanOfNewWindow) >> go(newWindow, tl)
    go(collection.immutable.Queue.empty, self)
```

In each of these functions, the accumulator type that was passed to the recursive driver function becomes the state type for `mapAccumulate`. We have to discard the final state by mapping over the result of `mapAccumulate`:

```
def countViaMapAccumulate: Pull[Int, R] =
  Output(0) >> mapAccumulate(0)((s, o) => (s + 1, s + 1)).map(_(1))

def tallyViaMapAccumulate[O2 >: O](using m: Monoid[O2]): Pull[O2, R] =
  Output(m.empty) >>
    mapAccumulate(m.empty): (s, o) =>
      val s2 = m.combine(s, o)
      (s2, s2)
    .map(_(1))

extension [R](self: Pull[Int, R])
  def slidingMeanViaMapAccumulate(n: Int): Pull[Double, R] =
    self
      .mapAccumulate(Queue.empty[Int]): (window, o) =>
        val newWindow = if window.size < n then window :+ o
                                           else window.tail :+ o
        val meanOfNewWindow = newWindow.sum / newWindow.size.toDouble
        (newWindow, meanOfNewWindow)
      .map(_(1))
```

■   **ANSWER 15.7**

One solution is mapping the supplied function over each element and combining all of the resulting Booleans using the logical OR monoid. This implementation traverses the entire source, instead of halting as soon as an element that passes the predicate is encountered:

```
def exists[I](f: I => Boolean): Pipe[I, Boolean] =
  src => src.map(f).toPull.tally(using Monoid.booleanOr).toStream
```

We define a halting version in terms of the nonhalting version by combining it with takeThrough and dropWhile:

```
def takeThrough[I](f: I => Boolean): Pipe[I, I] =
  src => src.toPull.takeWhile(f)
          .flatMap(remainder => remainder.take(1)).void.toStream

def dropWhile[I](f: I => Boolean): Pipe[I, I] =
  src => src.toPull.dropWhile(f)
          .flatMap(remainder => remainder).void.toStream

def existsHalting[I](f: I => Boolean): Pipe[I, Boolean] =
  exists(f) andThen takeThrough(!_) andThen dropWhile(!_)
```

Alternatively, we can replace dropWhile(!_) with last—a function that outputs the last value of a pull:

```
def last[I](init: I): Pipe[I, I] =
  def go(value: I, p: Pull[I, Unit]): Pull[I, Unit] =
```

```
    p.uncons.flatMap:
      case Left(_) => Pull.Output(value)
      case Right((hd, tl)) => go(hd, tl)
  src => go(init, src.toPull).toStream

def existsHalting[I](f: I => Boolean): Pipe[I, Boolean] =
  exists(f) andThen takeThrough(!_) andThen last(false)
```

ANSWER 15.8

Let's first define a `Pipe[String, Double]` that takes a line of input and converts it to
Celsius. We can define this as a pipeline of single-responsibility pipes and then compose them all into a single pipe:

```
def trimmed: Pipe[String, String] =
  src => src.map(_.trim)

def nonComment: Pipe[String, String] =
  src => src.filter(_.charAt(0) != '#')

def asDouble: Pipe[String, Double] =
  src => src.flatMap: s =>
    s.toDoubleOption match
      case Some(d) => Stream(d)
      case None => Stream()

def convertToCelsius: Pipe[Double, Double] =
  src => src.map(toCelsius)

val conversion: Pipe[String, Double] =
  trimmed andThen
  nonEmpty andThen
  nonComment andThen
  asDouble andThen
  convertToCelsius
```

We then use this pipe to convert the lines of an input file and write each converted
output to an output file. We need to write a driver function in the IO type; we open the
input and output files and use the conversion on the input lines, writing each transformed line to the output file:

```
import java.nio.file.{Files, Paths}

def convert(inputFile: String, outputFile: String): IO[Unit] =
  IO:
    val source = scala.io.Source.fromFile(inputFile)
    try
      val writer = Files.newBufferedWriter(Paths.get(outputFile))
      try
        fromIterator(source.getLines)
          .pipe(conversion)
```

```
            .fold(()): (_, a) =>
              writer.write(a.toString)
              writer.newLine()
      finally writer.close()
    finally source.close()
```

■ ANSWER 15.9

We use `Pull.Eval` to create a `Pull[F, Nothing, O]` and then `flatMap` on that with a
`Pull.Output`, resulting in a `Pull[F, O, Unit]`, which is equivalent to a `Stream[F, O]`:

```
def eval[F[_], O](fo: F[O]): Stream[F, O] =
  Pull.Eval(fo).flatMap(Pull.Output(_))
```

■ ANSWER 15.10

We can use `flatMap` along with `eval`. Since we're defining this inside the `Stream` companion, and as a result of `Stream` being an opaque type over `Pull`, we have to take care
to explicitly reference `Stream.flatMap` and not the `flatMap` method on `Pull`:

```
extension [F[_], O](self: Stream[F, O])
  def mapEval[O2](f: O => F[O2]): Stream[F, O2] =
    Stream.flatMap(self)(o => Stream.eval(f(o)))
```

■ ANSWER 15.11

The implementations are nearly identical—we `Eval(f(init))` and `flatMap` the
result, either terminating if the result signals termination or outputting the element
and recursing with the new state:

```
object Pull:
  def unfoldEval[F[_], O, R](init: R)(f: R =>
    F[Either[R, (O, R)]]): Pull[F, O, R] =
    Pull.Eval(f(init)).flatMap:
      case Left(r) => Result(r)
      case Right((o, r2)) => Output(o) >> unfoldEval(r2)(f)

object Stream:
  def unfoldEval[F[_], O, R](init: R)(f: R =>
    F[Option[(O, R)]]): Stream[F, O] =
    Pull.Eval(f(init)).flatMap:
      case None => Stream.empty
      case Some((o, r)) => Pull.Output(o) ++ unfoldEval(r)(f)
```

■ ANSWER 15.12

Let's first consider how `attempt` interacts with the accessible constructors (i.e., `unit` and `raiseError`):

```
unit(a).attempt == unit(Right(a))
raiseError(t).attempt == unit(Left(t))
```

Let's also see how `handleErrorWith` interacts with each constructor:

```
unit(a).handleErrorWith(h) == unit(a)
raiseError(t).handleErrorWith(h) == h(t)
```

And the following is how `raiseError` interacts with `flatMap`:

```
raiseError(t).flatMap(f) == raiseError(t)
```

We could also make some stronger demands on how exceptions are handled. For example, should `unit` catch exceptions thrown from its thunk argument?

```
unit(throw new Exception) == raiseError(new Exception)
```

Should exceptions be caught if thrown from the functions passed to `map` and `flatMap`?

```
fa.map(_ => throw new Exception) == raiseError(new Exception)
fa.flatMap(_ => throw new Exception) == raiseError(new Exception)
```

There's no wrong answer, only trade-offs.

index

exceptions *(continued)*
   Option data type 71–80
      composition, lifting, and wrapping 76–80
      usage patterns for 72–76
   possible alternatives to 70–71
ExecutorService 153–154, 159, 162, 164, 166
exhaustive test case generation 182
explicit forking 150–152
extension methods 52

F

F layers 371
F[Unit] type 436
factorial function 22
fibs function 106
File I/O 442
filter function/method 94–95, 104
filterM function 291
finalizers 436
find function 104
findFirst function 26
first-class loops 104
FlatMap constructors 364–365, 369–370
flatMap function 48, 127–129, 131, 170, 287–290, 370, 419
fold function 54, 200, 426
Foldable data type 270
foldLeft function 46, 145
foldMap function 259, 263
foldRight function 44, 266
for-comprehension construct 80
forAll function 184
forAllPar function 197
foreachM Monad function 360
forking
   explicit 150–152
   law of 160–161
format method 17
formatAbs function/method 17–18, 24
formatFactorial function 24
formatResult function 24–25
free monads 370, 388
free theorem 160
Free type 370, 376
Free[Console, A] type 372
Free[Console, Option[Int]] type 373
Free[Console, Unit] type 383
Free[F, A] type 375
function composition 30
function literals 26
function/method term 20
functional data structures
   data sharing in 40–50
      efficiency of 42–43
      lists 43–50

defining 35–38
pattern matching 38–40
trees 50
functional programming. *See* FP (functional programming)
functions, as values 21
Functor[F] instance 284
functors 283
   applicative
      advantages of 320–325
      applicative laws 325–329
      applicative trait 314–316
      generalizing monads 314
      monads vs. 317–319
   functor laws 285–286
   generalizing map function 284–286
   traversable
      overview of 329–331
      uses of 331–337
Future type 164

G

Gen data type 191, 284–287
Gen monad 292
generators
   laws of 200
   meaning and API of 186–187
   that depend on generated values 187–188
generic function 26
getOrElse function 73, 89
given keyword 264

H

handleErrorWith method 433
hasSubsequence function 107
higher-kinded type 266
higher-order functions 21–25, 266
   calling with anonymous functions 26–27
   recursion over lists and generalizing to 43–47
   testing 199–200
   writing 24–25
   writing loops functionally 21–23

I

I/O (input/output) 4
   avoiding StackOverflowError 363–368
      reifying control flow as data constructors 363–366
      trampolining 366–368
   capabilities 383–385
   factoring effects 356–357
   general-purpose I/O type 385–386